MARRIAGE RITES AND RIGHTS

Recent years have seen extensive discussion about the continuing retreat from marriage, the increasing demand for the right to marry from previously excluded groups, and the need to protect those who do not wish to marry from being forced to do so. At the same time, weddings are big business, couples are spending more than ever before on getting married, and marriage ceremonies are increasingly elaborate. It is therefore timely to reflect on the rites of marriage, as well as the right to marry (or not to marry), and the relationship between them.

To this end, this new interdisciplinary collection brings together scholars from numerous fields, including law, sociology, anthropology, psychology, demography, theology and art and design. Focusing on England and Wales, it explores in depth the specific issues arising from this jurisdiction's Anglican heritage, demographic development, current laws and social practices.

Marriage Rites and Rights

Edited by
Joanna Miles
Perveez Mody
and
Rebecca Probert

•HART•
PUBLISHING
OXFORD AND PORTLAND, OREGON
2015

Hart Publishing
An imprint of Bloomsbury Publishing Plc

Hart Publishing Ltd
Kemp House
Chawley Park
Cumnor Hill
Oxford OX2 9PH
UK

Bloomsbury Publishing Plc
50 Bedford Square
London
WC1B 3DP
UK

www.hartpub.co.uk
www.bloomsbury.com

Published in North America (US and Canada) by
Hart Publishing
c/o International Specialized Book Services
920 NE 58th Avenue, Suite 300
Portland, OR 97213-3786
USA

www.isbs.com

HART PUBLISHING, the Hart/Stag logo, BLOOMSBURY and the Diana logo are trademarks of Bloomsbury Publishing Plc

British Library Cataloguing-in-Publication Data
A catalogue record for this book is available from the British Library.

ISBN: 978-1-84946-913-5

Typeset by Compuscript Ltd, Shannon
Printed and bound in Great Britain by
Lightning Source UK Ltd

Foreword

St Augustine famously observed that he thought he knew what time was until someone asked him to define it; much the same might be said about marriage. And the heated debates over same sex marriage in the last couple of years have brought the problem into sharp focus. Are we talking simply about the public recognition of a sexual partnership that is meant to last? Or about the public affirmation of states of strong emotion? About what we now mean by 'household' and 'family' and how these are to be properly regulated and protected in law? About the purposes of God in creation? It is abundantly clear that speaking of marriage can involve any of these, often more than one—but that finding a single core of significance is remarkably difficult.

But of course this is not a situation unique to marriage. Many important social concepts are held together by 'family resemblances' rather than hard and fast definitions (what exactly is a game, to use a familiar philosophical example? or how exactly, in our society, do we define an industry?). The law can settle on helpful rules of thumb, but lawyers would be among the first to agree that the interesting questions arise when you are faced with something that challenges the most obvious definitions; and change happens as and when society's experience (granted that this is an intolerably vague phrase) pushes those definitions irredeemably out of shape. It has become a commonplace to say that marriage is changing in just such a way under just such pressures—and has been doing so for well over a century in the United Kingdom.

In a situation like this, it is inevitable that a lot of anxiety will be generated; and to take this anxiety seriously is not necessarily to collude with plain prejudice or unthinking reaction. Social institutions *ought* to be conservative; that's the point of them. And we ought to be able to ask whether this or that change alters their character fundamentally. To do this without presupposing that there is indeed a simple timeless definition is complicated; but it is a fair question to ask whether we are now talking about something different from what we started with. For a useful discussion of this, we need a lot of patient work both on legal and ideological understandings and on expectations and mythologies in the minds of people undertaking marriage. That patient work is abundantly in evidence in this excellent collection of essays.

The basic problem—you might say—is that human beings as far back as we can trace, seem to have regarded sexual partnership as a *cultural* matter, not just a biological one. Meanings, expectations and conventions surround sexual partnership in all societies we know about; whether we like it or not, marriage is involved with the symbolising capacities of human agents. To get married is to send a message of some sort. Of course there is a huge variety of messages, as there is a huge variety of ways of 'marrying'; but that does not imply that we can simply choose what we are going to mean by it or that we could easily imagine a world in which there were no cultural meanings attached to sexual partnership. At the very least, the existence of a cultural shape for sexual partnership announces that a society will, in one way or another, support partnerships that have this shape, simply by using the concept in its social vocabulary and by thus presenting it as a routine expectation. And—to touch on a neuralgic question—the heterosexual norm of marriage, assumed for most of human history, while bound up with parenting and, to a considerable extent, with the privileges of masculinity also, in its more flexible and imaginative modes presented marriage as a way of making sense of sexual *polarity*, as a symbol of the complementary gendered modes of human existence. For all the manifold ambiguities associated with this (eg complementarity seen as an 'equal but different' arrangement which often implied 'unequal and different'), there was and is a cultural issue here which a too simplistic account of 'equal' marriage bypasses. If marriage is inescapably cultural, we still have work to do as to what, if anything, we want to do about symbolising the working fusion of gendered difference if marriage as legally defined no longer does this job. To pick our way through this question is difficult: it is easy to see why some believe that the extension of the definition of marriage to same sex partnerships has irrevocably altered (or at least reduced) what our culture understands by marriage and what the symbolic vocabulary of marriage allows to be expressed—and why others see it as a vindication of the fundamental reality of marriage once an irrational and unjust attitude to homosexual identity and activity has been overcome. So, although the legal position is settled, we must expect a cultural dissonance to continue for a good while yet as to where the line is crossed between acceptable and questionable accounts of marriage; another illustration of the fact that law does not *create* culture or ethics.

In a context where it is assumed without question that sexual partnership has something to do with procreation, the protection or endorsement of marriage in society has a lot to do with the long latency period of the human child: a stable partnership is a stable background for the nurture of children, and that is self-evidently a good thing. But this begins to steer us towards further reflection on the role of law in relation to all this: if part of the law's responsibility is to protect the vulnerable in society, the well-being of children is manifestly a priority. In the past, this was widely interpreted to mean that the law should protect concerns about legitimacy and inheritance and simply reinforce the authority of the head of a household. With recognition of the weaknesses and abuses this could entail, the area has become more broadly defined; but few would dispute the desirability of a legal presumption that stability is a helpful thing, granted that other securities are in place. The law's interest in marriage is—like all proper legal interest—an interest in protection and redress. If it sanctions or defends a specific social/cultural practice, this must be on the grounds that someone needs protecting. In a cultural setting where marriage is closely bound up with childbearing and childrearing, this is obviously a rationale for the law's concern.

But there has also been a growing acknowledgement that long-term partnership, involving cohabiting and financial interdependence, entails risk to the contracting partners. The law clearly has a role in providing for redress here, if a partnership fails or becomes injurious. Arguably the most significant cultural shift in the understanding of marriage in the Western world in the last century and a half has been this acknowledgement—painfully slow and still uneven in many contexts: a partner, especially a female partner, may be severely disadvantaged through a failed, abusive or otherwise dysfunctional marriage, and the law has a clear interest in securing such a partner's well-being as far as possible. And this is a justification for the law to take the same interest in and make the same provision for same sex partnerships—just as it implicitly makes provision for childless heterosexual partnership through recognising the need to protect partners from the consequences of the failure of a relationship in which material and psychological goods have been invested.

Marriage is still partly, if not largely, about just what Georgian and Victorian novelists are so obsessed with—financial and personal security in the wake of a commitment that takes you outside your own kinship group and creates another set of kinship relations. The horrors of dowry-related crimes in some cultures (wives abused or killed because they have brought insufficient money to the marriage) is a grim reminder of the various risks entailed in partnership. And we should not forget that it took a remarkably long time for a minimally just treatment of married women's property to arrive on the statute book. It is a helpful corrective to merely sentimental discussions of marriage; and, as this book notes, it is now a serious question how far pre-nuptial anxiety over this can or should be incorporated into the social processes that surround marriage.

The current situation in our own culture is an odd one. We are bound to be aware of risks such as those just sketched, not least because of the statistics of marriage dissolution. Yet our language and practice are shot through with the most startlingly uncritical romanticism. The modern wedding has become the focus of unrestrained fantasy, an occasion for acting out dreams and dramas against theatrical backdrops of various sorts; and the language around it—as quite a lot of the discussion over same sex marriage illustrated—is simply about intense feeling being recognised and celebrated. It is certainly not a novelty that marriage, and in particular the wedding ceremony, attracts romantic fancy; what is new, and problematic both financially and psychologically, is the pressure to see the wedding as a flawless and unique performance of aspirations, to which no subsequent experience can quite live up. The law cannot exactly enact sumptuary restrictions on weddings; but the lawyer will note the effect of this ruthlessly marketed and marketised experience on the expectations of a human relationship and a shared household.

It is culture not law that makes 'good' marriages. The cultural debate needed is about why and how long-term partnership matters, not only for the nurture of children but for the nurture of *adults*, for adults to have a context in which they learn some of the most important aspects of human interdependence. The idea that we should culturally affirm the possibility of relationships that do not set conditions in advance, and are based on an unqualified promise of care is evidently still one that is felt as compelling by the majority, heterosexual and homosexual. The role of law is to bring to this also the realistic recognition that promises are risky and need some safety nets for when they break down. But the substantive work required is cultural and imaginative; which is why a culture of sentimentality and inflated expectation—not to mention monumental financial outlay—on the 'wedding experience' becomes a real challenge to seeing marriage as still having the meanings associated with unconditional care and fidelity.

Yet those meanings *are* still current, and, despite an environment in which individualism and a somewhat narrow picture of rights and entitlements have massive social and commercial endorsement, a steady stream of people choose to engage in the risky business of promising care and companionship in an exclusive bond, legally reinforced and culturally celebrated. Making sense of all this as part, in turn, of making sense of the distinctively human experience overall is what these essays address, with a fine blend of learning and insight. I hope they will make a real contribution to a debate still so often mired in confusion and unexamined emotion.

Dr Rowan Williams, FBA, FRSL, FLSW,
Master of Magdalene College,
Cambridge

Acknowledgements

The chapters in this inter-disciplinary volume were originally presented to fellow contributors at a workshop held at Trinity College, Cambridge under the aegis of the Cambridge Socio-Legal Group in April 2014. We are extremely grateful to the Cambridge Socio-Legal Group, the University of Warwick, and Trinity College, Cambridge for their financial support for this project, and to the staff of Trinity College who helped the workshop to run so smoothly.

In addition to the contributors themselves, whose biographies appear in the following pages, we must also acknowledge a huge debt to the following individuals for their contributions to discussion during the workshop: Clare Chambers, Paul Dominiak, John Eekelaar, Mavis Maclean, Jens Scherpe, John Oxley, and Linda Woodhead.

Finally, for kindly agreeing to write the Foreword we are especially grateful to Dr Rowan Williams.

Contents

Part III

Part IV

Notes on the Contributors

Rajnaara Akhtar currently teaches at the University of Warwick and received her doctorate from there in 2013. Her research area was Legal Pluralism, Dispute Resolution, *Shariah* Councils, British Muslims and Islamic Family Law. She is currently also a post-doctoral research fellow at London-based law firm Duncan Lewis, investigating the normative influences giving rise to unregistered Muslim marriages. She received her Masters in Human Rights Law from the University of Nottingham, and her undergraduate law degree from the University of Leicester. She is professionally trained as a solicitor.

Peter W Edge LLB, PhD (Cantab), joined Oxford Brookes University in 1999 as Reader in Law and Religion. His publications in that field include general texts, as well as more focused articles in areas as diverse as religious representation in democratic legislatures, and the application of consumer law to religion. His work on religion and marriage has developed in partnership with Dr Dominic Corrywright, also of Oxford Brookes.

Sarah Lucy Farrimond studied Geography at the University of Oxford and Theology and Pastoral Studies at the University of Leeds before completing a PhD at the University of Durham on 'Ritual and Narrative in the Contemporary Anglican Wedding'. She then undertook ordination training at the Queen's Foundation Birmingham, and was ordained deacon at Wakefield Cathedral in July 2014. She taught at Sheffield University and for the Yorkshire Ministry Course and the College of the Resurrection in Mirfield. She is now a full time curate in two parishes in Huddersfield, West Yorkshire. Her research interests are in the area of religion, ritual and material culture and she is now working with Professor Douglas Davies of the University of Durham on a book on Weddings and Partnership Ceremonies.

Rosie Harding is Chair in Law and Society at the University of Birmingham. She gained her LLB from the University of Edinburgh, her LLM from Keele University and her PhD from the University of Kent. Her research focuses on the everyday regulation and legal recognition of intimate and caring relationships. She uses social science methods including both qualitative and quantitative approaches to empirical data analysis to investigate the place of law in everyday life, including everyday understandings of law and legal discourse. Her work is grounded in feminist legal theory and gender, sexuality and law, and has been supported by research grants from the AHRC, ESRC and the British Academy. Her first book, *Regulating Sexuality* won the 2011 SLSA-Hart Book Prize and the 2011 SLSA-Hart Early Career Prize.

John Haskey has held a Visiting Senior Research Fellowship at the University of Oxford since 2000, and was head of the Family Demography Unit at the Office for National Statistics until 2005. He has published a variety of statistical studies and commentaries on the subjects of: marriage; divorce; cohabitation; Living Apart Together; ethnicity; adoption; families; households and relationships. One particular interest is the influence of legislative changes upon subsequent demographic behaviour. He has contributed articles to *Family Law* on: trends in divorce; the potential for court information to be better used for research purposes; and on profiles of surviving kin of different kinds of family member who die, as research for The Law Commission. John recently contributed a chapter to a book on the history of cohabitation and non-marital births in England and Wales. He is a past President of the British Society for Population Studies, and an Assistant Editor for the demographic journal, *Population Studies*.

Jonathan Herring is a Professor of Law at the University of Oxford and Fellow in Law at Exeter College, Oxford. He is the author of several textbooks including *Criminal Law: Text Cases and Materials*, 6th edn (OUP, 2014); *Criminal Law*, 8th edn (Palgrave, 2013); *Family Law*, 7th edn (Pearson Education, 2015) and *Medical Law and Ethics*, 5th edn (OUP, 2014). He has also written monographs on caring (*Caring and the Law* (Hart Publishing, 2013)); the law and older people (*Older People in Law and Society* (OUP, 2009)) and family law and human rights (*European Human Rights and Family Law* (with Shazia Choudhry) (Hart Publishing, 2010)). He has written widely on family law, criminal law, medical law and ethics, care law and elder law.

Joanna Miles is University Senior Lecturer and Fellow in Law at Trinity College, University of Cambridge, and an Academic Door Tenant at 1 Hare Court. She teaches and researches principally in family law and family justice issues, with particular expertise in the areas of legal regulation of adult relationships and financial and property issues on relationship breakdown. She is the co-author, with Sonia Harris-Short and Rob George, of *Family Law: Text, Cases, and Materials* published by OUP in its 3rd edition in 2015, and the current Chair of the Cambridge Socio-Legal Group, which generously supported the workshop at which the contributions to this volume were presented and discussed. She edited, with Rebecca Probert, a previous volume in the Group's series, *Sharing Lives, Dividing Assets: an inter-disciplinary study* (Hart Publishing, 2009).

Perveez Mody is a University Lecturer at the Department of Social Anthropology, and Senior Tutor and Fellow of King's College, Cambridge. She works on changes in South Asian kinship, marriage, gender, sexuality and care. She has written a monograph about the practice of love-marriage in urban India and the history of civil marriage legislation and practice from the colonial period into the present. Published by Routledge, *The Intimate State: Love-Marriage* *and the Law in Delhi*, provides an ethnographic account of self-chosen marriages across the class and caste spectrum. More recently, her work concerns the legal protections against the phenomenon known as 'forced marriage' in the UK. She has also published on 'marriages of convenience' amongst the South Asian diaspora.

Elizabeth Peel is Professor of Psychology and Social Change at the University of Worcester. Her research focuses on psychology and social change with respect to vulnerable and marginalised groups. She has published widely in the areas of sexualities diversity training, same sex relationships and families, type 2 diabetes, and latterly dementia care. In 2015 she is co-ordinating a BPS Research Seminar Series with Professor Michael Murray (Keele Initiative on Ageing) and Dr Carol Holland (ARCHA) entitled 'Beyond Boundaries: Exploring the Psychologies of Ageing'.

Rebecca Probert is Professor of Law at the University of Warwick. She has written on all aspects of modern family law, but has a particular interest in the history of marriage, divorce, cohabitation and bigamy, with recent books including *Marriage Law and Practice in the Long Eighteenth Century: A Reassessment* (2009), *The Changing Legal Regulation of Cohabitation: From Fornicators to Family, 1600–2010* (2012), both published by Cambridge University Press. She has also edited a number of collections of essays, including *Family Life and the Law: Under One Roof* (Ashgate, 2007), *Sharing Lives, Dividing Assets* (Hart Publishing, 2009), co-edited with Joanna Miles; *Responsible Parents and Parental Responsibility* (Hart Publishing, 2009) and *Landmark Cases in Family Law* (Hart Publishing, 2011), both co-edited with Stephen Gilmore and Jonathan Herring; and *Fifty years in Family Law: Essays for Stephen Cretney* (Intersentia, 2012), co-edited with Chris Barton.

Louise Purbrick is Principal Lecturer in the History of Art and Design in the School of School of Humanities, University of Brighton. Her research is devoted to the understanding of material culture and she has written about the meaning of artefacts within sites of conflict, industrial cultures and everyday domestic worlds. She is author of *The Wedding Present: Domestic Life Beyond Consumption* (Ashgate, 2007).

Ayesha Vardag read law at Queens' College, Cambridge, worked on expert research projects at the International Court of Justice in The Hague and at the UN (IAEA) Legal Division in Vienna, and is dually-qualified as both a solicitor and a barrister. She set up her own specialist family/divorce law firm, Ayesha Vardag Solicitors, in 2005, specialising in big-ticket financial and associated cases on divorce and family breakdown. She has acted for and against heirs and heiresses, tycoons, international footballers/polo players, celebrities and royalty. She regularly appears in the media as an expert on the leading cases and legal issues of the day.

Rowan Williams read theology at Christ's College, Cambridge, and studied for his doctorate at Wadham College, Oxford. His career combined both academic and parish work, with posts as Dean and Chaplain of Clare College, Cambridge and Lady Margaret Professor of Divinity and Canon of Christ Church, Oxford. In 1991 he was consecrated as Bishop of Monmouth, and in 1999 he was elected Archbishop of Wales. In 2002 he was confirmed as the 104th bishop of the See of Canterbury. In 2012 he stepped down from this role and took on the Mastership of Magdalene College, Cambridge. He is the author of numerous books of both theology and poetry.

Helena Wray is Associate Professor of Law at Middlesex University. She is a former solicitor and has a PhD from the University of London. Her interests lie in migration law and policy, particularly as it affects families, and citizenship. Her book *Regulation of Marriage Migration into the UK: A Stranger in the Home* was published by Ashgate in 2011 and she has published in leading law journals. She is editor of the *Journal of Immigration, Asylum and Nationality Law* and UK country expert for the *European Union Democracy Observatory on Citizenship*. She has provided expert evidence in a number of court cases including the landmark challenges to the pre-entry language requirement for partners and to the financial requirements for migrant spouses and partners.

1

Introduction

REBECCA PROBERT, JOANNA MILES AND PERVEEZ MODY

I. OVERVIEW

TWO DAYS AFTER the Marriage (Same Sex Couples) Act 2013 came into force, the BBC sitcom *Rev* showed the vicar Adam Smallbone struggling with the question of just what elements of a wedding ceremony he could allow in blessing the marriage of two of his gay friends.[1] The initial compromise pleased no one: the couple were disappointed by the fact that the words used were not sufficiently close to the wedding they wanted, while his immediate boss (ie the archdeacon, rather than God) was angered by the rumours that Adam had flouted the Church of England's prohibition on performing same sex marriages. The final scene showed Adam putting friendship above legal prohibition and performing the full (albeit legally ineffective) marriage service for the couple behind closed doors.

The episode brilliantly encapsulated how the rites of marriage matter as much as the right to marry. For, after all, what *is* marriage? Lawyers might tend to see it in terms of the rights that flow from it,[2] but the debates over the difference between civil partnership and marriage tell us that it is far more than a passport to legal rights. After all, would a marriage have the same significance if the couple could simply submit their details to the local Register Office and receive a certificate confirming their new status through the post?[3] Lee Badgett, commenting on the situation in the Netherlands, has suggested that same sex couples have 'reject[ed] the dry, accounting-like connotation of "registered partnership" and opt[ed] instead for the rich cultural meaning and emotional value of marriage' (Badgett 2009: 203). This is not to downplay the significance that entering into a civil partnership may have for those involved (see eg Shipman and Smart 2007; Heaphy, Smart and Einarsdottir 2013), but the introduction of this as an option was very much couched

[1] BBC2, *Rev*, first broadcast 31 March 2014.

[2] See eg, the definition of marriage as 'a contract for which the parties elect but which is regulated by the state ... because it affects status upon which depend a variety of entitlements, benefits and obligations' offered by Thorpe LJ in *Bellinger v Bellinger* [2001] EWCA Civ 1140.

[3] For discussion of this option see Peel and Harding (2004: 43).

in terms of state recognition for the purpose of *rights* rather than status, whereas the move to same sex marriage has been much more about status and social recognition.

Yet at the same time the rite *without* the rights has a very different significance. Same sex couples have been engaging in commitment ceremonies with no legal standing for some time, but having the right to the rite makes a profound difference, and not just because of the legal rights that flow from it.[4] As the psychologists Mary and Kenneth J Gergen have pointed out, 'when marriage vows are spoken between witnesses in a *sanctioned* setting, the nature of the relationship is suddenly and compellingly changed' (emphasis added) (Gergen and Gergen 2003: 469; see also Bourassa 2004: 58). The philosopher Elizabeth Brake similarly identifies this element of transformation, suggesting that the level of ritual adopted reflects the importance of the public and institutional aspects of marriage:

> It is because marriage is seen as a private and public transformation, a gateway to unique fulfillment, that it is an occasion for elaborate celebration ... it is the translation of love into a specific institutional form that gives the ceremony its meaning. (Brake 2013: 14).

Brake's allusion to 'elaborate celebration' encourages us to move our gaze beyond the legal rite that creates the marriage to the broader social rites associated with it that give the event its cultural and communal significance. Not all aspects of the celebration will merit the term but some helpful indicators are provided by Charlsey, in his study of the wedding industry in Glasgow in the 1980s: he suggests that if there is a perceived 'right way' of performing certain actions 'which is strikingly well known compared to any reason for doing them in that particular way', together with 'numerous sequences of action to be performed', taking the form of 'events which are not necessary for their avowed end', then a particular practice might well deserve the term 'rite' (Charlsey 1991; 179–80).

Serendipitously, at the time that this particular episode of *Rev* was broadcast, a group of lawyers, sociologists, anthropologists, psychologists, demographers, theologians, and art historians were gathering in Cambridge to reflect on the rites *of* marriage, as well as the right *to* marry (or not to marry), and how the two may relate to one another. The timing, of course, was not entirely coincidental. The proposed book that this group was gathering to discuss had been inspired in part by the widespread debates about the meaning of modern marriage that were occurring both in the media and within academia. While the 2013 Act had granted the right to marry to same sex couples, its tripartite distinction between marriages conducted in a

[4] As compared, for example, to those couples who *could* marry but instead choose a rite that has religious significance but no legal standing (see eg Akhtar, this volume).

civil ceremony (open to all), marriages conducted in an Anglican ceremony (explicitly limited to opposite sex couples) and marriages conducted according to the rites of other faiths and denominations (which can, but need not, be made available to same sex couples as well as to opposite sex couples) had opened up new questions and possibilities concerning the choice of *how* one can marry. At the same time, we wanted to broaden the focus of the discussion beyond same sex marriage, to think about what marriage means for those who have not had to fight for the right to marry, and who may as a result have devoted more thought to the rites to be followed in the marriage ceremonial. Such discussions in turn prompted consideration of how those who had just acquired the right to marry would exercise it: would the rites usually associated with marriage be embraced, adapted, subverted or rejected? In addition to considering the significance of particular rites of marriage, and how these might repel or attract, we also wanted to look at how the law conceptualises ceremonies that do not fit a particular form, and whether more radical reform is still needed.

Since our intention was to examine these issues from various disciplinary perspectives, we decided to focus solely on England and Wales, in order to explore in depth the specific issues arising from this jurisdiction's Anglican heritage, demographic development, current laws and social practices. We also decided to focus on key contemporary issues relating to marriage rites and rights. The history of particular developments is sketched in where necessary, but the focus is very much on how marriage has changed over the past 50 years, and more particularly in the last decade.

We begin, then, by exploring changes in the rite of marriage over the past decades. John Haskey discusses the significant demographic and social changes that have occurred, analysing not just changes in the numbers marrying, but also how they are choosing to marry. Pre-marital cohabitation, remarriage after divorce and the secularisation of the marriage ceremony all emerge as key changes. Pre-marital cohabitation is also the focus of Rebecca Probert's chapter: drawing on wedding magazines, television programmes and social surveys, she explores the extent to which the moment of marriage still constitutes a rite of passage when couples have been living together in advance of the ceremony. The ritual of giving and receiving wedding presents is another aspect that assumes a different significance where the couple are no longer having to equip a home for the first time, as Louise Purbrick shows in her chapter: it remains, however, an important way for the couple's kin and friends to demonstrate their approval (or not) of the union. The final chapter in this Part, Elizabeth Peel's empirical study of lesbian and gay couples, addresses the phenomenon of civil partnership ceremonies and holds out the possibility of more radical change to come as different groups innovate and perform marriage in different ways.

Part II then goes on to examine the interconnection between the rite of marriage and the rights that flow from marriage. Ayesha Vardag and Joanna

Miles assess whether the making of a pre-nuptial agreement should be seen as an emerging marriage rite in its own right. The possibility of redefining the rights that flow from marriage arguably reflects the degree of choice individuals have over whether to marry, how to marry, and what sort of marriage they want. Helena Wray then addresses the very different situation where immigration status, which may be claimed as a result of marriage, has become a central preoccupation of the state—with the result that not only the rights which flow from marriage, including the right to live in the UK, but also the marriage rites themselves are controlled in ways that would be regarded as unacceptably intrusive if they occurred in another context. For other couples, the rite may be more important than the rights: Rajnaara Akhtar discusses the practice among Muslim couples of going through a religious ceremony that is recognised by the community but which might not have any legal standing. The role of kin and community assumes a rather darker aspect in Perveez Mody's chapter on forced marriages: as Mody notes, there is also a right *not* to marry.

Language, ritual and the meaning of marriage are considered in Part III, with analysis of two very different sources. Sarah Farrimond examines the changing language of the Anglican ceremony and the symbolism of the ritual employed during the service. The very familiarity of the cultural script may often blunt our perception of the underpinning ideologies (for better or for worse). Rosie Harding then engages in a discourse analysis of the recent debates in the House of Lords over same sex marriage. Intriguingly, but perhaps not unexpectedly, the legacy of the Anglican liturgy can be seen in many of the concerns expressed, in particular the perception that husbands and wives have different roles within marriage and that marriage is inextricably linked with the procreation of children.

We close with two radical pieces calling for changes to the very language, performance and meaning of marriage. Peter Edge argues that we need to address the respective roles of religion and state more directly; after all, should a religious rite be capable of generating legal rights? He suggests that we should distinguish between the two both functionally and linguistically: religious organisations would be able to conduct marriage ceremonies, but only the state-organised civil partnership ceremonies would carry legal recognition and rights. Jonathan Herring, meanwhile, is content to retain the term 'marriage' but contends that it should bear a very different meaning: rather than being a union premised on the sexual relationship of two persons, it should be defined by the provision of care by the one to the other.

Having sketched out the approach of this collection and the content of the different chapters, it will be useful at this point to identify some of the common themes that have emerged and locate them in the existing literature on the topic.

II. CHOICE, INDIVIDUALITY AND IDENTITY

Fifty years ago, the exercise of choice as to whether and where to marry was rather more limited than it is today. At the most basic level, most couples who wanted to make a life together would not have seen themselves as having a 'choice' whether or not to marry. Marriage was expected, and those who lived together outside marriage would often face disapproval from kin and community—if, indeed, they even dared to make their unwed status known (Probert 2012). Those who did marry might choose to do so in a variety of ways—if, that is, they were marrying for the first time. Those who had gone through a divorce would find their options curtailed: as Haskey demonstrates in his chapter, some denominations were willing to conduct second marriages where one or both had been divorced, but the Church of England and the Roman Catholic Church were not, on the basis that marriages once entered into were indissoluble. Choosing a civil wedding, on the other hand, meant the local Register Office. Even wedding guides were prescriptive in tone: one 1964 wedding planner stipulated decisively that '[a] bride who has been previously married should not wear white' (Owen Williams 1964).

Fast-forward to the present day, and we find a very different picture. While it is still true that most couples who share a home are married, an increasing number are choosing not to marry (or even not to share a home: Haskey 2005; Haskey and Lewis 2006; Duncan and Phillips 2012) and the vast majority of those who do marry will have lived together beforehand (Haskey, chapter two of this volume). For those who have done so, marriage no longer operates as a rite of transition in the same way, since it is no longer marks the point at which it is assumed that couples will begin their joint lives together (Kalmijn, 2004: 583; Smock, Manning and Porter 2005: 680; Probert, chapter three of this volume; Heaphy, Smart and Einarsdottir 2013: 87).

Against this backdrop, all but a few now enjoy a genuine choice as to whether or not to marry, and so have to make a conscious decision to tie the knot (Lewis, 2001: 144). But given the degree of commitment that exists within many long-term cohabiting relationships (van Hooff 2013: 53), what does getting married actually signify? One couple pondering whether to marry identified the support which marriage provided to their existing commitment and concluded that it 'can promote stability (and from that mutual growth) within a relationship supported by formal commitment and peer acceptance' (Torien and Williams 2003: 435). Mary and Kenneth J Gergen similarly saw the public nature of marriage as contributing to the commitment being made, suggesting that '[b]y including within our "we" the relational tie of state and church, we emphasize the holding power of our vows' (Gergen and Gergen 2003: 470). While the state will no longer hold individuals to their vows, the act of marrying is at the very least a declaration of one's future intentions; a signal to the other spouse and the rest of the world that the relationship is intended to be lifelong (Fitzgibbon 2002; Garrison 2007; McGowan 2007; Farley 2007). As Milton C Regan notes, marriage 'still has powerful cultural power as the paradigm of intimate commitment' (Regan 1999: 7).

The importance attached by the state—and, perhaps, by one's family, partner and partner's family—to marriage as a signifier of commitment is clearly an important context within which individual choice is exercised. Of course, pinning down the motivations for the decision to marry may be difficult even in individual cases: Charlsey noted that the Glaswegian couples he observed marrying in the 1980s were doing so 'for a variety of perhaps typically tangled reasons, acknowledged and unacknowledgeable, admitted to all or not even to themselves' (Charlsey 1991: 27); as he added, this had always been the case. Some, even in the 1980s, were marrying to be married, and Eekelaar and Maclean's study of couples who had for the most part been entering into partnerships in that decade similarly found that a number gave conventional reasons for marrying, indicating 'an acceptance of the prescriptions of religion, cultural practices or family expectations as sufficient reason to enter marriage' (Eekelaar and Maclean 2004: 520). Even more recent research suggests that certain expectations still need to be navigated, with unmarried status being constructed as a temporary condition and women who had remained single into their late 30s and 40s needing to account for their status while younger single women were seen as 'not married yet' (Sandfield and Percy 2003). Clearly, 'choice' has to be seen in context.

At the same time, it should be borne in mind that the idea of two individuals choosing to make a commitment to each other is rooted in a Western view of marriage that presupposes a particular view as regards the position and agency of the individual. Other cultures do not necessarily share this view, but the dominance of the language of 'choice' in all aspects of marriage—from non-marriage, to cohabitation, ceremony, and rites—makes it perhaps unsurprising that a discourse of alterity in the shape of 'forced marriage' (characterised by assertions that in such marriages there is *no* choice) has simultaneously emerged as a pressing social and moral concern. The communities in which there may still be pressure not to cohabit before marriage, or to marry an approved spouse, now stand out, as the chapters by Rajnaara Akhtar and Perveez Mody show.

A second dramatic change has been from marriage as a religious rite to marriage as a largely secular rite. As John Haskey shows, civil marriages accounted for under a third of all marriages in 1964, and over two-thirds today. Significantly, it is the possibility of marrying on 'approved premises' that has proved popular, accounting for more than half of all weddings today. What has also changed is the *perception* of civil marriages. In Leonard's survey of 50 couples marrying in Swansea at the end of the 1960s, most reported that they wanted a 'proper' wedding, by which they meant a wedding in church (Leonard 1980). Significantly, even those who were not able to do so reported this as an aspiration. The idea of a 'proper' wedding still had a strong resonance for those getting married on the eve of the 1980s (Mansfield and Collard 1988: 102); indeed, religious marriages, which had been overtaken by civil marriages during the second half of the 1970s, narrowly reverted to being the choice of the majority during the following decade. Walliss, however, found a greater variety of views among those marrying in the final decade of the twentieth century. While the majority of couples who had chosen to marry in church justified this on the basis of it being the proper thing to do, this was often due to the influence of their parents (see also Farrimond, chapter ten of this volume). Those who married in a civil ceremony, by contrast, 'had tended to give the matter more thought than those who simply married in church because of some vaguely articulated notion of "tradition"' (Walliss 2002: 3.14). While a lack of any religious belief was a common reason, a desire 'to exercise a high level of control over their wedding' was another. Marrying on 'approved premises' offered the opportunity 'to make "their big day" an expression of their individuality rather than conforming to what they perceived as the "one size fits all" church ceremony'.

This idea that the rite of getting married (as well as, of course, choosing whether to marry at all) is increasingly about reflecting one's own individuality and identity has been noted by a number of writers (Gillis 1999: 52; Leeds-Hurwitz 2002; van Hooff 2013: 133). Wedding guides no longer dictate what should be done, but offer suggestions on how to personalise the occasion and make it 'different' and 'unique' (see eg ffitch 2000: 1). In recent years, the scope for customising one's wedding has been demonstrated through high-profile celebrity nuptials splashed in the pages of *Hello* magazine, an unprecedented number of magazines devoted to all aspects of the wedding, and popular television series such as *Don't Tell the Bride*, *Arrange me a Marriage* and *Wedding House*.

Yet there is perhaps an interesting distinction to be drawn between choice and individuality, in that couples are in many cases simply choosing from a range of options provided by the wedding industry. This can be seen in the changing attitudes to both the wedding dress and catering for the reception. The 1964 guide to *Planning Your Wedding Day From A to Z* assumed that '[m]any brides, for sentimental as well as economical reasons, will want to make their own wedding gown' (Owen Williams 1964). The guide also included a number of recipes as suggestions for catering at the reception. By contrast, a few decades on, Charlsey noted the ritualisation of the process of buying the wedding dress and the emergence of dedicated shops 'designed to celebrate the specialness of the wedding dress and to draw maximum profit from it': a bride was expected to identify with 'her' dress, but simply because it was the dress that would make her a bride, not because it represented her taste, personality or choice in the same way that her other clothes would (Charlsey 1991: 71). Similarly, while he commented that a keen baker might make the wedding cake at home, 'providing it with decoration of the expected elaboration and polish would defeat most home cooks' (ibid: 54).[5]

It is perhaps not surprising, then, that the last 50 years have also seen a significant change in the scale of the celebrations associated with marriage: as cohabitation has increased and the social significance of the wedding has diluted, there is a sense that weddings have become more elaborate to generate their own rationale (Charlsey 1991: 13; Probert, chapter three of this volume), while at the same time the availability of hotels, stately homes and castles means that many weddings are played out against a grand backdrop. The shift can be seen by looking back to an empirical study of weddings conducted before this period of change. Pierce, analysing marriages celebrated in the 1950s, noted that the white wedding, reception and honeymoon had 'become increasingly popular over the period in all social classes'; even so, only 57 per cent of weddings involved a white bridal dress and a reception (Pierce 1963: 219). By contrast, Otnes and Pleck speak of the right to the rite in modern North American culture, noting that 'except on the lowest rungs of the socio-economic ladder, the decision to plan and execute elaborate weddings is rarely questioned' (Otnes and Pleck 2003: 3). On this side of the Atlantic, Boden has identified the phenomenon of the 'superbride', responsible for project-managing the big day while she herself is 'picture-perfect' (Boden 2001): as she notes, the current emphasis is on the wedding as 'a cultural event or performance which generates its meaning primarily through consumption'. As Louise Purbrick shows in her chapter, this extends to the presents that guests are increasingly asked to give to the couple.

Some, understandably, are alienated by what they see as the emptiness of consumer weddings and either decide to eschew the ceremony altogether or opt for a more pared-down version.[6] Yet the exercise of choice is still inevitably constrained to a certain extent. For one thing, restrictions remain on where and how one can legally get married and on what can be included within the ceremony (see eg Edge and Corrywright 2011). In addition, quite apart from the legal aspect, certain elements are seen as so intrinsic to the process of getting married that without them the wedding would not be recognised as such. As Helena Wray notes in her chapter, weddings that do not fit the perceived norm may be more likely to be deemed to be 'sham' where they involve those subject to immigration control. Family members may equally have strong feelings about what constitutes a 'proper' wedding (see eg Peel, chapter five of this volume). The clear continuities between religious

[5] One of the authors, who did make her own wedding cake, can confirm this. But the icing was at least 'individual'.

[6] See eg V Elizabeth (2003: 428) noting that 'weddings seem such "show and tell" affairs'.

and civil weddings illustrate the hold of certain ideas: a number of couples marrying on 'approved premises' in the late 1990s revealed how they wanted a 'traditional' wedding ceremony but without the religious elements:

> As with couples marrying in church, this is also influenced by ideas of what is the 'correct' thing to do and also by cultural ideas of what is romantic and meaningful, such as walking down an aisle of some sort, being 'given away' and exchanging vows between loved ones. (Walliss 2002: 3.18; see also Farrimond, chaper ten of this volume).

Being 'given away' is of course one very obvious way in which the marriage ceremony continues to highlight gender differences,[7] which raises questions as to which aspects same sex couples might choose to adopt (or ignore). Smart, commenting on the then new option of civil partnership and the older but non-legal alternative of a commitment ceremony, noted that such decisions 'involve considerations of wider sexual politics, personal aspirations and desires, and ideas about how to retain integrity and principles concerning life-styles' (Smart 2008: 762; see also Heaphy, Smart and Einarsdottir 2013: 101). As Elizabeth Peel explains in her chapter, the participants in her study of new civil partners were 'creatively and reflexively adopting and remodelling ceremonial ritual'.

Yet Leeds-Hurwitz's study of inter-cultural weddings in the United States identified the dilemma faced by couples who want a different form of wedding: noting that the power of rituals comes from recognition, she commented that '[i]n an important way, it doesn't count as a "proper" wedding if few of the details match what you've experienced previously' (Leeds-Hurwitz 2002: 190). In her study of inter-cultural weddings, the parents of one bride did not even realise the nature of the event that was being planned and so did not attend. As the bride later reported:

> when they saw the photos, and they saw we had spent money on it ... they were surprised, and they said, oh, they didn't realize, and if they had known they would have come, but ... they didn't realize it was going to be a wedding, they just thought it was going to be a party, so they didn't come. (Leeds-Hurwitz 2002: 80; see also Peel, chapter five of this volume).

This brings us on to the important role that family and community play in the process of getting married.

III. FAMILY AND COMMUNITY

The rite of marrying is to some extent always a public one. Even the most pared-down ceremony still requires a third person to officiate, and the legislation directs that witnesses should also be present and should sign the

[7] Assuming that the parties want it to: it is not a required part of the ceremony.

register. In addition, marriage also offers the opportunity for the couple to make a public statement—to friends, family and the wider community—of their personal commitment (Eekelaar 2007). It also enables them to seek approval and guidance from those social networks: Kalmijn, for example, suggests in his study of marriages in the Netherlands that

> By celebrating the marriage in an elaborate fashion, newlyweds are helped to define their new identity; they obtain information on how to act in the new role, obtain approval from the social network in which they are embedded, and reduce the uncertainty they may feel about the new step they have taken. (Kalmijn 2004: 582).

Such approval may be all the more important for those who were previously barred from entering into a marriage: thus Kitzinger and Wilkinson, explaining why they had wanted to marry rather than enter into a civil partnership, felt 'that our continuing (and reaffirmed) centrality in each other's lives now stands some chance of being protected—even facilitated—by governments and states that have previously marginalized and condemned us for loving women' (2004: 139).[8]

Otnes and Pleck, musing on the meaning of 'ritual' in this context, noted the importance of the wedding as enabling those involved 'to feel connected to others' (Otnes and Pleck 2003: 4; see also Brake 2013: 14). Of course, the very fact of the marriage creates connections even between those not physically present: each spouse acquires a new set of 'in-laws'. But the role of kin in the making and shaping of marriages goes deeper than this. Family expectations may still play a role in influencing whether or not a couple marry (see eg Eekelaar and Maclean 2004: 520). For some, indeed, such expectations may determine the outcome: as the chapter by Perveez Mody illustrates, coercion may be most powerful when it is rooted in love on both sides.

Such expectations may also play a role in instigating and shaping a prenuptial agreement (see Vardag and Miles, chapter six of this volume). As we have already noted, the expectation of members of the family that a wedding should be celebrated in a particular way may also exercise an important influence on where and how it takes place (see eg Walliss 2002; Farrimond, chapter ten of this volume); in the case of Church of England weddings, family links to a particular parish may facilitate the couple's wedding in a church that is particularly meaningful to them even though they neither live in the locality nor worship there (see Farrimond, this volume). For other couples, meanwhile, the expectations of the family and community may

[8] At the time this was written, this was perhaps premature, as the UK government did not recognise their Canadian marriage as such, instead categorising it as a civil partnership, and their legal challenge to this failed (*Wilkinson v Kitzinger and Others* [2006] EWHC 2022 (Fam)). As a result of the Marriage (Same Sex Couples) Act 2013, Sch 2, Pt 3, para 5, however, they will be recognised as married.

mean that more weight is given to the religious rite than the state-sanctioned legal rights (Akhtar, chapter eight of this volume).

Members of the family also play an important role in the celebration of the marriage. The reactions of family members will be accorded particular significance: as Elizabeth Peel shows, some couples planning to register a civil partnership used the language of marriage to ensure that the nature of the event was understood and supported by their family (see also Shipman and Smart 2007). Close family will usually expect, and be expected, to attend the wedding: a decision whether or not to invite a particular relative is a statement of the perceived closeness of the relationship, while a refusal to attend is often rooted in disapproval of the union (see eg Heaphy, Smart and Einarsdottir 2013: 105). The father of the bride was once expected to foot the bill for the wedding (see eg Webley 1991), although increasingly the cost has been shared with the groom's family or assumed by the couple themselves. But support for the couple may still be demonstrated in tangible form by the giving of presents, and by what is given (see Purbrick, chapter four of this volume). The wedding itself will usually involve different members of the family in different ways, with the parents of the bride in particular having expected roles (see eg Charlsey 1991). Members of the family are often called upon to sign the register as witnesses of the marriage (Haskey, chapter two of this volume). During the wedding itself, the families of the bride and groom are symbolically separated on either side of the aisle but expected to mingle thereafter, reflecting the new relationship between them.

Identity, community and ritual are thus all intermingled in the marriage ceremony and accompanying celebrations: as Leeds-Hurwitz puts it:

> we use rituals as a way of telling ourselves stories about our identities (who we are), and our communities (the groups within which we find ourselves) ... Rituals have meaning for us because we conveniently forget that we ourselves have designed them. (Leeds-Hurwitz 2002: 29).

But even if '[w]e all love a good wedding'—as the MP Yvette Cooper claimed during the debates on the Marriage (Same Sex Couples) Act 2013—should we not be asking, as Harding suggests in the conclusion to her chapter, what is it ultimately about?

IV. LOVE AND LAW

Those who spoke in favour of extending marriage to same sex couples in the course of the debates in Parliament tended to celebrate its role in uniting two persons in love; those who spoke against, by contrast, argued that love could not be the sole defining feature and that the law (together with society and religion) had an important role to play in regulating who could marry. At the end of the Second Reading in the House of Commons, Hugh Robertson, the Minister of State at the Department for Culture, Media and Sport, managed to combine the two subtly by identifying the straightforward (if question-begging) proposition at the heart of the Bill as being that '[i]f a couple love each other, the state should not stop them from getting married *unless there is a good reason*' (emphasis added).[9]

Of course, as a number of commentators have pointed out, the idea of 'love' being integral to marriage is itself of relatively recent origin. Rosemary Auchmuty, for example has identified the modern form of marriage as being 'one that originates in romance and proceeds to companionship in a nuclear setting' (Auchmuty 2004: 122; see also Evans 2003: 21; Collins 2003; Stone 2007) and described this as being of relatively recent construction. It is also worth noting that for many British South Asians (pre-marital) love is not usually or necessarily a motive for marriage; instead, questions of suitability in terms of education, kinship, status and ethno-religious factors are important considerations for arrangement. The 'traditional' cultural expectation is that love flows between the couple after suitable marriage, not before.

An even more difficult issue was raised in the course of the Parliamentary debates by the Labour MP Robert Flello as to why the state should even be interested in registering and recording committed sexual unions.[10] The same basic question, with a rather different answer, has been posed by a number of commentators. Brake, for example, has coined the term 'amatonormativity' to challenge the assumption 'that a central, exclusive, amorous relationship is normal for humans, in that it is a universally shared goal, and that such a relationship is normative, in that it *should* be aimed at in preference to other relationship types' (Brake 2013: 89–90). Others have similarly questioned the need for the sexual relationship within marriage to be exclusive (Jackson and Scott 2004) or even to exist at all (Herring, chapter thirteen of this volume).

Brake's proposal was for a form of 'minimal marriage' which would allow individuals 'to select from the rights and responsibilities exchanged within marriage and exchange them with whomever they want, rather than exchanging a predefined bundle of rights and responsibilities with only one amatory partner' (Brake 2013: 156). She is not the first to talk of breaking marriage down into its constituent parts and assessing both the need for any given right and the needs of the would-be recipient (see eg Clive 1980, Krause 2000; McK Norrie 2000; Eichner 2007). Other commentators have focused on providing different forms of institutions for different purposes, whether this involves a menu of options for all couples (see eg Lifshitz 2012: 261), or limiting legal recognition to one neutral form such as civil partnership or civil union and leaving marriage as a matter for religious organisations (see eg Shanley 2004: 112; Thaler and Sunstein 2008: 224;

[9] Hansard, HC Deb, 5 March 2013, col 230.

[10] Ibid, col 146.

Presser 2012; Edge, chapter twelve of this volume). In some accounts, form and function are both challenged: Fineman, for example, has argued that legal regulation and protection should be focused on the 'caretaker-dependent' relationship rather than sexual unions, leaving marriage as a purely social or religious institution (Fineman 2004).

Such alternatives are, of course, easier to suggest than to implement. John Eekelaar, reviewing some of the more radical alternatives, gently suggested that 'given the benign nature of contemporary marriage in Western societies, and the fact that individuals can attribute to it as many meanings as they wish, it is hard to see how society would gain by losing it' (2012: 323). A more sustained defence of legal marriage comes from Hartley and Watson, who have evaluated it within the same terms of political liberalism that underpin Brake's work but have come to a rather different conclusion. They argue that arrangements other than marriage could support and recognise the caring relationships that commentators have identified as needing priority, but that there are good reasons[11] to recognise legal marriage 'to protect caregivers of dependents from problematic vulnerabilities that can result from domestic partnerships' (Hartley and Watson 2012: 203).

Whatever conclusions commentators come to on the purpose of, or need for, marriage, every year hundreds of thousands of individuals choose to tie the knot in England and Wales alone, and it is estimated that many tens of thousands travel overseas to marry (ONS 2010). That it remains an institution that so many individuals value is in itself good reason why it should be a matter of serious study, and we hope that the chapters that follow will illuminate why both rites and rights matter.

BIBLIOGRAPHY

AUCHMUTY, Rosemary, 'Same-Sex Marriage Revived: Feminist Critique and Legal Strategy' (2004) 14 *Feminism & Psychology* 101.

BODEN, Sharon, '"Superbrides": Wedding Consumer Culture and the Construction of Bridal Identity' (2001) 6 *Sociological Research Online*: www.socresonline.org.uk/6/1/boden.

BOURASSA, Kevin, 'Love and the Lexicon of Marriage' (2004) 14 *Feminism & Psychology* 57.

BRAKE, Elizabeth, *Minimising Marriage: Marriage, Morality, and the Law* (Oxford, Oxford University Press, 2013).

COLLINS, Marcus, *Modern Love: An Intimate History of Men and Women in Twentieth-Century Britain* (London, Atlantic Books, 2003).

[11] In the language of political liberalism, 'public reasons' that are 'justifiable in terms that can be shared by citizens as free and equal persons' (Hartley and Watson 2012: 185). See further Peterson and McLean (2013), who also analyse marriage from a perspective of political liberalism.

CLIVE, Eric, 'Marriage: An unnecessary legal concept?' in J Eekelaar and SN Katz (eds), *Marriage and Cohabitation in Contemporary Societies: Areas of Legal, Social and Ethical Change* (London, Butterworths, 1980).
DE WAAL, Anastasia (ed), *The Meaning of Matrimony: Debating Same-Sex Marriage* (London, Civitas, 2013).
DUNCAN, Simon and PHILLIPS, Miranda, 'People Who Live Apart Together (LATs)—New Family Form or Just a Stage?' (2012) 22 *International Review of Sociology* 513.
EDGE, Peter W and CORRYWRIGHT, Dominic, 'Including Religion: Reflections on Legal, Religious and Social Implications of the Developing Ceremonial Law of Marriage and Civil Partnership' (2011) 26 *Journal of Contemporary Religion* 19.
EEKELAAR, John, 'Review of Marriage Proposals: Questioning a Legal Status' (2012) *International Journal of Law in Context* 320.
EEKELAAR, John and MACLEAN, Mavis, 'Marriage and the Moral Bases of Personal Relationships' (2004) 31 *Journal of Law and Society* 510.
EICHNER, Maxine, 'Principles of the Law of Relationships Among Adults' (2007) 41 *Family Law Quarterly* 433.
ELIZABETH, Vivienne, 'To Marry, or not to Marry: That is the Question' (2003) 13 *Feminism & Psychology* 426.
EVANS, Mary, *Love: An Unromantic Discussion* (London, Polity Press, 2003).
FARLEY, Margaret, 'The Meaning of Commitment in K Scott and M Warren (eds), *Perspectives on Marriage: A Reader* (Oxford, Oxford University Press, 2007).
FFITCH, Diane, *Planning a non-traditional wedding* (Ipswich, Teach Yourself Books, 2000).
FINEMAN, Martha, *The Autonomy Myth: A Theory of Dependency* (New York, The New Press, 2004).
FITZGIBBON, Scott, 'Marriage and the Good of Obligation' (2002) 47 *American Journal of Jurisprudence* 41.
GARRISON, Marsha, 'The Decline of Formal Marriage: Inevitable or Reversible?' (2007) 41 *Family Law Quarterly* 491.
GERGEN, Mary and GERGEN, Kenneth J, 'Marriage as a Relational Engagement' (2003) 13 *Feminism and Psychology* 469.
HARTLEY, Christine and WATSON, Lori, 'Political Liberalism, Marriage and the Family' (2012) 31 *Law and Philosophy* 185.
HASKEY, John, 'Living arrangements in contemporary Britain: Having a partner who usually lives elsewhere and Living Apart Together' (2005) 122 *Population Trends* 35.
HASKEY, John and LEWIS, Jane, 'Living-Apart-Together in Britain: Context and Meaning' (2006) 2 *International Journal of Law in Context* 37.
HEAPHY, Brian, SMART, Carol and EINARSDOTTIR, Anna, *Same-Sex Marriages: New Generations, New Relationships* (Basingstoke, Palgrave Macmillan, 2013).
JACKSON, Stevi and SCOTT, Sue, 'The Personal Is Still Political: Heterosexuality, Feminism and Monogamy' (2004) 14 *Feminism & Psychology* 151.
KALMIJN, Matthijs 'Marriage Rituals as Reinforcers of Role Transitions: An Analysis of Weddings in The Netherlands' (2004) 66 *Journal of Marriage and Family* 582.
KITZINGER, Celia and WILKINSON, Sue, 'The Re-Branding of Marriage: Why We Got Married Instead of Registering a Civil Partnership' (2004) 14 *Feminism & Psychology* 127.

KRAUSE, Harry D, 'Marriage for the New Millennium: Heterosexual, Same-Sex—Or Not At All?' (2000) 34 *Family Law Quarterly* 271.
LEE BADGETT, MV, *When Gay People Get Married: What Happens When Societies Legalize Same-Sex Marriage* (New York, New York University Press, 2009).
LEEDS-HURWITZ, Wendy, *Wedding as Text: Communicating Cultural Identities Through Ritual* (London, LEA, 2002).
LEONARD, Diana, *Sex and Generation: A Study of Courtship and Weddings* (London, Tavistock Publications, 1980).
LIFSHITZ, Shahar, 'The Pluralistic Vision of Marriage' in M Garrison and E S Scott (eds), *Marriage at the Crossroads: Law, Policy, and the Brave New World of Twenty-First-Century* Families (Cambridge, Cambridge University Press, 2012).
MANSFIELD, Penny and COLLARD, Jean, *The Beginning of the Rest of Your Life? A Portrait of Newly-Wed Marriage* (Basingstoke, Macmillan, 1988).
MCGOWAN, Jo, 'Marriage versus living together' in K Scott and M Warren (eds), *Perspectives on Marriage: A Reader* (Oxford, Oxford University Press, 2007).
MCK NORRIE, Kenneth, 'Marriage is for heterosexuals—may the rest of us be saved from it' (2000) *Child and Family Law Quarterly* 363.
OFFICE OF NATIONAL STATISTICS, 'Population Estimates by Marital Status: Methodology Paper' (London, ONS, 2010).
OTNES, Cele C and PLECK, Elizabeth H, *Cinderella Dreams: The Allure of the Lavish Wedding* (Berkeley CA, University of California Press, 2003).
OWEN WILLIAMS, Betty, *Planning Your Wedding Day from A to Z* (London, W Foulsham & Co Ltd, 1964).
PEEL, Elizabeth and HARDING, Rosie, 'Civil Partnerships: A New Couple's Conversation' (2004) 14 *Feminism & Psychology* 41.
PETERSON, Scott and McLEAN, Iain, *Love and Law in the UK and the US* (Edinburgh, Edinburgh University Press, 2013).
PIERCE, Rachel M, 'Marriage in the Fifties' (1963) 11 *The Sociological Review* 215.
PRESSER, Stephen B, 'Marriage and the Law: Time for a Divorce?' in JA Nichols (ed), *Marriage and Divorce in a Multicultural Context* (Cambridge, Cambridge University Press, 2012).
PROBERT, Rebecca, *The Legal Regulation of Cohabitation: From Fornicators to Family, 1600-2010* (Cambridge, Cambridge University Press, 2012).
REGAN, Milton C, Jr, *Alone Together: Law and the Meanings of Marriage* (Oxford, Oxford University Press, 1999).
SANDFIELD, Anna and PERCY, Carol, 'Accounting for Single Status: Heterosexism and Ageism in Heterosexual Women's Talk about Marriage' (2003) 13 *Feminism & Psychology* 475.
SHANLEY, Mary Lyndon, 'Afterword' in M Lyndon Shanley (ed), *Just Marriage* (Oxford, Oxford University Press, 2004).
SHIPMAN, Beccy and SMART, Carol, '"It's Made a Huge Difference": Recognition, Rights and the Personal Significance of Civil Partnership' (2007) 12 *Sociological Research Online*.
SMART, Carol, '"Can I Be Bridesmaid?" Combining the Personal and Political in Same-Sex Weddings' (2008) 11 *Sexualities* 761.
SMOCK, Pamela J, MANNING, Wendy D and PORTER, Meredith, '"Everything's There Except Money": How Money Shapes Decisions to Marry Among Cohabitors' (2005) 67 *Journal of Marriage and Family* 680.

STACEY, JUDITH, *Unhitched: Love, Marriage and Family Values From West Hollywood to Western China* (New York, New York University Press, 2011).
STONE, Lawrence, 'Passionate Attachments in the West in Historical Perspective' in K Scott and M Warren (eds), *Perspectives on Marriage: A Reader* (Oxford, Oxford University Press, 2007).
THALER, Richard T and SUNSTEIN, Cass R, *Nudge: Improving decisions about health, wealth and happiness* (New Haven CT, Yale University Press, 2008; Penguin, 2009).
TORIEN Merran and WILLIAMS, Andrew, 'In Knots: Dilemmas of a Feminist Couple Contemplating Marriage' (2003) 13 *Feminism and Psychology* 432.
VAN HOOFF, Jenny *Modern Couples? Continuity and Change in Heterosexual Relationships* (Farnham, Ashgate, 2013).
WALLISS, John, '"Loved the Wedding, Invite Me to the Marriage": The Secularisation of Weddings in Contemporary Britain' (2001) 7(4) *Sociological Research Online*: www.socresonline.org.uk/7/4/walliss.
WEBLEY, Patrick, *How to Pay for the Wedding (written especially for the bride's father)* (Kimbolton, Attam Books, 1991).

Part I

2

Marriage Rites—Trends in Marriages by Manner of Solemnisation and Denomination in England and Wales, 1841–2012

JOHN HASKEY[1]

I. INTRODUCTION

A MARRIAGE RITE, conducted according to a prescribed service or form, has general public acceptance, legal authority or ecclesiastical sanction, and usually a combination of these elements. Marriage, and the way it has been celebrated, particularly in its rituals, has varied considerably throughout the centuries and across countries, the inevitable result of social, economic, cultural, political, and religious forces and influences. In any era, there is undoubtedly a basic human psychological need for ritual.

To the great majority of those of us who are neither theologians nor anthropologists, the term 'marriage rite' probably conjures up in our mind a sacred ritual for solemnising marriage—with an inevitable religious, or at least mystical, connotation. Indeed, the dictionary defines a 'rite' as: 'a ceremonial form or observance, especially religious: a liturgy'.[2] A study of marriage rites, including their history, therefore should certainly include all forms of marriage which were solemnised in the different Christian denominations, and in other faiths too. The newcomer might question whether civil marriages should also be included, although the definition implies that the ceremonial form does not necessarily have to be religious. And the fact that civil marriages are *solemnised* indicates their ceremonial form and therefore their proper inclusion.

[1] Thanks are due to the Department of Social Policy and Intervention, University of Oxford, who provided a range of facilities, and to the Bodleian Library for retrieving enumerable books. The author is grateful to Professor Linda Woodhead who kindly provided useful information and advice, and to John Ribbins, formerly Deputy Registrar General, who provided helpful background details. Any errors remain the responsibility of the author, and, similarly, any opinions expressed are those of the author alone.

[2] *Chambers 20th Century Dictionary* (Edinburgh, Chambers, 1983).

Given that a 'marriage rite' is essentially a liturgy, either religious or secular, and that the different faiths, denominations and manners of solemnisation each have their own distinct liturgy or form of service, marriages by marriage rite may be studied by distinguishing marriages by these different forms of marriage celebration—for which statistical information is available.

In this chapter, marriage rites will be considered from the advent of civil registration in England and Wales in 1837. With the exception of 1538, when a Mandate was issued by Thomas Cromwell to keep parish records of every marriage, christening, and burial, 1837 was the year when marriages were first registered, through legislation (Registration Act 1836 and Marriage Act 1836) not only establishing the General Register Office for registering births, deaths, and marriages, but also instituting civil marriage. The legislation also allowed places of religious worship to apply to be registered for solemnising marriage. The Church of England, the Quakers and the Jews could already solemnise and register their marriages, but marriages in Roman Catholic and Non-conformist churches, once registered for marriages under this new legislation, had to be attended by a Registrar to record the event. These two Acts marked a considerable advance in state involvement in regulating and solemnising marriage, and, more especially, introduced a new non-religious rite. It was the first time, apart from a short time during the Commonwealth, that non-religious marriages were solemnised by the state, and legally recognised as such.

Copies of the marriage entries—which are made in the marriage registers—as well as constituting a legal document which provides evidence of marriage, also yield information about the marriage: the manner of solemnisation, and, if religious, the denomination or faith; the basic characteristics of the bride and bridegroom; the place of marriage; etc (Haskey 1991). Hence the marriage entries record some information on the spouses (but not their denominations or faiths), and some on the marriage ceremony (including the manner of solemnisation, denomination or faith in which the marriage was celebrated). An important implication is that marriage rates of men and women by denomination or faith cannot be derived from marriage registration records. This particular limitation is a result of the fact that, although civil registration has brought the advantage of statistical information on marriages, such data are only a *by-product* of the prime objective of recording the legal event; the details of the bride and bridegroom are required solely to identify the spouses uniquely. Hence occupation is recorded as an additional means of aiding identification, and not for the analytical purposes of, say, investigating socio-economic or social class differentials[3] in marriage.

[3] Though such differentials have been estimated from this source (Haskey 1983), and a statistical analysis made of all the information recorded in marriage entries (Haskey 1991).

Furthermore, the design of the marriage entry—the standard form on which the details of the marriage are recorded—has not changed or been updated since 1837, so that more modern features of marriage in which researchers might be interested, such as pre-marital cohabitation, whether the couple already have children (or step-children-to-be), etc, are not recorded—even if they would further aid identification of the couple (and the children brought into the marriage). Nevertheless, marriage registration records are unrivalled as a reliable source of the basic and consistent information on marriages by manner of solemnisation and denomination[4] over almost two centuries.

Using all the available series of marriage statistics—which have been extracted from the Annual Reports of the Registrar General, and their latter-day equivalents—this chapter will trace from 1841, when calendar-year statistics were first published, the statistical trends in the patterns of marriage in England and Wales, primarily according to their manner of solemnisation and denomination. This examination will then be followed by a statistical analysis of various factors associated with *recent* marriages[5] to explore their various differentials by manner of solemnisation and denomination, as a means of glimpsing the social and cultural factors associated with the different marriage rites. It will be shown that there have been profound changes not only in the numbers who marry in the different denominations, but also in the proportion marrying with a civil, rather than a religious, rite.

II. OVERALL TRENDS IN MARRIAGE FROM 1841 TO 2012

In order to set the scene for more detailed analyses to come, Figure 1 provides an overall picture of the trends in marriages by manner of solemnisation and denomination between 1841 and 2012. It must be emphasised that this is not a definitive graph, since numbers of marriages by manner of solemnisation and denomination were missing for a total of 41 years within the entire period of 172 years; the relevant numbers were not published in the appropriate Annual Reports of the Registrar General, and have had to be estimated. For the period between 1914 and 1934, and between 1952 and 1962, numbers were only available for every fifth year. In addition, there was a much longer gap of 17 years between 1934 and 1952.

To the knowledge of the author, such a long historical series of marriage statistics by manner of solemnisation and denomination has not been assembled before, let alone completed by estimating the missing data to give an uninterrupted overview.[6] The method by which the numbers were estimated

4 As 'denomination' strictly means class or group, 'by denomination' will be taken throughout to include 'by faith'.

5 All statistics for 2012 marriages are provisional.

6 Floud and Thane (1979) graphed Anglican, (total) Non-conformist, and civil marriages to 1911, without estimation.

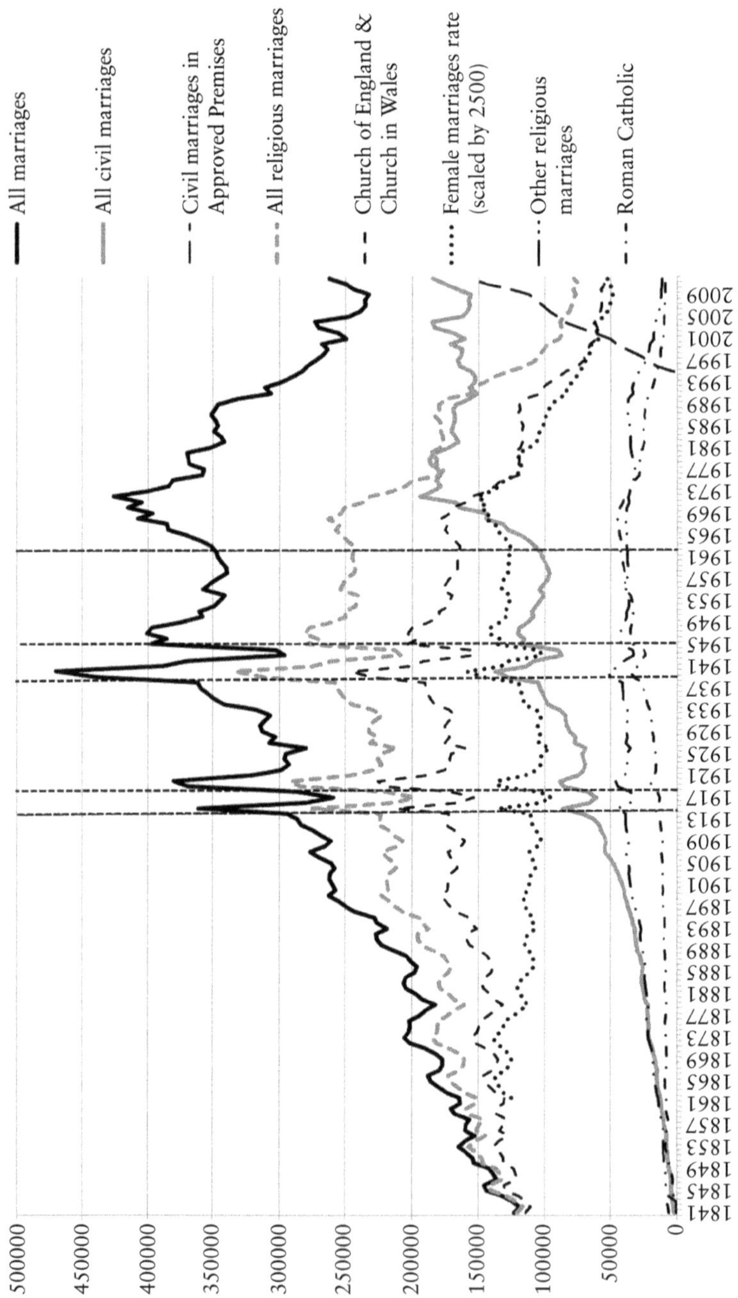

Figure 1: Marriages by manner of solemnisation† and denomination†, and female marriage rate*, 1841–2012, England and Wales

† including estimates using interpolations (see Appendix, Part (a))
* women marrying per 1000 unmarried women aged 15 and over

for the missing years is given in the Appendix (Part (a)); of course, alternative methods of estimation might give slightly different results.

It is unfortunate that estimates had to be made for all the years of both World Wars—during which there was great social disruption with many marriages being brought forward, others postponed, and perhaps yet others foregone. The two pairs of vertical dotted lines in Figure 1 indicate the two World War periods, and the outer two lines, for 1914 and 1962, contain the period within which estimates had to be made for the 41 years for which the relevant statistics are missing.

Whether the pattern of peaks in the number of marriages in 1915 and 1920, with a deep decline in between, shown in the (known) *total* number of marriages, was *indeed* replicated in a corresponding pattern for each category of marriage shown in Figure 1 is far from certain, though may be plausible. Similar considerations apply to the estimates for the years during, and surrounding, World War II, and, indeed, there is more uncertainty concerning these estimates as they fall within the longer period of missing data. It is perhaps not surprising that limited statistics were produced during the war years when national survival was at stake, and that the production of the full range of statistics was not resumed immediately afterwards.

Recognising these uncertainties, attention will be focused on the two major periods during which no estimates, or very few, have had to be made: 1841 to 1914, and 1952 to 2012, respectively. Wherever possible, the trends will be examined and discussed in historical order, introducing at the appropriate moment relevant statistical data on related subjects, such as divorce, cohabitation, and individuals remaining unmarried, to give background and possible explanation to the observed trends.

III. HISTORICAL BACKGROUND TO THE STATISTICAL TRENDS IN MARRIAGE

Since the mid-nineteenth century, starting with the Matrimonial Causes Act 1857, which allowed divorce to be granted in civil courts for the first time, there have been several Acts of Parliament concerning divorce, almost all of which have influenced the trend and pattern of those divorcing. In contrast, as far as may be discerned, the Marriage Acts which have been enacted since the 1836 Marriage Act—concerning the permitted hours of marriage solemnisation, the minimum age at marriage, and the introduction of Authorised Persons to record marriages in Registered Buildings, etc—have had little effect upon the overall numbers, or the profile, by denomination, of marriages in England and Wales. (The only possible exception was the comparatively recent introduction of marriages in 'Approved Premises',[7] which, it may be

[7] Marriage Act 1994.

argued, increased the popularity of civil marriage and further eroded the already long-standing decline in the number of religious marriages.) Ironically, it can be argued that the various Acts of Parliament concerning *divorce*, the legal *ending* of marriage, have had much greater impact on marriages by denomination than legislation on the arrangements for solemnising marriage.

Instead, events such as the two World Wars, demographic changes and economic and social changes—such as feminism, women's equality and participation in the labour force—coupled with a few ecclesiastical developments (such as the formation of the United Reformed Church in 1972), have played a much more decisive role in influencing the patterns of marriage. But perhaps the most important factor of all has been the increasing secularisation of individuals, families, and society, as part of the decline in traditional religious belief and practice.

A. Trends from the Mid-Nineteenth Century up to World War I

From just after the start of the registration of the vital events of births, marriages, and deaths, up to the outbreak of World War I, the number of marriages rose remarkably steadily, albeit punctuated by regular minor peaks and troughs (Figure 2). Even though the number of marriages increased considerably owing to the large and consistent growth in the population during the Victorian era, the marriage rate for women was lower at the end of the period than at the beginning, indicating that the population rose slightly faster than the number of marriages. Indeed, the population of England and Wales more than doubled between 1831 and 1901.[8] Earlier, Malthus had warned about population growth, and had posed the question as to who should desist from marriage to stem the increase (Malthus 1817: 282). There were large variations across the country in marriage, both in the age at marriage, and the proportion who ultimately married (Ogle 1890; Woods 2000).

The era was one of railway building, expansion of industry, and invention (Hewitt 2006). The rural economy was heavily dependent upon agricultural labour; in 1831, 29 per cent of all families in England and Wales were employed 'chiefly in agriculture'.[9] There were limited opportunities for skilled or professional work by women. In 1841, 89 per cent of men aged 20 or over in England and Wales were recorded as having an occupation or trade, whereas the corresponding proportion of women was less than one quarter, 23 per cent. Of these working women, almost one half,

[8] *1831 Census, Enumeration Abstract, 1831, vol I, Abstract of Answers and Returns, Part 1* (1833), House of Commons Preface p xii; *Census of 1901, General report, England and Wales, 1901*, Population and rates of increase, p 15. (London, HMSO, 1904).

[9] Ibid. Re-evaluating 1851 Census data, agricultural workers are estimated to have formed 25 per cent of the total workforce in 1851, and women 27 per cent of the agricultural workforce (Higgs 1995).

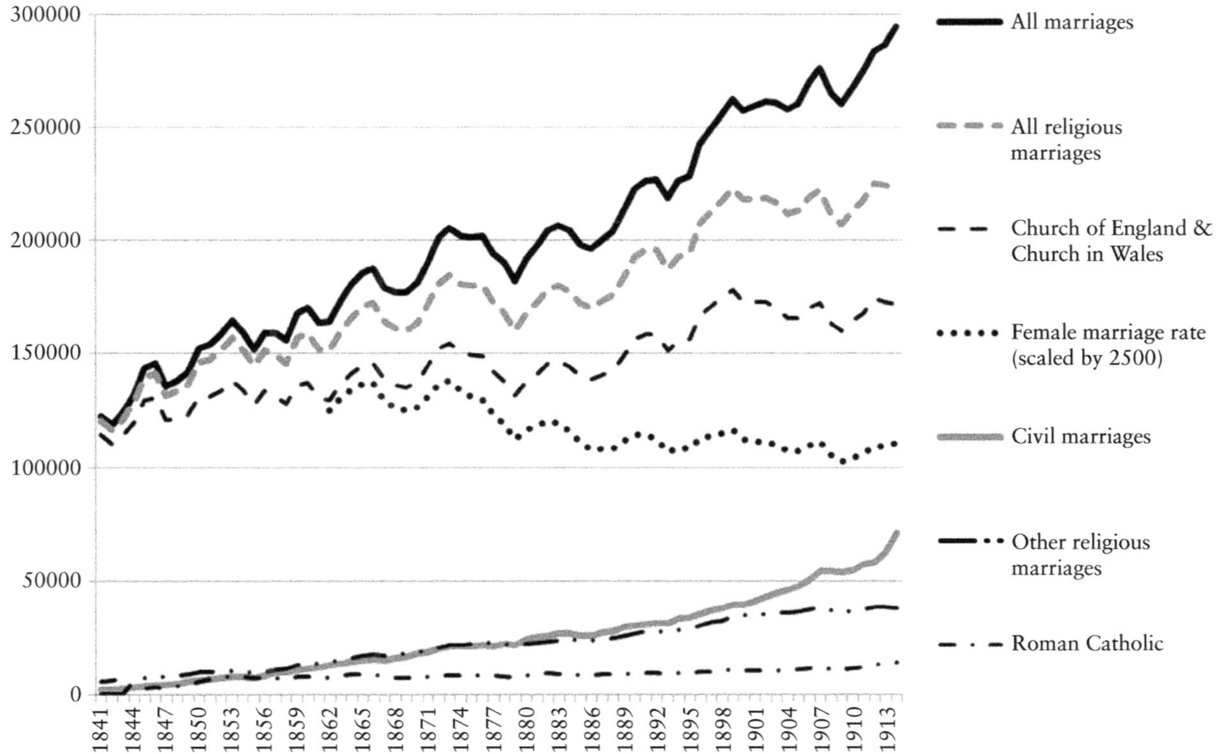

Figure 2: Marriages by manner of solemnisation and denomination, and female marriage rate*, 1841–1914, England and Wales

* women marrying per 1000 unmarried women aged 15 and over

46 per cent, were in domestic service; the next most numerous occupations were, in turn, dressmaking, cotton manufacturing, and laundry keeping, and overall almost two thirds, 64 per cent, of working women were engaged in these four types of occupation.[10] Society was heavily patriarchal: 'A dual economy can be discerned (in society), comprising the family economy and a superimposed capitalist market. The former is "manned" by women and the latter dominated by men' (Higgs 1987). Darwin's exposition of natural selection led him to the idea of sexual selection[11] (Darwin 1859), which fired Galton to invent, and study, the subject of eugenics (Galton 1883); in theory, both sexual selection and eugenics had implications for marriage, although probably neither influenced overall marriage patterns. Social reformers, often fired by the zeal of Christian ideals, led campaigns to alleviate or improve the conditions of the poor. The Non-conformists were in the ascendant (Hewitt 2006); by 1851, attendance at Non-conformist chapels had matched that at Anglican churches (Floud and Thane 1979). And the Oxford Movement, effectively led by John Henry Newman, whose tracts were the torchbearers of the Movement, reinvigorated the Catholic tradition within the Church of England. Religion played a central role in Victorians' lives, albeit attended by denominational rivalry.

The cyclical variations in the numbers of marriages, also reflected in the marriage rate, were attributed in 1854 by Dr William Farr—who had been appointed in 1837 as the 'Compiler of Abstracts' in the General Register Office—as primarily due to the success or failure of the harvest, the economy then being particularly dependent upon the health or otherwise of agriculture (GRO 1854). Farr measured the success of the harvest by the price of wheat; in good years the price of wheat was low, and the marriage rate was high; conversely when the price of wheat was high, the marriage rate tended to be lower. Farr also investigated the relative proportions of couples marrying by banns and by licence in the Established Church and discovered that proportionately more couples married by banns than licence (marrying by licence being more expensive) in years in which the price of wheat was low or moderate, and, conversely, relatively more tended to marry by licence when the price of wheat was high. Farr explained this variation by 'the pressure of the high prices of provisions ... [which] depressed the poorer classes of society more than the classes who usually marry by licence'.

In 1841, virtually all marriages were religious marriages; civil marriages got off to a very slow start, forming only 1.7 per cent of all marriages. In addition, of all religious marriages which were solemnised, 95 per cent were in the Church of England or the Church in Wales, and only five per cent

[10] *1841 Census, Occupational Abstract, 1841, Part I, Abstract of Answers and Returns* (London, HMSO, 1844) 31, 44.

[11] Sexual selection is a section within Chapter IV, Natural Selection, of the Volume: *Origin of Species*.

were in Roman Catholic or Non-conformist churches (Haskey 1987). At the start of civil registration in 1837, 11,694 Church of England clergymen—and 817 Registrars—had been furnished with Marriage Register Books (GRO 1839), but, by the end of 1838, a total of only 1,332 buildings had been registered for solemnising marriages (GRO 1841). By mid-1842, of such buildings which were so registered, 42 per cent were Congregationalists';[12] 24 per cent were Baptists'; 14 per cent were Roman Catholics'; and 9 per cent each were Presbyterians' and Methodists'[13] (GRO 1842: 15). Given that Non-conformist chapel attendance was fast catching up with Anglican church attendance, the rate of registering Non-conformist chapels for solemnising marriages appears to have been slow. The number of buildings registered for marriage did increase annually, but it would only be towards the close of the century, the start of 1897, that the number would reach 11,716, close to the initial number of marriage register books issued to Anglican clergy, some 60 years earlier (GRO 1897). Evidence exists that the Non-conformist denominations may have been content with having won their battle to marry in their own chapels, with some continuing to marry within the Church of England, at least for a while (Krause 1969)—perhaps appreciating the liturgy and beauty of Cranmer's English. A more prosaic explanation, though, is that marriage in Non-conformist chapels was the most complicated (administratively), and often the most expensive, form of marriage throughout the whole nineteenth century (Floud and Thane 1979).

Civil marriages rose steadily, but at a much slower pace than all marriages for most of the 1800s. The numbers accelerated somewhat up to 1914, when they formed 24 per cent of all marriages. In the early days, civil marriage was associated with the Poor Law Unions. At the very start of civil registration, the clerk to the Board of Guardians in every (Poor Law) Union could accept the office of Superintendent Registrar and by the end of 1838, 81 per cent had done so (GRO 1839). Although it was the duty of Guardians to provide a Register Office and furnish it, in many districts the Register Office was established at the Union workhouse, an arrangement justified on the grounds of saving expense to ratepayers and of convenience to officers, but often repugnant to the feelings of the public, and causing civil marriage to carry some stigma (Hammick 1873). The association with the workhouse is also evident from an 'Instructional letter' sent in 1838 by the Poor Law Commissioners to the 'Boards of Guardians and Clerks' that 'the expenses incurred by the Guardian of a Union in providing and upholding a register-office, are to be charged in the same way to the several parishes of the Union, as the expenses of providing and upholding a workhouse' (Poor Law Commission Office 1838).

[12] Includes 'Independents'.
[13] Includes Calvinistic Methodists.

The 1836 Marriage Act required notice of every marriage, except Anglican marriages by banns, licence, and special licence, to be given to the district's Superintendent Registrar who was to copy each notice into a 'Marriage Notice Book'. Every notice of intended marriage was to be read on three occasions at successive weekly meetings of the Guardians of the Poor Law Union by their Clerk (often the Superintendent Registrar). This link with Poor Law Unions was subsequently broken, however, when the 1856 Marriage Act expressly prohibited notices of marriage to be read, or published, before the Guardians of any Poor Law Union or transmitted to the Clerks to such Guardians. From the start of 1857, notice of marriage was to be 'suspended or affixed in some conspicuous place' in the Superintendent Registrar's Office for three weeks before the marriage could be solemnised; this extra publicity obviated the need for the readings at the Poor Law Union. There is no sign that this change made any difference to the existing gradual upward trend in annual numbers (see Figure 2).

B. Trends Since World War II

As mentioned earlier, between 1914 and 1962, the numbers of marriages *by denomination and manner of solemnisation* were not published annually. However, because they *were* available for 1952, 1957 and 1962 (and each subsequent year), it was considered that the period from 1952 to 2012, which approximates to the post-War era, could usefully be studied, since it involved using estimated numbers for only eight years—see Figure 3.

(i) Trends in Anglican, Roman Catholic, Religious and Civil Marriages

As Figure 3 shows, the trends are completely different from those for the period leading up to World War I. There was an increase in the total number of marriages from the early 1950s to the late 1960s/early 1970s, which was almost entirely the result of the growth in civil marriages. Thereafter, the total number of marriages fell quite steeply, almost entirely due to the decline in religious marriages, the annual number of civil marriages remaining fairly constant. Religious marriages were relatively more numerous than civil marriages during the 1950s and 1960s, but declined comparatively until 1976 when the two main forms of marriage converged in numbers. Religious and civil marriages were roughly equal in number from 1976 until 1992, after which civil marriages grew at the expense of religious marriages. By 2012, civil marriages accounted for 70 per cent of all marriages, and religious marriages 30 per cent.

The high point of post-World War II marriages occurred in 1972 (the second largest annual number of marriages ever recorded, the highest being in 1940). Around that time marriage was very popular, and the ages at

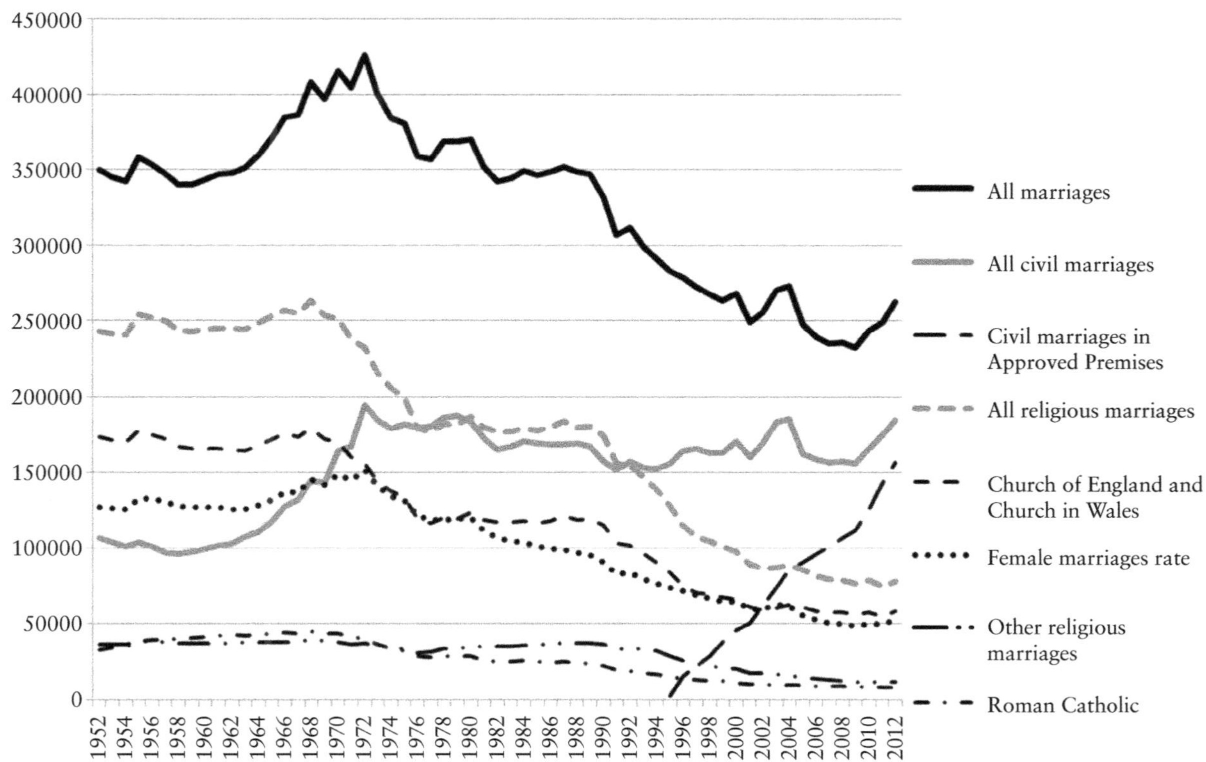

Figure 3: Marriages by manner of solemnisation and denomination, and female marriage rate*, 1952–2012, England and Wales

* women marrying per 1000 unmarried women aged 15 and over

marriage were at their youngest. In addition, as may be seen from the minor peak in civil marriages in 1972, many men and women who had availed themselves of the recently enacted Divorce Reform Act 1969, which allowed divorce on the newly available fact of separation, subsequently remarried (Haskey 1983). Overall, remarriages involving one or both partners being previously divorced reached an unprecedented 22 per cent of all marriages in 1972, and 44 per cent of civil marriages. The peak in religious marriages occurred a few years earlier in 1968, with the large numbers of first marriages of the 'baby boomers' who were born just after World War II. Shortly afterwards, the Family Law Reform Act 1969, which came into effect in 1970, lowered the age at which marriage could take place without parental consent, from 21 to 18. The effect was to sustain the large numbers of marriages at that time, especially through teenage marriages, but the subsequent fall in annual numbers is partly explained by successively fewer marriages of those in their early twenties.

Overall, the subsequent decline in the annual number of religious marriages was dramatic, with large falls between 1968 and 1977, and from 1989 onwards. In 2012, religious marriages were less than one third of their number in 1968, with a similar fall in Anglican marriages, and an even steeper decline in Roman Catholic marriages, which, in 2012, were less than one fifth of their 1968 number. Anglican marriages have fairly consistently formed just over 70 per cent of all religious marriages for more than half a century, from 1952 to 2012.

In contrast to religious marriages, civil marriages in 2012 were only five per cent below their peak of 1972. In 1995, the Marriage Act 1994 came into force—it introduced two major new facilities for civil marriage: (i) the option to marry with a civil ceremony in a place other than a Register Office—in Approved Premises; and (ii) the ability of couples to marry outside their district of residence by civil ceremony—either in an Approved Premises or in a Register Office. This latter option made it possible to marry in any Register Office or Approved Premises in England and Wales and represented an historical change, second only to the introduction of civil marriage in 1837. But in stark contrast to the introduction of civil marriage, which was accompanied by deterrents to civil marriage promoted by militant churchmen and Non-conformists, such as the association with the Poor Law Guardians and the workhouse (Anderson 1975), the motivation of the 1995 changes was primarily one of extending choice.

Approved Premises had to meet various requirements with their local authority, and fairly quickly hotels, stately homes, places of historical interest, sports and leisure venues, etc, applied and were granted approval (Haskey 1998). The two facilities of the 1994 Act, the ability to marry in Approved Premises, and being able to marry in *any* Register Office, or, indeed, any Approved Premises, considerably bolstered the number of civil marriages. Indeed, against all other trends, marriages in Approved Premises have grown phenomenally in popularity since their introduction, as may be seen from Figure 3; by 2012, 60 per cent of all marriages were solemnised in Approved Premises and such marriages formed 85 per cent of all civil marriages. Using data for 21 months following the Act, it was estimated that 42 per cent of Approved Premises marriages would otherwise have been solemnised with a religious ceremony (Haskey, 1998). In addition, there was early evidence that the introduction of Approved Premises marriages was accompanied by a growth in Register Office marriages, probably partly due to couples newly being able to marry in any Register Office, and partly due to local authorities making their Register Offices more attractive places in which to marry (Haskey 1998).

(ii) Trends in Non-conformist and Jewish Marriages

Marriage statistics for the Non-conformist denominations and the Jewish faith have been published every fifth year from 1952 until 1967, and then annually from 1970 onwards. A second set of estimates was made for the numbers of these marriages for the missing years (see Appendix, Part (b)).

As Figure 4 shows, the annual number of marriages in the Methodist Church remained fairly level from the early 1950s to around 1990, after which the numbers plunged (Figure 4). The United Reformed Church, URC, was formed in mid-1972 from the union of the Presbyterian Church and around three quarters of the Congregational Churches in England, the remaining Churches continuing independently. As a result, there was an abrupt fall in Congregationalist marriages in 1972 which then plateaued at a lower level. The combined numbers of marriages in the URC and the (independent) Congregational Churches after 1972 follow the same fairly level trend as that of the Congregationalists before 1972, but at a slightly higher level, the difference presumably being the numbers of marriages in the Presbyterian Church up to 1972 (for which information is not available).

Marriages in Baptist churches declined fairly consistently over the entire period, unlike most other denominations, more than halving in number. A similar pattern occurred for Jewish marriages, although an unknown number of Jews will have married with a civil ceremony, which will have been recorded as a civil marriage. It has been estimated that nearly one half of Jews marry outside their faith, and with the Jewish population declining by about one fifth in 15 years, it is not surprising that the number of Jewish marriages has fallen appreciably. However, despite the *number* of Jewish marriages falling considerably since 1952, they actually increased slightly as a proportion of all religious marriages. Baptist weddings showed a similar pattern after 1952: although the number fell appreciably, Baptist marriages as a proportion of all religious marriages held up fairly well.

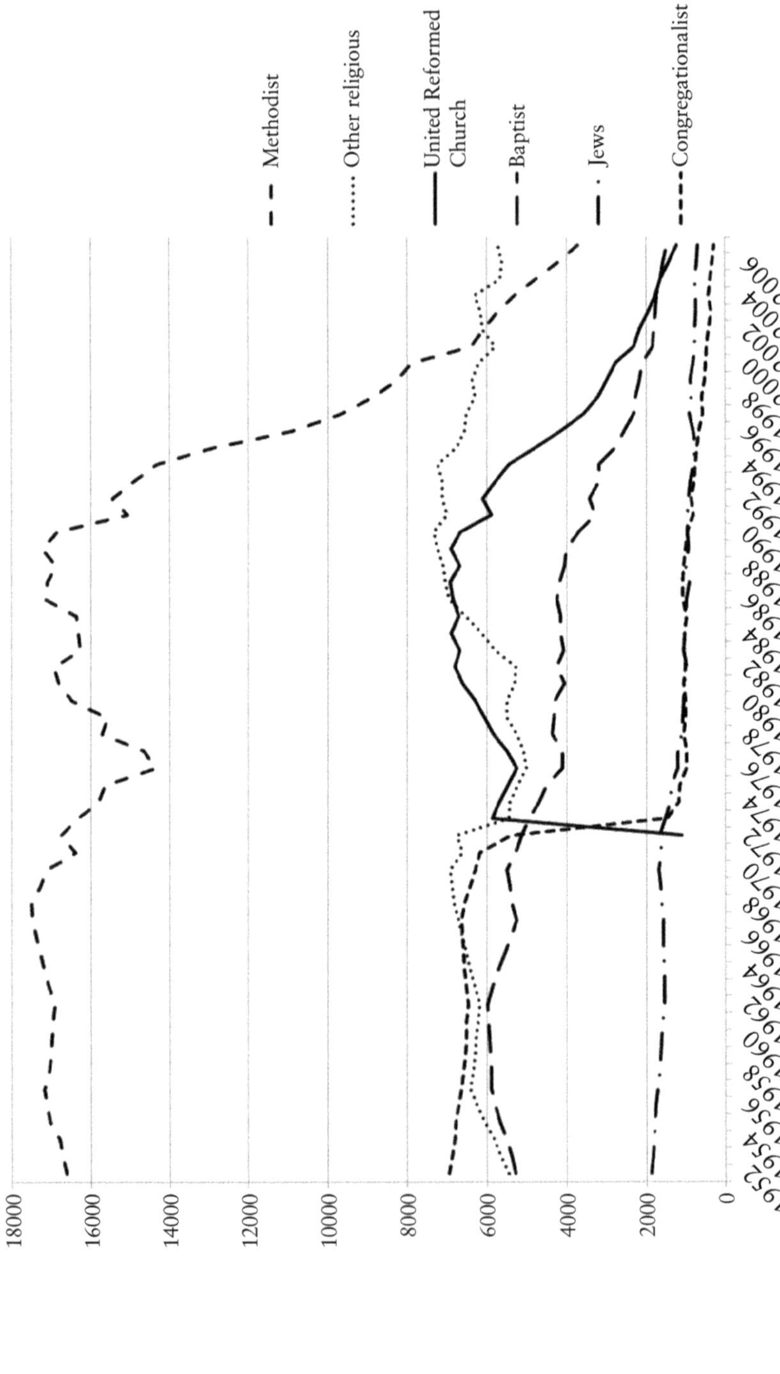

Figure 4: Other* religious marriages, by denomination, 1952–2007, England and Wales

* other than Church of England, Church in Wales, and Roman Catholic

Marriages in all other denominations and religions combined—which include those solemnised by Presbyterians, Calvinistic Methodists, Quakers, The Salvation Army, Jehovah's Witnesses, other Christian bodies, and other religious organisations—were fairly constant in number between the early 1950s and the late 1980s.

IV. MARRIAGES IN THE DIFFERENT DENOMINATIONS AND FAITHS

Figure 5 shows the numbers of marriages celebrated in both 1971 and 2007 in all the denominations and faiths coded[14] from copies of the marriage entries. As marriages peaked in the early 1970s and dipped to their lowest point in the mid-2000s, the two years compare a post-War peak with a post-War trough. Because the numbers of marriages vary from 12 to over 400,000, the numbers in Figure 5 have been plotted on a *logarithmic* scale—so that each horizontal band is 10 times the band below. Hence six orders of magnitude of numbers appear in Figure 5, as indicated along the y-axis. It may be seen that the number of marriages has fallen for each of the Nonconformist denominations: Methodist; (independent) Congregationalist; Baptist; Presbyterian and Calvinistic Methodist. Similarly the numbers have declined for the Quakers, the Jews, Salvation Army, and Brethren marriages.

In apparent contrast, Muslim and Sikh marriages have each increased by a factor of 10, as may be appreciated from the histogram bar being one band taller in 2007 than 1971. However, on closer inspection, the numbers are comparatively small; Muslim marriages seemed to increase from 12 to 197, and Sikh marriages from 117 to 1,276. In fact all these numbers, though correct, are misleading; they are not the total numbers of Muslim and Sikh *couples* who married, but the number of marriages legally *solemnised by these faiths* (see chapter eight in this volume for further information on this subject).

The vast majority of Muslims and Sikhs who marry under English law do so with a *civil* ceremony, which constitutes the legal marriage, and their marriages therefore appear in the statistics as *civil* marriages. As the Marriage Acts 1856 and 1949 recognise and allow, couples often have a subsequent religious ceremony in their places of worship, most of which are not registered for marriage. Statistics of these religious ceremonies, not being the legal marriages, are not collated nationally. Many Muslims view the Islamic (religious) ceremony as the *actual* marriage, not the (legal) one at the Register Office (Maqsood 2009). Although mosques are places of worship, relatively few are registered as places for solemnising marriages.

[14] Coding is restricted to 19 different major denominations/faiths, which include some 'other' groups, ie not all denominations/faiths can be separately identified.

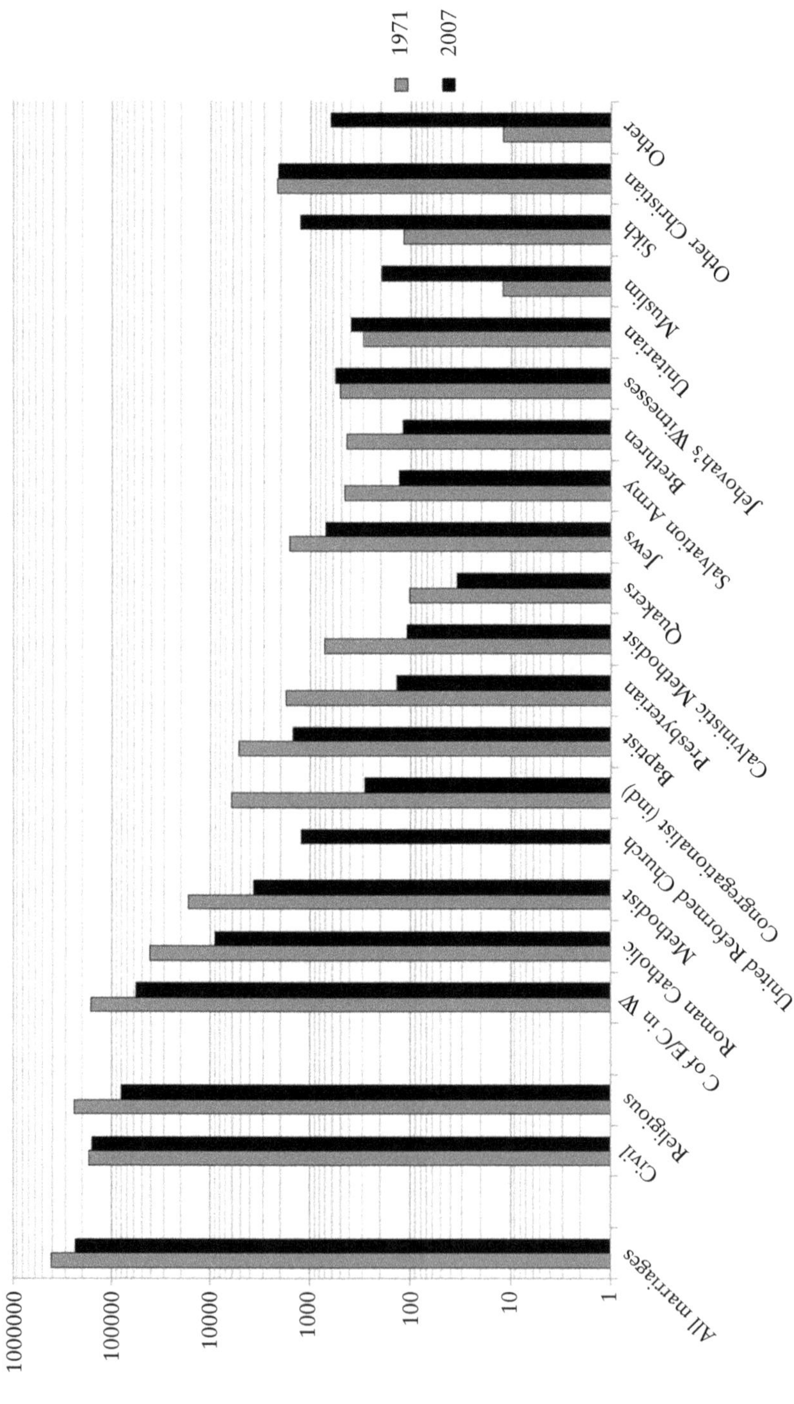

Figure 5: Number of marriages (log scale) by manner of solemnisation and denomination, 1971 and 2007, England and Wales

For example, in 2007, 806 mosques were registered for public worship, but only 164 for solemnising marriages (in which the 197 couples married). In the 2011 Census for England and Wales, just under 1½ million Muslims recorded themselves as of marriageable age (16–49), and the corresponding number of Sikhs was just under ¼ million, so the total number of Muslims and Sikhs marrying each year must therefore be very much larger. As indicated earlier, the true total number of Muslims and Sikhs—or indeed of any faith—marrying cannot be ascertained with any accuracy since the religion of the spouses is not recorded in the marriage entry, only the faith in which the marriage is solemnised.

V. MARITAL STATUS BEFORE MARRIAGE AND MANNER OF SOLEMNISATION

Religious faiths and denominations have always been concerned with the morality of sexual behaviour, and have viewed marriage as channelling natural desires aright and buttressing the stability of family and society. Many faiths take marriages which have ended by divorce very seriously, since one or both spouses have broken the solemn vows they made before God. In the Christian denominations, the priest or minister needs to consider whether the spouse concerned might be the 'innocent' party. Also, the state wishes to ensure that a divorced person really has been legally divorced before a legal remarriage can be undertaken. The legal marital status of individuals who wish to marry is therefore of considerable importance, since it may dictate to a large extent the manner of solemnisation of their marriage and the denomination in which it is—or can be—celebrated.

Some statistical information on the previous marital status of marriage partners—which illuminates certain trends in civil and religious marriages—is shown in Figure 6. Statistics on marriages by the combined marital status of the partners are available for every year from 1845. Figure 6 plots the proportions of all marriages for three constituent marital status combination groups: (a) first marriages for both partners (traditionally termed 'bachelor/spinster marriages', and referred to as 'first marriages'); (b) all remarriages involving either a divorced man or a divorced woman (or a divorced man marrying a divorced woman); and (c) the 'remainder group', marriages involving either a widowed partner with a single (never-married) partner, or both partners having previously been widowed, referred to as the 'widowed group' (however, this group excludes marriages between a widowed partner and a divorced partner, which are included in (b)). Widowed partner/divorced partner marriages accounted for less than one per cent of all marriages for each year up to the end of World War II, but recently increased to around 14 per cent.

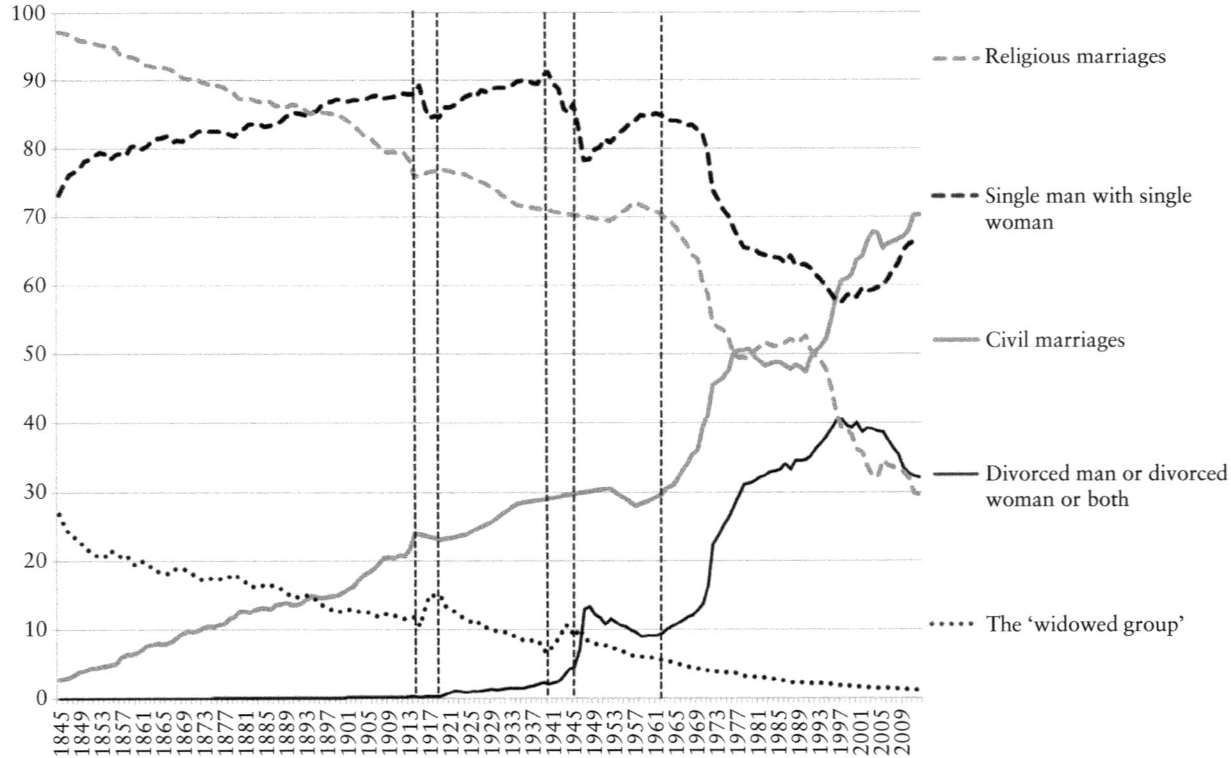

Figure 6: Marriages by previous marital status, and religious* and civil* marriages, as a percentage of all marriages, 1845–2012, England and Wales

* interpolations between certain years for religious and civil marriages proportions—see Figure 1

A. First Marriage for Both Partners

Marriages which were the first for both partners formed 73 per cent of marriages in 1845, but, by 1915, the first full year of World War I, reached a peak of 89 per cent. The proportion fell back between 1914 and 1918, as the proportion of the 'widowed group' who remarried increased. Marriages which were the first for both partners rose again as a proportion of all marriages to an even higher peak in 1939, the beginning of World War II, but fell fairly consistently during the following decade, and then fell for 35 years from a post-War peak in 1961.

B. Remarriage of the Divorced

In contrast to the other two categories discussed here, remarriages involving one or both partners who were divorced formed an insignificant proportion, around 0.3 per cent of all marriages each year, until 1915, the first full year of World War I. The right to divorce was very limited under the prevailing law: with no civil divorce at all until 1858, and only around 500 couples divorcing annually in the closing years of the nineteenth century (Haskey 1987), the numbers who might wish to remarry were necessarily small. But remarriages of the divorced grew slowly, exceeding one per cent of all marriages in 1922, and eventually reaching the largest proportion ever recorded, 40 per cent, in 1996. The large increase in the divorced population, and in those wishing to remarry, became a difficult issue for the various faith groups, as will be discussed below.

C. Remarriage of the Widowed

Marriages of the 'widowed group' accounted for just over one quarter, 27 per cent, of all marriages in 1845, but this proportion declined gradually throughout the nineteenth century. Historically, the widowed have tended to marry with a religious rather than a civil ceremony, and traditionally widows remarried only following a suitable time lapse after being bereaved. In Victorian times, widows were numerous, and many did not remarry, largely because there were insufficient numbers of men. In 1845, there were approximately three remarriages of widowers for every two remarriages of widows (GRO 1848). Life expectancy was around 40 in 1837, and just under 50 in 1901 (Woods 1982: 374), so that losing one's spouse often meant that the surviving spouse was a lone parent, responsible for children. (Queen Victoria herself fell in this category, having been widowed in 1861 in her early forties, with nine children.) Widows tended to be heads of household and home-based, which allowed them to combine domestic occupations, such as laundry work, with child care. Widows and spinsters shared the same problem as they grew older of not having a husband to support them; often they had insufficient funds, and had to live with relatives, usually their children (Rose 1988) or in institutions (Curran 1993).

The proportion of marriages accounted for by the 'widowed group' declined steadily, and quite markedly, over the entire period from 1845. However, despite life expectancy improving during the Victorian era, more than one in eight marriages involved the remarriage of at least one widowed partner in the late 1890s. After 1915, the proportion increased, and between 1917 and 1919 plateaued at a higher level of around one in seven of all marriages. A substantial number of widows and widowers remarried just after the end of World War I; women were widowed largely as the result of men dying in the War, and men were widowed largely as a result of the influenza and tuberculosis epidemics of 1918 (Haskey 1982). There was also an increase in the number of remarriages of the widowed just after World War II. More recently, since the early 1970s, the annual numbers of widows and widowers remarrying have been nearly equal.

D. Proportions of Religious and Civil Marriages

Figure 6 also shows the proportions of all marriages which were solemnised with religious and civil ceremonies, derived from the estimated numbers of civil and religious marriages shown in Figure 1. The purpose of including these extra two lines on the graph is to show the broad similarity between the trends in the proportions of (i) first marriages for both parties and religious marriages, and (ii) remarriages of the divorced and civil marriages.

Overall, the period from the mid-1840s up to just before World War II generally marked an era of relative stability in marriage patterns, both by manner of solemnisation and by previous marital status, albeit accompanied by steady long-term trends. The subsequent period up to the present-day has witnessed more rapid and radical changes.

While the proportion of religious marriages declined steadily from 97 per cent in 1845 to 72 per cent in 1934, the proportion of first marriages for both parties grew slowly from 73 per cent to 90 per cent. Nevertheless, religious and first marriages each accounted for at least 70 per cent of all marriages over this period of some 90 years. The similarity in the pattern of trends is more apparent after the early 1950s and up to around 1996: the trend in the proportion of religious marriages follows almost exactly that of first marriages (albeit at a slightly lower level). Similarly, the proportion of civil marriages very closely tracks that of remarriages of the divorced.

After the mid-1990s, however, the correspondence between the two trends in each pair ended: civil marriages increased from around 50 per cent to almost 70 per cent of all marriages, whilst the proportion of marriages involving the remarriage of a divorced partner fell. A converse picture applied to religious marriages and first marriages: the former declined, whilst first marriages increased a little. A combination of factors is likely to have caused these changes. From the mid-1990s, although the number of the divorced in the population continued to grow, their rate of remarriage plunged. Furthermore, civil marriages in Approved Premises grew from under one per cent of all marriages in its first year of 1995, to 60 per cent of all marriages in 2012, and, from the start, just under one half of Approved Premises marriages were first marriages for both parties, marriages which, in earlier times, would have been expected to be solemnised with a religious ceremony.

VI. COHABITATION, DIVORCE, AND BIRTHS OUTSIDE MARRIAGE

It has been mentioned that the peaks in the annual numbers of marriage occurred during World Wars I and II—there was a third peak in the early 1970s. Indeed a visitor from another planet on viewing the annual numbers in Figure 1 might have concluded that the third peak was due to yet another World War. In fact, it marked the start of a period of enormous social upheaval, as reflected in large changes in many demographic series on sexual and partnership behaviour, and alternative living arrangements. For example, there was a sharp increase in births outside marriage, a growth in cohabitation, lone parenthood and divorce, and a decline in marriage (Haskey 2014). These changes have collectively been called 'The Second Demographic Transition'[15] on the basis that they shared common factors as their root cause (Lesthaeghe and van de Kaa 1986; van de Kaa 1987; Lesthaeghe 1995).

These changes since the early 1970s have all undoubtedly influenced the patterns of marriage. At first, the growth in divorce resulted in increasing numbers of remarriages, but the *rate* of remarriage of the divorced declined rapidly, most likely because cohabitation began to replace possible remarriage, or at least delayed it for a proportion of couples. Others lived alone, or as a divorced lone parent. In addition, some couples who would otherwise have married for the first time started cohabiting instead, with some marrying subsequently, whilst others did not marry at all. Pre-marital cohabitation is thought to have been very low in the 1960s and 1970s but grew considerably; nine per cent of women marrying at ages under 25 in 1970 had pre-maritally cohabited, but the corresponding proportion was 68 per cent of women who married in the mid-2000s (Beaujouan and Ní Bhrolcháin 2014), and the proportion for those marrying at older ages in the mid-2000s was even higher.

[15] The First Demographic Transition refers to a change from high fertility and high mortality, first to lower mortality, followed by a fall to lower fertility. Generally, developed countries experienced this transition decades ago or even longer ago, whilst developing countries have yet to do so, or are in the process of doing so.

During the 1960s and early 1970s, the number and proportion of births outside marriage started to increase, as did the proportion of births within marriage which were pre-maritally conceived—that is, births legitimised with a 'shot-gun wedding'. As a proportion of all marriages, 'shot-gun weddings' reached a peak in the mid-1960s, when they formed 22 per cent of all marriages, but this proportion declined during the 1970s, falling to 12 per cent in 1976. During this period, contraception use grew exponentially, and abortions rose in number, resulting in the increase in births outside marriage being temporarily slowed. Increasingly, mothers whose child was conceived extra-maritally resorted either to abortion or gave birth to a child outside marriage. Some of these latter mothers began to live with their partner, forming a cohabiting couple family with children, without marrying, whilst others became lone mother families; successively fewer subsequently married the father. Also, some married women with children became lone mother families through divorce. Both cohabiting couple families and lone mother families grew in relative numbers and at the expense of the proportion of families which were married couple families with children (Haskey 2014).

The overall growth in cohabitation and its effect upon marriage may be appreciated from Figure 7 which gives 'snapshots' each year of the proportions of women aged under 50 who were single (ie never married), cohabiting, and married, irrespective of how long they had been in that state. It may be seen that there has been a steady increase in the proportion who were cohabiting (the bottom line); and a declining proportion who were married (second line from the top). The top line shows the proportion of women who were living in a couple—either being married or cohabiting. The proportion of women living in a couple has been declining gently, which is consistent with the growth of the proportion of women who are single (shown by the middle line in Figure 7) (although an increasing proportion of those single in successive 'snapshots' would have been cohabiting at those instances—it being possible to be *both* single, ie never-married, *and* cohabiting).

These trends have inevitably played a large part in the patterns of marriage by manner of solemnisation and denomination. Collectively, they put the decline in marriage into a broader social context, and, along with increasing secularisation, help explain the growth of civil marriage. However, those denominations which have been more attuned to these developments and sympathetic to those experiencing them have generally experienced a smaller decline in marriages. Undoubtedly the different denominations have been challenged by these enormous social changes, and experienced a dilemma of whether to adjust to them (with emphasis on pastoral care), or whether to be faithful to traditional teaching (holding fast to doctrine) and effectively resist them. The reaction of the different denominations and faiths is reflected in the different profiles of marriages which they have solemnised, most particularly by the previous marital status of the spouses.

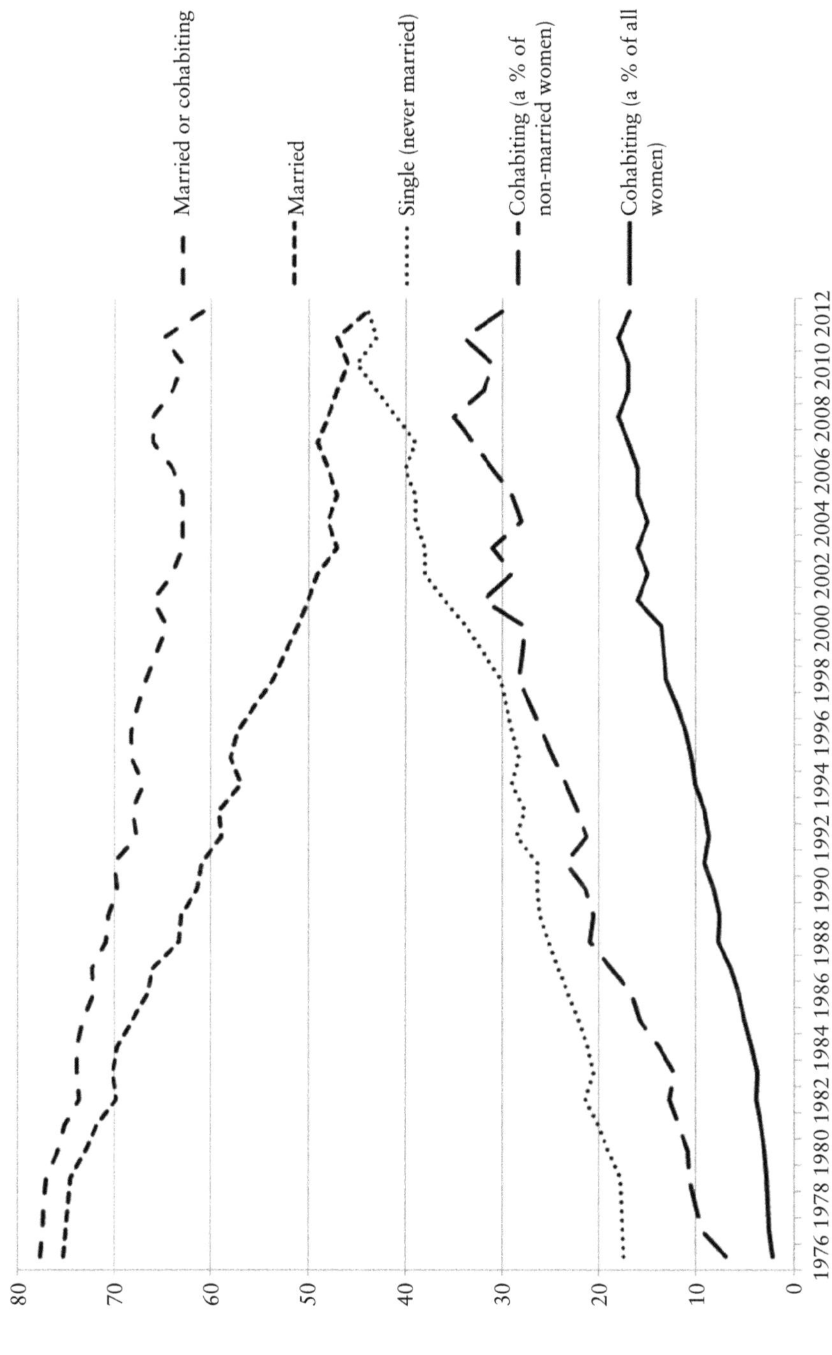

Figure 7: Percentage of women aged 18–49 who were: cohabiting; married; single, 1976–2012, Great Britain

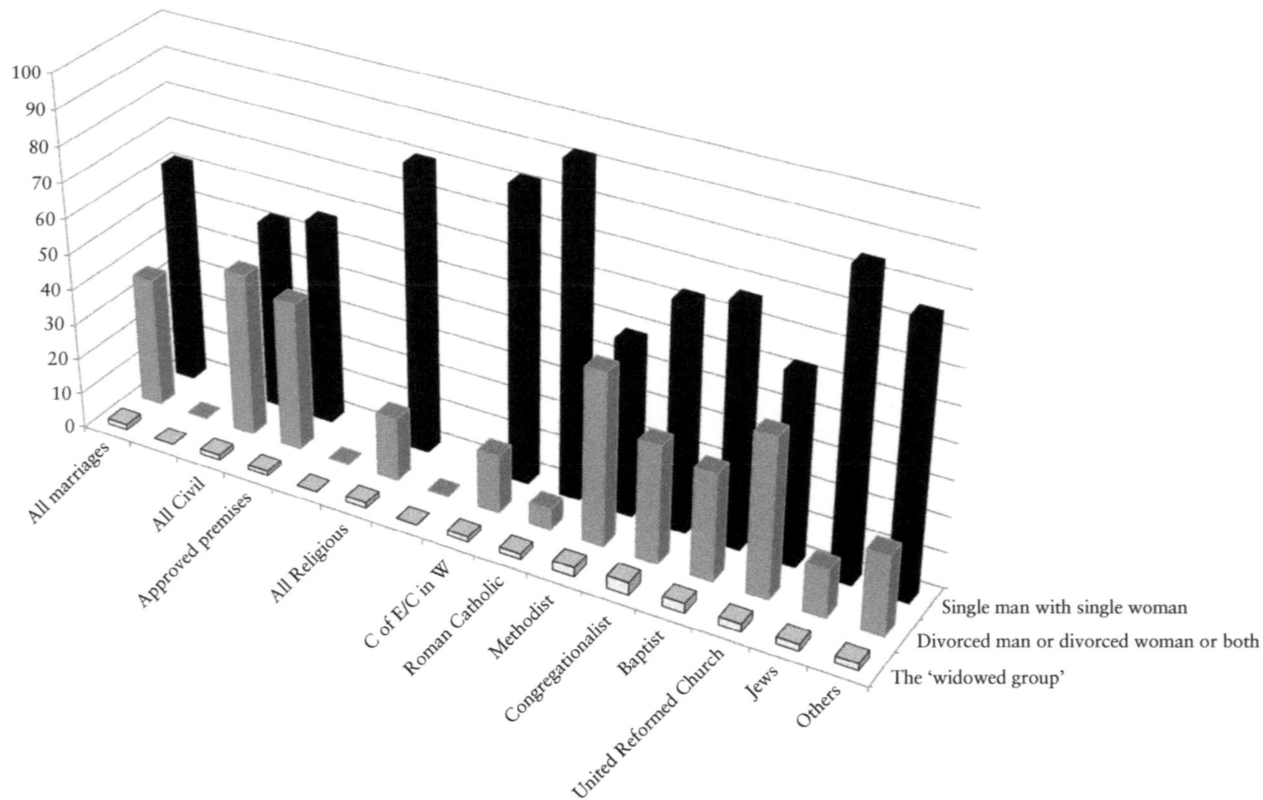

Figure 8: Percentage of marriages by combined marital status before marriage of the spouses, by manner of solemnisation and denomination, England and Wales, 2007

Using recent 2007 data, Figure 8 depicts these profiles, using the same three broad combined marital status groups as employed in Figure 6. The vast majority of marriages were either first marriages for both parties or involved a divorced person remarrying; scarcely any marriages involved widowed spouses. Just over one third, 36 per cent, of all marriages involve the remarriage of a divorced partner, but this proportion is much larger amongst civil marriages (almost one half, 46 per cent), and much smaller (18 per cent) amongst religious marriages. The proportion of remarriages after divorce is particularly high amongst Methodist and United Reformed Church marriages, 48 and 45 per cent, respectively.

VII. REMARRIAGE OF THE DIVORCED—A DIFFICULT ISSUE FOR THE CHRISTIAN DENOMINATIONS

A. The Established Church

Only 16 per cent of marriages in the Anglican Church involve the remarriage of a divorced person—a smaller proportion than for almost all other denominations, see Figure 8. The growing divorced population has prompted debates in the Anglican Church on the remarriage of the divorced in church. Whilst biblical teaching, tradition and ethical considerations have been central to the debate, there has been strong disagreement over whether remarriage should be allowed by the Church and, if so, on what grounds. It is widely accepted—and the Church believes—that there is a legal requirement on Anglican clergy to marry *never-married* parishioners whatever their denomination, a duty traceable back to Lord Hardwicke's Act of 1753. By contrast, following the introduction of civil divorce in the Matrimonial Causes Act 1857, clergy did not have to remarry the 'guilty party' where adultery had been proven and the former spouse was still alive (Woods 2006). The Matrimonial Causes Act 1937 granted much more discretion to clergy, allowing them to refuse to solemnise the marriage of any divorced person, regardless of the reason for the divorce, if their former spouse was still alive (Buckler 1941: 343; Jones 2014). The 1957 Act of Convocation of Canterbury reaffirmed this principle (though not making it canon law), but some Anglican clergy did start solemnising remarriages of the divorced, as they were legally entitled to do, albeit against the guidance of the 1957 Act. In 2002, however, Synod abolished the Church's ban on the remarriage of a divorced person whose former spouse was still alive, and accepted that decisions to remarry such individuals would have to be taken by the clergy concerned. Even this conclusion was not entirely clear-cut (as with previous deliberations on the subject); it was agreed that such remarriages should be 'exceptional' (presumably infrequent), a concession to those opposed to the change (Woods 2006).

So, for both Anglicans and non-Anglicans who are divorced and who wish to remarry in the Church of England, although it has become somewhat easier over the years, there remain conditions to be met, and certainly not all who wish to can remarry in church. In general, the Church of England uses ritual to encourage behaviour it commends (Farrimond, chapter ten in this volume), while simultaneously promoting Anglican church weddings.[16]

B. The Roman Catholic Church

For Roman Catholics, the position of remarriage after divorce is straightforward: the Church's teaching is that no one who was validly married can remarry in the Roman Catholic Church if their former spouse is still alive.[17] Nor can a Roman Catholic partner who has never married marry someone who is divorced. In the Church's eyes, divorce is a civil action and legal outcome, quite distinct from the Church's judicial process to determine the validity of a marriage, which involves an ecclesiastical tribunal's investigation and decision on the marriage's nullity (or not).[18] A Roman Catholic who has divorced in a civil court, or wishes to marry someone who has, may therefore be tempted (unless their faith and allegiance to the Church is sufficiently strong) to marry in another denomination or with a civil ceremony instead of in the Church, so avoiding the necessity of submitting to the deliberations and delay of another court. Once a marriage has been annulled by the Church, the parties are free to marry as though for the first time, since it is as if their original marriage never existed.[19] Thus, from the Church's viewpoint, which is very much grounded in belief that marriage is indissoluble and a sacrament, the terms 'remarriage' and 'divorce' are inapplicable.

Undoubtedly the Church's position has affected the number of Roman Catholic marriages. From the early 1950s up to the early 1970s, Roman Catholic marriages formed around 10 per cent of all marriages, but subsequently declined, accounting for just three per cent in 2012. This decline is all the more significant given the boost in numbers attending church caused by the recent mass migration of Catholics from Poland and Romania (Brierley 2011).

Both the Catholic Church's teaching and the debate in the Church of England on remarriage of the divorced have resulted in increasing numbers of the divorced remarrying with a civil ceremony. However, some have remarried in the Non-conformist churches, which—as the next section discusses—have

[16] www.yourchurchwedding.org/youre-welcome/did-you-know.aspx.

[17] www.aboutcatholics.com/beliefs/catholic-marriage-and-beliefs/divorce-annulments-and-remarriage

[18] www.beginningcatholic.com/catholic-annulment.html.

[19] See n 17 above.

traditionally adopted a more liberal policy permitting such remarriage, including those from other denominations. Different requirements of church membership by the different denominations have also played a part. Certainly, though, there has been concern in the Roman Catholic and Anglican Churches—and also in the Jewish faith—over the loss of those who 'marry out'—ie, who leave their church or faith on marrying someone of a different denomination or faith.[20]

C. The Non-conformist Churches

The relative numbers of the divorced who have remarried in the Non-conformist churches are generally large compared with those in other denominations, as was shown in Figure 8. 1968 marked the start of a decade of rapid growth in remarriages of the divorced as a proportion of all marriages (see Figure 6); by 1978, just under one half of all Non-conformist marriages involved the remarriage of a divorced partner (Haskey 1980). In 2011, an estimated 33 per cent of all Non-conformist marriages involved at least one partner remarrying after divorce, compared with only 16 per cent of Anglican marriages. (The former proportion is not much smaller than that of 39 per cent for all civil marriages.)

As was seen in Figure 4, the annual number of marriages in the Methodist Church fell dramatically after 1990. In 1993, the Methodist Conference considered the issue of human sexuality and reaffirmed the teaching on marriage and sexuality: 'chastity for all outside marriage and fidelity within it' but at the same time celebrated 'the participation of lesbians and gay men in the church'.[21] Until 1998, ministers had to evaluate who was the 'guilty' and 'innocent' party in a divorced couple where one of the partners wished to remarry. In 1998, the Methodist Conference introduced several changes concerning the Church's response to requests by divorced people to remarry in the Methodist Church.[22] In general, the Methodist Church has been willing to marry the divorced—even if their previous spouse is still alive—provided that there are no important reasons for not doing so.[23] Those wishing to marry, or remarry, in the Methodist Church do not have to be members of that Church, but a confirmed member of another denomination can become a member of the Methodist Church by a simple act of welcome; furthermore, that person does not have to renounce their membership of

[20] Past personal communications with the churches, etc, and their statistical researchers enquiring about commissioning special marriage tabulations to investigate this phenomenon.

[21] www.methodist.org.uk/downloads/ne_derbyresolutionsmethrec_130207.pdf.

[22] www.methodist.org.uk/downloads/conf-marriage-in-the-methodist-church-2002.pdf.

[23] www.methodist.org.uk/who-we-are/baptisms-weddings-and-funerals/weddings.

their *original* church.[24] Indeed, many couples who marry in the Methodist Church are from different denominations, neither being a Methodist.[25]

Remarriages after divorce also figure prominently in the United Reformed Church (URC), the individual minister alone deciding, after discussions with the couple, whether to marry them. The URC is probably second only to the Methodist Church in performing proportionately so many such remarriages.

VIII. PRE-MARITAL COHABITATION AND DENOMINATION OF MARRIAGE

Since the 1970s, couples have increasingly cohabited before their marriage, with previously divorced partners more likely to do so than those marrying for the first time (Beaujouan and Ní Bhrolcháin 2014). Also, more recently, there has been some evidence that if both wedding partners give the same residential address immediately before marriage (as recorded in the marriage entry), then that is a good proxy indicator for the couple having pre-maritally cohabited (Haskey 1990). Table 1 gives the proportion of marriages in which the partners gave identical addresses before their wedding in 2007, by manner of solemnisation and denomination.

Overall, in 81 per cent of marriages the couple may be supposed to have pre-maritally cohabited. There is a large differential in the proportions between religious and civil marriages—66 per cent and 88 per cent of such marriages, respectively, which is not surprising given that most denominations vary between being strongly opposed to pre-marital cohabitation, to reluctantly accepting it. The denominations with larger proportions of identical address marriages include the Roman Catholics, perhaps surprisingly, with 80 per cent, and also the Non-conformists: United Reformed Church, 81 per cent; Methodist, 77 per cent; Calvinistic Methodist, 75 per cent, etc, each exceeding the overall proportion of 66 per cent for all religious marriages combined. As mentioned above, divorced partners are more likely to cohabit before remarrying, and, as has been seen, divorced partners tend to remarry in the Non-conformist churches.

This association is borne out by the other results in Table 1 (right hand column): the proportion of remarriages involving at least one divorced partner in which the partners gave identical residential addresses is larger than that for both first marriages and remarriages of the 'widowed group', whether the subsequent marriage is solemnised with a religious or a civil ceremony. The largest proportion pre-maritally cohabiting by this measure, 91 per cent, occurs for the divorced remarrying with a civil ceremony in Approved Premises.

[24] www.methodist.org.uk/who-we-are/membership#1.

[25] www.methodist.org.uk/who-we-are/baptisms-weddings-and-funerals/weddings.

Table 1: Percentage of marriages in which the bride and bridegroom gave identical addresses for their residences before marriage, by manner of solemnisation, denomination, and faith, and by previous marital status in combination, 2007, England and Wales

All marriages	%	Religious marriages	%	Civil marriages	%
All marriages	81	**All religious marriages**	66	**All civil marriages**	88
First marriage for both parties	78	First marriage for both parties	65	First marriage for both parties	87
Remarriage of at least one divorced partner	87	Remarriage of at least one divorced partner	73	Remarriage of at least one divorced partner	90
Remainder: 'widowed group'	68	Remainder: 'widowed group'	52	Remainder: 'widowed group'	77
		Church of England	68	Register Office	86
		Church in Wales	54	Approved Premises	90
		Roman Catholic	80		
		Methodist	77	**Civil marriages in Approved Premises**	90
		United Reformed Church	81		
		Congregationalist (Independent)	71	First marriage for both parties	89
		Baptist	52	Remarriage of at least one divorced partner	91
		Presbyterian	71		
		Calvinistic Methodist	75	Remainder: 'widowed group'	78
		Unitarian	88		
		Salvation Army	62		
		Brethren	25		
		Jehovah's Witness	8		
		Society of Friends (Quakers)	86		
		Jews	40		
		Muslim	27		
		Sikh	5		
		Other Christian body (incl. Mormon)	46		
		Other unattached body	27		

Note: The 'widowed group' excludes marriages between a widowed person and a divorced person

IX. MARRIAGES BY DAY OF THE WEEK AND DENOMINATION

Contemporary culture tends to think of weddings as Saturday events, but it was not always so, and is not always so today. In 1864, the most popular day was Sunday, when 32 per cent of couples married, as revealed by an analysis of marriages in certain districts and counties by the Registrar General (GRO 1866: Table VIIIc, p xv). In 1864, 92 per cent of marriages were religious, of which 85 per cent were solemnised in the Anglican Church. Monday was the next most popular day, 21 per cent, followed by Saturday, chosen by 17 per cent of couples. In contrast, Figure 9 illustrates the profile of marriages by day of the week for weddings in 2002, with separate profiles for civil and religious marriages, and also for each denomination and faith. There are some interesting differences in the patterns. From the profile for all marriages (the first set of histograms on the far left) almost two thirds, 63 per cent, of marriages took place on a Saturday. Hence over the last 140 years, Saturday weddings have risen from being the third most popular day to marry to being the most popular (Haskey 1996).

Amongst marriages solemnised by the major Christian denominations, Saturday is the choice which dominates, accounting for at least 80 per cent of weddings. Roughly one half, 49 per cent, of civil marriages in Register Offices take place on a Saturday, and slightly more, 57 per cent, of marriages in Approved Premises.

Not surprisingly, the pattern for Jewish weddings is very different, with Sunday being the most popular day, and virtually none on Saturdays, which—as Saturday is the Sabbath—might be expected. The proportions of Saturday weddings amongst Muslim and Sikh weddings (ie those where the Muslim and Sikh spouses marry in their own faiths, rather than with a civil ceremony) are smaller than those of Christian denominations, but still account for at least one third of all their weddings.

Overall, after Saturday, Friday is the next most popular day, with Friday weddings being more than twice as numerous amongst civil marriages than religious ones (21 per cent and eight per cent of weddings, respectively). Interestingly, Sunday weddings account for 10 per cent of all marriages in Approved Premises, larger than the corresponding proportion for each of the Christian denominations, and twice the proportion of five per cent for all religious marriages. As mentioned above, the Act which introduced marriages in Approved Premises also allowed couples to marry by civil ceremony *outside* their district of residence. Such 'away marriages' in Approved Premises are even more likely to be solemnised on a Sunday than the corresponding 'home marriages'; the proportions were 12 per cent and nine per cent, respectively (Haskey 2002).

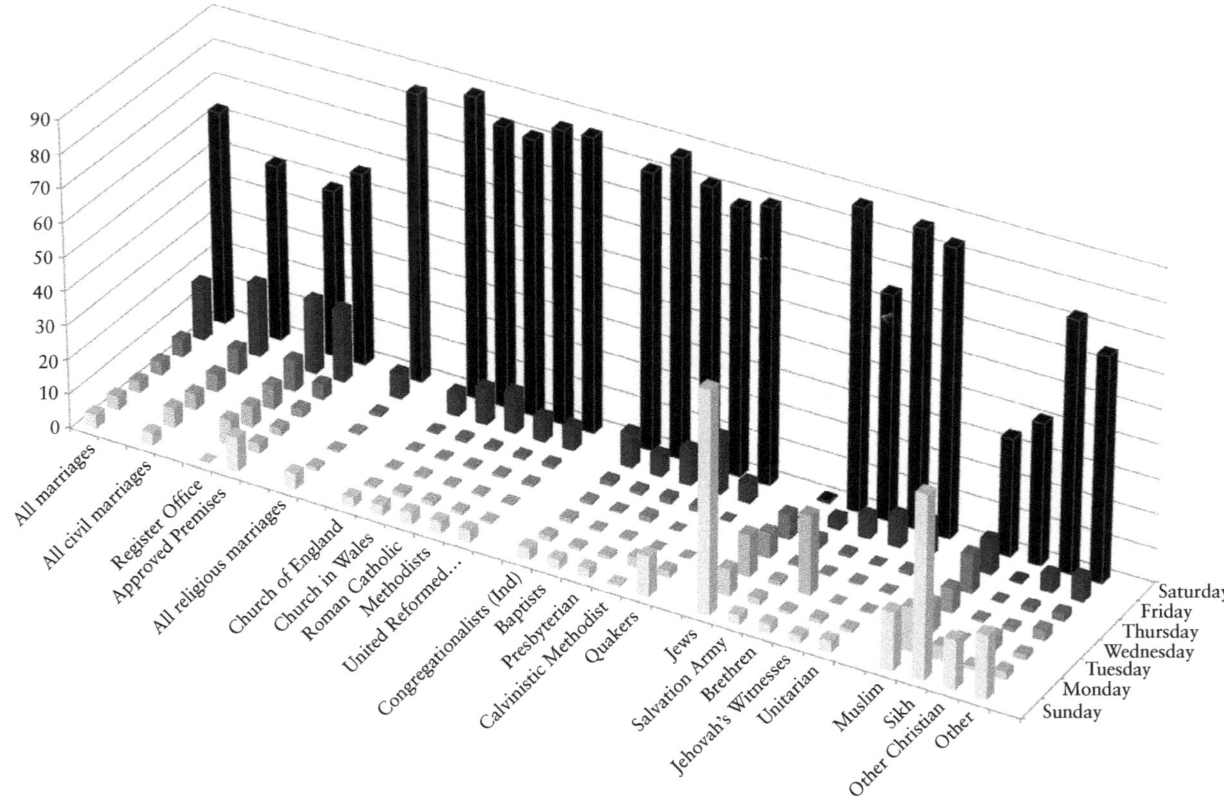

Figure 9: Percentage of marriages solemnised by day of the week, by manner of solemnisation and denomination, 2002, England and Wales

X. THE SPOUSES' FATHERS ACTING AS WITNESSES TO THE MARRIAGE

The marriage entry records the names of the fathers of the bride and bridegroom, and also of the witnesses to the marriage. To study the involvement of kin in the ceremony, a sample of marriages in 1979 examined the names of the witnesses to see whether they included the fathers of the spouses (Haskey 1991). The spouses' fathers were much more likely to act as witnesses at religious weddings than civil weddings. The bride's father was a witness in 65 per cent of religious marriages, but only in 15 per cent of civil marriages, and the bridegroom's father a witness in 51 per cent, and 10 per cent, respectively. *Both* fathers acted as witnesses in 24 per cent of religious ceremony marriages, but in only three per cent of civil ceremony marriages. However, on checking whether the witnesses included someone with the same *surname* as the bride or the bridegroom (other than their fathers), such witnesses were found to be present slightly more often at civil weddings than religious weddings.[26]

Of all the religious denominations, marriages in the Church of England and the Church in Wales were the most likely to be witnessed by the spouses' fathers: the bride's father was a witness in 76 per cent of weddings, the bridegroom's father in 58 per cent. It is perhaps not surprising that the father of the bride should act as a witness more frequently since he is traditionally likely to be present in order to 'give the bride away' (see Farrimond, chapter 10 in this volume).

XI. DISCUSSION

It is evident that religious marriages have suffered a sustained and substantial decline over at least the last 150 years. Secularisation has usually been attributed as the root cause. Secularisation is a somewhat nebulous term and concept, and has been described as 'the impact of what sociologists called modernisation and what historians ... labelled as a mixture of urbanisation, industrialism, and the impact of the Enlightenment' (Brown and Snape 2010). Nevertheless its influence upon religious affiliation, church attendance and involvement, which might be taken to include church weddings, has long been the subject of study and debate. One explanation is that adherence to religious faith has declined because advances in knowledge, technology, and objective thought have secularised attitudes and beliefs. As Bruce has expressed it: 'crucial to the marginalisation of religion has been the combination of egalitarianism, individuality and diversity'; also that 'technology (rightly or wrongly) gives us a sense that we are masters of our own

[26] There are obvious challenges in identifying the relatives of females (and female relatives) due to the convention of women changing their surname on marriage: see Haskey (1991).

fate' (Bruce 2006). Among social historians, a consensus grew up that 'the growth in industrial cities in the 19th Century caused a decline in religiosity ... (and that) within cities ... the working classes became alienated from organised religion and were the leading edge of secularisation' (MacIntyre 1967). This interpretation was challenged by Brown as being too simplistic, and that other social factors were at work. He also argued that, in more recent times, the cultural revolution of the 1960s marked the first generation to forsake religious affiliation, and the first not to absorb Christian beliefs into their lives as part of their identity (Brown 2009). Yet other researchers, supported with statistical survey evidence, have proposed that the change is from traditional Christian beliefs to a more general, if somewhat nebulous, spirituality, rather than to secular unbelief (Gill, Hadaway, and Marler 1998).

The turning away from traditional Christian denominations has occurred at the same time as a steadily increasing prevalence of cohabitation and growing individualism. Increased individualism—which is perhaps what cohabitation more easily affords—does not necessarily imply lack of commitment; the relationship between these two factors has been the subject of study (Lewis 1999). In addition, the formulation of the theory of the Second Demographic Transition (Van de Kaa 1987) involved relating a variety of respondents' values, including those of individualism and self-fulfillment, to the new forms of living arrangements, such as cohabitation. Cohabitation has also led to the 'privatisation' of coupledom and, with the absence of a public ceremony, even some close members of the couples' families are unsure of the status or permanence of such relationships. However, there has been a contrasting trend in that couples who *do* wish to marry want their wedding to be a 'full flourish' with many guests and accompanied with all the social trimmings; there is a reluctance to have an 'economy wedding'. Indeed, a common reason cohabiting couples give for *not* marrying is the cost of a 'proper wedding' (Barlow and James 2004: 158).

The advent of marriages in 'Approved Premises' has provided the opportunity for a 'big splash' at a prestigious location—there is no religious connotation and the setting is admirable for a large social gathering and celebration. Furthermore, the legal and social sides to the marriage follow on seamlessly. Marriages in picturesque churches in idyllic settings have always been popular, but until recently the Anglican Church insisted that at least one of the parties should be either resident in the parish or else on the electoral roll for a period of time beforehand, which prevented couples from choosing any church other than their own for their wedding. These requirements have now been relaxed, though there still must be one or more pre-existing 'connections' to the parish church in question.

Perhaps because of the loss of couples marrying in their denominations, churches have made renewed efforts at encouraging and welcoming couples considering marrying there. The Church of England on its website lists all the conditions the couple do *not* have to fulfill: no need to be a member of the church (and can marry whatever your beliefs); no need to have been christened; no need to be married in white; no need to promise to obey, etc.[27] In former times, one suspects that the emphasis might have been on requirements which *were* necessary. Other denominations certainly accentuate a warm welcome to prospective couples on their websites. Meanwhile, the Roman Catholic Church has conducted a consultative survey to gauge Catholics' views worldwide on a wide range of social and sexual issues;[28] the recently published summary document, *Instrumentum Laboris*,[29] summarises the responses and recognises the difficulties Catholics face in their relationships, marriages—and divorces. And, already, there are signs of a change in attitude and tone towards gay and lesbian couples, at least amongst some bishops. The various other denominations are reconsidering their position over divorce and cohabitation, whether for the pastoral care of the divorced and the cohabiting in their congregations, or to accommodate the wishes of the divorced to remarry in church.

Most recently, of course, the Churches are now also being challenged on their attitudes to all aspects of same sex relationships, not least as a result of the passage of the Marriage (Same Sex Couples) Act 2013 (see Harding, chapter 11 in this volume). Religious groups are exempted from having to solemnise same sex marriages, but—with the exception of the Church of England—have the opportunity to 'opt in' and solemnise same sex marriages if they so wish. Amongst some denominations and faiths, positions are divided. Whether the Churches can reconcile the different theological stances taken towards these issues amongst their own clergy and laity, and meet the challenges posed by all these changes, is another matter—though perhaps with appropriate guidance, they will.

[27] www.yourchurchwedding.org/youre-welcome/did-you-know.aspx.

[28] www.vatican.va/roman_curia/synod/documents/rc_synod_doc_20131105_iii-assemblea-sinodo-vescovi_en.html.

[29] www.vatican.va/roman_curia/synod/documents/rc_synod_doc_20140626_instrumentum-laboris-familia_en.html.

APPENDIX

Estimating the Number of Marriages by Manner of Solemnisation and Denomination for Years of Missing Statistics

(a) *Numbers of Civil, 'All Religious', Anglican, Roman Catholic, and 'Other Religious' Marriages Shown in Figures 1–3.*

Numbers of marriages were unavailable for: 1915–18; 1920–23; 1925–28; 1930–33; 1935–51; 1953–56; 1958–61.

Numbers were available for: 1914; 1919; 1924; 1929; 1934; 1952; 1957; 1962.

Method: The method may be illustrated with an example in the case of a four-year gap, which shows the general principle; that is, the method also applied to the 17-year gap. The numbers of marriages by manner of solemnisation and denomination are known for both 1952 and 1957, but not for the intervening years. The estimated number of *civil* marriages for each year between 1952 and 1957 was estimated by linear interpolation between the known numbers of civil marriages in 1952 and 1957. Similarly, the estimated number of 'all religious' marriages in each year was obtained in the same way. Then, for each denomination in turn, estimates were derived for each year, also by linear interpolation.

The resulting set of estimates for each year inevitably contained inconsistencies; for example, the sum of the estimated numbers of civil marriages and of 'all religious' marriages did not agree with the known, published, *total* number of marriages. To correct for this mismatch, the number of civil marriages, and the number of 'all religious' marriages, were both scaled by the same factor, whose size was determined to ensure agreement with the total. Then, the revised estimate of the 'all religious' marriages was inevitably inconsistent with the sum of the estimates for the individual denominations. Again, the estimates by denomination were scaled so that their sum coincided with the total estimated number of 'all religious' marriages. This procedure was carried out for each year between 1952 and 1957; it should be noted that the two correction factors—one for consistency with the total number of marriages, and the other for consistency with the 'all religious' marriages—varied from year to year.

This whole estimation exercise was repeated for each set of years with missing data.

(b) *Numbers of Marriages for the Second Set of Denominations Shown in Figure 4—Methodist, Congregationalist, etc.*

Numbers of marriages were unavailable for: 1953–56; 1958–61.

Numbers were available for: 1952; 1957; 1962.

Method: For each denomination separately, the number of marriages was estimated for each missing year by interpolating between the known numbers of marriages in the two years just before, and just after, the missing period. Then, for each 'missing' year, the estimated number of marriages for each denomination in this second set was added together, and also added to the estimated numbers of Anglican and Roman Catholic marriages, estimated in (a) above. This total should be the estimated 'all religious' marriages for that year. It was then compared with the estimated number of 'all religious' marriages derived in (a) above, (which was taken to be definitive) and usually differed slightly. For each 'missing' year, the estimate of each denomination in the second set was factored to ensure that their total, together with the estimates for the Anglican and Roman Catholic denominations matched the definitive estimated 'all religious' number of marriages.

BIBLIOGRAPHY

ANDERSON, Olive, 'The incidence of civil marriage in Victorian England and Wales' (1975) 69 *Past and Present* 50.

BARLOW, Anne and JAMES, Grace, 'Regulating marriage and cohabitation in 21st Century Britain' (2004) 67 *Modern Law Review* 143.

BEAUJOUAN, Éva and NÍ BHROLCHÁIN, Màire, 'Cohabitation and Marriage in Britain since the 1970s' in R Probert (ed), *Cohabitation and Non-Marital Births in England and Wales, 1600–2012* (Basingstoke, Palgrave MacMillan, 2014).

BRIERLEY, Peter, *UK Church Statistics 2005–2015* (Tonbridge, ADBC Publishers, 2011).

BROWN, Callum G, *The Death of Christian Britain: Understanding Secularisation 1800–2000* (Abingdon, Routledge, 2009).

BROWN, Callum G and SNAPE, Michael, 'Introduction: conceptualising secularisation 1974–2010: the influence of Hugh McLeod' in CG Brown and M Snape (eds), *Secularisation in the Christian World* (Farnham, Ashgate, 2010).

BRUCE, Steve, 'Secularisation and the impotence of individualized religion' (2006) *The Hedgehog Review* 35.

BUCKLER, FW, 'The establishment of the Church of England: its constitutional and legal significance' (1941) 10 *Church History* 299.

CURRAN, Cynthia, 'Private women, public needs: middle-class widows in Victorian England' (1993) 25 *Albion* 217.

DARWIN, Charles, *On the origin of species by means of natural selection, or the preservation of favoured races in the struggle for life* (London, John Murray, 1859).

FARRIMOND, Sarah, 'Rights and rites: Church of England weddings and ritual symbolism' in this volume.

FLOUD, Roderick and THANE, Pat, 'The incidence of civil marriage in Victorian England and Wales' (1979) 84 *Past and Present* 146.

GALTON, Francis, *Inquiries into human faculty and its development* (London, Macmillan, 1883).

GENERAL REGISTER OFFICE, *First Annual Report of the Registrar-General of Births, Deaths and Marriages in England (1837–38)* (London, HMSO, 1839).
——, *Second Annual Report of the Registrar-General of Births, Deaths and Marriages in England (1838–39)* (London, HMSO, 1840).
——, *Fourth Annual Report of the Registrar-General of Births, Deaths and Marriages in England (1840–41)* (London, HMSO, 1842).
——, *Eighth Annual Report of the Registrar-General of Births, Deaths and Marriages in England (1845)* (London, HMSO, 1848).
——, *Seventeenth Annual Report of the Registrar-General of Births, Deaths and Marriages in England (1854)* (London, HMSO, 1856).
——, *Twenty-seventh Annual Report of the Registrar-General of Births, Deaths and Marriages in England (1864)* (London, HMSO, 1866).
——, *Sixtieth Annual Report of the Registrar-General of Births, Deaths and Marriages in England (1897)* (London, HMSO, 1899).
GILL, Robin, HADAWAY, C Kirk and MARLER, Penny Long, 'Is religious belief declining in Britain?' (1998) 37 *Journal for the Scientific Study of Religion* 507.
HAMMICK, James, *The marriage law of England* (London, Shaw and Sons, 1873).
HARDING, Rosie, 'Playing "House of Lords Bingo": A critical discourse analysis of *Hansard* debates on the Civil Partnership Act 2004 and Marriage (Same Sex Couples) Act 2013' in this volume.
HASKEY, John, 'Trends in marriage: church, chapel and civil ceremonies' (1980) 22 *Population Trends* 19.
——, 'Widowhood, widowerhood and remarriage' (1982) 30 *Population Trends* 15.
——, 'Remarriage of the divorced in England and Wales—a contemporary phenomenon' (1983) 15 *Journal of Biosocial Science* 253.
——, 'Social class patterns of marriage' (1983) 34 *Population Trends* 12.
——, 'Trends in marriage and divorce in England and Wales: 1837–1987' (1987) 48 *Population Trends* 11.
——, 'Identical addresses at marriage and pre-marital cohabitation: results from linking marriage registration and census records' (1990) 59 *Population Trends* 20.
——, 'Social and family characteristics of marriage in England and Wales: information derived from marriage registration records' (1991) 23 *Journal of Biosocial Science* 179.
——, 'The day of the week on which couples marry' (1996) 85 *Population Trends* 45.
——, 'Marriages in "Approved Premises" in England and Wales: the impact of the 1994 Marriage Act' (1998) 93 *Population Trends* 38.
——, 'Marriages in approved premises and register offices in England and Wales: the proportion who marry away from home' (2002) 107 *Population Trends* 35.
——, 'Cohabitation and births outside marriage after 1970: a rapidly evolving phenomenon' in R Probert (ed), *Cohabitation and Non-Marital Births in England and Wales, 1600–2012* (Basingstoke, Palgrave MacMillan, 2014).
HEWITT, Martin, 'Why the notion of Victorian Britain *does* make sense' (2006) 48 *Victorian Studies* 395.
HIGGS, Edward, 'Women, occupations and work in the Nineteenth century censuses' (1987) 23 *History Workshop* 59.
——, 'Occupational censuses and the agricultural workforce in Victorian England and Wales' (1997) 48 *The Economic History Review (New Series)* 700.

JONES, Philip, 'Comments on Ecclesiastical Law' (2014): www.ecclesiasticallaw.wordpress.com/tag/divorce-and-matrimonial-causes-act-1857/.

VAN DE KAA, Dirk J, 'Europe's Second Demographic Transition' *Population Bulletin 41* (Washington DC, Population Reference Bureau, 1987).

KRAUSE, JT, 'The changing adequacy of English registration, 1690–1837' DV Glass and DEC Eversley (eds), *Population in History* (London, Arnold, 1969).

LESTHAEGHE, Ron and VAN DE KAA, Dirk J, 'Twee demografische transities' in R Lesthaeghe and DJ van de Kaa (eds) Bevolking: *Groei en Krimp?* (Deventer, Van Loghum, Slaterus, 1986).

LESTHAEGHE, Ron, 'The second demographic transition in Western countries; an interpretation' (1995) *Gender and family change in industrialized countries* 17.

LEWIS, Jane, *Individualism and commitment in marriage and cohabitation* (London, Lord Chancellor's Department, Research Series 8/99, 1999).

MACINTYRE, Alasdair, *Secularization and moral change: the Riddell memorial lectures, 36th series* (London, Oxford University Press, 1967).

MALTHUS, Thomas, *An essay on the principle of population; or a view of its past and present effects on human happiness with an enquiry into our prospects respecting the future removal or mitigation of the evils which it occasions*, 5th edn with important additions, vol II (London, John Murray, 1817).

MAQSOOD, Ruqaiyyah, 'Weddings' (2009) available at www.bbc.co.uk/religion/religions/islam/ritesrituals/weddings_1.shtml

OGLE, William, 'On marriage-rates and marriage-ages, with special reference to the growth of population' (1890) 53 *Journal of the Royal Statistical Society* 266.

POOR LAW COMMISSION OFFICE, *Fourth Annual Report of the Poor Law Commissioners for England and Wales* (London, HMSO, 1838).

ROSE, Sonya O, 'The varying household arrangements of the elderly in three English villages: Nottinghamshire 1851–1881' (1988) 3 *Continuity and Change* 101.

WOODS, Robert, 'The structure of mortality in mid-nineteenth Century England and Wales' (1982) 8 *Journal of Historical Geography* 373.

——, *The demography of Victorian England and Wales* (Cambridge, Cambridge University Press, 2000).

WOODS, Timothy, 'Marriage after divorce: the challenge for the Church of England' (2006) 17 *Islam and Christian-Muslim Relation* 343.

3

From this Day Forward? Pre-Marital Cohabitation and the Rite of Marriage from the 1960s to the Present Day

REBECCA PROBERT

I. INTRODUCTION

FIFTY YEARS AGO marriage marked an important rite of passage in a number of respects. It was a central part of the transition to adulthood: marriage was both expected and entered into at an early age (Leete 1979: 16). It was the point at which the vast majority of couples set up home together, usually moving from the parental home rather than from an independent abode (Leonard 1980: 61–62; Rosser and Harris 1983: 183). And for many couples it was the point at which they embarked on a full sexual relationship. As one woman who had married in 1955 told Mass Observation, after 'the great day of the engagement',

> in most cases, a period of saving began so that there was a nest-egg to put towards the future home. About a year to eighteen months after the engagement came the wedding and the couple started life together and in most cases also started their sexual relationship after marriage. I know this was true in my own case, and in the cases of my close friends. (Quoted by Langhamer 2013: 152).

But since the early 1960s the proportion of couples who have lived together before marriage has increased to the point where it is highly unusual *not* to do so (Haskey 1997, 2015). Those who do marry do so at a significantly older age, often after having children together. Against this background, the rite of marriage has lost much of the social significance it once had. Not only has it 'lost its potency as a rite that marks the transition from adolescence to adulthood' (Otnes and Pleck 2003: 5), but, for many, it is simply a transition from living as if married to being legally married.

This chapter accordingly explores how pre-marital cohabitation became part of the process of marrying—a rite in its own right, one might say—and how the rite of marriage has been altered by the emergence of pre-marital cohabitation and its evolution from avant-garde practice to acceptability and then to near-universality. To do so, it draws on a range of sources. Surveys from the late 1970s onwards began to provide nationally representative data about the extent of cohabitation, while the British Social Attitudes Survey captured changing attitudes to marriage and cohabitation. For the more recent past, in-depth qualitative studies of individual couples also exist, while for earlier decades a particularly rich source of information about expectations, understandings and perceptions can be found in the magazines aimed at teenagers and aspiring brides. Indeed, it is worth noting that these were overlapping constituencies at the start of the period under consideration: *Honey*, aimed at those in their teens and twenties, had a short-lived spin-off entitled *Honey's Bride Guide*, and even magazines aimed at younger teenagers might include advertisements for engagement rings (Comer 1974: 36). Both *Honey* and its rival *19* regularly dealt with the topic of marriage in the 1970s and early 1980s, although by the time the former folded in 1986 its coverage was becoming more theoretical and less a matter of practical reality for its readers. The weekly *Woman* magazine was aimed at a broader age range, and was more likely to deal with those already married or living together than those embarking on the process, but useful insights can still be drawn from occasional letters to its regular agony aunt, while its sister publication, *Woman Bride & Home*, published between 1968 and 1972, envisaged a slightly younger audience. Rather longer lasting was *Wedding Day & First Home*, first published in 1976 and continued from 1986 under the title *Wedding & Home*. As will be discussed further below, the changes in titles are themselves significant indicators of changing social reality over the period from the late 1960s to the early 1990s, and examining material published on a monthly basis allows for the timing of changes to be identified with a fair degree of precision. Finally, two television series broadcast in the late 1970s—*Robin's Nest* and *Rings on their Fingers*—both depicted the transition from cohabitation to marriage and provide insights into what was regarded as novel and funny at the time.

II. EMERGENCE OF PRE-MARITAL COHABITATION

Early bridal magazines and other guides to wedding planning assumed that the couple would be setting up home together *after* the wedding. Betty Owen Williams' 1964 guide to *Planning Your Wedding Day from A to Z* included 'A Few Hints on Buying a House', while seven years later *Planning Your Wedding With Woman Bride & Home* devoted separate chapters to 'Finding a Home' and 'Moving in'. Marriage preparation classes made similar assumptions: one magazine noted that the classes for engaged couples run by the National Marriage Guidance Council 'usually … start with practical topics connected with setting up a shared household' (*Woman* 19 February 1972: 76). Younger readers were given similar information: *Honey's Bride Guide* may have focused on fashion—'What will trendy brides be wearing?' asked the Spring/Summer issue of 1967—but also contained 'hints for homemakers', along with advice on mortgages and budgeting (*Honey's Bride Guide* Spring/Summer issue 1967: 41, 43 and 45). The assumption was, as one headline put it, that couples would be 'Starting from Scratch' (*Honey's Bride Guide* Spring 1969: 55). In a similar vein, the first issue of *Woman Bride & Home*, published in Spring 1968, began by saying 'It's the happiest time of your life, they say, planning a wedding and putting together your first home'. Its focus was very much on the household rather than the wedding, with articles in the Easter 1968 issue on household appliances, recipes, budgeting, and the necessity of a trip to the family planning clinic appearing alongside a rather short section on wedding dresses and an analysis of whether white weddings were worth it. The cover of the Winter 1968 issue invited readers to consider 'New ways with casseroles', while that published for New Year 1969 tried to tempt them with a 16-page booklet promising 'all you need to know about CURTAINS'.[1]

Contemporary sociological surveys suggest that these editorial assumptions reflected the reality of readers' lives. Diana Leonard's survey of couples getting married in Swansea between 1968 and 1969 found little evidence of cohabitation, even among those marrying for a second time (Leonard 1980). The general pattern was for young people to live at home until marrying in their early twenties (ibid: 19): 45 of the 50 women marrying for the first time were living at home, as indeed were all four of those marrying for a second time. The living arrangements of their husbands-to-be were only slightly different, with 40 out of 49 of those marrying for the first time being at home, and three of the five marrying for a second time (ibid: fig 3). Those not living at home did not necessarily enjoy any greater freedom from supervision, with six (one woman and five men) living in institutional residences (whether college, hospital residence or the army), and another two living with relatives. Only four couples had lived together before marriage: one married man had moved in with the woman he wished to marry and her mother, marrying the former as soon as his wife divorced him; an 18-year-old had lived with her fiancé and his parents while consent for their marriage was obtained from the magistrates' court; and two students had shared a flat in their second year. And there was only one case of a couple who had set up home together in the same town as their parents—this 'single, revealing exception' being 'a couple who were refused consent to

[1] Anxious brides-to-be may well have welcomed such advice. In an article on engaged couples, Betty, who had been engaged to Gerald for eight years, worried about how they would cope when they married, since '[h]is mother was such a splendid housewife and he had been living at home all the time': 'How long is too long?', *Woman Bride & Home* Autumn 1969, p 65.

marry, and who then "ran away" and got a flat together. Their ménage lasted five days before they were marched to the register office' (ibid: 49).

The influence of parental disapproval of cohabitation—actual or dreaded—was clearly an important influence on marriage. Beyfus' 1968 survey of contemporary marriages found one self-avowedly unconventional couple who had lived together in Bournemouth before marrying but who had soon decided to marry. In the words of 'Rosie': 'it didn't really work. I wasn't ready to live with him. I had told my parents that I was going away for a holiday by the sea, and I felt guilty because I knew they wouldn't approve' (Beyfus 1971: 15). In the same year, *Woman Bride & Home* carried an interview with a woman who had married at the age of 16: in a nice blend of radicalism and conventionality she confessed that 'I wouldn't have minded just living together but of course my parents would only agree to me leaving home if we got married' (*Woman Bride & Home* Winter 1968: 81).

But this was about to change. Pre-marital cohabitation increased three-fold from the late 1960s into the early 1970s (Leete 1979). Even the more home-oriented magazines were discussing cohabitation. While early articles tended to be defensive—'Marriage may be changing but it's still the best arrangement we've got!' proclaimed one piece in *Woman* in 1970 (*Woman* 20 June 1970: 25)—before long the new flexibility was being presented as an advantage. Women, it was noted, 'are now able to live openly with their partners' (*Woman* 15 July 1972: 27). The range of choices had expanded: '[y]ou can live with someone for a while, marry them later or not marry them at all' (*Woman* 12 May 1973: 28).

The issue of cohabitation featured as a 'talking topic' in *Woman* in December 1972 under the heading 'Where do you draw the loving line?' (*Woman* 9 December 1972: 18), and revealed the diversity of views even among the young and between members of the same family. One young man of 21 thought it acceptable to go on holiday with his fiancée but rejected the idea of living together on the basis that he felt the need to set an example to his younger siblings (in spite of, or perhaps because of, the fact that his older sister had lived with a man for five years before marrying). Nineteen-year-old Susan, a typist, agreed that '[t]o go away together is one thing. To live with somebody is another', but her 18-year-old sister took the more pragmatic line that it depended on whether the couple could afford to live together.

Yet despite such widespread discussion, increasing acceptability, and the removal of many of the practical obstacles to living together unwed (on which see Probert 2012: ch 7), pre-marital cohabitation remained a minority practice during the 1970s (Brown and Kiernan 1981: 8, table 8). One study of newly-weds carried out on the cusp of the 1980s found that

> although sexual intimacy in courtship was widely accepted by courting couples (and even their parents) as natural, and beneficial to marital happiness, cohabitation prior to marriage was still generally not accepted by them. Even though a quarter of the newly-weds lived together before marrying, they did not regard this as an alternative

> to marriage. For the remaining three-quarters of newly-weds (and especially their parents) the idea of living together was unacceptable, even when considered as a final phase of courtship. (Mansfield and Collard 1988: 86).

And for those who did live together—or at least those who did so when young and single—it was 'largely a childfree, relatively short-lived, transitional form of behaviour preceding marriage' (Kiernan and Eldridge 1987: 60).

As cohabitation before marriage became more common, wedding magazines also began to feature couples who had lived together before marrying, although the fact that they had done so was initially seen as a matter for comment. At the start of 1986, *Wedding Day & First Home* ran an article on 'real life weddings', with a picture of Sue, John and baby Daisy revealingly captioned 'marrying a little late for convention, perhaps—but happy nonetheless' (*Wedding Day & First Home* New Year Preview 1985–86: 132). A second couple featured, Debbie and Roger, had lived together for six years, and it was noted that after he had proposed 'as if to make up for lost time, they rang the vicar the next day' (ibid).

But by the Spring issue the title of the magazine had tellingly changed to *Wedding & Home*, reflecting the fact that the marital home would now often not be the *first* home. Having invited readers to fill in a survey to discover the nature of the 'bride of the 80s' (*Wedding Day & First Home* Autumn 1985: 84), it reported that 31 per cent of those who responded were already living together (*Wedding & Home* Autumn 1986: 122). When checked against national-level studies for the period it would appear that levels of cohabitation among readers of bridal magazines were only slightly lower than the norm: Haskey and Kiernan found that 34 per cent of those who married between 1980 and 1984 had cohabited first (Haskey and Kiernan 1989). And as this increased to 50 per cent or more in the second half of the decade (Beaujouan and Ní Bhrolcháin 2011), readers of *Wedding & Home* kept pace with the national trend, with the magazine reporting in 1989 that 47 per cent of those responding to the now-annual survey had lived together before the wedding (*Wedding & Home* Autumn 1989: 79), and a year later noting that this had risen to 53 per cent (*Wedding & Home* October/November 1990: 76). Pre-marital cohabitation had simply ceased to be a matter for comment.

III. PRE-MARITAL COHABITATION AS PART OF THE RITE OF GETTING MARRIED

The extent to which pre-marital cohabitation can be seen as part of the rite of getting married depends to a great extent on the expectations of the individual couple. Buying or renting a home and moving in together shortly before the wedding is a different matter from living together specifically to test one's compatibility for marriage—and different again from those cases where couples who have been cohabiting eventually decide to marry.

A. Pre-Marital Cohabitation as a Short-Term Precursor to the Wedding

Examples of pre-marital cohabitation as a short-term precursor to the wedding can be found primarily in the early part of the period. It was still sufficiently novel to be used as a gag in BBC TV's *The Good Life*, with Tom Good remarking that he and Barbara moved into their Surbiton house 'a week before they were married'. 'Surely you mean the week after?' asks their more straight-laced neighbour Gerry. 'No—before', responds Tom, to the accompaniment of much (admittedly canned) laughter.[2] The practicalities of obtaining a home might influence the timing: Leonard's survey of Swansea couples found that those buying a new home had generally paid a retainer six to nine months in advance of the wedding, while those buying older houses obtained them between one and six months beforehand and worked on them in the meantime; by contrast, those who were renting the matrimonial home began to do so only one or two weeks before the wedding (Leonard 1980: 239–40).

This form of cohabitation is best seen as part of the rite of marrying, since it occurred only when the decision to marry had been taken. Kiernan, writing in 1983, commented that:

> One could speculate that young couples, having decided that they wish to marry, organise their future home and are increasingly likely to live together before the nuptial ceremony instead of living apart with their respective parents or paying two rents. Such a pattern of behaviour may account for the fact that the time spent cohabiting before marriage is relatively short (Kiernan, quoted in Fletcher 1988: 64).

And in the early part of the period this was the predominant model of pre-marital cohabitation: in a study of newly-weds '[o]nly a quarter of those who cohabited had begun living together in advance of a commitment to marriage' (Mansfield, quoted in Chester 1986).

B. Longer-Term Cohabitation as a Means of Determining Suitability for Marriage

At the same time, a second type of cohabitation was emerging, one that was entered into as a means by which a couple could test their relationship and suitability for marriage. In the summer of 1972 *Honey* posed the question: 'Those Whom Love has Brought Together Will Marriage Put Asunder?' and told readers that 'It's better to learn your limitations through a trial marriage

[2] I am grateful to Chris Barton for alerting me to this.

than to find out when it's too late that marriage is a trial' (*Honey* August 1972). A few months earlier it had noted the

> increasing popularity of the trial marriage, which is threatening to take the place of the engagement, even among nicely brought-up boys and girls. The apparent advantage of the trial marriage is that it gives both partners a chance to test the inevitable rigours of marriage without actually committing themselves finally to a long-term relationship. (*Honey* October 1971: 83).

Some individuals described their decision to cohabit in precisely these terms. Suzanne, a sociology student who married a fellow student after living together for a few months, confidently told *Woman Bride & Home* that 'I knew that marriage was the completely logical step for me. By living together first I had found out all that marriage entails which I couldn't possibly have done if we had simply been engaged' (*Woman Bride & Home* Autumn 1969: 65). Others displayed some anxiety: the young woman who wrote to 'Evelyn Home', the agony aunt of *Woman* magazine, to explain that she had been living with her fiancé for the previous four months declared that 'I don't see anything really wrong in this; it's the only way to find out if marriage will work out'. But she added that her mother didn't know, and that she would not want the neighbours to find out, and ended with a plea: '[d]o you think I am doing wrong?' (*Woman* 18 July 1970: 61).[3]

It was somewhat ironic that the 'trial marriage' emerged against the backdrop of a substantial increase in divorce. Logically, one might expect greater ease of divorce to make marriage seem less of a 'final irrevocable step', and to reassure couples that if they subsequently found that they were incompatible there would still be a way out for them. But the increase in divorce clearly created a sense of insecurity among those contemplating marriage. *Honey* noted how marriage had become 'practical', with couples wanting 'to know the score before it's too late, before a judge in the divorce court has to spell it out' (*Honey* October 1971: 83), while *Woman* featured a recently married couple, Shirley and Gerald, who 'had lived together before they married and decided to make their union legal just before she became pregnant with twins. They wanted to be absolutely sure they could live together permanently' (*Woman* 28 October 1972: 26). Some were wary because their parents had divorced: one girl seeking advice from *Woman* noted that her 19-year-old boyfriend was 'frightened of marriage because he comes from a split-up home' (*Woman* 8 April 1972: 100), while a new bride whose parents had recently divorced told the researchers 'we lived together before we got married for about five months to sort of just give it

[3] 'Evelyn Home' was unwilling to offer any comfort: 'What I think doesn't matter: you think you are doing wrong by living a lie and it makes you thoroughly uneasy. Must you go on being a mistress when you so much want to be a wife? A wedding needn't be costly or ceremonial, takes little time to arrange and would settle your troubled conscience'.

a try—so that if either of us changed our minds we wouldn't have all that legal binding sort of thing' (Mansfield and Collard 1988: 93). *Rings on their Fingers* gently satirised this view, with Oliver Pryde suggesting that one of the benefits of cohabitation was that if they split up they could 'float out of each other's lives … like an open prison' (*Rings on their Fingers* 13 October 1978).

Others simply wanted to make sure that they would not be adding to the divorce statistics themselves. As Barbara, living with Neville in Solihull, told *Woman*: 'Perhaps one day we will get married, but we'll have to be absolutely sure we will never split up'. *Robin's Nest* captured this concern by making the central female character the daughter of divorced parents: turning down Robin's proposal of marriage in the very first episode, broadcast on 11 January 1977, she points out that her parents were married—'that's why they got divorced'. Marriage was clearly being taken very seriously by these couples, real and fictional, with the possible failure of a marriage being seen as somehow worse than the ending of the relationship.

Not that the trial marriage was presented as entirely attractive. *Honey* highlighted a potential downside, suggesting that

> unmarried couples frequently have more tensions. In most cases the girls are ready to marry before the men; they want to make a permanent relationship, and when a girl feels a bit on trial it can make her anxious. (*Honey* August 1972).

Such anxiety would hardly have been allayed by the warning that '[t]he inescapable self-consciousness of a situation where both partners are watching each other's every move for the slightest hint of discontent creates a building sense of insecurity' (*Honey* October 1971: 83). And the suggestion in *Woman* that 'living with someone at the "Who left the top off the toothpaste" and dirty socks level is seen as part and parcel of getting to know that person' seemed calculated to put more fastidious readers off the idea altogether, even if the article was billed as 'Sex—the new liberation' (*Woman* 13 October 1973: 8).

Nonetheless, surveys confirmed the growing perception that it was a good idea to live together before marrying. The National Marriage Guidance Council amassed information from various regions on this point. In Guernsey, 74 per cent of boys and 63 per cent of girls 'thought it was a good idea to live together before marriage', while in Purley, 12 out of the 50 engaged couples in the sample surveyed were living together, with 'almost all' saying that it was to 'test the relationship' (Guy 1983: 3, 12). In Walsall, by contrast, a distinction emerged between younger and older couples:

> The feeling of a group of 17 to 25 year olds from Walsall, who were attending a voluntary marriage preparation course, was that living together was not really part of the plan—it was engagement, wedding, marriage. By contrast, some of the older couples from the same area, many of whom were teachers, had all lived together for anything up to six years before marrying (ibid: 11).

By the end of the decade the British Social Attitudes Survey had found that 43 per cent of the population—or at least a nationally representative sample of it—would advise a young woman to live with a man first and then marry, although 37 per cent were still advocating marriage without living together and only four per cent favoured cohabitation without marrying (Kiernan and Estaugh 1993: 6–7). Within a few years the proportion thinking that 'it was 'a good idea to live together before marriage' had risen to 58 per cent (ONS 1997: table 1.8).

Yet the idea of trial marriage still presupposed that the parties moved in with the deliberate intention of marrying if they felt that the relationship worked, and there were hints that this was beginning to change. When, in early 1987, *Wedding & Home* ran an article on living together asking whether it was '[s]inful or sensible, a good trial for marriage or simply a matter of convenience?', Renate Olins, Director of the London Marriage Guidance Council, suggested that many couples simply drifted into living together: '[v]ery few couples see living together as a trial marriage' (*Wedding & Home* Spring 1987: 90).

C. Cohabitation that Ended in Marriage

Of course, there had always been couples who lived together without thought of marriage (*Honey* March 1974: 48), or who saw living together as a trial not merely of their compatibility with the other person but also a test of whether they could marry at all. *Woman* ran a series of stories on this theme as early as 1975:

> In a world where convention no longer makes the rules for us, life becomes much harder. There are few excuses now for drifting into marriage. Our short season of love stories concerns people who have reached a point where, free of social pressures, they must decide for themselves if they really are ... the marrying kind. (*Woman* 12 April 1975: 20).

And in 1977 *Rings on their Fingers* depicted the transition from long-term cohabitation to marriage where the male partner had often voiced ideological objections to marriage.

Over the course of the 1980s, however, while most cohabiting couples did go on to marry (on which see Buck and Scott 1994: 69–70), there was a new concern that such relationships were characterised by 'drift'. The mocking note of the 'cautionary tale' related in *Honey* under the heading 'Look before you live together' suggests that certain stereotypes had already emerged:

> Bunty met Boris at her best friend's wedding. She said. 'I hate this bourgeois parade of an anachronistic romantic myth.' He said 'Marriage is the death of true love.' The consequence was: they ended up living together ... their reasons,

> of course impeccable: they'd known each other for months—three at least. And it was eminently practical—Bunty was fed up with traipsing backwards and forwards from her flat in town to his shared house in the suburbs ... they'd only have to pay one lot of rent, and they'd be able to save. (*Honey* November 1980: 27).

In 1987 a study carried out by a group from Sheffield polytechnic found that while some were living together because they couldn't marry, others

> had followed a clear pattern of becoming gradually more committed to each other, starting off by living in the same house as students, or one half of the couple moving into the other half's flat. The next stage was buying a house together, and the third stage was getting married; so what started off as a temporary arrangement, ended up as permanent. (*Wedding & Home* Spring 1987: 90).

American researchers have subsequently dubbed the practice 'sliding' rather than 'deciding' (Stanley, Rhoades, Markman 2006).

By this time the pressure to marry was much reduced. Those interviewed in McRae's study of cohabiting mothers in the late 1980s were specifically asked whether they had ever felt under any pressure to marry: 'only 10 long-term cohabiting mothers replied that they had, with 84 per cent replying negatively' (McRae 1993: 65). Some even felt that there was peer-pressure *not* to marry: Sally Jones, writing for *Honey* in 1982, noted that:

> There are also my friends to think of. All are single for reasons of principle. If I got married they'd think me a coward; they wouldn't respect me; they'd think I'd let the side down. Peer-group approval is more important than we think (*Honey* November 1982: 99).

And '[a]round 1990, the probability of a cohabitation spell ending without marriage became greater than the reverse for the first time' (Murphy 2000: 51).

IV. PRE-MARITAL COHABITATION CHANGING THE RITE OF MARRIAGE

A. Rite of Sexual Initiation

The first issue of *Woman Bride & Home*—'For tomorrow's happiest young marrieds', as the strapline proclaimed—included an article reassuring readers that 'Honeymoons can be happy' (*Woman Bride & Home* Spring 1968). Mrs Phyllis Marks, somewhat dauntingly described as a 'Marriage Guidance Counsellor, Magistrate and Lecturer on human relationships', discussed the issue with four girls who were about to be married—nervous Pamela, who had never seen a naked man, 'starry-eyed' Yvonne, eagerly looking forward to sexual fulfillment, prosaic Jenny, who was willing to dispense with the honeymoon altogether and move into their new home, and 'cool and sophisticated' Frances who had actually had sex with another man (although the article was quick to stress that she had been engaged to the man in question at the time). Mrs Marks dispensed advice and reassurance to all four, gently warning that Yvonne might not experience the 'instant ecstasy' she was hoping for, and suggesting that Jenny should go away for the honeymoon:

> It is a time set aside for a couple, between their single and married life, to get to know each other physically and emotionally in a way that was not possible before. For the marriage status bestows security on the couple within which they can joyfully and freely come into possession of each other.

Honey's Bride Guide similarly felt that readers might be in need of advice on the sexual implications of marriage. Under the heading 'The physical side of marriage' it warned that:

> Planning a wedding, making a home, buying a house—these things take pride of place during an engagement, and not enough is learned about the physical relationship between men and women (*Honey's Bride Guide*, Autumn/Winter 1967: 68).

But the backdrop was changing rapidly. A few months later, *Woman Bride & Home* ran an article on 'Sex and the engaged girl', in which a marriage guidance counsellor (in a presumably unintentional double entendre) noted that the issue of sex before marriage is 'bound to come up sooner or later', although her advice was that girls shouldn't feel pressured into it (*Woman Bride & Home* Autumn 1968: 89). In an example that can be seen as being designed to warn young women of how the rite of marriage would be affected, one bride who had slept with her husband-to-be 'fairly regularly beforehand' was quoted as saying that 'on my wedding night I did wonder if I wasn't missing something' (ibid: 90). Another, pregnant with her cohabitant's child, told *Honey* that 'Once we decided to marry, I wanted to stop sleeping with Jon until our wedding night … I guess it was silly, but I wanted it to be special in some way' (*Honey* August 1972). Sandra Bennett in *Rings on their Fingers* clearly had a similar idea of what was appropriate, putting up the camp bed for Oliver in the sitting room after his reluctant proposal but reassuring him it was 'only till after we're married, darling' (*Rings on their Fingers* 13 October 1978). And while they do end up in bed together at the end of the following episode, she makes him go back to the camp-bed to sleep (*Rings on their Fingers* 20 October 1978).

By the early 1970s the assumption was that the honeymoon was no longer a time of sexual initiation (*19*, January 1969: 9; *19*, October 1970: 145). Admittedly, at the start of 1971 *Woman Bride & Home* was still presenting marital sex as different from pre-marital sex—'It doesn't matter if they've had intercourse before, or even lived together for a time, they've still only been playing at a marriage relationship'—and noting that the honeymoon might be difficult if one of the partners was sexually inexperienced, warning that 'Honeymoons aren't all honey' (*Woman Bride & Home* New Year 1971: 30). But by the end of the year it was suggesting a new difficulty: noting that the marriage of two virgins 'is now comparatively rare' it pointed out that 'there's always the temptation to compare the performance of your partner with that of a previous lover' (*Woman Bride & Home* Winter 1971: 58).

Just over a decade later, the *Bride's Complete Guide to Planning Your Wedding* could confidently declare that '[t]he majority of today's newly-weds have lived together or slept together long before the wedding' (1983: 134).

Of course, it should never be assumed that a trend has become universal. In 1977 *Honey*, having commissioned a survey of sexual habits, reported that one in three of those surveyed claimed to be a virgin (*Honey* May 1977: 40).[4] Half of them said that they simply hadn't met the right man but over a third declared that they preferred to wait until marriage. The proportion who wanted to wait was, however, dropping rapidly: 10 years later *Wedding Day & First Home* found that only four per cent of respondents to its annual survey would be virgins on their wedding night (*Wedding & Home* Autumn 1987: 93). The variations in the questions asked of readers reflected this shift. In 1980 a quiz designed to test readers' readiness for marriage had, when asking 'have you and your fiancé made love', given the following options: '(a) Yes (b) No, he respects me (c) No, we are both agreed that it is morally wrong before marriage' (*Woman Bride & Home* Summer 1980: 24). *Wedding & Home*'s annual surveys asked a number of questions about readers' sexual experience, reporting in 1987 that 32 per cent of brides had said their fiancé was their first lover, and eight per cent that they were engaged when they first made love to him (*Wedding & Home* Autumn 1987: 93), but the dwindling proportion of virgin brides meant that by 1991 those who admitted to this state were asked a follow-up question: 'why?' (*Wedding & Home* October/November 1991: 43).

The changing significance of the honeymoon was noted in *Honey*, in an article questioning the point of the excursion 'now the idea of "saving yourself for marriage" has become a thing of the past'. What, it demanded,

> will the honeymoon mean to those modern couples? Will it just be a relaxing holiday, free of 'first-night nerves' and other pressures? Just a fun excuse to get away after the 'mere formality' of the marriage itself, a carefree, indulgent celebration of an already established, consummated relationship? (*Honey* February 1982: 70).

One couple interviewed for the piece said that 'it didn't feel any different from just a very good holiday'—although since they had booked this particular holiday before deciding to get married this was perhaps to be expected. Another 'added spice by having their honeymoon in the hotel where they'd spent their first dirty weekend'. But a third expressed some discomfort with the perceived expectations of the occasion: 'even if you've "done it" before, now it's legal you've got to do it properly—or that seems to be the feeling'. And as late as 1985 one book was advising couples that the honeymoon

> is also a time for making love. Even if you have lived or slept together before the wedding, you will probably find that lovemaking is more enjoyable, in more relaxed circumstances, than in the tense months before the wedding. (Moss 1985: 124).

[4] The survey, commissioned from a professional organisation, involved a representative sample of 290 unmarried women aged between 18 and 26.

As the period of time for which couples live together before marrying has lengthened significantly since the 1980s, one would expect that even this remnant of difference will have disappeared. Sex has become so thoroughly decoupled from marriage over the past four decades that it is difficult to imagine researchers today solemnly asking couples whether their experience of 'lovemaking' was different after marriage: we have moved very swiftly from a time when the question would have been too embarrassing to ask to a time when it is simply irrelevant.

B. The Rite of Setting Up Home

It might seem obvious that cohabitation has replaced marriage in terms of the rite of setting up home. Yet it is not necessarily an exact replacement, since cohabitants' housing and domestic arrangements are not always the same as those of their married counterparts (Miles, Pleasance and Balmer 2009: 42; Purbrick 2007). The evidence here is not as comprehensive as that available on couples' pre-marital sexual experience, but there are nonetheless some suggestive findings from the literature.

For one young couple who married in the late 1960s, the transition from the man's flat to a mortgage and a house was the trigger for their marriage: 'Sarah' reported that 'I refused to live with him in a house that my parents knew about so I wanted our relationship to become official. I suppose I sulked him into marrying me' (Beyfus 1971: 140). Alternatively, marriage might be the trigger for a new home: one of Oliver Pryde's many objections to marriage in *Rings on their Fingers* is that it would mean moving, since one couldn't carry the bride 'over a threshold of sin' (*Rings on their Fingers* 13 October 1978). When he does marry Sandra, her mother almost immediately turns up with proposals for the complete redecoration of their flat, referring to their previous situation as being 'impermanent' (*Rings on their Fingers* 10 November 1978).

There was a strong sense that what was acceptable during a period of cohabitation was not necessarily suitable for married life. *Wedding & Home* commented in 1987 that those who married and then moved in together

> are most likely to have bought a flat or house and renovated, decorated and furnished it, ready to move into. Couples who live together first are more likely to share the home of one or the other, and to put up with less than perfect (often cramped) conditions. (*Wedding & Home* Spring 1987: 90).

This is of course linked to the evidence that financial stability was often seen as a prerequisite for marriage, and those who were cohabiting were less able to afford their own home. Wallace's study of the Isle of Sheppey in the 1980s found that 'a higher proportion of young people cohabited before marriage in this employment-stricken community than the 24 per cent cited for 18–34 year-olds in the General Household Survey' (Wallace 1987: 179).

Kiernan and Estaugh's analysis of the 1989 General Household Survey data confirmed that cohabitants were less likely than married couples to own their home and further revealed that they were also less likely to have central heating, a car, a telephone or a colour TV (Kiernan and Estaugh 1993: 14–15). There may also have been a feeling that a home and the purchase of consumer durables spelled commitment, as is nicely illustrated in the case of John and Lil, whose differing expectations of what moving in together meant came to a head when they went to buy a cooker together. Lil noted that, for her, moving in together

> was a sign of permanency. We were now a 'couple' and I wanted it to be our home. I thought this is it—marriage and everything. But John doesn't think anything is permanent so the move in was very fraught.

The immediate matter was 'resolved when John's feeling that a second-hand cooker was somehow less of a commitment foundered on the fact that the price was much the same' (*Honey* August 1983: 24); sadly, we don't know whether the relationship did or did not prove to be permanent.

It is also worth noting that moving in together is still not celebrated by the giving of presents in the same way that a wedding is (Purbrick 2007: ch 6). Housewarming gifts may be given, but as yet there is no institution of the 'living together list' whereby a couple can circulate their needs and requirements to family and friends for their new home to be stocked. And, of course, the fact that the couple have been living together before the wedding changes the nature of the wedding list as well, as it ceases to be a way of equipping a new home.

C. The Rite of the Wedding Ceremony

Did the fact that a couple had lived together before marriage change the way in which they married? The period since the 1970s has seen a profound change in the way that marriages are celebrated, but the trends, and their relationship with cohabitation, are complex.

Broadly speaking, though, it would seem that in the early part of the period pre-marital cohabitation was more likely to be followed by a simple Register Office wedding. The number and proportion of those marrying for the first time who chose to do so in a religious ceremony decreased over the course of the 1970s (Haskey 1980). For some this was an active and positive choice: one bride-to-be explained that they were getting married in the Register Office because '[w]e're not religious, and I've always hated the idea of just using a church for weddings and christenings. It seems too much like organising a stage show' (*Woman Bride & Home* Midsummer 1971: 10). But there was also a perception that a white wedding—whether in church or Register Office—was not appropriate for those who had anticipated the marriage.

Lorna Sage recalled marrying as a pregnant teenager on 26 December 1959 in a deliberately low-key and secretive ceremony:

> I had on my new winter coat, whose fur collar didn't reconcile me to the concealing lines that had attracted my mother ... [M]y father ... drove us through the empty early-morning streets to the town hall, where a dyspeptic registrar pronounced the words and we signed the right forms ... No one took any pictures. (Sage 2000: 248).

Scarcely more festive was the 'hasty register office wedding' of a man and his pregnant girlfriend. The only guests were their parents: '[w]e went for a drink afterwards, to try and make it into an occasion, but it wasn't a howling success' (*Woman Bride & Home* Autumn 1971: 62). Similarly, Diana Leonard noted of her study of couples getting married in Swansea in the late 1960s that most wanted a 'proper' wedding—ie a white wedding in church—but that since seven brides were pregnant, and five men and four women had been married before, only seven out of the twenty couples were 'eligible' to marry in church (Leonard 1980: 206). A year or so later, one woman wrote to *Woman* in 1970 to say that she had got pregnant at 15 and married at 16—adding that 'It wasn't a proper white wedding, of course' (*Woman* 21 March 1970: 68). Another asked 'Can I be married in white in a church even though I have had an illegitimate baby?' (*Woman* 24 July 1971: 61). The reassuring answer from *Woman*'s advisor was 'yes', but, tellingly, advice on other colours was also given. A 1972 advert for *Woman Bride & Home* also posed the question 'They're already living together—should they have a pure white wedding?' (*Woman* 1 April 1972). And in *Rings on their Fingers* Oliver Pryde responded to his partner's wistful confession of her dream of walking up the aisle in white with the caustic rejoinder: 'White? More like deep purple' (*Rings on their Fingers* 13 October 1978).

But as pre-marital sex became the experience of the majority, brides were reluctant to allow the white dress to remain the preserve of the dwindling number of virgins. One daughter clashed with her mother over the appropriate choice of rites when the latter discovered that she had been on the pill and told her that she should get married in the Register Office (*Woman* 8 May 1976: 58). The reply was that she could get married in white if she wanted. The first series of *Robin's Nest* closed with Vicky deciding not to marry Robin in the Register Office, as planned, because she wants to do it 'properly' (*Robin's Nest* 22 February 1977); the second series culminated on 30 March 1978 with a white wedding in church.

Pre-marital cohabitation might pose other challenges for the eventual wedding. Some parents were embarrassed by the very fact of the wedding as they had been pretending that their son or daughter was already married. Others refused even to attend. In Mansfield and Collard's study of newlyweds one father whose daughter was living with her husband-to-be 'called me all the names he could lay his tongue to and just said that he didn't want anything to do with it' (Mansfield and Collard 1988: 93). And as late as 1987 *Wedding & Home* reported that '[a]lthough living together out of wedlock has become far more socially acceptable, especially in the south of England, it is still frowned on in some areas', giving the example of one set of parents who were 'so upset' that they refused to attend the wedding (*Wedding & Home* Spring 1987: 90).

Yet over the same period the nature of the Register Office wedding also began to change, as can be seen in the changing ideas about what should be worn for the ceremony. In the 1960s the assumption had been that bridal wear for a Register Office wedding would be simpler. The author of one early book on wedding planning advised readers that either a coloured dress or a suit 'should be chosen for a Registry Office wedding' (Owen Williams 1964: 30). The Easter issue of *Woman Bride & Home* ran a feature advising on short dresses and suits for those who wanted a quiet wedding:

> Getting married quietly, with the minimum of fuss and flurry? In a register office perhaps, with just a few close family and friends? Still want to look super for the great day and later? (*Woman Bride & Home* Easter 1969: 32).

A decade later, *Wedding Day & First Home* noted the controversy about 'what should or should not be worn to a registry office wedding', and, while reassuring readers that 'it really is up to you', suggested that it was a good opportunity to buy a designer outfit that could be worn again (*Wedding Day & First Home* Late Autumn 1982: 26). Most readers, however, seem to have disdained such advice. The following year, the first of its annual surveys on the cost of weddings noted that: 'Over half of register office brides not surprisingly bought a traditional bridal gown. Why should couples who choose a civil ceremony dispense with the finery traditionally associated with church weddings?' (*Wedding Day & First Home* Spring 1983: 14).

While those marrying in the Register Office were still cautioned to avoid 'anything too full and flouncy' (*Wedding Day & First Home* Autumn 1985: 84) and to dispense with the train and veil 'which might look over-elaborate' (Moss 1985: 70), the long white (or at least pale) dress had clearly become established as the norm for civil as well as church ceremonies. As one couple told *Honey*, 'Even though we'd been together for four and a half years before, we wanted a traditional wedding, a white dress and a romantic honeymoon' (*Honey* Feb 1982: 70).

Just as pre-marital cohabitation was no longer seen as a reason for not wearing white, so too it was increasingly no bar to marrying in church, although some still harboured residual anxieties. One 'real life wedding' featured in *Wedding & Home* in the autumn of 1986 involved Mandy and Steve, who had been living together and had a baby daughter. Mandy was quoted as saying 'I asked the vicar if he thought a white wedding dress would be hypocritical: he said he didn't mind what I wore, as long as I wore something!' (*Wedding & Home* Autumn 1986: 122). The evident overlap between those living together (over half by the end of the 1980s, according to *Wedding & Home* October/November 1990: 76) and those intending to have a church ceremony (nine out of ten respondents to the same survey) suggests that there was no longer any perceived institutional objection to marrying those who had lived together.[5]

As a final reflection, it is interesting to note that it was as pre-marital cohabitation emerged as the norm in the 1980s that the cost of weddings also suddenly increased. Was it that the costs were rising anyway—perhaps in response to the lavish wedding of Prince Charles and Lady Diana in 1981, or even the fact that wedding magazines, by publishing information on the 'average' spend on weddings, raised the bar as to what was expected—and that this acted as a disincentive to those who would otherwise have married (see eg Eekelaar and Maclean 2004; McRae 1993: 48)? Or did those who had lived together feel the need to make more of a statement about their wedding to emphasise that a transition of sorts was occurring? Otnes and Pleck have suggested that the lavish wedding has 'captured imaginations and incomes within contemporary Western culture' on account of its capacity to offer a magical transformation if only for a day (Otnes and Pleck 2003: 8). After all, now that marriage is detached from the rite of sexual initiation and the rite of setting up home, in order for the wedding to signify something it has to derive its meaning from its own mode of celebration (see also Charlsey 1991: 13).

Certainly weddings have become both more elaborate and more individualistic in recent years. The choice about whether to marry has been accompanied by a far greater choice about where and how to marry, illustrated in particularly dramatic form in the popular BBC3 series *Don't Tell the Bride*. The 'traditional' wedding is represented by the brides' dreams of receptions at minor stately home (cue shots of Doric pillars, sweeping staircases and chairs with chiffon bows tied on). The grooms tasked with organising the wedding, however, tend to have more exotic ideas, with particularly notable examples being an alien-themed wedding, sky-diving, and a mountain-top ceremony. Little attention is paid to whether the venue is one that is actually licensed for marriages, although the voice-over is usually careful to point out when this is not the case. Bridal reactions vary from indignation—as encapsulated by the immortal line 'What the hell am I doing at Thorpe Park on my wedding day?'—to tears (practically every episode), anger (ditto),

[5] Although personal objections remained: *Wedding & Home* New Year Preview 1987–88, 116, featured in its 'real life weddings' Deborah and Michael, who had been living together and didn't go to church regularly and so felt that a Register Office wedding would be more honest. Over a decade later, in a sample of 172 engaged individuals from North Staffordshire and Cheshire in 1998–99, 56 per cent of respondents who were cohabiting chose a religious venue, as compared to 74 per cent of those who were not cohabiting with their spouse-to-be (Hibbs, Barton and Beswick 2001: 200).

resignation and (sometimes) happiness that the groom has devoted so much thought and effort to the event. One particularly sweet-natured bride said that she would 'probably' not have chosen a bucking bronco machine had she been planning the wedding, but was very enthusiastic about the bouncy castle (Series 6, Episode 2, 21 August 2012). And despite the fact that virtually all of the couples depicted on the programme have lived together for some time, all clearly find the actual wedding day to be profoundly significant and moving.

V. CONCLUSION

As noted in the introduction, marriage was once a central part of the transition to adulthood. Mansfield and Collard, whose book *The Beginning of the Rest of your Life?* was based on interviews with couples marrying on the cusp of the 1980s, could still comment that

> [w]hen the couples had made their commitment to marriage, they had recognised that they were beginning their adult lives … almost all of them were brimming over with a sense of 'becoming', and were imbued with hope for the future. (Mansfield and Collard 1988: 199).

Increasingly, however, marriage was coming to be seen as a final step rather than 'the first day of the rest of your life'; a celebration that confirmed an existing state of affairs rather than signalling a new one (Eekelaar and Maclean 2004: 520). The now-prevalent practice of living together before marriage has profoundly and permanently altered the meaning of the rite of marriage. Yet, as Charlsey has pointed out, the fact that something is being done for the first time does not make it a rite of passage; rather, 'it is the representing of transition which is' (Charlsey 1991: 35). While those making vows to each other 'from this day forward' will often have a long shared past, it is clear that the wedding does remain a meaningful, if now radically altered, rite for all those involved.

BIBLIOGRAPHY

Brides Complete Guide to Planning Your Wedding (London, Octopus Books, 1983).

Planning Your Wedding With Woman Bride & Home (London, IPC Magazines, 1971).

BEAUJOUAN, Éva and NÍ BHROLCHÁIN, Máire, 'Cohabitation and marriage in Britain since the 1970s' (2011) 145 *Population Trends* 35.

BEYFUS, Drusilla, *The English Marriage: What it is like to be married today* (London, Penguin, 1971).

BROWN, Audrey and KIERNAN, Kathleen, 'Cohabitation in Great Britain: evidence from the General Household Survey' (1981) 25 *Population Trends* 4.

BUCK, Nick and SCOTT, Jacqueline, 'Household and family change' in N Buck, J Gershuny, D Rose and J Scott (eds), *Changing Households: The BHPS 1990 to 1992* (ESRC Research Centre on Micro-social change, 1994).
CHARLSEY, Simon R, *Rites of marrying: The wedding industry in Scotland* (Manchester, Manchester University Press, 1991).
CHESTER, Robert, 'The Myth of the Disappearing Nuclear Family' in D Anderson and G Dawson, *Family Portraits* (London, Social Affairs Unit, 1986).
COMER, Lee, *Wedlocked Women* (Leeds, Feminist Books, 1974).
EEKELAAR, John and MACLEAN, Mavis, 'Marriage and the moral bases of personal relationship' (2004) 13 *Journal of Law and Society* 510.
FLETCHER, Ronald, *The Shaking of the Foundations* (London, Routledge, 1988).
GUY, Catherine, *Asking About Marriage* (Rugby, National Marriage Guidance Council, 1983).
HASKEY, John, 'Trends in marriages: church, chapel and civil ceremonies' (1980) 22 *Population Trends* 19.
———, 'Spouses with identical residential addresses before marriage: an indicator of pre-marital cohabitation' (1997) 89 *Population Trends* 13.
———, 'Marriage Rites—Trends in Marriages by Manner of Solemnisation and Denomination in England and Wales, 1841–2012' chapter two in this volume.
HASKEY, John and KIERNAN, Kathleen, 'Cohabitation in Great Britain: characteristics and estimated numbers of cohabiting partners' (1989) 58 *Population Trends* 23.
HIBBS, Mary, BARTON, Chris and BESWICK, Joanne, 'Why Marry?—Perceptions of the Affianced' [2001] *Family Law* 197.
KIERNAN, Kathleen and ELDRIDGE, Sandra 'Age at marriage: inter and intra cohort variation' (1987) 38 *British Journal of Sociology* 44.
KIERNAN, Kathleen and ESTAUGH, Valerie, *Cohabitation: Extra-marital childbearing and social policy* (London, Family Policy Studies Centre, 1993).
LANGHAMER, Claire, *The English in Love: The Intimate Story of an Emotional Revolution* (Oxford, Oxford University Press, 2013).
LEONARD, Diana, *Sex and Generation: A Study of Courtship and Weddings* (London, Tavistock Publications, 1980).
LEETE, Richard, *Changing patterns of family formation and dissolution in England and Wales 1964–76* (London, HMSO, 1979).
MANSFIELD, Penny and COLLARD, Jean, *The Beginning of the Rest of your Life? A portrait of newly-wed marriage* (Basingstoke, Macmillan, 1988).
McRAE, Susan, *Cohabiting Mothers: Changing marriage and motherhood?* (London, Policy Studies Institute, 1993).
MILES, Joanna, PLEASANCE, Pascoe and BALMER, Nigel, 'The experience of relationship breakdown and civil law problems by people in different forms of relationships' (2009) 21 *Child and Family Law Quarterly* 47.
MOSS, Susannah, *Brides Wedding Planner* (London, Octopus Books, 1985).
MURPHY, Michael, 'The evolution of cohabitation in Britain, 1960–95' (2000) 54 *Population Studies* 43.
OFFICE OF NATIONAL STATISTICS, *Social Focus on Families* (London, The Stationery Office, 1997).
OTNES, Cele C and PLECK, Elizabeth H, *Cinderella Dreams: The Allure of the Lavish Wedding* (Berkeley CA, University of California Press, 2003).

OWEN WILLIAMS, Betty, *Planning Your Wedding Day from A to Z* (London, W Foulsham & Co Ltd, 1964)

PROBERT, Rebecca, *The Changing Legal Regulation of Cohabitation: From Fornicators to Family, 1600–2010* (Cambridge, Cambridge University Press, 2012).

PURBRICK, Louise, *The Wedding Present: Domestic Life Beyond Consumption* (Aldershot, Ashgate, 2007).

ROSSER, Colin and HARRIS, Christopher, *The family and social change: A study of family and kinship in a South Wales town* (London, Routledge & Kegan Paul, 1983).

SAGE, Lorna, *Bad Blood* (London, Fourth Estate, 2001).

STANLEY, Scott M, RHOADES, Galena K and MARKMAN, Howard J, 'Sliding versus Deciding: Inertia and the Premarital Cohabitation Effect' (2006) 55 *Family Relations* 499.

WALLACE, Claire, *For Richer, For Poorer: Growing up in and out of work* (London, Tavistock Publications, 1987).

4

No Frills: Wedding Presents and the Meaning of Marriage, 1945–2003

LOUISE PURBRICK

I. INTRODUCTION

RIGHTS AND RITES are different. A right is a definite object fixed in order that it that cannot or should not be easily removed; a rite is a momentary practice, part of a process that is often characterised as a journey, a rite of passage. A right may be adjudicated in limited places, state sanctioned offices, while a rite, an act within a ritual practice, is often collectively organised and performed in spaces of everyday life, according to the calendars of family and community. The adjudication of rights and the performance of rites intersect at a wedding, in a Register Office or a church. Rights are substantially important since their award constitutes a documented change in the status of a person, from unmarried to married, and the rest may appear as decorative detail. However, as Sarah Farrimond points out in this volume (chapter ten), the material culture of weddings, the special clothing, flowers, rings and more, used in the performance of marriage rites are 'important or meaningful' to the participants in the wedding despite carrying no religious authority whatsoever (Farrimond 2015). Wedding presents, the subject of this chapter, are an integral part of the wedding ritual; indeed, they are a consistent component, or rite, in what has been defined as the dominant western tradition (Boden 2003; Ingraham 1999; Otnes and Pleck 2003) performed in a variety of ways in Britain over the last 50 or more years.

II. THE CASE OF THE WEDDING PRESENT

Giving gifts at weddings is not a matter of choice. Many gifts are carefully considered objects but people also give in ways they dislike and to those they may not know intimately or at all. Wedding presents are obligatory. This is, according to the gift's theorist Marcel Mauss, the character of all gifts: their exchange initiates circuits of reciprocity and therefore obligation (Mauss 1990). But wedding presents are a special case. The ritual of giving might appear as superfluous and redundant, since a wedding could take place and a marriage become legalised without gifts. But, this chapter argues, gifts are necessary to the marriage rite and thus to the status of the marriage itself; they are a material endorsement, a 'ritual adjunct' in Mary Douglas' words, in the recognition of marriage (Isherwood and Douglas 1979). The type of marriage gift has changed over time but gifts have remained a stable and essential marriage rite and wedding ritual. Gifts permit the incorporation of the married relationship into family and community life. A couple may be legally wed after a ceremony without gifts but it would be a materially and socially unrecognised union.

This chapter has a number of sections. The first is a discussion of the sources of the study, Mass Observation correspondents. The subsequent sections examine the significance of the gift within the wedding ritual, how gifts may define a marriage and provide the material means of its recognition. There is an attempt to plot the shifting patterns of wedding gifting, the adaptation of rituals with social and economic change from the post-War period to the early twenty-first century. Changed forms, emerging alternative ritual practices, wedding spectacles and commercial lists are examined alongside the continuity of giving and receiving 'deeply domestic' objects upon marriage.

III. MASS OBSERVATION: WRITING THE EVERYDAY

My investigation of wedding presents is based upon responses to a Mass Observation 'directive' entitled 'Giving and Receiving Presents', collected in Autumn 1998. Mass Observation writing is the subject of methodological and theoretical enquiries in anthropology, sociology, social and cultural history (Bhatti 2006; Highmore 2002; Hurdley 2006; Hurdley 2013; Pollen 2013; Sheridan, Street and Bloome 2000; Stanley 2001). It is one of the most thoroughly debated collections of documents of the twentieth and twenty-first centuries. Mass Observation writing, either that generated by its founders Tom Harrison, Charles Madge and Humphrey Jennings through their 1930s documentary collages announced as 'anthropology of ourselves', or that of the thousands of participants, 'correspondents' in the Mass Observation Project that have created a record of 'everyday life in Britain' initiated in the 1980s (Mass Observation 2014),[1] is multivalent: it can be read as life history, historical document, sociological data or

[1] Mass Observation, 'Welcome' page and 'Brief History': www.massobs.org.uk/index.htm and www.massobs.org.uk/a_brief_history.htm.

ethnographic description. Its strength or richness, to use the ill-fitting terms to describe evidence, derives from its immediacy; it is a relatively unmediated act of documentation, everyday life recorded by the people who live it. Dorothy Sheridan, Brian Street and David Bloome in their analysis of Mass Observation correspondents as literary subjects, *Writing Ourselves* (2000), have identified how the description 'ordinary' is used to evoke both a common experience of being part of an everyday world and a shared position outside institutions of cultural and political influence, particularly the professional media.

The Autumn 1998 'Giving and Receiving Presents' directive, a series of questions and prompts, invited Mass Observation correspondents to write about gifting. One section, which I co-wrote with Dorothy Sheridan, then Director of the Contemporary Mass Observation Project and the Archivist of the Mass Observation Archive, was solely devoted to wedding presents. Correspondents, who then numbered 354, were invited to 'be as detailed as possible' about the objects they received when they married, who gave them, when they were given, whether they were requested, where they have been kept, how they have been used and if they held any memories. There were 254 responses to the 'Giving and Receiving Presents' directive and the accounts of wedding presents within were very detailed, frequently running to two pages of handwritten or typed script, with many correspondents writing much more. Extensive detail was more often provided by female Mass Observation writers than male ones. Responses to the directive extended the gender bias within the 1998 cohort of correspondents, which comprised 252 women and 102 men. Women not only wrote more but more women replied: 194 women compared to 60 men. Clearly, female correspondents have more to say about wedding presents than their male counterparts. This is not surprising. These things become their responsibility. Wedding presents may be initially jointly received by brides and grooms but become the preserve of wives. Gift giving and receiving is a gendered practice; it is usually women that manage the gifting for the family (Komter 1996). Wedding presents are also part of material culture of domesticity that is gendered within its boundaries, subject to familial division of labour (at the time of writing British women spent twice as much time doing housework than British men (OECD 2014)).

The collected responses to the 'Giving and Receiving Presents' directive contain accounts of marriages that took place over a 60-year period, from the late 1930s to the late 1990s. My study, the one upon which I draw in this chapter, covers a slightly different period, 1945 to 2003. Because a large number of Mass Observation correspondents who replied to the directive were married in the immediate post-War austerity period, it seemed logical to begin there. In 2003, after some five years reading and re-reading the directive, I wrote a follow-up letter to 23 Mass Observation correspondents who were unmarried or recently married in 1998, at the time of responding to the original directive. These letters elicited 11 replies, which provided details of marriage and cohabitation up until 2003, indeed, one long-term cohabitee got married in that year.

The geographical scope of the study reflects the focus of Mass Observation. It is a British case study in which populous England dominates; fewer than 10 per cent of the recorded weddings took place in Wales and Scotland. Civil marriage ceremonies are common, especially immediately post-War and again from the 1980s onwards. In both instances, they are regarded as a no-fuss, practical way to get married and as an explicit alternative to tradition. Thus, as we would expect, most correspondents who wed in the middle years of the period of this study did so in a church of some kind.[2] But the religious aspect of wedding rituals features very little in the accounts of marriages across the period as a whole. Church represents an idea of tradition rather than the importance of Christian theology. Performing a wedding in a church or chapel of one of the various Christian denominations referred to within the directive responses was more indicative of belonging to a particular community than holding a set of beliefs. Religion does not define these weddings. The indicative phrases used by correspondents to discriminate between types of weddings are the 'small' or the 'big' do, the 'quiet' or the 'posh' affair. Thus regardless of whether it took place in a church or registry office, a wedding is categorised according to its sociability, by the number of people who were there and the ways in which they endorsed the match. Marriage is a social and material act, defined by the participants and their consumption practices.

IV. SOCIAL AND MATERIAL: THE WEDDING AND THE GIFT

A pattern of a large church wedding followed by a smaller Register Office one can be discerned, however, between the mid-1950s, when communities had emerged from the disruption of war and austerity, and the end of the 1980s. This scaling down from church to Register Office, big wedding to simple ceremony, recurs over the lifetimes of many twice-married Mass Observation correspondents. An Exeter primary school teacher's two weddings are typical of this pattern:

> Wedding number one—1969, religious, Church of England, big wedding for my family rather than me—though if we had communicated properly perhaps everyone would have been happy with something smaller. We had a wedding list but not at particular shop because I felt that was far too commercial (R1227).[3]

[2] Marriages recorded within the responses to the 'Giving and Receiving Presents' directive were performed in Anglican, Church of Scotland, Catholic, Methodist, Presbyterian and Baptist churches or chapels. Two ceremonies took place in Synagogues. After weddings in Anglican churches, civil ceremonies were the most common form.

[3] The bracketed number and letters refer to the Mass Observation Archiving system, which protects the anonymity of its correspondents.

Despite reservations about asking for consumer purchases as marriage gifts this teacher received numerous fashionable goods: 'all the "right" things for the sixties bride', as she rather wryly observes, including a black basalt Wedgewood coffee service and Jonelle towels and sheets. Her subsequent marriage ceremony, following divorce and cohabitation, was a less traditional affair but also typical of an emerging alternative ritual form:

> Second wedding, 1989, civil, 9 people including ourselves. This is much simpler. We had already been living together with our children for some time. I think both lots of parents gave us some money. About a month after we were married my friends gave us a lunch party (everyone brought something to eat). We received presents then (R1227).

The type of gifts she received in 1989 related to the type of wedding: fewer in number and more informal. The teacher describes her second marriage gifts with the affection for the everyday item: 'All lovely things which we are still using'. In contrast to a high ceremony associated with a classically designed coffee set, she was given a 'Habitat blue and white ceramic bowl'. Towels featured as marriage gifts again but these were appliquéd, a homespun aesthetic. She also received plants and bulbs. Gifts for the garden, presentations of living and organic objects for the borders of home become a marker of a second wedding or a post-cohabitation union and could be considered as characteristic of a ritual endorsement of a different kind of marriage. By the 1990s couples marrying after divorce, cohabitation or both regularly received garden plants (see A1646, L1504, W1918). The effect of cohabitation on wedding rituals is closely considered by Rebecca Probert in chapter three of this volume; she suggests cohabitation may have contributed the loss of 'social significance' evident in this case in the scaling down of ceremony to informal gatherings (Probert 2015).

The wedding trajectory of big religious ceremony followed by a smaller secular one, as indicated by this Mass Observer's two marriages that also follows the path of a family affair overtaken by a friendship ritual, chimes nicely with established interpretations of social changes in Britain in the second half of the twentieth century. But it is not the only discernible pattern of change, nor representative of the breadth of lived experience. First, there are many examples of simple, quiet and quick church weddings. For example, a Mass Observation correspondent, a counsellor from Grimsby, notes: 'I married in 1970. I was pregnant'. 'It was a small religious wedding', she explains. 'We were both C of E, regular worshippers'. Her wedding presents reflected, and were, the necessities of married life: 'practical gifts which were well appreciated and well used' (L2835). Secondly, Register Office weddings can become big affairs. A librarian married in 1976 relates:

> The wedding was registry office after 6 months of cohabiting. What a rebel I was in those days. It was to be a vv quiet do but my mother invited all her relatives. Prob c 25+ people, for a sit down meal at an elegant restaurant (G2640).

She and her groom received gifts from 'Friends, family + colleagues—before and at the wedding'. Both the role of the bride's mother, her desire to mark the significance of the wedding with substantial numbers of people of her generation and their material offerings may be understood as assertion (and insertion) of a residual traditional form in a changing ritual.

Two weddings from the next decade, the 1980s, best illustrate the continuity and change or the difference and similarity in social and material forms of wedding rituals. These Mass Observation accounts also demonstrate that while gifting is a constant, the materiality of the wedding ritual becomes subject to the styling of an expanding consumer culture. One Mass Observation correspondent, an East Sussex classroom teaching assistant, describes how she 'Married April 1982 at a register office because we wanted a quick, quiet, no frills non-religious wedding'. Even in this pared-down wedding practice, presents are still expected. Indeed, this part of the ritual was carefully planned. 'I had a made a list', states the teaching assistant, of which there were two copies, 'one held by my mother and one by me which we produced only on request as I did not want to look pushy'. She received over 30 gifts that were, she writes, 'deeply domestic & practical', a collection that included wooden spoons and dusters, kitchen knives and towels, a bucket and two pillow cases. Her gifts embodied the utilitarian nature of the wedding; they were essential items in more ways than one, no frills but not extras. Gifts appear more than adjuncts; they are of the ritual itself. The occasion of not offering an object is an exception and worthy of note. 'We had presents from all the guests at the wedding ceremony, husband's friends were invited to the reception & two did not give us presents' (H2577). Proper participation in the wedding is constituted by the gift. The importance of material culture to the ritual practice of the wedding persists in its reduced form and is simply more obvious in conspicuously fashionable weddings, such as that celebrated by another Mass Observer, who lived in Devizes, worked as a secretary and wed towards the end of the decade: She writes:

> We got married in 1988 and it wasn't a religious wedding although it took place in church. The wedding itself was rather big, with 150 guests, 7 bridesmaids and 5 page boys; all the boys were dressed up in top hats and tails and the bridesmaids had the same dresses but all in different colours—a rainbow wedding, I'm told! My own dress was fabulous, rose coloured with pink embroidery around the skirt and very along the lines of a 'Diana' wedding dress, bows and pearls, very princessy ... we received absolutely loads of gifts (P2819).

This wedding embraced frills. It is an example of the beginning of scaling up, rather than down, of the wedding of ceremony from the late 1980s that continued apace into the twenty-first century. A large affair, carefully costumed and choreographed, it drew upon a popular visual culture of consumption to reproduce details of televised royal or cinematic fairy-tale weddings. With such attention to the performance of marriage ceremony, it could be described as a wedding spectacle in which the church becomes a setting that evokes tradition rather than a religious space. The entwined acts of consumption and marriage are evident in dress and location as much, if not more, than the acquisition of gifted goods. Certainly, like the large lavish wedding, the gifts are greater in number and expense. Over the decade, consumption was increasing and was increasingly individualised. Two gifts most indicative of this trend, received by the Devizes secretary, were a Panasonic microwave, a new kitchen technology, and Marks and Spencer tokens, a means for the bride and groom to have their own choice of gift. Nevertheless, the majority were, albeit fashionably, within the limits of traditional wedding presents: they were household goods.

IV. THE DEFINING OBJECT

Within my study, whatever the type of wedding, civil or religious, large or small, and whenever it occurred, there was, almost without exception, a gift. Of the total of 254 Mass Observation accounts of weddings, just three recorded no gifts. These are quite different cases, and I discuss two in conclusion to this chapter. Here, it is important to note that over a period when the script of the ritual of marriage diversifies, changing from religious to secular, standard to individualised, and the social necessity of marriage declines as the acceptability of cohabitation increases, gift giving remains: it is the most consistent component of the wedding and a defining act of marriage. Indeed, those seeking to avoid marriage gifts are rarely able to do so. Upon the most discreet weddings, presents are offered and accepted. One Mass Observation correspondent, a female fire brigade control worker from Somerset who married in 1985 after cohabiting for 17 years, stated: 'we had a very small, quiet affair, in fact we only told one close friend, who acted as a witness', adding 'We obviously didn't expect any wedding presents and had owned our own home about 12 years'. They received two gifts of money (with which she bought a food processor and washing machine), towels and bed linen, rose plants and goblet wine glasses (W1918). 'We got married very quietly' explains another correspondent, a Glasgow housewife. 'Just 2 witnesses who were warned not to buy us anything. (They did—2 crystal glasses)' (M1171). Thus the practice of gifting is upheld despite expectations or instructions to the contrary. The obligation to give is powerful and overrides the specific circumstances of different weddings. A number of explanations can be offered for this. First, participants in the wedding perform known and therefore traditional, understood and thus established, rituals, including giving gifts, because these practices comprise the wedding; they are the ways through which people are wed, and recognised as being wed. As gifts arrive, at various points in the wedding ritual according to specific circumstance, they acknowledge that the marriage will happen, is happening or has taken place. Secondly, all, or a sufficient number of discrete wedding practices, the rites that constitute the ritual so to speak, such as speaking the vows, signing the register, wearing appropriate clothing or accepting gifts—have to be performed in order for the marriage to be complete. This is the point where rites and rights rub together: a rite, such as wearing a white dress, putting on a gold ring, receiving more china than two people could ever use at any meal, may appear as more important both at the time of the wedding and over the duration of the marriage than the rights accorded to married people, financial and physical care, tax status or property ownership. Thirdly, gifts are necessary to express the meanings of marriage: how financial and physical care will be arranged on an everyday basis: typically, in a family and through a gendered division of labour.

From a twenty-first-century perspective, all forms of present giving have increased in quantity and complexity. We, or rather those of us who live in the wealthy west, are saturated by commodities: inundated with goods purchased for us on an fast spinning cycle of commercialised events, a popular ritual calendar of birthdays, Christmas, Mothers' Day, Valentine's Day, Fathers' Day, wedding anniversaries. The life-cycle events, birth and marriage, are of greater significance than the regular repeatable calendar and accrue even more gifts. However, the upward trajectory of gifting or the avalanche of objects it generates (depending on how you visualise it) does not, in the case of wedding presents, follow a linear pattern; it is not quite so straightforward. At elite weddings in the early twentieth century, goods in greater quantity and of higher value were received and recorded in county newspapers than were offered to people of the working or lower middle class who wed later in the same century. Consumption is differently practised according to class: the forms of familial exchange are part of the distinctive cultures of class. My study, based on Mass Observation writers who define themselves as 'ordinary', is one of popular practice of giving and receiving presents. Within this popular practice, the types of marriage gifts have altered and it is safe to estimate that overall their number has increased between 1945 and today. Things are shaped by the encroachment of consumer culture into all aspects of life, including its rituals: we adapt what is available to us. This is easy to argue. Passing on pewter or silver upon marriage has long been overtaken by buying china. A linen tablecloth might still be given to express hopes for longevity of family life but polyester cotton sheets in a contemporary pattern could be a stylish but more short-lived substitute. Weddings and marriage are always a matter of consumption when consumption is defined more generally and anthropologically as a form of exchange and therefore a form of cultural production. Thus changes in the rituals or patterns of giving occur at the intersection of the practice of marriage and the practice of consumption and are best understood in relation to both.

V. THE GENERAL VIEW OF CHANGES OVER TIME: WEDDING, MARRIAGE, HOME

In the immediate post-War period, the disruption to family life caused by army demobilisation and aerial bombardment led to hastily arranged marriages and weddings without elaborate ceremony. The period of austerity, characterised by shortages of all kinds, especially lack of consumer goods in highstreet shops, lasted into the early 1950s: there was little to give at any wedding. A carpenter from Peacehaven, who married in 1945, noted that he and his wife received 'three glass water jugs, a five pound note, cannot remember anything else' (T2741). Of 'the magnificent sum of £50' that a female correspondent received from her parents on her marriage of the same year, £10 were spent on a 'tin chest full of second-hand household goods, many of them pre-War, which had been advertised in the local paper' (P2546). The 'parents and in laws' of a pregnant bride of 1947 'gave furniture, etc, to start us off'. Now a social worker from Hertfordshire, she also remembers 'I had some money as a gift from work colleagues' (B1533). A school secretary from Hemel Hempstead, who wed in 1949, received 'plain tableware'. Her 'most expensive' gift was an 'Ekco Model A104 radio' (R2136). She explains:

> We didn't want—and couldn't afford—a big 'do'. Our parents and a friend of mine attended. Travel was difficult and friends and family were scattered in different parts of the country ... My husband, recently demobilised, had just started work after failing to obtain a grant to continue his higher education full-time. Although I had a well-paid job, living away from home left very little spare cash. We didn't have a 'proper' home until January 1957 when we moved into this New Town (R2136).

Significantly, rather than simply income, it is property ownership, the type of home (in this case living in rented accommodation) that determines the forms of giving. Another correspondent, a housewife from Staines, who married a year later in 1950, received similar gifts, including a 'radio & china'. She had 'a civil wedding, but in a very pleasant room'. She explains: 'I was 19' and 'We were hard up & non-religious so it suited us'. She points out that she and her husband 'couldn't have many presents as we were starting life in furnished rooms' and concludes by saying that it 'was not until we were buying our own home, about 2 years later that we bought furniture, on Hire Purchase mainly' (B2605).

These accounts of the post-War weddings convey the contingency of times in which the act of marriage is compromised; it did not assume its ideal form; it was not a 'big do'. Of necessity, the wedding took a reduced form but nevertheless gifts were offered and accepted. From the later 1950s through to the 1980s, what may be understood as the popular, traditional or dominant ritual practice of giving wedding presents emerges and is sustained as acquisition of consumer goods escalates. At the same time, the availability of contraception, accessibility of divorce and acceptance of cohabitation undermine the status and significance of marriage.

The following account tells of the popular ritual of marriage. A Mass Observation correspondent who was working at the 'old Bingley Building Society, Head Office (now it is the large Bradford & Bingley B. Soc)' when she married in 1958 received '72' wedding presents. Her 'parents and my husband's parents bought us, or gave us big presents', she states. These included a gas oven, a top-filling washer with mangle attached, a bedroom suite and 'green Spode Tea service'. The parents also gave 'cleaning materials & other bits and pieces'. Her uncle's family 'bought us a Combination Dinner/Tea Service, fruit set etc—from the most expensive china shop in Bradford … It was Royal Doulton, "Frost Pine"'. From the Staff Association of the Bingley Building Society she received a bedroom lamp with a pink shade. 'I was told to go out and choose a present to a certain value and then hand it over to them' and 'the afternoon before my wedding, they presented me with this'. Those she worked alongside, 'the girls in my department', also gave her pink blankets and pink sheets. The Mass Observation correspondent then lists gifts from 'relatives, friends, friends of both sets of parents, and neighbours': weighing scales, pairs of towels, egg cups, a rolling pin, wooden spoon set, pans, casserole dishes, wood and ceramic salad servers, a metal swan brand teapot, a teapot and tea cosy to match the green Spode tea set. She adds 'We even received gifts from people we hardly knew' (W571).

The twentieth-century ritual practice of wedding presents is characterised by a particular type of object given by a particular gift community. That community is kindred based but extends to kin friendship networks. Family members must give; indeed, they assume their particular place in the family and gift community by the scale of their giving. The former building society employee is clear on this point: her and her husband's parents presented the largest items of necessity in a home, including the cooker, the washing machine, the bedroom furniture. It is a pattern of parental giving frequently reported by Mass Observers who married in this mid-twentieth-century period. There are, then, hierarchies of giving within the family: the closer the relationship the larger the size of gift; the more distant the smaller. Compare weighing scales, which the Bingley Building Society bride received from her cousin's family, to any of her parent's gifts. Friends are usually less significant givers than family, at least in this period. Importantly, the limit of the gift community is not defined by the marrying couple's own friendship circle but that of their parents. This is why the former building society employee and her groom did not know all givers very well. The presence of the parent's generation at the wedding and its influence over types of gifts is repeated in other Mass Observation writing. The older generation gives the largest and the most to the younger generation. Thus marriage gifting is an intergenerational transfer of wealth and knowledge. It may be best understood as an act of reproduction. Indeed, the role of the bride or groom's mother in managing gifts through a list of appropriate things was so common it was often assumed. 'I suppose I must have made a list', wrote a Grimsby counsellor, 'it may have been organised by my mother-in-law who was good at such things' (L2835).

The particular type of gift offered by wedding guests, the gift community, is often the same, or to be more historically specific, there is very little variation in type at this point in time. All gifts are of a type, domestic objects; the ritual adjunct that materialises the meaning of marriage. An HGV driver also married in 1958 confirms that 'In the tradition of the time all the presents were household goods' (R470). 'We could not have set up home without them' wrote an information assistant who married six years later in 1964 (B1180). Setting up home, a recurring phrase in Mass Observation writing about weddings, is the purpose of gifts because it is that of marriage and the home is created, or recreated through intergenerational giving in particular ways. Mass Observers may refer to 'useful' or 'practical' things as if their meaning is obvious or absent. Nevertheless, the gift exchange is a transfer of wealth and materialisation of knowledge: the newly wedded building society employee was supplied with objects that instructed her on matters of making and managing a home; it is a place where clothes should be cleaned, tea should be served and bedrooms are pink, the feminine colour of romance.

Wedding presents embody the idea of marriage. These gifts, particularly those from one generation to another, project past married life into the future. This is not only a matter of attempting to secure the continuity of a particular family by contributing to its economic survival, although this is precisely the aim of gifts of money for renting properties or deposits to buy them. Gifts upon marriage also reproduce family life itself. They sustain the social organisation of the household; they maintain the gendered spaces that provide respite from the world outside and uphold divisions between work and home, public and private: soft fabrics to invite rest (and the feminine labour devoted to cleanliness); the sparkling ceramic series, all those sets of shining matching cups and plates, afford the familial respectability of sociable eating (and the gendered practice of food preparation).

At weddings three decades later, these same practices of giving persist despite the decline in the social importance of marriage and its secularisation. In the 1980s, traditional and alternative forms of wedding ritual collide. A Durham housewife wed in 1982. Her groom's parents and his aunts and uncles, that is, relatives of his parent's generation, presented them with cutlery, a full dinner and tea service, a 'continental quilt', covers, sheets, pillowcases, saucepans, frying pan and a Hoover. Their friends gave a jug and glasses, wine glasses and a kitchen clock. The ritual of offering and accepting the most substantial gifts from an older generation continued, but in this instance was practised by only one family. The bride's brother, 'the only member of my family who was speaking to me', gave a coffee machine. The Durham correspondent wrote: 'I was alone, with next to no family left; I was fighting through the courts to get my daughter back'. Her wedding illustrates both the relevance and irrelevance of marriage in the late twentieth century, its unstable status: it was not the bride's first relationship of significance for she had a child but it was a declaration of the propriety and permanence of her current familial affiliation. It was through the giving of gifts, she reflects, that 'everyone we knew were trying to show us that we were not alone and that they supported us'. The gifting by all of the groom's family compensated for the absence of the bride's. His relatives deployed the gift ritual to recognise the significance of their relationship and legitimacy of their marriage. The importance of their giving not only relates to marriage as a second union but also to the matter of home ownership. They were buying a new house and therefore needed all the appropriate domestic things for those 'starting out' (M1201).

Five years later, in 1989, a forensic consultant married 'in a register office'. She explains: 'It was a small "do"—I didn't believe in marriage and didn't want to make a big song and dance about it, and my husband had been married before and couldn't have a church wedding' (J2830). Despite her declaration that 'there weren't many people obliged to give us presents' those that did so offered objects according ritual of marriage: hierarchical intergenerational exchanges of domestic material culture. 'Our gifts came from family and a few friends, plus some old friends of our parents'. Parents of the forensic consultant gave money for a pine bed and pink carpet. Her grandmother funded a chest of drawers and china tableware. From friends they also received sheets, tablemats, a thermometer, chopping board, bathroom weighing scales, teapot, letter rack, salad bowls, a 'fairly-traded ethnic needlework from Central America' and clocks, one from Amnesty International, which was on the mantelpiece nine years later when she replied to the Mass Observation directive. This is an unconventional wedding between a male divorcee and wedding-refuser with anti-consumerist leanings. Yet, the gifts defined a conventional household devoted to the sexual and social labour of reproduction: objects were for the bedroom (which retained the romantic pink colour) or the kitchen, indeed, most were tools of essential cooking and fashionable eating; they proposed skills and knowledge of food consumption.

It is difficult to isolate a turning point in marriage gifting, since the practice of wedding rituals is amended through the lived experience of historical change: everyday life does not immediately follow the legal rulings, such as making divorce more accessible, or economic policies, including the promotion of home-ownership, that may affect it. Also, traditions persist into the 1980s (and beyond). Nevertheless, it is possible to identify two emergent ritual practices in this decade: the alternative anti-consumerist wedding and the wedding spectacle. The latter, because of its size, appears to be traditional.

VI. THE COMMERCIAL LIST AND DIFFERENT ORDER OF MARRIAGE

Costume and choreography, the dress of bride, bridesmaids, groom and best man, the flowers, rings and music, the movements of the wedding couple are, Sarah Farrimond argues, important performances in the Anglican wedding ritual that have been transferred to secular contexts to create a '"proper wedding"' (Farrimond 2015: **) (Figure 1). The wedding spectacle's purchase upon tradition is realised by enacting this performance in Anglican churches or licensed locations that evoke rural parishes. The performance of tradition is usually underwritten by the attendance of large numbers of guests and by gift offerings. However, gifting at these large weddings is substantially different. At the end of the twentieth century and the beginning of the twenty-first, the practice of giving upon marriage has significantly changed. It is the act of gift exchange that has altered; the way in which the transfer is enacted destabilises the meanings of the wedding present and the recreates the wedding present ritual. The rise of the commercial gift list is the cause.

The commercial gift list developed apace in the 1990s. Once an exclusive shop or elite department store service, it expanded onto the high street stores and populated internet shopping companies. It operates in the following way: a couple planning a wedding select goods from a store, which constitutes their list; they are usually advised by a personal shopping assistant who works for the shop that manages the list and supplies the goods; the wedding guests are informed where the list is held and they deal directly with the shop, selecting from the list and paying for the goods. The quantity and expense of objects listed in this way is characteristically high. But there are important continuities in the types of objects: domestic things still dominate. The composition of the gift community also remains the same, since the list is sent to family and friends who are expected to give; however, the hierarchies of familial giving lose their place in the widely distributed commercial list.

It must be noted that commercial gift lists are not entirely new in the late twentieth century. Some Mass Observation correspondents who wed in the late 1950s to mid-1960s stated that lists were used and, moreover, that they were expected to carry out gift transactions in this way. 'Because it was the normal fashion in our social circle', states a chartered surveyor who married in 1956, 'we did have a wedding list and we did earmark a department store in Manchester where it could be found' (B1509). An audio typist whose marriage took place in the same year explains that she also followed the practices of her social group and had a list. 'Like most of my contemporaries, I made out a list and people ticked off what they had decided to buy me and my husband (B89)'. A list was an unquestioned marriage convention for another correspondent whose wedding took place in 1965. 'We had a wedding present list at Peter Jones and a china shop in Regent Street' states a 'carer' living in Hampshire (C2078). These Mass Observation accounts represent the very few among the 254 that tell of a mid-twentieth-century use of the commercial list. For most Mass Observers, as might be expected given their identification as 'ordinary' and the history of gift lists as elite, the use of the commercial list appears new at the time of the 'Giving and Receiving' directive, at the moment of writing their response in 1998. Commercial gift lists were also generally, almost universally, unpopular.

Many Mass Observation correspondents state they did not have a list. Of her first marriage in 1958, a teacher form Norwich wrote: 'We did not have a formal list—never would have thought of such a thing' (B2258). Many also wrote about being asked to select from a list and used the directive to declare their opposition. One correspondent, who was unemployed and single at the time of writing, announced:

> I intensely dislike wedding lists, even though I can see the point of them, especially these days when the couple have most likely furnished a home so don't want to duplicate items in their possession. I feel a bit insulted & intimidated by being told what to buy. Every list I've seen has contained maybe one item I could actually afford so I find it all very embarrassing (A2801).

Another, an engineer from Gloucester, made his case:

> One comment—the cold, calculating 'Wedding List' that nowadays arrives with an invitation from a distant relative I've not seen in years (and who is unlikely to acknowledge a gift anyway) makes me cross—particularly when it takes the form of 'Our wedding list is at Marks and Spencers: you can see it at your local branch'. I regard it as a form of blackmail. Not only that, but it means the would-be recipient is too distant for us to have some idea of what they might like or for us to discuss it with them or their parents. Despite which, we do give wedding presents (L2669).

And, a clerical worker insisted that lists were not necessary for her:

> Let me say straight away that I do not like being told that a certain shop contains such and such china etc & that's the only sort they want buying. Hinting that is what you'd like would not offend me at all, but the choice at the end of the day would be mine. I don't like being made to feel that any other purchase would be unwelcome. Nevertheless I think having a present list is sensible & handy & very practical if someone is at a loss what to buy. But it shouldn't be shoved at people (H1703).

The terms of opposition to lists, according to these accounts, are: the imposition of expense, the exploitative barter, the overly demanding request, the assertion of possession. In their, the correspondents' words, lists are: intimidating, cold, an act of blackmail, an offence. The list affects people: its makes them frightened, cross, offended. To claim that all this arises from the intrusion of the market into a family affair is true, but it misses a step. The physical reaction and written opposition to the list is an embodied and intellectual response to ritual undermined; an unwritten order unsettled. The decision about the exact type of object, the particular form of the ritual adjunct, has been taken from the giver and allocated to the receiver. The giver has lost the means to express their particular understanding of the meaning of marriage through their gift. An object prescribed by the receiver cannot contain the giver's understanding of the necessary things of life. This has a particular affect upon intergenerational gifting as a projection of a past family life into the future. A family affair has re-materialised as an individual demand, as the transfer of wealth has been disentangled from the transfer of knowledge. Guidance from the parents and parents' generation about how a home may be managed with appropriate objects is rejected by their children and children's generation as the former are told by the latter what to buy.

The form of the list rather than the practice of making a list is the source of opposition. Form, the material specificity of the ritual adjunct is, of course, a register of differences in a ritual practice. The traditional, old, acceptable, proper list was handwritten, held by the mother of bride or groom and never reproduced, but its listed objects were closely negotiated within the parents' generation; they deliberated about what to get and thus debated how to spread their wealth and knowledge through their gifts. The commercial list is printed and distributed; it disallows participation and projection

Figure 1: The spectacle of the proper wedding (2010s)

BRIDES

WEDDING LIST

FOR THE TABLE	Make	Design	Colour		Make	Design	Colour
Dinner service				**Cutlery**			
Dinner plates				Place settings			
Dessert plates				Coffee spoons			
Side plates				Teaspoons			
Tea plates				Serving spoons			
Cereal/dessert bowls				Steak knives			
Serving dishes				Butter knives			
Sauce boats				Fish knives and forks			
Soup bowls				Fish slice			
Soup tureen				Cake slice			
Other				Carving set			
Tea/coffee service				Ladles			
Teapot				Salad servers			
Milk jug				**Miscellaneous**			
Sugar bowl				Butter dish			
Teacups and saucers				Candlesticks			
Plates				Cheeseboard and knife			
Coffee pot				Egg cups			
Cream jug				Jam pot and spoon			
Coffee cups and saucers				Mugs			
Glassware				Napkin rings			
Goblets				Nutcrackers			
White wine glasses				Pepper and salt mills			
Claret glasses				Place mats/coasters			
Champagne flutes				Toast rack			
Tumblers				Trivet			
Brandy balloons				Other			
Sherry glasses				**Drinks accessories**			
Liqueur glasses				Bottle opener			
Water jug set				Ice bucket			
Decanters				Wine coasters			
Fruit bowl				Wine cooler			
Vases				Wine rack			
Other				Other			

LINEN	Make	Design	Colour		Make	Design	Colour
Bathmat				Napkins			
Bathrobe				Oven set			
Bath sheets				Pillowcases			
Bedspreads				Pillows			
Blankets				Sheets			
Duvet				Tablecloths			
Duvet cover				Table-mats			
Electric blanket				Tea-towels			
Facecloths				Throw/quilt			
Hand-towels				Valance			
Mattress cover				Other			

Figure 2: 'Wedding List' 1997 *Brides and Setting up Home* courtesy of Brides © Condé Nast

of proper household management. All is decided in advance of the gift and not by the giver but the receiver. It could be understood as an assertion of the rights of the individual (Figure 2). And, discourses of consumption are most assertive in this respect: advertising has long screamed out 'You can have it!' The formula has been applied to the marriage ritual.

It is not all the fault of consumption. Gift lists are an intersection of the commercial and social; economic decisions and moral values play a part in their use. Both the imperative to buy a house rather than rent rooms in order to establish the life of a married household and the incremental establishment of a household before marriage have set the conditions for the gift list. Lists facilitate filling up the empty space of an unfurnished new home and the recreation of a pristine household collection to replace that casually arranged through cohabitation. The distribution of lists can be attributed to changes in the propriety of marriage and of home ownership as well as the escalation in consumption. Since marriage is less of a social necessity, it is has become a matter of individual choice exerted in the bride and groom's own space. The gift now confirms the individualism of marriage: they no longer embody the past practices of family life but assert the style of the person who receives them. The desirability of style, not just being stylish but adopting a particular style, is a pervasive discourse of consumption that is manifested most often in youth fashion but is now evident in the wedding industry that cultivates wedding spectacles.

VII. A NEW MEANING: WITHOUT PARENT APPROVAL?

One Mass Observation account illustrates the individualisation of the wedding as well as how a bride and groom's friendship networks can become as important in gifting rituals as their parent's generation, if not more so, and how, ultimately, the meaning of marriage has changed. A London-based film producer's 1980s marriage occurred at that moment when old and new wedding practices, traditional and modern, established and innovative, jostled awkwardly together. She described her 1988 wedding as 'a very private affair'. It took place in the Caribbean to avoid the social pressures of a large wedding, thereby exerting individual rather than familial control over the ritual practice, or at least over one part of its script. Nevertheless (but, of course, not unexpectedly) presents were given and received: a bottle of champagne, a food processor, a zester, a bowl, a pestle and mortar. The film producer is far from affectionate about these things. Only the coffee cups remind her of the wedding and they are never used. She had cohabited before her marriage but her detachment from her marriage gifts also relates to her rejection of intergenerational giving:

> Because we had already shared a flat together, we had many items that traditionally people give for presents; I do remember getting irritated with my Mother, whose friends, very kindly, wanted to give us presents, and at the time I rather scoffed at this; I felt they didn't know me and in fact they were giving to her in a way, or at least 'for' her, and that it was nothing to do with me … At some point

> I must have collected all these presents, because my oldest friend was around, and I do remember putting all the presents together, in a piss-taking kind of way, like the end of The Generation Game, when all the stuff that the contestants have won off the Conveyor Belt is put together, and we took a photograph of it all! (D2239, 1998)

Of the gifts she does recall, at least two are from her parent's generation: the food processor from her father's foreman and the zester from her mother's friend. Five years later in her reply to my 2003 follow up letter, the film producer confessed, 'I actually feel rather ashamed of my attitude towards the wedding presents I received in 1988, well some of them, at any rate' (D2239, 2003). She reflects:

> My mother's friends wanted to buy me gifts. At the time I was irritated by this. I realise now, of course, they were doing it for her, and actually it was really kind of them ... The only truly duff present was from mum's friend Ann who embroidered a 'D' on some linen napkins. The 'D' was badly embroidered; but even though we never used them, it was kind of her to put the effort in!

It was ridiculing the gifts and thus refusing to recognise these relationships between her, her mother and her mother's friends that she now regrets. Arranging her wedding in the style of the Generation Game was 'a horrible piss-taking kind of way' and 'It's that that I am ashamed of!' She also adds her 2003 reply that the decision to marry abroad to have a civil ceremony was because 'he had been married before and neither of us were religious'.

The new form of the wedding ritual is attributable to a series of changes. Her discomfort and initial rejection of gifts from her mother's friends, an older generation, indicates that she does not seek their material guidance nor require them to confer legitimacy upon her marriage. She explains her actions as a thoughtless manifestation of a desire to escape the demands of her own family, but they are also indicative of how marriage was no longer a rite of passage to adulthood whereby a younger generation accepts wealth and knowledge from an older one and is permitted to share their familial authority by adopting their practices of home-making. The increased number of unmarried households and living arrangements that differed from traditional parental homes (the multiple occupancies of students or a young mobile workforce, cohabitation that precedes marriage or follows divorces as well as same sex partnerships) changed the significance and meaning of marriage. No longer a prerequisite or social necessity in the establishment of a household, it has become associated with a very particular type of home: permanent and purchased. At the same time, consumption has continued to escalate but become more individualised. The collective practices of home-making realised through useful domestic objects has been re-directed towards creating a home as a site of pleasure and personal display (Figures 3 and 4).

VIII. A CONCLUSION: THE (EXPLANATORY) EXCEPTIONS TO THE RULE

I would like to offer a conclusion that emphasises the defining role of gifts in the wedding ritual and considers the importance of ritual in the making of a marriage by examining two exceptions. 'I got no presents' states a Suffolk housewife, 'because both marriages were not approved by any sets of parents' (W1835). Nothing could make the status of her marriages clearer. Not to give is to not to engage in the wedding ritual and a rejection of the marriage, regardless of its legal status. This exception indicates the necessity of the gift, the integral importance of this material practice in the wedding ritual and in the recognition of the marriage.

A London local government officer also received no wedding presents. She described herself as 'single but with male partner and children' at the time of the 'Giving and Receiving Presents' directive in 1998, but she married him in 2003 (B2728). Back in 1998, she distanced herself from marrying types. 'Because of my age and the attitudes of my peer group, I have been to remarkably few weddings', she claimed. Her own wedding in the early twenty-first century shunned all ceremony and was almost conducted without involving any family members at all:

> We did it for purely practical reasons to do with pensions, security and children and did our utmost to avoid the trappings of the traditional wedding ceremony. Our approach involved using the very unromantic local registry office, telling no one apart from our three children and the two witnesses and the banning (no pun intended!) of all additional extras such as photos, hen parties, presents, etc. We disagreed about telling the children. My partner didn't think it was necessary but I felt that because it required a change to their birth certificates it did concern them and it would be better to tell them in a matter of fact way than let them find out later on and think we had concealed our marriage from them (B2728, 2003).

It seems that she and her partner wanted to be married without getting married, or rather to continue cohabiting with the legal reassurances of a marriage. Since she and partner sought neither material nor symbolic equivalence to marriage, wanting merely to preserve their cohabitation, no gifts were a requirement of their wedding. Thus, to get married is to receive gifts. It is a distinguishing difference between marriage and cohabitation.

Between 1945 and 2003, wedding rituals have taken different forms: from no frills to wedding spectacles or from the enforced intergenerational sociability to a pared-down ceremony accompanied by an informal celebration with only a close peer group. As wedding rituals alter so does giving and receiving gifts; it is an essential material form through which the ritual is performed. The 1980s has proved to be the most complex and revealing decade to study because the acceptability of divorce and cohabitation, the increase in property ownership and, towards the end of the decade and beginning of the next, the escalation of consumption, have greatly affected the patterns of marriage, forms of weddings and acts of gift exchange. The gift 'rite', here tagged onto the end of a sentence as its 'adjunct', may be as revealing of a marriage as its 'rights'. For example, the selection processes of the commercial list that replace maternal and parental knowledge of household management in the traditional handwritten list may seem a small matter, which is nevertheless indicative of a significant shift in the meaning of marriage at the end of the twentieth and beginning of the twenty-first century: less a family matter and more an individual affair.

BIBLIOGRAPHY

BHATTI, Mark, '"When I'm in the Garden I can Create my Own Paradise": Homes and Gardens in Later Life' (2006) 54 *The Sociological Review* 318.

BODEN, Sharon, *Consumerism, Romance and the Wedding Experience* (Basingstoke, Palgrave, 2003).

DOUGLAS, Mary, and ISHERWOOD, Baron, *The World of Goods: Towards an Anthropology of Consumption* (London, Allen Lane, 1979).

FARRIMOND, Sarah, 'Church of England Weddings and Ritual Symbolism' chapter ten in this volume.

HURDLEY, Rachel, 'Dismantling Mantelpieces: Narrating Identities and Materialising Culture in the Home' (2006) 40 *Sociology* 717.

HURDLEY, Rachel, *Home, Materiality, Memory and Belonging: Keeping Culture* (Basingstoke, Palgrave Macmillan, 2013).

HIGHMORE, Ben, *Everyday Life and Cultural Theory: An Introduction* (London, Routledge, 2002).

INGRAHAM, Chrys, *White Weddings: Romancing Heterosexuality in Popular Culture* (London, Routledge, 1999).

KOMTER, Aafke, 'Women, Gifts and Power' in A Komter (ed), *The Gift: An Interdisciplinary Perspective* (Amsterdam, Amsterdam University Press, 2006.

MAUSS, Marcel, *The Gift: The Form and Reason for Exchange in Archaic Societies* (London, Routledge, 1990 [first published 1925]).

ORGANISATION FOR ECONOMIC CO-OPERATION AND DEVELOPMENT, 'Balancing paid work, unpaid work and leisure' (2014): www.oecd.org/gender/data/balancingpaidworkunpaidworkandleisure.htm.

OTES, Cele and PLECK, Elizabeth, *Cinderella Dreams: the Allure of the Lavish Wedding* (Berkeley CA, University of California Press, 2003).

POLLEN, Annebella, 'Research Methodology in Mass Observation Past and Present: "Scientifically, about as valuable as a chimpanzee's tea party at the zoo"?' (2013) 75 *History Workshop Journal* 213.

PROBERT, Rebecca, 'From this day forward? Pre-marital cohabitation and the rite of marriage from the 1960s to the present day' chapter three in this volume.

SHERIDAN, Dorothy, STREET, Brian and BLOOME, David, *Writing Ourselves: Mass Observation and Literacy Practices* (Cresskill, NJ, Hampton Press, 2000).

STANLEY, Liz, 'Mass Observation's Fieldwork Methods' in P Atkinson, S Delamont, A Coffey, J Lofland and L Lofland (eds), *Handbook of Ethnography* (London, Sage, 2001).

Figure 3: 'Your Gifts, Your Way' 2013 © Prezola Ltd Reproduced with kind permission

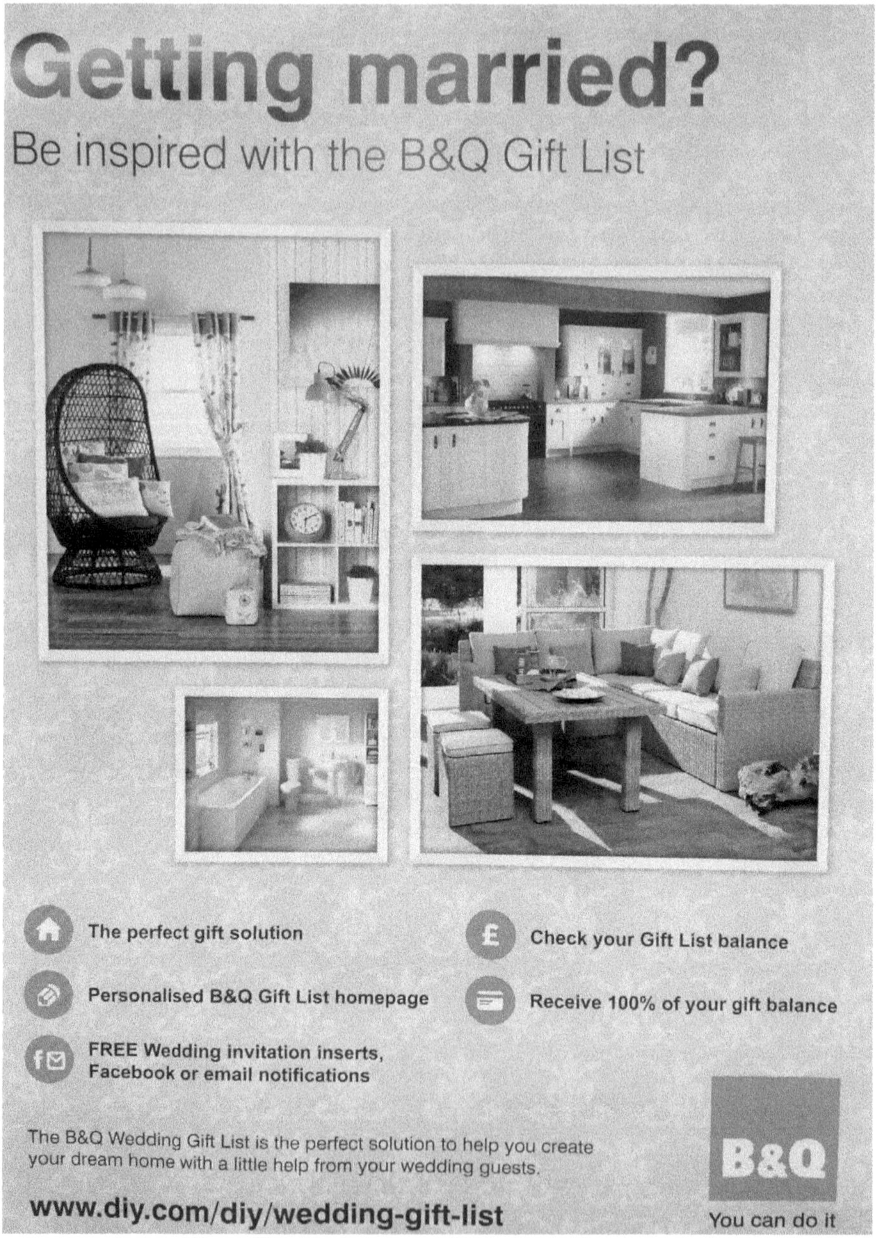

Figure 4: 'Getting married?' (2013) © B&Q Reproduced with kind permission

5

Civil Partnership Ceremonies: (Hetero)normativity, Ritual and Gender

ELIZABETH PEEL[1]

'What is clear is that we cannot simply argue that same-sex marriage always challenges or never challenges heteronormativity'. (Kimport 2012: 895)

I. INTRODUCTION

GAY WEDDING IMAGERY is replete with women in near-identical white dresses and men in matching suits; 'his and his' and 'hers and hers' cake toppers, and buttonholes and bouquets. The homogeneity of the visual representation of same sex marriage with different sex marriage is striking, but this tells us little about how same sex couples articulate the enactment of their civil partnerships (at a time before same sex marriage was available). Katrina Kimport found from her analysis of wedding photographs from same sex weddings compiled by the *San Francisco Chronicle* in 2004 that men always presented themselves in accordance with gender normative expectations (ie, no dress wearing). Women, she found, were more varied in their gender presentation and she notes that 'more than two-thirds confirmed to the wedding standard of a bride and groom, albeit with a woman groom' (Kimport 2012: 876). She suggests on the basis of this that there is 'the persistence of normative conventions in lesbian and gay couples' wedding practice' (ibid). But, of course, the visual representation of weddings is but one aspect of marriage rites, and accounts of same sex couples' decision-making processes are a valuable adjunct which can be both paradoxical (Rolfe and Peel 2011) and offer different insight into, as Kimport (2012: 894) puts it, the 'odd puzzle' of same sex wedding photographs.

[1] Acknowledgements: With grateful thanks to the participants and to Adam Jowett and Nicki Hayfield for their research assistance. This study was support by a British Academy small grant (SG-43697) awarded to Victoria Clarke and Elizabeth Peel.

On the one hand, it has been argued that wedding rituals are overwhelmingly heteronormative and that they perpetuate the cultural production of heterosexuality as inevitable, normal and natural (Ingraham 1999; Kimport 2012). On the other, it has been suggested that there has been a rise in more innovative rites of passage that have 'become more individualized, reflected in rites that are tailor-made, at least in part, by the individual or individuals concerned' (Cook and Walter 2005: 367). In this chapter my focus is on the accounts that (predominantly) lesbian and gay couples provide about how, and in what ways, they construct their civil partnership ceremonies. My overarching argument is that we are moving to a position in the United Kingdom whereby notions of heteronormativity—that is denoting a perspective that promotes heterosexuality as the preferred sexuality—are being fractured by the ways in which non-heterosexual individuals are 'cherry picking', and potentially therefore subverting, traditional elements of wedding ceremonies. The aim is to demonstrate, through a discursive analysis of same sex couples' descriptions of ceremonies, that much can be learned generally about the public and private display of marriage rites.

The Civil Partnership Act (2004) came into force at the end of 2005 and, for the first time in the UK, provided a legally recognised status for same sex relationships. It marked a historical shift in the legal and societal landscape for same sex couples from being able to undertake the ceremonial aspect of marking commitment without legal consequences attached (Lewin 1998) to ostensibly having civil marriage, at least in terms of the legal consequences attached to civil partnership if not the label (Jowett and Peel 2010). The terrain has shifted in the intervening period with the advent of the Marriage (Same Sex Couples) Act 2013 whereby same sex couples, as of 29 March 2014, can enter into full civil marriage. The Act grants all religious organisations, save the Church of England, the opportunity to 'opt in' to solemnise same sex marriages through their own ceremonies. In the first three months of the law changing just over 1,400 same sex marriages took place, and from 10 December 2014 couples in civil partnerships are able to convert to marriage (McCormick 2014). Nevertheless, equal marriage is now only available for same sex couples in sixteen countries worldwide, and widespread inequality and persecution persists in many jurisdictions.

The formal equality argument has underpinned much of the lobbying and lesbian, gay and bisexual (LGB) activism around the establishment of same sex marriage. For instance, Stonewall's poster campaign traded on liberal humanist slogans such 'People are people. Marriage is marriage' (Stonewall 2014). This public discourse does not take into account findings from the social science literature which foreground the complex, and sometimes paradoxical, relationship lesbian, gay, bisexual, trans and queer (LGBTQ) people have with marriage and marriage-like institutions (Harding and Peel 2006; Harding 2011; Rolfe and Peel 2011) not least because of the heterosexism associated with weddings (Oswald 2000) and the reification of the coupledom norm, that is two—and just two—adults in an intimate relationship (Harding 2008). However, many members of LGBTQ communities greatly value the legitimacy and recognition afforded by marriage and/or marriage-like frameworks (Harding and Peel 2006), and for the 60,454 couples (as of end 2012, ONS 2013) who have entered into a civil partnership this, invariably, constitutes a personally important event in their lives. Carol Smart (2008) has, for example, argued that lesbian and gay commitment ceremonies take four distinct forms: 'regular weddings', 'minimalist weddings', 'religious weddings' and 'demonstrative weddings', and that each of these ceremonial forms reflects the distinct personal, ethical and political journeys of those participating in them. The literature, however, on lesbian and gay couples' interpretations, and accounts of their civil partnership ceremonies is still fairly limited.

This chapter extends this focus on participant accounts of enactment of civil partnership by drawing on qualitative data from around the time civil partnership was introduced. Given the timing of the research, all participants were amongst the 'first wave' of civilly partnered couples, making their plans before any 'norms' for how to celebrate civil partnerships had become established. These data come from interviews (52) and qualitative questionnaires (72) undertaken with 124 lesbian, gay or bisexual (LGB) people who were either planning or in a civil partnership. Of the 62 couples who participated, 75 per cent (47) had had civil partnership ceremonies, which were mostly conducted in 2006. Five couples were interviewed both before and after they had had their civil partnership ceremony. Following University ethical approval, the semi-structured in-depth interviews were conducted jointly with the couple; the questionnaires could be completed by each partner individually, both partners together, or by one partner on behalf of the couple. All three response options were used by questionnaire respondents. Akin to most research on LGBTQ populations (Clarke, Ellis, Riggs and Peel 2010), no claims can be made as to the representativeness of the sample as an opportunistic sampling strategy was used. This involved advertisement in the gay press (eg, Pink paper, Diva magazine) alongside use of academic listservs (eg, British Psychology Society Psychology of Sexualities email list) and University and personal networks. Questionnaire respondents were not required to specify which part of the UK they were in, but the interviews were conducted in the Midlands, North West, South and South West of England and central Scotland. With regard to the demographic characteristics of participants, 59 per cent were women, of whom 94 per cent identified their sexuality as lesbian. The women who did not identify as lesbian were bisexual or did not label their sexual identity, describing themselves, for example, as 'just me'. All of the men identified as gay. All of these LGB people had 'come of age' when no legal status was conferred on relationships between people of the same sex (cf, Heaphy et al 2013). Their mean age was 42.6 years (range 20 to 83 years) and the average length of their relationship was 11 years 4 months (range 1.5 to 36 years). Nearly all participants were white and did not classify themselves as disabled. Eighty-five per cent self-identified as middle class (15 per cent working class) and most (75 per cent) had experienced University level education and were employed (78 per cent). Nearly half the sample reported their religion/belief was Christian (49 per cent) and most did not have children (76 per cent) (see further Table 1).

Utilising the qualitative questionnaire data and semi-structured interviews with these couples, I unpack some of the gendered dimensions embedded in lesbians' and gay men's understandings and enactments of civil partnership ceremonies. In so doing, I offer some thoughts on the intersection of gender and sexuality with regard to relational practices, as understanding gendered processes and practices in lesbian and gay male relationships can be neglected in favour of viewing same sex relationships solely through the lens of sexuality. As Clarke and Peel (2007: 20) suggest, it is 'important to examine lesbian and gay men as gendered beings: we emphasise how lesbians and gay men negotiate living in a heterosexist world, and neglect how they live as women and men in a gendered world'. First then, I discuss the forms of language these lesbian and gay couples used to describe their civil partnership; and second, I explore their accounts of the ritual and ceremonial aspects of their civil partnerships. I end this chapter by suggesting that while

Table 1: Demographic Information

Gender	41% (50) men, 59% (72) women (including 1 transgender woman)
Sexuality	100% of the men identified as gay, 94% of women identified as lesbian
Age	Average age 42.6 years (range 20–83 years)
Ethnicity	99% (121) White, 1% Thai Chinese
Class	85% (95) self-identified as middle class, 15% (17) as working class
Disability	96% (115) not disabled
Religion/Belief	49% (19) Christian, 44% (17) non-religious, 8% (3) 'spiritual'
Children	76% (88) had no children, 24% (28) had children
Relationship status	Average relationship length 11 years 4 months (range 1 year 6 months—36 yrs); 98 per cent (61) co-habiting
Education	75% (72) University-level education, 9% (9) A-Level, 6% (6) GCSE or equivalent
Employment status	78% (97) employed, 12% (15) retired, 4% (5) student, 2% (2) unemployed

marriage rites are indelibly normative—in terms of both their ubiquity and enduring cultural standing—it is more fruitful to view rites undertaken by people in a relationship to someone of the same sex as remodelling what normative means (ie, shifting what contemporary marriage and married life 'looks like' and can be) rather than continuing to view marriage as an unchanging and unchangeable *hetero*normative phenomenon.

II. MARRIAGE AS A LINGUISTIC OR SYMBOLIC FRAMEWORK FOR CIVIL PARTNERSHIP

As I noted above, these data were collected from lesbian and gay couples at the point where civil partnership was becoming a legal reality in Britain and there was little appetite for same sex marriage (but see Kitzinger and Wilkinson 2004). Most of these participants did, however, discuss drawing on different aspects of wedding rituals when discussing the creation of their own civil partnership ceremony. As one male participant suggested: 'I think civil partnerships have offered a really good opportunity for people to be creative and for people to do the things they want to do and not to be bound by a marriage ceremony' (James).[2] Thus, there was a recognition that the 'marriage ceremony' provided the broader landscape or cultural reference for civil partnership, but that the advent of civil partnership as a new institution provided an 'opportunity' for creativity, increased flexibility and not being 'bound' by convention. As exemplified here, it is not that civil partnership merely created an opportunity to re-invent or re-imagine marriage rituals, but the significance of this is communicated ('really good') and the more idiomatic phrase 'bound by convention', that might have been expected, is not used, the participant instead specifying a desire not to be bound by a marriage ceremony (specifically). The contrast here is between active choice ('things they want to do') and 'marriage ceremony', which connotes convention and constraint even though this is not explicitly articulated. Clarke et al (2013) highlight in their small-scale study of 22 same sex couples that their participants emphasised creativity in how they enacted their celebrations, and were able to 'spin it' in ways which met with their own requirements rather than necessarily conforming to (hetero)normative expectation. Similarly, in these data a smorgasbord approach to civil partnership celebration was presented. For instance, Michael reported that 'we've just cherry picked mercilessly'. But more than this, Michael's neat phrase conveys not only a commitment to individual choice in selecting what one wants from the package of marriage ceremony rituals, but 'mercilessly' suggests doing so in a way that is unsympathetic to the tradition as a whole.

[2] All participant names are pseudonyms and other potentially identifying information has been changed. Questionnaire data extracts are reproduced as they were written.

In terms of the language and specific terms participants used to describe their civil partnership there was an overall preponderance in adopting traditionally heterosexual terms like 'wedding' and 'marriage' to refer to their civil partnership. In the questionnaire data set the word 'wedding' was used 50 times and the word 'marriage' was used 57 times. In the interview data set, 'wedding' was used 594 times and 'marriage' 812 times. In total these terms were used generously (1513). Therefore, if a straightforward content analysis can be used evidentially, these participants were drawing heavily on the language of marriage, rather than creating a new set of terminology to describe the new legal framework. Other key terms that were used were 'civil partnership', 'civilly partnered', 'hitched' and reference was made to our 'do'. The male interviewees used the language of marriage more, on average, than female interviewees (men: mean usage 59; women: mean usage 49).

As we will go on to see in the data analysed below, the usage of these terms was not merely unreflective or blanket adoption. It was actually about an active appropriation of this terminology—often for different ends in different contexts, for example, to increase support for the relationship from family, or in a deliberately parodying way. Interestingly, although many participants emphasised the creativity afforded by the (then) new civil partnership framework there was generally less enthusiasm about the term 'civil partnership' itself—which was often referred to as being 'cold' or 'clinical'. It was also the case that the number of times that marriage terms were used was lower, on average, amongst interviewees who had already experienced their civil partnership ceremony (before civil partnership ceremony, mean 54; after civil partnership ceremony, mean 40). There are a number of possible interpretations for this decrease in reference to marriage and weddings once in a civil partnership. It may be that marriage terminology is less salient for those who have experienced civil partnership because the legal and social reality of a civil partnership status eclipses referring to the relationship in these terms. Or it may be that marriage terminology has more utility in the run up to a civil partnership ceremony as it provides an accessible shorthand for capturing the activity of conceptualising and planning such an event.

Let us turn now to larger data excerpts which display a range of reasons for why the language of marriage offers a useful currency for describing civil partnership ceremonies. By way of context, Miriam and Jill had been together 13½ years and were both in their 50s. Their civil partnership was 10 years after a commitment ceremony they had had in 1996. They both wore cream (as opposed to white) trouser suits for their ceremony. Miriam had a ring but Jill had a 'bangle' that they exchanged during the ceremony, which was held in the city Register Office. Both their items of jewellery were engraved with the words 'on and on and on' from the Greenham Common women's peace camp song (circa 1984) lyrics 'you can't kill the spirit, she's just like a mountain old and strong she goes on and on and on' (Roseneil 2000). After their ceremony, they enjoyed champagne and canapés with their friends and family at a bar; they had a lavender coloured cake decorated with rainbow icing and stars. Miriam's son and daughter were their witnesses and they both made speeches. That evening they had a night's stay in a hotel close to their city centre flat. Three weeks later they went on a trip to Tanzania with friends—which had already been organised. Upsettingly, their relationship was invisible in this context, and, ironically, Jill received three marriage proposals from men. In response to a question about whether they felt positive about language like 'marriage' and 'wedding' or whether they thought it was good to 'appropriate' those terms 'and make them less associated with straight people', Miriam stressed the importance of 'terminology' but suggested that the variation in language—and its associated status—should be delineated on the basis of Register Office versus church ceremonies rather than sexuality. Jill, on the other hand, conveys the importance of using marriage terminology:

Extract 1: Miriam and Jill (civil partners—interview)

Miriam: I like the idea that all the terminology could be interchangeable one day. Wouldn't it be nice if you had civil partnership as the registry office wedding and if you have a wedding because you've gone the whole shebang and had the meringue and the church and whatever. I don't know it would be nice to think that the terminology wasn't separated by sexuality, you know, I think that would be a real milestone somehow. I've never really thought about it before but you asked me the question. I think that's what I think about it.

Jill: Yeah I don't want us to be—you know, because otherwise it feels like it has not got the same status almost. If you can't use the same meanings or words.

We can see here, then, a complexity in interpretations of language, and its significance, even within a long-standing couple. Miriam foregrounds a potential cultural sedimentation of language associated with civil partnership so that, ultimately, there is interchangeability between two different but equal frameworks—leaving 'wedding' as associated with 'the whole shebang', 'meringue' and 'church', and 'civil partnership' as the term for a Register Office civil ceremony. She hedges this though, by signalling lack of prior thought on this issue—articulating that her thinking has been prompted directly by the question rather than being a considered view. And then softens this position further through the phrase 'I think that's what I think'. Jill, on the other hand, perhaps sensitive to being heard as challenging the perspective Miriam has just articulated cuts off at the point where she could have said 'second class citizens' and alludes to the framework of civil partnership (as a separate legal entity just for same sex relationships) demarcating a lack of legitimacy when not expressed through 'the same meanings or words'. In other words, Jill suggests that utilising the language of marriage confers an elevated status on civil partnership without directly suggesting that civil partnership, and by extension same sex relationships themselves, are in any way lesser to different sex ones.

The broader 'currency' of wedding and marriage terminology was highlighted by Grace and Diane, and like many of the women in this study they either implicitly or explicitly voiced awareness and critique of the problematic patriarchal and anti-women legacy of marriage. Grace and Diane were in their late 20s and early 30s and had been together for two years 10 months. They called their civil partnership a wedding, but they included definitions of wedding and partnership and marriage on their invitations because 'we wanted people to think about that (aware that some would not consider it either a wedding or a marriage)'. They exchanged rings and vows in a chapel ceremony, in addition to registering their civil partnership, and went on honeymoon. They described their civil partnership as 'a spiritual ceremony followed by a fairly traditional reception' that involved 120 family and friends of 'all ages all persuasions'. In Extract 2, Grace illustrates the intelligibility of the language of marriage for heterosexual family, and how that is translated into enthusiasm and support (see also Peel 2012), and Diane highlights the transformational potential of same sex marriage in response to the question 'Are you treating your civil partnership as a marriage?':

Extract 2: Grace and Diane (civil partners—questionnaire)

> Yes. Well, difficult question ... in the sense of its social and legal weight yes, in terms of the gendering of roles, no. I know that that is how our friends and family talk about it and understand it. I am struck by an incident when we told my brother and sister-in-law about our plans to have a civil partnership ceremony. They were pleasant but muted. At some point later in the conversation I said, 'and we will have to think about where to hold the wedding...' and my sister-in-law said 'What wedding?' As the penny dropped they both got extremely excited and said 'Oh my god you're getting married!!! We must have champagne!!!'. That for me illustrates the importance of language in this situation. I believe our commitment deserves that excitement and context. (Grace)
>
> I definitely view it as a marriage—because in all practical terms that's what it is. I have issues with some of the negative anti feminist notions of marriage down the ages ... In one way I'd like to think that we could establish a new, less compromised, tradition of union between two people and leave behind the connotations of patriarchy and exploitation, but I'm a big believer in the power and weight of history and I think that 'marriage' is what is taken seriously by most people ... and is thus the word that best expresses our partnership. (Diane)

In both Grace and Diane's response we can see the disaggregation of civil partnership from the 'gendering of roles', 'negative anti feminist notions' and 'connotations of patriarchy and exploitation' of women. But they simultaneously embrace the language of marriage because of its cultural gravitas ('taken seriously by most people'), both in the abstract and in reference to their own familial context. I have discussed elsewhere (Peel 2012) the heterosexism that lesbians and gay men invoke through describing 'muted' reactions of friends and family to the announcement of civil partnerships, but what is interesting here is that Grace, through the use of active voicing, multiple exclamation marks and explicit reference to 'the importance of language' highlights the practical significance of utilising terminology that garners an 'appropriate' level of enthusiasm from family. Therefore, for Grace and Diane making a decision to use the language of marriage in the context of their commitment deploys a 'power and weight' that generates a validation and support, and simple understanding, from their family of origin that 'civil partnership ceremony' lacks.

Similarly, Paul and Josh, in response to the same question about whether they were treating their civil partnership as a marriage provided an affirmative response:

Extract 3: Paul and Josh (civil partners—questionnaire)

> 'Yes, absolutely. We don't even like to call it a civil partnership. As far as we are concerned we had a wedding day and we are married ... We consider ourselves to be married and although the law and others don't allow it to be called that, we still put that on forms'

Paul and Josh were in their mid-30s and had been together 11 years 5 months. They had talked about marriage about six months into their relationship and bought and exchanged rings at that point, but shelved their plans to have a commitment ceremony after 'getting very negative responses from services, organisations and some friends too!'. In contrast to Grace and Diane, this couple definitively and unequivocally claim 'we are married', both in linguistic terms and with respect to their interactions with legal or official entities ('we still put that on forms'). Therefore, for these male participants there was a wholesale claiming of marriage as the framework for their relationship status.

For the majority of participants the language—and by extension status—of marriage was conveyed as offering a range of positive benefits to their civil partnership. Some participants were, however, critical of heterosexual marriage as a template for civil partnership and emphasised that they 'didn't want to model it on that at all'. Matthew and Louis, who were in their 40s and had been together for 15 years and were planning their civil partnership at the time of interview, had had an 'affirmation ceremony' five years previously involving 140 people, which they suggested was 'in fact much more like a wedding in a way than what we're going to be doing [for] the formal day'. They emphasised that while their previous commitment ceremony had 'looked very conventional from the outside' they had self-consciously adapted ritual elements 'for our experience and our relationship' such that their ceremony was not 'mimicking'. Their response to the question 'How relevant for you is heterosexual marriage as a template for conducting your civil partnership?' emphasised the disaggregation of civil partnership from a heterosexual framework:

Extract 4: Matthew and Louis (before civil partnership—interview)

Louis: Just completely irrelevant I would have thought. I mean I don't even give it a moment's thought would you?

Matthew: I'm just trying to think whether I have. No, it is absolutely irrelevant.

What is striking about Louis and Matthew's response here is their direct refuting of the social significance of heterosexual marriage in the context of their impending civil partnership ceremony. They are both emphatic ('completely', 'absolutely') about the immateriality and un-connectedness of what they are doing from marriage, and they do this in a way that foregrounds a lack of cognitive engagement ('thought', 'think') which is experientially strong and difficult to contest. Other participants also emphasised the distinctiveness of civil partnership, and resisted their civil partnership being incorporated into a heteronormative framework even though this was, at times, difficult. For example, Beatrice and Naomi, who were in their late 40s and early 50s and had been together six years, were treating their impeding civil partnership 'as a commitment to each other, although the majority of our friends seem to refer to it as a marriage!'. They had met when Beatrice was still married to her ex-husband and they were not planning 'a large bash':

Extract 5: Beatrice and Naomi (before civil partnership—questionnaire)

Society is generally slow to change, and acceptance of civil partnerships will take time. Certainly the lady in the cake shop at Little Sodbury needs to get up to speed—when we enquired about a cake for our civil partnership she was most unhelpful and said that she'd have to call it a wedding cake as that was the only type of cake they made there!

We can see here that rather than use marriage-like language their preference was to pursue civil partnership as a distinct framework—and they position the woman in the cake shop as 'most unhelpful' in not re-naming their cake as a civil partnership cake. This, then, is an alternate approach to that expressed by Grace and Diane, wherein using 'intelligible' language garners support. For Beatrice and Naomi it is about people 'get[ting] up to speed' with the new framework and language of civil partnership. Dean and Mick were in their early 60s and early 50s and had been together 19 years having originally met shortly after Mick had married a woman. Dean was against campaigning for same sex marriage and wrote that he 'would like to retain a difference and have CP as a gay only thing—straights do marriage, gays and lesbians do CP—rights should be equal though'. They had '25 best friends and some family' come to the Register Office and then afterward to lunch at a restaurant. They went on holiday after their civil partnership for three days to Spain but this was 'Not a honeymoon! That word also banned!'. But Dean also wrote 'I'm afraid we sometimes lapse and call it our wedding—as some of our friends did—tried to ban the W and M words at the time'. This illustrates the power and ubiquity of the language of marriage even in the context of an explicit disavowal of a marriage-like or wedding ceremony.

One of Mitchell et al's (2009: vii) observations based on interviews with 47 same sex couples was that 'there was universal agreement that the language of civil partnership did not lend itself to developing an everyday vernacular that was elegant or easy to use'. These data echo that sentiment, but also highlight complex and sometimes contradictory positions on the significance of marriage and marriage-related terminology regarding civil partnership ceremonies at both a linguistic and symbolic level. In the next section, I further explore how these participants produced their ceremonies, and suggest that there was a gendered dimension to their ideological and practical stance on wedding rituals.

III. RITUAL, CEREMONY AND GENDER

Male and female participants often talked about their civil partnership ceremonies differently and displayed a contrasting ideological and practical stance on 'wedding rituals'. For instance, gay male couples often described creating lavish weddings embodying both the trappings and the language of heterosexual marriage. The materialism that inhered to this more extravagant approach was commonly redirected as a resistance to camp, for example 'pink limos or anything "too much"' (Mark and Daniel). By contrast, lesbian couples were more critical of the heteropatriarchal associations of marriage and, in contrast to notions of brides wanting their big day, often articulated a preference for 'low-key' civil partnership ceremonies: not wanting a 'big do' (Rachel and Salma) or a 'large bash' (Beatrice and Naomi). The women were generally (but not exclusively) more critical of the consumerism and materialism associated with public relationship celebration than the men, and stressed differences between heterosexual marriage and civil partnership. Jane and Rachel, who were in their late 30s and early 40s and had been together 14 years, had 'gone an' done it on such a low budget and low key and my jeans cost more than—I bought some new jeans to get married in and um they cost more than the ceremony'. They had two friends as witnesses and then afterwards went for lunch with them. While Jayne and Rachel articulated feeling more 'powerful' and having 'legitimacy 'cos we're married now', as we can see in Extract 6, there was reticence about the ritual and public display of weddings even though they were debating whether to have a celebration of their civil partnership in the future:

Extract 6: Jayne and Rachel (after civil partnership—interview)

Rachel: But for me, um I don't want it to be a spectacle of kind of pretending to have a marriage in their world. For me it's a completely different thing; for me it's a commitment to Jayne in front of our friends which is what the words of the ceremony said and our friends and family know that we're committed. So I don't need or particularly want to make that commitment in front of our family and friends. I want to celebrate it but just not—I don't want to have a pseudo marriage if you like.

Jayne: I have to admit I was really pleased that there were only two people there because I think I would have felt quite humiliated [laughs].

Rachel: But I mean Jayne [and I] are quite—we're not cynical about marriage or weddings but we have been heard to say over a glass of champagne, you know, 'oh Christ', you know, 'same shit, different day' ... it feels just synthetic, it's just so put on ... And I mean I guess perhaps other people don't see it maybe but Jayne and I kind of do rather cynically sit there like the two old guys in the Muppets in the box.[3]

For some of the women participants their ceremony 'escalated' or 'spiralled' into a larger scale event than they had originally planned or anticipated. Nicola and Emma were in their mid-50s and early 40s and had been together for ten years. Nicola had been previously married for 25 years to a man and had two children from that relationship. Emma wrote that 'we started off planning a small affair just for the piece of paper. However, once we told a few people of our plans their genuine excitement for us helped me, and I then went into planning a perfect day'. Emma was explicit about Nicola not being very 'out', whereas Nicola referred to herself as 'shy':

One issue that had been stressing Nicola was what we would do once we had been c.p.'d. As Nicola is less out than me and finds being in the lime light difficult we agreed that I would kiss her on the cheek and hug her. (Emma)

While there was a political objection to the trappings of marriage for some women on feminist grounds, in some cases, such as Emma and Nicola's, the small-scale nature of their ceremony was, in part, about managing the scope of the event so it would be a wholly positive occasion:

Extract 7: Nicola and Emma (civil partners—questionnaire)

We had 40 guests who came to the registry office and to the lunch reception. They were carefully picked and had to be behind us. This meant not having a son in law, a friend's husband or my father. I have no intention of telling him he now has a daughter in law as he is bigoted and not very pleasant when he visits. We also excluded some people who just wanted to say they had been to their first gay wedding. (Nicola)

Nicola and Emma's experience highlights a dilemma with respect to the public and ceremonial aspect of civil partnership (see also Rolfe and Peel 2011). This is not to say that decisions are not made with respect to all

[3] Rachel is referring here to Statler and Waldorf who were disagreeable old men who appeared in the television series *The Muppet Show* (broadcast in Britain from 1976 to 1981) and heckled the rest of the cast from their balcony seats.

weddings about the scope and nature of those invited, but the exclusion of one of the women's father 'as he is bigoted' and those who they felt would attend on almost prurient grounds to 'say they had been to their first gay wedding' are issues particular to the advent of civil partnership ceremonies. Diane and Grace, discussed earlier, had a larger scale ceremony, which Diane described as 'the most amazing demonstration of love and support', but she also wrote about '"holding" a lot of emotion for a lot of people—in a way that we might not have been doing had it been a straight wedding'. Therefore the scope and scale of women's ceremonies were mediated by ideological issues, feminist concerns about aping marriage, and also a concern for deliberately planning their ceremony in such a way as to maximise the pleasure of the occasion and minimise the risk of real or perceived heterosexism and homophobia.

Many of the male participants, by contrast, discussed organising more visible, larger scale ceremonies and seemed more comfortable with, and invested in, using the language and the rituals of marriage. Paul and Josh, who were discussed earlier, are illustrative of this perhaps more grandiose manifestation of ceremonies:

Extract 8: Paul and Josh (civil partners—questionnaire)

> We started rethinking the whole wedding idea about 2.5–3 years before we actually did it ... We decided to try and take some of the stress out of the whole thing by having a Wedding Co-ordinator ... We eventually found a venue and booked it 2 years in advance ... We had a big celebration, it was our wedding day! We wanted all of our friends and family to be a part of our day. We sent official invitations to everyone we knew ... We chose 6 men and 10 women and asked them all to do something on the day. To make this more special we arranged 3 separate events prior to the wedding to help them to get to know each other before the big day. We paid for a dress maker to make individual dresses for the women (to their own personal design), but we bought the fabric to ensure that they all had the same colour ... We bought suits for the men and the dressmaker tailored these to fit ... The wedding day was more of a wedding weekend, as we booked to stay in a large hotel near to the venue ... There were 146 people there.

We can see in the account of their ceremony that Paul and Josh offer a representation of their 'wedding day' that ostensibly appears to utilise conventional marriage ritual and rites, is fully public and not mediated by any concerns about broader acceptance from friends and family—they report inviting 'everyone we knew'.

It is interesting to reflect on the variation in understandings of the significance of language for these couples having had civil partnerships in the early days of the institution, and also how they planned, constructed and explained their ceremonies. Same sex relationships are sometimes conceptualised as devoid of gender and gendered power relations, however, drawing on these data from 124 LGB people, I have suggested that same sex couples' accounts of, and approaches to, their civil partnerships demonstrate the implicit but thoroughgoingly gendered nature of civil partnership. Of course, this crucial gendered dimension also intersects with class and monetary privilege, as well as women's and men's differential relationships with marriage norms and practices. Another observation relates to the positioning of these ceremonies in the relationship trajectory of these couples—who, on average, had been together 11 years—some of whom had undertaken or had considered having non-legally recognised commitment ceremonies prior to the existence of civil partnership. For these couples (and increasingly also for different sex couples) the traditional positioning of marriage as a rite of passage *marking* relationship commitment, or occasioning a change in living arrangements or sexual behaviour was essentially redundant. That is, relationship commitment, from the perspective of many of these participants, very much pre-dated engagement in the new framework of civil partnership rather than it being signalled through this marriage rite.

IV. CONCLUDING COMMENTS

In this final section, I want to return to the notion offered by Kimport (2012: 895) and others, that it is not possible to argue that 'that same-sex marriage always challenges or never challenges heteronormativity'. Neither do the polarised positions of assimilation to, or transformation of, marriage capture what is going on when same sex couples enter into civil partnerships and account for the rituals they do, or do not, adopt to demonstrate relationship commitment (see also Clarke et al 2007; Peel and Harding 2004, 2008). One of the gay male couples in this study described the situation thus—'there seems to be a bit of a split within the LGBT community about it all ... there are certainly some people who think that it conforms to "heterosexual values" and shouldn't be done despite the legal rights'. The complexity and nuance with which couples themselves discuss their civil partnership ceremonies signals the transformative potential that the legally-recognised public celebration of same sex relationship has now and in the future; but not merely on the representation of 'marriage as a heterosexual business' (Jowett and Peel 2010). There has certainly been change in the UK legal and social landscape for LGBT people and same sex couples in the years since these empirical data were collected. There has also been momentum within LGBT scholarship to emphasise a growing schism 'between the socially acceptable "good gays" and the "dangerous queers" who refuse to "settle down" and "fit in"' (Clarke et al 2007: 175).

Conversely, I would like to suggest that this perspective on same sex marriage rites and rights is ultimately unhelpful, as well as divisive. There is a tendency to view weddings and marriage, however they are constructed and enacted, as archetypal indicators of heteronormativity. Following and furthering Kimport (2012), a decade down the line from the Civil Partnership

Act (2004) I would argue that same sex marriage can no longer be claimed to be invariably *hetero*normative. In contrast to those who have coined the term 'homonormative' (eg, Duggan 2003), which is understood as the mimicry by lesbians, gay men and others in same sex relationships of heteronormative standards, it may be that a de-coupling of hetero from normative is what the sedimentation of same sex marriage rites and rights means within British culture. Many of the participants in this study were creatively and reflexively adopting and remodelling ceremonial ritual, even though civil partnership was 'new', and 'full' same sex marriage legislatively labelled as such was not then on the horizon. As one participant wrote: 'It did not occur to us not to have a celebration reception. I do not think this is socially acceptable'. So, in other words, the interesting question now becomes what is normative and how is normativity transformed when marriage is no longer implicitly or explicitly codified as relating to heterosexuality and different sex relationships? I have not suggested that same sex relationships are devoid of gendered norms and practices, but that the (hetero)normativity of marriage rites are fractured and reconfigured by the ongoing business of queer folks getting hitched.

BIBLIOGRAPHY

CLARKE, Victoria, BURGOYNE, Carol and BURNS, Maree, 'Unscripted and Improvised: Public and Private Celebrations of Same-Sex Relationships' (2013) 9 *Journal of GLBT Family Studies* 393.

CLARKE, Victoria, BURGOYNE, Carol and BURNS, Maree, 'Romance, Rights, Recognition, Responsibilities and Radicalism: Same-Sex Couples' Views on Civil Partnership and Marriage' in V Clarke and E Peel (eds), *Out in Psychology: Lesbian, Gay, Bisexual, Trans and Queer Perspectives* (Chichester, Wiley, 2007).

CLARKE, Victoria, ELLIS, Sonja J, PEEL, Elizabeth and RIGGS, Damien W, *Lesbian, gay, bisexual, trans and queer psychology: an introduction* (Cambridge, Cambridge University Press, 2010).

CLARKE, Victoria and PEEL, Elizabeth, 'From lesbian and gay psychology to LGBTQ psychologies: A journey into the unknown (or unknowable)?' in V Clarke and E Peel (eds), *Out in Psychology* (Chichester, Wiley, 2007).

COOK, Guy and WALTER, Tony, 'Rewritten Rites: Language and Social Relations in Traditional and Contemporary Funerals' (2005) 16 *Discourse & Society* 365.

DUGGAN, Lisa, *The Twilight of Equality: Neoliberalism, Cultural Politics, and the Attack on Democracy* (Boston, Beacon Press, 2003).

HARDING, Rosie, *Regulating Sexuality: Legal Consciousness in Lesbian and Gay Lives* (London, Routledge, 2011).

——, 'Recognizing (and Resisting) Regulation: Attitudes to the Introduction of Civil Partnership' (2008) 11 *Sexualities* 740, 760.

HARDING, Rosie and PEEL Elizabeth '"We Do"? International Perspectives on Equality, Legality and Same Sex Relationships' (2006) 7 *Lesbian & Gay Psychology Review* 123, 140.

HEAPHY Brian, SMART, Carol and EINARSDOTTIR, Anna, *Same Sex Marriage: New Generations, New Relationships* (Basingstoke, Palgrave Macmillan, 2013).
INGRAHAM, Chrys, *White Weddings: Romancing Heterosexuality in Popular Culture* (New York, Routledge, 1999).
JOWETT, Adam and PEEL, Elizabeth '"Seismic Cultural Change?": British Media Representations of Same-Sex "Marriage"' (2010) 33 *Women's Studies International Forum* 206.
KIMPORT, Katrina, 'Remaking the White Wedding? Same-Sex Wedding Photographs' Challenge to Symbolic Heteronormativity' (2012) 26 *Gender & Society* 874.
KITZINGER, Celia and WILKINSON, Sue, 'The Rebranding of Marriage: Why we got Married instead of Registering a Civil Partnership' (2004) 14 *Feminism & Psychology* 127.
LEWIN, Ellen, *Recognizing Ourselves: Ceremonies of Lesbian and Gay Commitment* (New York, Columbia University Press, 1998).
MCCORMICK, Joseph Patrick, 'UK: Over 1,400 same-sex weddings have taken place so far in England and Wales' (2014) *Pink News*, available at: www.pinknews.co.uk/2014/08/21/uk-can-you-guess-how-many-same-sex-weddings-have-taken-place-so-far/
MITCHELL Martin, DICKENS, Sarah and O'CONNOR, William, *Same-Sex Couples and the Impact of Legislative Changes* (London, NatCen, 2009).
OFFICE OF NATIONAL STATISTICS, *Statistical Bulletin: Civil Partnerships in the UK, 2012* (ONS, 2013), available at: www.ons.gov.uk/ons/dcp171778_329457.pdf.
OSWALD, Ramona Faith, 'A Member of the Wedding? Heterosexism and Family Ritual' (2000) 17 *Journal of Social and Personal Relationships* 349.
PEEL, Elizabeth, 'Moving Beyond Heterosexism? The Good, the Bad and the Indifferent in Accounts of Others' Reactions to Important Life Events' (2012) 3 *Psychology of Sexualities Review* 34.
PEEL, Elizabeth and HARDING, Rosie, 'Divorcing Romance, Rights, and Radicalism: Beyond Pro and Anti in the Lesbian and Gay Marriage Debate' (2004) 14 *Feminism & Psychology* 584.
———, 'Recognising and Celebrating Same Sex Relationships: Beyond the Normative Debate' (2008) 11 *Sexualities* 659.
ROLFE, Alison and PEEL, Elizabeth, '"It's a Double-Edged Thing": The Paradox of Civil Partnership and Why Some Couples are Choosing not to Have One' (2011) 21 *Feminism & Psychology* 317.
ROSENEIL, Sasha, *Common Women, Uncommon Practices: The Queer Feminisms of Greenham* (London, Cassell/Continuum, 2000).
SMART, Carol, '"Can I Be Bridesmaid?" Combining the Personal and Political in Same-Sex Weddings' (2008) 11 *Sexualities* 763, 778.
STONEWALL, *Equal Marriage to become Law—Thank You!* (2014), available at: www.stonewall.org.uk/what_we_do/parliamentary/5714.asp.

Part II

6

The Rite that Redefines the Rights? The Contemporary Role and Practice of Pre-Nuptial Agreement

AYESHA VARDAG[1] AND JOANNA MILES

I. SETTING THE SCENE...

THE COUPLE HAVE decided to marry. They have made each other promises about their relationship. They sign the document recording these promises before presiding officiants and witnesses. The video camera may be rolling. The families are awaiting the conclusion with bated breath. A wedding? No, the solemn signing of a marriage contract, or 'pre-nup'.

What has happened is the formal crystallisation of the bargain struck around the couple's profound commitment to each other. Negotiating the bargain may have been an arduous and lengthy process, and the fear and risk of loss of the beloved high. The promises made are the as-yet unmarried couple's terms for their impending marriage and/or any possible future divorce, the 'officiants' are their lawyers, the filming is optional (but a convenient source of evidence that no duress or other undue pressure was applied: Skoloff et al 1996: Part X-G),[2] and their wider families may have been closely involved in instigating or even negotiating the agreement. But while an ostensibly 'ceremonial' signing may not be recommended (Skoloff et al 2012-2: XIII-22) and the parties may not dress up for the occasion or entertain guests, it may not be stretching a point to regard the conclusion of a pre-nuptial agreement as sharing at least some features of a 'rite' of marriage. Pre-nups now even have their own dignified page on Debrett's wedding website, listed last amongst other pre-wedding financial planning issues (after insurance for the big day).[3]

[1] The lead author wishes to thank John Oxley, Barrister, for his assistance in the research and preparation of this chapter.

[2] A web search quickly pulls up firms in the US advertising their services specifically for this purpose, eg: www.kurtzvideo.com/nuptial.htm.

[3] www.debretts.com/weddings/engagements-and-invitations/wedding-money/pre-nuptial-agreements.

II. INTRODUCTION

At one level, pre-nups are the epitome of the practical and pragmatic. At another, however, they go to the very heart of how human beings deal with those they most love, how they negotiate their relationships with those with whom they hope to spend their lives, and the delicate, high-stakes balance of giving themselves wholeheartedly to another while each retaining a vital and precious element of self.

This chapter explores the current role and practice of pre-nuptial agreement in England and Wales, drawing on the professional experience of the lead author together with examples from reported case law and empirical research findings. We begin by placing English pre-nuptial agreements in the wider context of contracting around marriage under other legal systems and then identify the status of and principal role played by secular 'English' agreements. We move on to consider who might be interested in obtaining a pre-nuptial agreement under English law and why. We then address some of those aspects of pre-nuptial agreement that might justify its being construed as a novel form of marriage rite, in particular the involvement of wider kin and the process of negotiating an agreement the function of which will be to (re)define the rights which the spouses will enjoy in the event of a future divorce.

As getting married at all becomes an increasingly distinctive statement in many parts of British society, the emergence of pre-nuptial agreements in contemporary discourse around marriage—even if they are not as yet widely adopted[4]—serves to re-emphasise the distinctively legal nature of the bargain being struck on marriage, whether that bargain is defined by the parties' own pre-nuptial agreement or by the general law that would otherwise define that bargain for them.

III. PRE-NUPTIAL AGREEMENTS: THE WIDER PERSPECTIVE

Pre-nuptial agreements are a relatively new—and controversial—phenomenon in the secular English environment, but they have a long pedigree in other territorial and religious legal systems.[5] The recognition that marriage

[4] As seems to be the case both here and in Australia: see in England & Wales, Hitchings (2011: 31), and in Australia, Fehlberg and Smyth (2002).

[5] Cf the historical use of marriage *settlements* in English law, particularly in order to create, protect and preserve property rights (in equity) for the soon-to-be wife who, at common law, would lose her legal and property-owning identity on marriage: see generally Cretney (2003: ch 3). Terms of such settlements which anticipated a future divorce were liable to be struck down as void on grounds of public policy in so far as they provided either party with a financial incentive for guilt-free separation: see case law discussed by Miles (2009: 520).

is a socio-economic and even a political contract has its roots in ancient history. The Old Testament book of Kings records:

> Solomon arranged a marriage contract with Pharaoh, king of Egypt. He married Pharaoh's daughter and brought her to the City of David. (1 Kings 3, 1–3)

This recognition of marriage as a contract permeates many cultures of the modern world. In both Islamic and Talmudic law, articulating the (gendered) financial duties of (and provision for) one[6] or both parties has been a long-established part of the marriage ceremony itself. That ceremony acts both as the formation of a private contract between the parties[7] and a public act which attests to the couple's union. It both negotiates the relationship between the two parties (during marriage and following its end, whether through death or dissolution,[8] and potentially including financial and domestic terms) and serves a vital purpose within the wider kinship and community context.

The ceremonial place of the contract is most pronounced in Jewish marriage rites, the *ketubah* forming a key part of Jewish culture. The marriage contract is intended to reflect the covenant between God and the Israelites. The document is signed at the climax of the marriage ceremony, in sight of all the attendees. It is often lavishly decorated and will be displayed in the couple's home during their marriage; under stricter interpretations of Talmudic law, its loss or damage requires that the spouses cease to cohabit until it is replaced.[9] In Islamic law, the Arabic *Katb-al-kitab* and Urdu *Nikah-nama* serve a less symbolic but equally practical role, allowing the couple to agree between them to depart from the default provisions of Sharia law, for example to preclude further marriages or to allow wives to initiate divorce (Qudamah 1986: 483).

Both cultures have seen their traditional marriage contracts evolve as they interact with secular law, particularly amongst diaspora communities. The Islamic contract has come to be seen as a 'morally enforceable' contract bound up in the community's customs and traditions, parallel to the legal rights which accrue on marriage in a non-*Sharia* secular legal system.[10] The Jewish community has been innovative in its use of the interface between traditional and secular law, particularly in the United States where it is not

[6] The Talmudic *ketubah* imposes duties on the husband only.

[7] See Sharia law's *Katb el-Kitab* and Jewish law's *ketubah*.

[8] See the function of the *mahr* in Islamic law, the transfer of money from husband to wife on marriage (or deferred). For a concise outline of Sharia marital practices see Tribe (2013: 661–64).

[9] *Shulchan Aruch, Even ha-Ezer*, 66:3. For outline of the Talmudic basis of Jewish marital agreements, see Broyde and Reiss (2004).

[10] For example, the British Islamic Institute has produced a 'model' *Katb el-Kitab* for use by British Muslims. The document has no legal force, but remains an important part of the marital rite even if the spouses' rights are determined by secular law.

uncommon for Orthodox couples to use a secular pre-nuptial agreement to refer the dissolution of their marriage to a rabbinical court, or *Beth Din.*[11] This has been recognised by the courts as a permissible route, similar to commercial arbitration agreements, both in the United States and the United Kingdom.[12] Such arrangements permit a couple to use the legal rights conferred by a pre-nuptial agreement to re-establish the Jewish community's rite of marriage, and to negotiate between traditional marriage rites and modern family law rights.[13]

It is not, however, only amongst these religions that the contractual aspects of marriage are closely tied to the legal process of marriage, or even the ceremony itself. Pre-nuptial agreements are used in secular legal systems all over the world, in particular to permit the parties to modify the property and financial consequences of a future divorce (see generally Scherpe 2013). For example, in several European civil law 'community property' jurisdictions couples are obliged to elect a property regime prior to marriage—though this commonly entails simply sticking with the default regime offered by the law. In many jurisdictions this decision not only determines how property will be divided on the dissolution of the union, but also how it will be held during the marriage, with wide-ranging implications, for example, for issues of tax and insolvency. Commonly, the agreement selecting the applicable regime (or departing from it in favour of a bespoke property solution) has to be executed before a notary (who in many jurisdictions is a state official), and/or be otherwise registered or lodged with the state. The rubric of the French secular wedding ceremony itself entails the public identification of the type of property regime selected, with any pre-nuptial agreement reached having to be presented to the person officiating at the wedding and recorded on the marriage certificate.[14] In such jurisdictions, it is considered perfectly normal for rich individuals to conclude a pre-nuptial agreement; a significant factor in the *Radmacher*[15] case was the fact that the parties hailed from monied French and German families—in both of which countries their pre-nuptial agreement would have been binding—and could have been expected to be familiar with the implications of signing one.

[11] See, for example, the agreement in *N v N* [1999] 2 FLR 745.

[12] For a recent example of the use of religious arbitration (albeit not pre-ordained by a pre-nuptial agreement) coming to the attention of English courts, see *AI v MT* [2013] EWHC 100 (Fam).

[13] See for example the use of pre-nuptial agreements in the US to overcome the problem of Jewish husbands declining to grant a *get* on divorce (to secure a religious as well as secular divorce), for example by including a 'Lieberman Clause' which imposes a financial penalty (usually around US$150 per day) if the husband refuses to grant the *get*: Rabinowitz (1998); Willig (2012). For general discussion of the interplay between secular and Talmudic matrimonial law, see Leichter (2009).

[14] Code Civil, Art 1394.

[15] *Radmacher v Granatino* [2010] UKSC 42.

IV. PRE-NUPTIAL AGREEMENTS: THE ENGLISH LAW CONTEXT

By contrast with the centrality of the pre-nuptial agreement to the marriage ceremony and the publicity entailed in the execution and/or registration of pre-nuptial property agreements under some of these religious and secular legal systems, the nascent English practice of pre-nuptial agreements follows the common law tradition that such agreements are a private matter: concluded out of sight, and often kept confidential (at least until the point at which one party seeks to rely on it in the event of divorce). Moreover, though stories abound of pre-nuptial agreements including terms imposing penalties for adultery, or setting out conjugal entitlements and housework rotas, such terms are only slowly entering practice (adultery clauses being at the fore of these), and remain untested by the courts. However, despite the private, property-focused nature of pre-nuptial agreements in England and Wales, there are plenty of parallels between them and their foreign and religious law cousins.

A. The Basic Legal Position: Financial Remedies on Divorce and the Role of Marital Agreements

The 'state marriage contract' effectively provided under English law defines the financial rights and obligations which flow from marriage and which arise on divorce, albeit in somewhat discretionary terms.[16] The nature of those rights and duties has evolved since the introduction of judicial divorce in the mid-nineteenth century. Key developments include the empowerment of judges in the 1960s to make awards of capital as well as needs-based periodical payments,[17] and the judicial introduction (in the cases *White* and *Miller, McFarlane*) of a principle of equal sharing of capital, modified as necessary to meet the parties' competing needs and to compensate for relationship-generated disadvantage. This latter approach replaced the previously prevailing needs-oriented principle that only the claimant spouse's 'reasonable requirements' should be met,[18] though even a 'needs-based' award may be eye-wateringly high.[19] It was the introduction of the sharing principle that has particularly fuelled the market for pre-nuptial agreements. For wealthier spouses, it has become increasingly important to seek to moderate or entirely displace the sharing principle, in particular, and limit

[16] Matrimonial Causes Act, Part II.

[17] First introduced by the Matrimonial Causes Act 1963; see generally Cretney (2003: ch 10).

[18] *White v White* [2001] 1 AC 596, *Miller v Miller, McFarlane v McFarlane* [2006] UKHL 24.

[19] See eg, *Mills-McCartney v McCartney* [2008] EWHC 401.

needs in advance (see further below). Without a pre-nup, it may be said that 'divorce can work like a 50 per cent tax on your total wealth'.[20]

In one sense at least, pre-nuptial agreements are just another part of the wider, long-standing promotion of private ordering on divorce, without which the family justice system would grind to a halt. Certainly at the point of divorce, parties have since the 1970s been actively encouraged to make their own agreements regarding the financial consequences of their separation.[21] It remains advisable to have that agreement enshrined in an order of the court (a 'consent order') in order to make it fully binding: the courts have retained the power to superintend these arrangements,[22] and if one party wishes to resile from their bargain before a consent order has been made, they remain in theory free to apply to the court for financial provision different from what they signed up for.[23] Around 65–70 per cent of applications for financial orders on divorce are for consent orders and around 95 per cent of all orders ultimately made are based on the parties' agreements. However, it seems that only a little over a third of divorcing couples go to court for a financial order at all (whether or not by consent)—most of the financial bargaining that happens around divorce is therefore entirely off-radar (MOJ 2014: table 2.5).

But while private ordering on divorce has long been encouraged, until very recently pre-nuptial agreements—providing *before marriage* for the hypothetical event of its demise—were viewed with such suspicion that they were regarded as void on grounds of public policy. The reasons underpinning this objection changed over time: once, as the older cases had it, it was because they were thought to undermine the state-governed, status-based institution of marriage; then, as more recent cases tended to emphasise, because holding the parties to agreements that may have been made many years before they came to be relied upon, at a time when their situation at the point of divorce could not have been foreseen, risked leaving economically vulnerable parties in dire straits on divorce.[24] Whatever its basis, in the widely publicised[25] case of *Radmacher v Granatino* in 2010, the Supreme Court lifted the public policy objection,[26] putting pre-nuptial agreements on the same footing as other types of marital agreements providing for the

[20] www.divorcesaloon.com/2014/06/11/interview-with-uk-divorce-solicitor-ayesha-vardag-just-call-her-the-diva.

[21] See Ingleby (1989) for a useful survey of the early history, drawn on and developed into the last two decades by Hitchings, Miles and Woodward (2013: ch 1).

[22] MCA 1973 s 33A.

[23] *Hyman v Hyman* [1929] AC 601.

[24] For an analysis of the various ways in which that public policy objection could be construed, see Miles (2009).

[25] Though apparently not to an extent that fixed in the minds of respondents to the contemporaneous research study conducted by Barlow and Smithson (2012: 306): only one of 26 respondents had heard about the case, decided just before the study commenced, despite its blanket media coverage accompanied by stylish photographs of the successful appellant.

[26] *Radmacher v Granatino* [2010] UKSC 42.

financial incidents of divorce, whether made at separation[27] or during the marriage.[28] The position for all such agreements is now that

> The court [considering an application for financial relief on divorce] should give effect to a nuptial agreement that is freely entered into by each party with a full appreciation of its implications unless in the circumstances prevailing it would not be fair to hold the parties to their agreement.[29]

What is regarded as 'fair' is not yet fully defined, but it seems relatively clear from the lead author's current experience in practice that one can by pre-nuptial agreement exclude the equal sharing principle altogether, in addition to restricting (though not failing to meet) the 'needs' of the financially weaker spouse. Needs may still be more or less 'generously interpreted',[30] but the trend in practice is to honour properly entered agreements increasingly, even tough ones, providing that they do not engender real hardship. The Law Commission has recently made recommendations to put a scheme for the enforcement of 'qualifying nuptial agreements' on a statutory footing (Law Commission 2014). If implemented, such reform would further raise the profile of such agreements in contemporary culture—though whether it would make their use much more common remains a moot point.

B. Autonomy versus Paternalism—For Better or Worse?

This development in English law has not been uncontroversial. In the Court of Appeal in *Radmacher v Granatino*, Wilson LJ regarded as 'patronising' what he saw as the premise of the law which made pre-nuptial agreements void, in its

> assumption that, prior to marriage, one of the parties, in particular the woman, is, by reason of heightened emotion and the intensity of desire to marry, likely to be so blindly trusting of the other as to be unduly susceptible to the other's demands even if unreasonable.[31]

Reflecting Wilson LJ's view, the eight-Justice majority of the Supreme Court held that:

> [T]here should be respect for individual autonomy. The court should accord respect to the decision of a married couple as to the manner in which their financial affairs should be regulated. It would be paternalistic and patronising to override their agreement simply on the basis that the court knows best.[32]

[27] *Edgar v Edgar* [1980] 1 WLR 1410.
[28] *MacLeod v MacLeod* [2008] UKPC 64.
[29] *Radmacher v Granatino* [2010] UKSC 42, [75].
[30] For generosity see eg, *Z v Z (No 2)* [2011] EWHC 2878.
[31] [2009] EWCA Civ 649, [127].
[32] [2010] UKSC 42, [78].

However, the lone dissenting Justice in the Supreme Court, Lady Hale, expressed strong concern about the implications of her male colleagues' decision for the position of women, which had been so advanced by the judges' earlier development of the principle of equal sharing:

> [T]he court hearing a particular case can all too easily lose sight of the fact that, unlike a separation agreement, the object of an ante-nuptial agreement is to deny the economically weaker spouse the provision to which she—it is usually although by no means invariably she—would otherwise be entitled.[33]

One commentator remarked that the *Radmacher* decision marked the 'death knell of marriage' (Herring 2010),[34] like Hale nervous about its contractualisation of marriage and the autonomy it thereby conferred on spouses to avoid the gender equality underpinning equal sharing on divorce that had only recently (somewhat belatedly) been introduced into English matrimonial law.

It is not the purpose of this chapter to rehearse the arguments for and against the greater legal status now enjoyed by pre-nuptial agreements in English law, though we shall encounter several of those arguments along the way. For better or worse, these agreements are now part of the English matrimonial law landscape. The concern of this chapter is to examine the way in which pre-nuptial agreements may be viewed as a form of pre-marriage rite in which couples come together, usually with input from their advisors and wider family and often encompassing a variety of unique and bespoke interests, to (re)define the rights flowing from the marriage that they are about to contract, where formerly they would have been required to take the state's 'off the peg' institution without bespoke alterations.[35] As we shall explore, they permit couples to tailor their legal relationship to a range of situations involving not just their own interests but also those of their family. The process of negotiating the pre-nuptial agreement may itself form an important part of the engagement, requiring couples to consider issues (good and bad) that might not have otherwise been discussed and altering the spirit in which they enter into the marriage. It arguably also creates a union that is more the product of considered choice than the passive acceptance of marriage rights defined by the state. This transforms the marriage itself from traditional, publicly defined rite into a product of tailor-made personal and inter-kin group negotiation, in which individual requirements that may not be readily or reliably accommodated by the generally applicable law may find expression in the parties' vision of marriage.

33 Ibid, [137].

34 See also the arguments made by George, Harris and Herring (2011).

35 Contrast tailor-made partnership deeds or articles of association that displace the standard form terms for partnerships and companies that otherwise apply by default.

V. WHO CONCLUDES PRE-NUPTIAL AGREEMENTS IN ENGLAND AND WALES TODAY AND WHY?

Pre-nuptial agreements in English law and practice are predominately about the allocation and preservation of property on divorce. At their simplest they are used to agree what assets will fall into the matrimonial 'pot' in the event of divorce and how those assets will be apportioned. Yet this simplicity belies the wide variety of couples who choose to enter into such agreements, their varied motivations, and the advantages that they perceive may accrue from having a pre-nup. In practice, every pre-nuptial enquiry is different from the last, with each couple approaching lawyers from different backgrounds and with different intentions for the future.

The classic public perception of a pre-nuptial agreement, fuelled by tabloid speculation about celebrity nuptials and divorces, is based around the wealthy man marrying a less wealthy (usually younger) woman. For the time being, it remains the case that men continue to dominate high-earning professions and businesses, and are more likely to be the party bringing substantial assets to the marriage. The London family court in particular has garnered a reputation for generosity towards wives, something which high net-worth husbands wish to avoid by entering into pre-nuptial agreements. They often therefore try to use pre-nuptial agreements to ring-fence assets in ways the court will not (or cannot be relied on to do, as discussed further below). Many of the most publicised divorces of the past few years are believed to have been quickly settled by 'water-tight' pre-nups; Charles Saatchi, Tom Cruise and Rupert Murdoch to name but a few. The lead author's firm is often approached by husbands in such a position, amongst them sports stars, executives and entrepreneurs. They rarely arrive thinking that their fiancée is marrying them for money, but wish to opt out of a court process that could see them subject to a huge award after even a very short marriage. The act of asking for a pre-nup may be taken as questioning the motives or integrity of the financially weaker party, but the stigma may reduce as pre-nups become more common and the diversity of circumstances and intentions giving rise to them become known.

However, as empirical research both here and overseas has identified,[36] pre-nuptial agreements are not the preserve of the high-earning husband seeking to erect defences against the 'gold-digger'. Increasingly, as couples marry later, both will come to the relationship with existing assets and wish to preserve their position. It is not uncommon for parties to want an agreement which serves to extinguish both parties' claims, as in *Radmacher v Granatino*, where both parties were wealthy prior to marriage (albeit that

[36] See in England & Wales, Hitchings (2011: 31); and in Australia, Fehlberg and Smyth (2002: 134).

the wife was rather more so, from her inherited wealth).[37] The lead author's own pre-nup was made in balanced financial circumstances and with a mutual desire to substitute private agreement for the court process (Vardag 2014). Even those with relatively modest wealth may wish to plan their affairs to try to minimise the risk that a future divorce will jeopardise assets with sentimental value.[38] The parties can try to structure their affairs knowing what sum will be payable on divorce, avoiding the risk of a much-loved home needing to be sold, or art and antiques being auctioned off rather than kept in the family.[39] The less money in the pot, the more creative the solution needed—to have this planned in advance and with a cool head can be much more reassuring than risking arbitrary decisions in the heat of divorce.

Quite beside their role on breakdown of a marriage, even in the English context pre-nuptial agreements may also be used to settle financial affairs during the marriage, rather than just at the end, for example with an eye to tax efficiency and succession management. Agreements accordingly often incorporate provisions relating to the couple's wills, and how assets are to be held during the marriage. In such cases, as in continental European regimes providing for immediate community of property, the pre-nuptial agreement therefore acts as an important part of the marriage, rather than something which is merely kept on standby in case of separation.

Moreover, pre-nuptial agreements may be motivated by concerns beyond mere wealth preservation. Whilst the lump sums paid out on divorce can be daunting, so too can the process of litigating such cases on divorce if agreement cannot be reached at that point, both in terms of the time such cases can take to reach resolution and the costs incurred along the way. This is especially true of litigation in which high-value assets are being disputed. Whilst proportionate case management is required in all cases,[40] high-value cases may be especially lengthy, complex and costly, involving the instruction not only of lawyers but also a variety of financial experts, valuers and forensic accountants. Of course, in a jurisdiction where such agreements cannot oust the jurisdiction of the court entirely, having a pre-nuptial agreement does not rule out litigation further down the line, for example over the validity of the agreement or the justice of departing from it. The problem of 'satellite litigation' around pre-nuptial agreements has been noted by various commentators (Fehlberg and Smyth 2002: 128–29; George, Harris and Herring 2009: 935–36). However, just as instructing a good conveyancing solicitor can potentially save vast sums of money if something goes wrong

[37] See also *Crossley v Crossley* [2007] EWCA Civ 1491.

[38] Though it is recognised by practitioners that agreements have little if any relevance in cases that will be governed by the needs principle: see Hitchings (2011: 102).

[39] The Law Commission made much of this sort of example: (2010: para 5.49).

[40] See comments by Mostyn J on the costs incurred by the wife in *Young v Young* [2013] EWHC 3637 (Fam), [4]–[14].

with the purchase of a house, so a properly drafted pre-nuptial agreement has the potential to avoid costly matrimonial litigation. And parties who wish to litigate at the point of divorce should be required to show good reason why such a claim should be considered. As Mostyn J remarked recently,

> It must be obvious that the principal object of the exercise in this case (as indeed in every case where a nuptial agreement is signed) is to avoid subsequent expensive and stressful litigation; and it is for this reason ... that the law adopts a strict policy of requiring the demonstration of something unfair before it will open the Pandora's box of litigation where there has been an agreement of this nature.[41]

A related source of difficulty which may incline some individuals towards making a pre-nuptial agreement is the inherent uncertainty of matrimonial law in this area. As the Law Commission has acknowledged, there are 'significant unresolved issues of principle' in the law, such that lawyers can find it 'extremely difficult to advise on outcomes' (Law Commission 2010: para 5.35). Many approaches to family solicitors begin with a familiar refrain: 'What are my rights?' When couples only consider their rights on family breakdown when the breakdown has occurred, they can be thrust into a bewildering *terra incognita*. On the one hand, the inherent flexibility in English law's approach to financial settlements on divorce offers scope to accommodate parties' clearly agreed preferences about which assets should be available for division at all and how their assets should be divided—for example enabling them to protect inherited or other family wealth, or particular assets of a sentimental or family significance whose liquidation to fund a cash settlement would be particularly deleterious to wider family interests.[42] On the other hand, that same flexibility—or, less flatteringly, uncertainty—gives parties strong motivation to achieve some certainty for themselves before they even embark on marriage by setting out in advance what will happen in the event of divorce, and so—it will be hoped—not expose themselves to the vagaries of judicial discretion should divorce come to pass. Just as a marrying couple would not want a third party to pick the wedding venue or the flowers for them, they can use a pre-nuptial agreement to ensure that a third party will not be deciding their property rights for them.

Seeking to examine these issues up front, before marriage, carries the inevitable risk that the parties will not be able to foresee the economic circumstances that they end up confronting at the point of divorce and so will reach an agreement which, with the benefit of hindsight, might be regarded

[41] *BN v MA* [2013] EWHC 4250 (Fam), [17]. Cf concerns expressed prior to *Radmacher* by some practitioners in Hitchings' study about the unpredictability of judges' responses to the presence of a pre-nuptial agreement should the case be litigated on divorce: Hitchings (2011: 44 et seq).

[42] Cf the outcomes in *Y v Y* [2012] EWHC 2063 (Fam) and *Robson v Robson* [2010] EWCA Civ 1171.

by some as 'unfair', particularly if they are under pressure of time to reach agreement. The reported cases give several examples of what might be dubbed 'shotgun pre-nups' concluded by pregnant brides at short notice.[43] For some critics, this—together with the general propensity of agreements to provide less generously for the economically weaker spouse than would the general law, and the inherent difficulty of crystal ball-gazing when attempting to draft a fair agreement[44]—is ample reason to deprive pre-nuptial agreements generally of binding force.[45] However, in less fraught circumstances, parties may see advantages in attempting to reach agreement prior to marriage, when times are good, rather than at the emotionally turbulent time of separation. In principle (though reality may, of course, sometimes be different), the agreement will be concluded in good faith and, when managed correctly, in good spirits. If properly advised and if proper disclosure has been made, both parties will have the security of knowing what their rights are before they marry, the monied spouse seeking to limit the exposure of their assets in the event of divorce, while the poorer party seeks the reassurance that they will be financially secure on separation (even if not as lavishly provided for as they might have been without the agreement).[46] In short, as Lord Wilson writing extra-judicially has put it, a pre-nuptial agreement 'replaces an undefined outcome, dependent on the future exercise of a court's discretion, with a defined outcome' (Scherpe 2013, foreword). A pre-nuptial agreement has the potential to allow a couple to cement their rights in an uncertain world and to deal with their finances in a flexible and pragmatic way that is bespoke to their relationship.

Lastly, it is not insignificant that in the English context (by contrast with some of the systems explored in the introduction) the pre-nuptial agreement also grants the couple a greater degree of privacy than litigation on divorce might provide. Whilst the divorce will be a matter of public record, the terms of the pre-nuptial agreement, even if in due course enshrined in a consent order, will not. For much of the last century the family courts have captivated tabloid interest and continue to do so, especially in the case of household names. It is standard practice for a pre-nuptial agreement to contain comprehensive non-disclosure clauses, which help prevent the parties from being dragged through the press should the marriage end. Even

[43] See eg, *M v M* [2002] 1 FLR 654; *K v K* [2003] 1 FLR 120; *Ella v Ella* [2007] EWCA Civ 99.

[44] See reservations noted by respondents in Hitching's study (2011: 31 and 41); George, Harris and Herring (2009: 936).

[45] Note also the Law Commission's striking characterisation of the nature of the autonomy protected by a binding pre-nuptial agreement: in part, the 'freedom to force one's partner to abide by an agreement when he or she no longer wishes to do so': (2010: para 5.31).

[46] Though this is not always so. Some pre-nups in the reported cases are more generous than the provision that would otherwise have been made by the governing law: eg *AH v PH* [2013] EWHC 3873.

when the couple are not famous, the case can be publicised in law reports and the mainstream press, potentially disseminating embarrassing financial or other details. A confidentiality agreement reached prior to marriage can help remove this risk.

VI. THE PLACE OF WIDER KIN IN PRE-NUPTIAL AGREEMENTS

We turn now to the place of wider kin in these cases, both as a further source of motivation for concluding a pre-nuptial agreement and as more or less active characters in the pre-nuptial narrative. Marriage is often about more than just the betrothed couple. The union of two spouses necessarily involves the juncture of two families, and the process of marriage is usually firmly connected to the wider kinship network. The same is true of pre-nuptial agreements. The wider family can be closely bound up in the creation of an agreement, as instigators, negotiators and beneficiaries.

It is common for the push for a pre-nuptial agreement to come from one or both of the parties' families, rather than from one or other of the happy couple themselves. This is particularly true when the assets involved are predominantly from a family business or large family settlement. In the *Radmacher* case, for example, the pre-nup was drawn up at the instigation of the bride's father as a precondition to advance transfer of their ultimate share of the family fortune. In one qualitative study in this jurisdiction, Hitchings (2011: 31) found that third party involvement was the most frequently reported factor in requests for pre-nuptial agreements. Indeed, it is common in practice to find that the agreement was initiated or even effectively required by the parents of one party, who may often contact solicitors before they have even raised the issue with their child.[47] Just as parents are likely to be involved in the wedding itself, they may take a lead role in planning for issues that the couples do not wish to countenance, in particular what would happen to property should the marriage fail, especially if they are more cautious, even dubious, about their prospective son- or daughter-in-law than is their enamoured child.

In some cases, the degree of parental involvement and resulting family pressure to conclude a pre-nuptial agreement might be regarded as constituting duress on one or both parties (a concern expressed in one of Hitchings' focus groups: Hitchings (2011: 66–67)). However, in other circumstances parents can play a useful role in the theatre of pre-nuptial negotiations. For many couples, discussion about pre-nuptial agreements is uncomfortable. It raises serious issues—of trust, commitment and money—none of which

[47] For a particularly striking example of a family very much in the driving seat, see *K v K* [2003] 1 FLR 120, where both father and mother of the bride were actively involved in the entire process.

individually, never mind taken collectively, is likely to be a welcome topic of discussion in romantic relationships. As hard as it might be to propose marriage at all, the question 'Will you enter into a pre-nuptial agreement with me?' is even harder to ask. The spouse who wants a pre-nuptial agreement may, as noted above, feel that they are accusing their future spouse of being a potential 'gold-digger' or that the approach suggests that they are not fully committed to the relationship. For this reason, many parties use their families as an excuse for launching into such a process.[48] The suggestion that the initial impetus behind the approach has come from a relative can help allay these suspicions and more smoothly introduce the idea of an agreement. This is much more convincing when the parent has already approached a solicitor. So in practice, it is not uncommon for an engaged person to discuss the potential pre-nuptial agreement with their family, and even with lawyers, before broaching the subject with their future spouse. It is certainly not uncommon for solicitors to be initially approached by a relative in the first instance. Often, the approach about a pre-nuptial agreement might be rather tentative—it is an area about which people are generally poorly informed—and a family member is often better placed to obtain initial information without alerting or alarming the opposite party.

It is not just in cases of inheritance and 'old money', or as instigators or even negotiators of the pre-nuptial agreement, that the wider family have a role to play. The involvement of the wider family as *beneficiaries* of a pre-nuptial agreement can be particularly important in cases of 'self-made' parties. In the lead author's experience, it is quite natural for a party who becomes wealthy by their own endeavours to seek to look after their extended family. It is not uncommon therefore to see such parties buy properties and provide investments for their parents, siblings or other kin. This is particularly common when dealing with sports stars and celebrities who have enjoyed a meteoric rise from humble backgrounds to exceptional affluence. Many clients like this come to the marriage having bought houses, cars and other items for their family. Without the protection of a pre-nuptial agreement, these assets can be vulnerable in a divorce.

Moreover, as the modern family evolves, there can be a number of competing claims on a party's wealth, particularly for those entering into second marriages.[49] Parties to second and subsequent marriages may in any event be motivated by their enhanced sensitivity to the issues of marital breakdown, having been through the divorce process once already, and a desire to protect the wealth that they—at a later stage in life—may already have

[48] It was suggested that the wife in *Radmacher* used her family's concerns as cover for securing her pre-nuptial agreement: [2008] EWHC 1532, [23]. See also the more positive members of Hitchings' focus group: (2011: 67).

[49] In the reported cases, see *S v S* [1997] 2 FLR 100, *M v M* [2002] 1 FLR 654, *Crossley v Crossley* [2007] EWCA Civ 1491. This issue was also highlighted by respondents in Hitchings' study: (2011: 32–33).

accumulated. But the concerns of the 'first' family also regularly play a role, and may be readily acknowledged by the new spouse.[50] This is particularly the case when adult children are involved. Though the children of the first marriage may be grown up and self-sufficient, parents may want to support them in some practical way by preserving a portion of their property for their adult children or some other dependent relative.[51] This can take effect on dissolution of the marriage, or at a point within it—perhaps providing a bounty on a certain birthday or providing a first property.

In all of these cases, without an agreement about the treatment of such assets, such arrangements might come under scrutiny in divorce proceedings (does the spouse still have a beneficial interest in that asset?), and so be vulnerable to being redirected to the claimant spouse by the courts. A pre-nuptial agreement can help ring-fence such arrangements, both during the course of the marriage and on divorce, and so protect the future interests of the wider kinship group.

It is notable that these sorts of cases encourage us to pull away to some extent from the marriage-centric approach of English family law which increasingly vaunts the nuclear spousal relationship above other family relationships. The extended family has been increasingly distanced from couples since the sexual emancipation and focus on individual autonomy of the sixties and seventies. But it is not immediately obvious that a divorcing spouse should have the priority claim of an individual's assets when there are other dependants (not directly connected to that marriage as 'children of the family') for whom it is entirely reasonable for the property-owning spouse to want to make provision.[52] The pre-nuptial agreement is therefore not merely a tool for controlling entitlements between the spouses, but also for regulating a spouse's claim in relation to the wider family. In the process, it has brought the wider kin, and a measure of caution, circumspection and no-frills financial bargaining, back into the pre-marriage process. It has brought back the sense that marriage involves more people than just the spouses, as well as the sense that marriage involves money and property alongside love and desire.

In a sense, this links up with Jonathon Herring's chapter (chapter thirteen of this volume). His concept of care as the central idea of marriage, rather than sex or romantic love, is not a million miles from the concept of familial alliance or indeed of pooling of resources, including financial resources. At a time when divorce rates arguably attest to the fallibility of the 'when you know, you know', Romeo-and-Juliet idea of love, society is endeavouring to

[50] See eg, the views of 'Tamzin' in Barlow and Smithson's study: (2012: 317).

[51] See eg, the dependent disabled nephew of the husband in *K v K* [2003] 1 FLR 120.

[52] This is recognised to some extent on death by the range of persons entitled to succeed on intestacy (under the Administration of Estates Act 1925) and to bring claims under the Inheritance (Provision for Family and Dependants) Act 1975.

work out what underlies a deeper and more sustainable bond. The pragmatic and reasoned involvement of family, mutual understanding of financial expectations, and agreement to contingent arrangements in case of potential divorce, can arguably help to form and reflect a strong dynamic of mutual care between the spouses.

VII. NEGOTIATING THE PRE-NUPTIAL AGREEMENT

Blood relations are not the only third parties who may be drawn into the process of negotiating a pre-nuptial agreement. The professionals and advisers that surround wealthier clients can often involve themselves in negotiations. Business advisers, wealth managers and agents are increasingly aware of the potential advantages of an agreement and frequently are the ones to suggest it. Quite often a solicitor will be approached via a referral, or cold-called, by an individual's professional advisers, and (as in family cases) sometimes before the matter has even been raised by the client. The first pre-nup brought to the lead author's firm after the *Radmacher* judgment came via a telephone call from a football agent. Whilst this may seem deeply unromantic, it usefully highlights the way marriage today interacts with every part of life, particularly for high net-worth individuals. In so far as marriage or cohabitation really is now a matter of legitimate social and cultural choice in many communities (see Probert, chapter three of this volume), the decision to marry is not just a romantic decision but also a practical economic decision. Entering into a marriage can be a form of investment, and an inherently risky one. It therefore raises the same concerns and considerations as any other major investment, and so can to some extent be approached in the same way. However, the process of negotiating a pre-nuptial agreement is in many respects self-evidently very different from other 'business' transactions. After all, in approaching the pre-nuptial agreement, the couple are setting not only the financial groundwork for their marriage, but also engaging in discussions which can affect their personal relationship—for better or for worse.

The pre-nuptial process can be a time when much is revealed about the couple in question and their relationship, beyond merely financial matters. How each party *approaches* negotiations is itself revelatory about their attitude towards their new partner and impending marriage. When it comes to issues of disclosure, the parties' willingness to be frank and honest can say a lot about their long-term intentions. In the lead author's experience, parties are usually co-operative, laying out their assets in an open way, in stark contrast to many contested divorces. But of course this is not always the case. Some wealthy parties can be exceptionally reluctant to share full information, taking the view that the more they share, the more their partners may request. They can often be surprisingly frank to solicitors about the assets they want to leave outside the pre-nuptial agreement, even when advised that poor disclosure is likely to render the agreement unenforceable. At the extreme end, some clients even ask if their future spouse needs to sign, or even see, the pre-nuptial agreement for it to be binding. Such attitudes often betray a lack of trust or seriousness about the marriage. The less wealthy party can also demonstrate much about themselves in the negotiation process. More often than not this is to their credit, though one might be concerned about the reality or otherwise of the autonomy being exercised by some of these parties.[53] The 'I'll sign anything' approach is often noted in practice, with spouses seeking only the minimal economic safety-net.[54] Equally though, the process can reveal ugly attitudes of greed and accusations of 'gold-digging'.

Seeing how the other side approaches the process can reveal unwanted things about a partner's approach to the relationship. The pre-nuptial agreement can cut through the excitement of the engagement and show incipient cracks within the relationship. On some occasions, the process of creating a pre-nuptial agreement can highlight such disparate opinions and conflicting moods that the couples realise they are not suited to a relationship together.

The lead author has seen couples split over a pre-nuptial agreement. One prospective husband felt such a mismatch between what he considered to be a generous and fair approach on his part and a greedy and unreasonable approach on the part of his wife-to-be that he called off the wedding. Another relationship foundered on the examination, during the course of working on the pre-nup, of the day-to-day financial arrangements the couple had in place for their cohabitation and which they expected to continue during their marriage. The wife-to-be was unhappy about their respective contributions but felt unable to talk to her husband-to-be about money. An arrangement was brokered but the marriage was subsequently called off, the mismatch between their attitudes and expectations running too deep.

Unromantic as it may be, it is hard to reject the proposition that such mismatches of perspective and expectation are likely to throw a marriage awry at some stage, and that it is better to flush them out at this early stage than to gloss over them and deal later with divorce, especially once there are children born to the couple. The role of lawyers, in those cases, is rather like that of an old-fashioned matchmaker, who will try to explore the possibility

[53] See concerns of George, Harris and Herring (2009: 937) regarding the potential dangers of negotiating away important rights, and the various concerns about the reality of the 'autonomy' being exercised in these cases: Law Com (2010: para 5.27 et seq).

[54] See also the concern of the wife in *AH v PH* not to appear greedy in the run-up to the marriage: [2013] EWHC 3873 (Fam), [63(a)].

of a union but advise withdrawal if the couple seem mismatched. To some extent, the 'unromanticism' of the pre-nup may arguably be a useful counter to a society where 'love' is often infatuation and is hormonally driven rather than based on real compatibility of character, interests and shared goals. To those who wish to encourage marriage and reduce divorce, a culture whereby pre-nups become a standard premarital rite might be seen as a welcome development.

So, even where the wealth disparity between parties is not that great, the pre-nuptial agreement can throw differences into sharp focus. In the course of negotiating a thorough pre-nuptial agreement, couples are forced to confront aspects of their marriage which might otherwise be avoided. The associated discomfort is precisely what prompts many people, perhaps naively, to oppose pre-nuptial agreements (Barlow and Smithson, 2012: 316). Whether it is discussing potential children, investments, or other aspects of their life together, the process can reveal problematic disagreements and attitudes. This can be both to the detriment of and beneficial to the couple's relationship. The pre-nuptial process can therefore be a useful test of whether the couple are right for marriage, and so act as a helpful part of marriage preparation. The process of negotiating the pre-nuptial agreement may itself form an important part of the engagement, requiring couples to consider issues (good and bad) that might not have otherwise been discussed and altering the spirit in which they enter into the marriage. The pre-nuptial negotiation process can therefore become like a form of marriage preparation, in which couples explore the contentious issues within their relationship, a practice akin to the long-standing, routine use of marriage preparation classes by religious organisations and community groups, and the growing private sector market (particularly in the United States) amongst therapists providing 'pre-marital counselling' to engaged couples. The premise of such approaches is a sensible one: confronting difficult issues from a position of happiness. A pre-nuptial agreement entered into in the same spirit can be used as positive foundation for marriage.

Indeed, it would be wrong to see pre-nuptial agreements in a purely unromantic way. On the contrary, as Elizabeth Gilbert commented in relation to her own pre-nup (quoted in Foley 2010), 'drawing up a pre-nup was almost a way of reassuring each other if this relationship ends, you are not going to be left devastated by who I am and who I turned out to be'. In her book, Gilbert (2010: 115–16) also states that:

> I must ask you to believe me when I say that we shared some truly tender moments during these conversations—especially those moments when we find ourselves arguing on behalf of the other person's best interests.
>
> If you think it's difficult to talk about money when you're blissfully in love, try talking about it later, when you are disconsolate and angry and your love has died.

The lead author's account of signing her own pre-nup (Vardag 2014), attended by celebratory wine and witnessed by mutual friends, is in similar vein.

> At that moment, after all the stress and grumpiness … for the first time, we really felt we'd taken the first real step of getting married. It was an amazingly emotional moment. We'd signed a binding contract, before our friends, crystallising the basis upon which we were entering into our lives together. We'd done that as independent equals, making our own choices together about how we want to plan things, for better or for worse, and expecting to be held to them.

Signing the pre-nup was a moment of very deep respect for each other, and gave us a real sense of the reality and seriousness of what we were doing in getting married. Contrary to what everyone might think, it was incredibly romantic.

Although research in Australia found that 'one of the major factors inhibiting entry into agreements is difficulty experienced at a personal level during the process of negotiating agreements' (Fehlberg and Smyth 2002: 135; see also Hitchings 2011: 39), most practitioner-respondents to Hitchings' study in England and Wales suggested that their clients were neither put off marrying nor put off concluding the agreement by the process (2011: 28). The discussion of matrimonial finances in such a context can, and in the lead author's experience usually does, act to strengthen and affirm the relationship. The negotiation process allows couples to be upfront about what they want from the marriage—how they envisage family life being managed and what they might want if the marriage were to dissolve—and allay any fears. They can discuss the thorny issues such as money, children and relationship to the wider family in a proactive manner, finding common ground before launching into the marriage.[55] They can reassure themselves about their partner and lay the groundwork for a married life built on discussion and compromise. Such discussions can be harmful, but often they can be helpful and constructive, especially when parties are approaching a second marriage (Hitchings 2011: 33).[56]

Indeed, it is striking in practice how many couples feel their marriage is stronger for having had such discussions before the wedding ceremony, rather than feeling that the ready-made divorce settlement makes it weaker. It can be said that negotiating a pre-nup enables couples to negotiate with each other in a way which they will have to learn to do in order to have a successful marriage. Indeed that process of negotiation may enable them to feel more in control, more empowered, within the relationship and thereby

[55] Cf the Law Commission's observation that the absence of binding pre-nuptial agreements does not *stop* people from having such discussions in any event: (2010: para 5.21).

[56] Note also her findings re the use of collaborative law techniques to negotiate pre-nuptial agreements, in place of a more traditionally partisan style of lawyer-led negotiation: (2011: 77–78).

experience more genuine partnership.[57] Couples who can take the active step of altering the legal rights involved in marriage may thereby alter their approach to the union, undertaking a form, if you will, of 'conscious coupling'.[58]

This in turn shows a rather overlooked aspect of pre-nuptial agreements in contemporary English debates. In popular opinion, the pre-nuptial agreement is commonly seen as the thing that gives one party an easy get-out clause, but this is rarely the case. Far more often, a pre-nuptial agreement is the thing which gives a party, particularly a wealthy one, the confidence to enter into marriage at all.[59] While Hitchings' research in England and Wales identified several practitioners with experience of clients who had not gone through with the agreement but had gone ahead with the marriage (2011: 28), in the lead author's experience, it is rare that a party chooses between a marriage with no agreement in place or a marriage with a pre-nup, but rather between a pre-nuptial agreement and no marriage at all. Reassured that their partner has the same approach to marriage as they do, a party can feel more able to enter into a binding union than if these were issues not discussed and agreed. Prior to the *Radmacher* decision, the advice of the lead author, and, anecdotally, of other practitioners, to monied parties was not to marry save for religious or cultural imperatives (Vardag, online). Now the advice, for those who wish to marry, is to go ahead and do so with a pre-nup, and numerous clients have now approached her firm from long-term cohabiting partnerships stating that they have long wished to marry and feel only now that they can do so.

It should be acknowledged that in some cases, the pressure on the other party to agree to the pre-nup in order to secure the marriage may be immense, as in the 'shotgun pre-nup' cases where the female party has fallen pregnant—often very early in the parties' relationship—and the wedding date (often picked early to avoid a visible pregnancy or at least to ensure it happens pre-birth) is looming large.[60] Some practitioners have reported inserting clauses into pre-nuptial agreements reciting the fact that the wedding would not have gone ahead had the agreement not been signed, in an attempt to signal the existence of pressure on the parties to proceed in the hope that it may be taken into account in any future legal proceedings

[57] See eg, Robert Benjamin, www.mediate.com/articles/Benjami.cfm.

[58] Reference to the intended 'conscious uncoupling' declared by G Paltrow and C Martin (2014) on Goop blog, available at: www.goop.com/journal/be/conscious-uncoupling.

[59] In a number of reported cases, the narrative suggests that the pre-nup was a 'but for' condition of one party contracting the marriage: *S v S* [1997] 2 FLR 100, *M v M* [2002] 1 FLR 654, *Radmacher v Granatino* [2010] UKSC 42, *Z v Z (No 2)* [2011] EWHC 2878, *V v V* [2011] EWHC 3230, *AH v PH* [2013] EWHC 3873. See also anecdotal evidence reported to the Law Commission: (Law Commission 2010: para 5.19).

[60] See eg, *M v M* [2002] 1 FLR 654, *K v K* [2022] 1 FLR 120, *Ella v Ella* [2007] EWCA Civ 99.

concerning the agreement (Hitchings 2011: 65–66). However, given the lack of stigma now attaching to cohabitation outside marriage (which makes marriage or not a true choice) and the lack of remedies following separation from cohabitation, securing marriage on the limited terms of the pre-nuptial agreement may be the best choice open to the pregnant party who will otherwise have no claim at all against the father of her child in her own right and only (comparatively limited) claims for the child's benefit.

In 'shotgun' cases, the parties may not have the luxury of the time which can make the process of negotiating a pre-nuptial agreement so potentially valuable in the ways discussed above.[61] However, in less pressured circumstances—and provided the clients approach the solicitors in timely fashion[62]—the very process of creating a pre-nuptial agreement can help the parties work through the difficult issues in a safe, non-confrontational environment that is supportive of their relationship. Negotiations for a pre-nuptial agreement will usually be done between two sets of lawyers, each would-be spouse dealing with their legal team rather than directly with each other.[63] This model of negotiation allows each spouse to explore their ideas and wishes in confidence and without the pressure of being with their intended spouse, facilitating a frankness and openness that might otherwise be absent. As the lawyers shuttle between the two and carry out the negotiation, the issues can be discussed calmly and without emotional escalation. In the lead author's experience, it is not uncommon for parties to take assertive positions in private but to blame these on lawyers, so that they can thrash out their issues whilst remaining amicable with each other once the negotiation has ended.

If conducted in line with best practice, the process can therefore be a positive and cathartic experience for the couple. It can allow them to explore issues that affect marriage in a positive way based on reaching a solution rather than creating conflict. The pre-nuptial agreement and the process of negotiating it can be posited as the foundation for the marriage, something which sets out the couples' views and wishes for their future relationship, rather than as a tool to facilitate any future divorce. This is something that can be reflected in the practicalities of the process, with negotiations taking place in comfortable settings, such as the client's home or an upscale hotel. When the document is signed it is usually without ceremony, but symbolically sees the couples coming together after being with their separate legal

[61] Conversely, the process would ideally not take the years apparently consumed in *BN v MA* [2013] EWHC 4250.

[62] This was reported as a difficulty by some of Hitchings' respondents: if clients only come to the solicitor shortly before the long-since-planned wedding, the time available for negotiation (and associated processes such as disclosure) is necessarily confined. Some practitioners accordingly have a minimum permissible lead-in period for conducting pre-nup negotiations: (Hitchings 2011: 62 et seq).

[63] Contrast the examples of collaborative law practice identified by Hitchings (2011: 77–78).

teams. A well-managed pre-nuptial process can thus become an integral part of the parties' engagement and marriage, rather than being part of the (at that point hypothetical) breakdown.

VIII. CONCLUDING THOUGHTS: A NEW RITE OF MARRIAGE?

It may be argued that developments in the law and practice of pre-nuptial agreements in England and Wales have come to affect not only the rights that accrue on marriage, but also the rite of marriage itself. As couples are given the ability to set out and define their property rights in ways which affect both married life and potential divorce, they change the way marriage is thought of and approached, allowing them to centre their relationship within the wider context of their lives in novel and innovative ways. Business interests or family legacies can be protected. Children from prior relationships and other dependants can be provided for and their interests safeguarded. Couples can use pre-nuptial agreements to try to avoid the pitfalls of previous marriages or allay fears (whether their own or their family's) about their future spouse. In crafting their own document, on their own terms, parties can create a bespoke set of marriage (and divorce) rights, which may depart to a greater or lesser extent from the default position that the law would otherwise supply for them, whilst (under the current law) always ensuring a safety net of needs-based provision. Rather than being entirely alien to the concept of marriage, there are aspects of these agreements which arguably resonate with the old use of marriage settlements to protect wider family interests.

In doing this, couples executing pre-nuptial agreements reflect the changing position of marriage within society. Couples have become increasingly free to choose the formal rites by which their marriage is created (see Haskey, chapter two of this volume), as well as the attendant social 'rites', such as wedding gifts (see Purbrick, chapter four of this volume) and other aspects of the celebrations. Granting couples greater autonomy over the rights conferred by the status of marriage—whilst more profoundly undermining the public aspect of the institution than the choice of ritual—may be regarded as just a natural development along the same spectrum of choice.

Moreover, as previous decades have seen the decoupling of sex and marriage (see Probert, chapter three of this volume), as well as the diminishing link between marriage and family, pre-nuptial agreements allow couples to reconfigure the economic rights that will arise in the event of divorce, and reconsider the relative place of marriage within the broader family. Whilst they might or might not remain a minority marriage practice, the increased use of pre-nuptial agreements and their appearance in public discourse around marriage serve to re-emphasise the concept of marriage as a legal bargain. Rather than being a forgotten part of the nuptial process—a set of implications neglected until a potential divorce might bring them into play—the financial and legal obligations that marriage entails are highlighted. For couples who choose to enter into a pre-nuptial agreement, these implications are just as important as any romantic, sexual or familial aspects of marriage. Re-emphasising these aspects of marriage reminds us that, whilst marriage may no longer mark initiation into sexual relations, home-building or children—all of which may already have commenced—it does still mark a significant change in the legal status of the parties.

For its part too, we have seen that the pre-nuptial agreement is arguably emerging as a rite in itself. Though relatively informal, it is for an increasing number of couples an important part of the process of engagement and marriage, bringing wider kin into the equation again. It can consume a good deal of time and emotional energy and has to be carefully managed. The signing of a pre-nuptial agreement is not just an exchange of contracts, but the culmination of a process that involves a deep exploration of the relationship. In examining the rights asked for and volunteered, couples are forced to examine many issues that would otherwise lay undisturbed. While the result is often a strengthening of the union, it can also mark the end of a relationship. Ultimately though, pre-nuptial agreements redefine the rite of marriage by moving it away from the generally defined civil law into something more bespoke and controlled. In defining their own rights of marriage, the couple individualise and privatise the rite of marriage.

BIBLIOGRAPHY

BARLOW, Anne and SMITHSON, Janet, 'Is modern marriage a bargain? Exploring perceptions of pre-nuptial agreements in England and Wales' (2012) 24 *Child and Family Law Quarterly* 304.

BROYDE, Michael and REISS, Jonathan (2004) 'The Ketubah in America: Its Value in Dollars, its significance in *Halacha* and its Enforceability in Secular Law' (2004) 47 *Journal of Halacha and Contemporary Society* 101, available at: www.jlaw.com/Articles/KETUBAH.pdf.

CRETNEY, Stephen, *Family Law in the Twentieth Century* (Oxford, Oxford University Press, 2003).

FEHLBERG, Belinda and SMYTH, Bruce, 'Binding pre-nuptial agreements in Australia: the first year' (2002) 16 *International Journal of Law, Policy and the Family* 127.

FOLEY, Dylan, 'Author Elizabeth Gilbert finds peace with marital chapter' (14 February 2010) *The Denver Post: Lifestyles*, available at: www.denverpost.com/lifestyles/ci_14385399.

GILBERT, Elizabeth, *Committed: A Love Story* (London, Viking, 2010).

GEORGE, Robert, HARRIS, Peter and HERRING, Jonathan, 'Pre-nuptial agreements: for better or for worse?' (2009) 39 *Family Law* 934.

——, 'With this ring I thee wed (terms and conditions apply)' (2011) 51 *Family Law* 367.

HASKEY, John, 'Marriage Rites—Trends in Marriages by Manner of Solemnisation and Denomination in England and Wales, 1841–2012' in this volume.

——, 'Ante-nuptial agreements: fairness, equality and presumptions' (2011) 127 *Law Quarterly Review* 335.

HERRING, Jonathan, 'The Death Knell of Marriage' (2010) *New Law Journal* 1551.

HERRING, Jonathan, 'Why Marriage Needs to be Less 'Sexy' in this volume.

HITCHINGS, Emma, *A study of the views and approaches of family practitioners concerning marital property agreements* (Bristol, Bristol University, 2011), available at: www.bristol.ac.uk/law/research/researchpublications/2013/maritalpropertyagreements.pdf.

HITCHINGS, Emma, MILES, Joanna and WOODWARD, Hilary, *Assembling the jigsaw puzzle: understanding financial settlement on divorce*, available at: www.bristol.ac.uk/law/research/researchpublications/2013/assemblingthejigsawpuzzle.pdf.

INGLEBY, Richard, 'Rhetoric and Reality: Regulation of Out-of-Court Activity in Matrimonial Proceedings' (1989) 9 *Oxford Journal of Legal Studies* 230.

LAW COMMISSION, *Marital Property Agreements,* Law Com CP 198 (London, TSO, 2010).

——, *Matrimonial Property, Needs and Agreements,* Law Com No 343 (London, TSO, 2014).

LEICHTER, Alexandra, *The Effect of Jewish Divorce Law on Family Law Litigation*, available at: www.iaml.org/cms_media/files/the_effect_of_jewish_divorce_law_on_family_law_litigation.pdf (published 2009).

MILES, Joanna, '*Radmacher v Granatino*: Upping the ante-nuptial agreement' (2009) 21 *Child and Family Law Quarterly* 513.

MINISTRY OF JUSTICE, *Court Statistics Quarterly, Main Tables Jan-March 2014,* available at: www.gov.uk/government/statistics/court-statistics-quarterly-january-to-march-2014.

PROBERT, Rebecca, 'From this Day Forward? Pre-Marital Cohabitation and the Rite of Marriage from the 1960s to the Present Day' in this volume.

PURBRICK, Louise, 'No Frills: Wedding Presents and the Meaning of Marriage, 1945–2003' in this volume.

QUDAMAH, Mawaffaq, *Al-Mughni, vol 9* (Saudi Arabia, Hajr, 1986), translation of relevant excerpt available at: nikaahplanner.files.wordpress.com/2011/01/what-a-woman-may-stipulate-in-contract.pdf.

RABINOWITZ, Mayer E, *Agunot (Abandoned Wives)*, Comments to the Agunot Conference (Jerusalem, 1998).

SCHERPE, Jens (ed), *Marital Agreements and Private Autonomy in Comparative Perspective* (Oxford, Hart Publishing, 2013).

SKOLOFF, Gary N, SINGER, Richard H, and BROWN, Ronald L, *Drafting Prenuptial Agreements* (Wolters Kluwer, looseleaf service).

TRIBE, Alexandra, in J STEWART (ed), *Family Law—Jurisdictional Comparisons* (London, Sweet & Maxwell, 2013).

VARDAG, Ayesha, 'Why I'm having a pre-nup, by the lawyer who made them work in England', *The Telegraph* (8 March 2014), available at: blogs.telegraph.co.uk/news/ayeshavardag/100262189/why-im-having-a-pre-nup-by-the-lawyer-who-made-them-work-in-england/.

——, 'Pre nuptial advice', available at: presswire.com/pr/avs/tramp1.pdf.

WILLIG, Mordechai, 'The Pre-nuptial Agreement: Recent Developments' (2012) 1 *Journal of the Beth Din of America* issue 1, available at www.jlaw.com/Articles/ThePre-nuptialAgreement.pdf.

7

The 'Pure' Relationship, Sham Marriages and Immigration Control

HELENA WRAY

'What first attracted you to short, balding millionaire Paul Daniels?' (Mrs Merton, parody chat show host to Debbie McGee, younger wife of celebrity magician Paul Daniels)

'"... Will you tell me how long you have loved him?"

"It has been coming on so gradually, that I hardly know when it began. But I believe I must date it from my first seeing his beautiful grounds at Pemberley"'. (Jane Austen, *Pride and Prejudice*, Penguin Classics, p 301)

I. INTRODUCTION

THIS CHAPTER INVESTIGATES the circumstances in which marriage rites that involve a non-EEA migrant spouse are subject to additional controls or do not give rise to the right to live together in the UK. Marriages which involve immigration, here called cross-border marriages (Williams 2012: 24), are one of the few instances in which it is considered acceptable to impose added conditions, reflecting, as Abrams (2012) has observed, the particular interest that the state has in immigration control and the substantial benefits which are presumed to flow from immigration status. There are many such conditions (financial, good character etc) but the focus here is on those that aim to detect whether a marriage is only for immigration purposes: a sham marriage.[1] Few people would dispute the right of the state to withhold immigration rights from parties to a sham marriage even though, if such a marriage occurs between two citizens, it generally has the same legal consequences as any other marriage.[2]

[1] Sham marriages are also called bogus marriages, marriages of convenience or immigration marriages. For convenience, the term 'sham marriage' is used throughout this chapter.

[2] See, for example, *Silver v Silver* [1955] 1 WLR 728; *Vervaeke v Smith* [1983] AC 145.

Sometimes, a marriage is entered only for immigration purposes, 'with the sole aim of circumventing the rules on entry and residence'.[3] Commonly however, sham marriage controls capture marriages where one or more of the elements associated with a 'genuine' marriage (such as sexual relations, the raising of children, cohabitation, financial support, affection) is present but the relationship is regarded as tainted by immigration considerations and to be insufficiently 'genuine'. This judgement involves scrutiny of the character of the marriage, from how the parties meet to the wedding celebrations to their daily post-marriage life, but also of their personal characteristics: their age, social and immigration status and ethnicity. It may be adapted to reflect understandings of cultural difference—so that, for example, an arranged marriage is held to a different standard—but it is problematic. First, it is normative and will tend to dismiss marriages that are unconventional, not sham. Secondly, the breadth of regulation and the subjectivity of the assessment process mean that controls expand to include marriages where immigration is one reason but not the only reason for the marriage or where the migrant is otherwise regarded as undesirable. Thus, sham marriage controls permit 'moral gatekeeping' (Wray 2006), protecting the cultural and moral heart of the nation from invasion through exploitation of the naive and against corruption from within by foolish citizens intent on making unsuitable matches. This chapter aims to build on the 'moral gatekeeping' concept, through a closer examination of what is actually determined by sham marriage controls.

Governments often hold migrant families to standards that do not apply where there is no immigration element (Strasser et al 2009). The analysis here suggests that sham marriage controls are also used to identify not only 'poor quality' marriages but 'poor quality' marriage migrants. These controls cannot be detached from the wider functions of immigration control. The last few years have seen, particularly in Northern and Western Europe, the importation into the regulation of family migration of criteria more commonly associated with economic migration, such as high financial thresholds, integration conditions and language tests (Bonjour and de Hart 2013; Wray 2014). Spousal migrants are now being assessed in similar ways to labour migrants and for the same purposes, to ensure that they will be of value to the host society. Controls against sham marriage are a part of that process, a means of detecting not only those who do not sufficiently value the institution of marriage but those whose presence is otherwise undesirable. 'Moral gatekeeping' is not separate from but inherent to the wider gatekeeping functions of immigration control.

Legal definitions of sham marriage may rely on the reasons for the marriage, its present character or both. The definition used in EU law, a marriage

[3] Council Resolution of 4 December 1997 on measures to be adopted on the combating of marriages of convenience ([1997] OJ C382/01 of 16 December 1997).

entered 'with the sole aim of circumventing the rules on entry and residence', relies on the former.[4] Section 24 of the Immigration Act 1999 adopts a similar test but excludes the word 'sole' thus potentially broadening its application. The current test in the immigration rules considers the present character of the marriage, requiring both that a marriage be 'genuine and subsisting' and that the parties intend to live together permanently in the UK.[5] The most recent definition, in section 55 of the Immigration Act 2014, considers both the purpose of the marriage and the current nature of the relationship. When this chapter refers to a sham marriage, it will mean a marriage that is sham according the EU test, that it was entered solely for immigration purposes. This is a useful starting point because it includes only marriages which have no content other than an immigration motive.

Assessing the number of sham marriages is difficult and contentious. Section 24 of the Immigration and Asylum Act 1999 requires marriage registrars to report suspected sham marriages to the Home Office. In 2001, the first year of implementation, 756 such reports were received, rising to 2,712 in 2003 and 2,251 in the first half of 2004, after which the government introduced the certificates of approval scheme discussed later in this chapter (Wray 2011: 161–63). The number of reports dropped substantially after that but rose again, reaching 2,135 in 2013.[6] These figures are often said to be an underestimate, although the inaccuracy could also go the other way, as they are reports of suspicions and it is unknown how many are later confirmed. Widely reported claims of larger numbers, such as the well-publicised estimate made in 2004 that one in five register office marriages in London (or 8,000 marriages per year) were sham, often turn out to be speculative (Wray 2006: 314–15). In April 2011, the Prime Minister made a familiar elision of categories when he claimed that many student visa applications included bogus dependants:

> Consider this: a sample of 231 visa applications for the dependants of students found that only twenty-five percent of them were genuine dependants. The others? Some were clearly gaming the system and had no genuine or loving relationship with the student. Others we just couldn't be sure about.[7]

The most recent Home Office estimate is that 3,000 to 10,000 applications to stay in the UK are made each year on the basis of sham marriages, although how that figure was reached is not clear (Chief Inspector 2014a: 8).

The focus of control has expanded in the past decade. In the past, questions about the marriage were asked only at the point that immigration rights were claimed. This still occurs but, increasingly, it is also the marriage

4 See n 3 above.

5 'State of Changes to Immigration Rules HC 395 as amended', Appendix FM, paras E-ECP.2.6 and E-ECP.2.10.

6 HC Deb, 18 June 2014, col 604W.

7 www.bbc.co.uk/news/uk-politics-13083781.

ceremony itself which is subject to regulation. It is true that the fact of marriage strengthens rights in European law (both Article 8 ECHR and EU law) but such rights do not flow from sham marriages. It is certainly more convenient from an immigration control perspective to prevent marriages from taking place but it is not necessary. However, the wedding ceremony itself and not just its consequences have increasingly become enmeshed in the immigration process. As controls have rarely been confined only to the detection of sham marriages as defined here, the effect is that any marriage involving non-EEA migrants is now controlled at multiple points both before and after the wedding.

The next section of this chapter identifies four broad and porous categories of marriage, placed on a spectrum according to the degree to which immigration considerations played a part in their formation and trajectory. Of these four categories, only one conforms to the definition of 'sham marriage' in the sense of a marriage entered only for immigration purposes. However, marriages in the other categories are often caught by sham marriage controls. The chapter then draws on various episodes in the control of spousal migration in the UK to demonstrate this wider impact before, during and after marriage and argues that it is not an accidental by-product of controls but a central feature.

II. SHAM MARRIAGES: DETERMINING THE (ALMOST) INDETERMINABLE

The concept of a sham marriage assumes that there is a binary divide between marriages entered for 'good' reasons (such as emotional intimacy, sexual fulfilment, raising children) and 'bad' reasons (such as financial gain, immigration, social status). Except where a marriage is entered solely for immigration purposes, a comparatively unusual occurrence which sometimes involves organised crime, this is a false dichotomy (for a discussion, see Wray 2006) and one that is rarely drawn when marriages do not have an immigration aspect to them. While Mrs Merton's mischievous question to Debbie McGee cited at the start of this chapter implied an obvious dominant reason for her marriage, she and Paul Daniels have been married, apparently successfully, since 1988, a long time by entertainment industry standards. Elizabeth Bennet is, as usual, teasing her sister, and her marriage to Mr Darcy is one of the great romances of English literature, but it is hard to imagine Mr Darcy as romantic hero without the grace, power and ease that Pemberley confers.

Sham marriage controls aim, so far as possible, to neutralise the immigration incentive to enter a marriage so that only relationships which are sufficiently untainted are granted immigration advantages. The implied contrast is with a 'pure' marriage (Giddens 1991: 1992), an individualistic relationship based on voluntarism, mutual self-disclosure, equality and the absence of ulterior or instrumental motives: 'the relationship exists solely for whatever rewards that relationship can deliver' (Giddens 1991: 6). Although the social reality of the 'pure relationship' and its correlation with intimacy have been questioned (see Eggebo 2013 for a discussion), it is nevertheless seen in modern European culture as the ideal condition. It is not only the immigration authorities who rely on this model. Applicants may also place their relationship within the template of a 'pure' relationship, existing independently of conventional criteria for compatibility, as a defence against what they consider to be unfair conclusions about their relationship based on its external characteristics (Eggebo 2013: 785).

The powerful hold of the 'pure' marriage ideal is problematic for those who marry within different cultural frameworks, notably those who enter arranged marriages where both the reasons for choosing a partner and the nature of the marital relationship are different (see, for example, Ballard 2008). However, immigration laws can adapt (and have done so to some degree) to accommodate these; the problem is that the underlying suspicions of international arranged marriages mean that such adaptations are often rigid and based on stereotypical assumptions (Shah 2010) so that, just as with non-arranged marriages, those whose relationships do not conform to pre-defined norms have difficulty in meeting expectations (see Carver 2014 for an example). To be acceptable, an arranged marriage must tread a sometimes narrow path between being too 'modern', and thus rejected as lacking credibility, and too traditional, and therefore risks being designated as a forced marriage. There is also a tendency to believe that some things must be true of all 'genuine' marriages, whatever the cultural background (see, for example, Satzewich 2014).

The other problem with the 'pure marriage' ideal is that it treats the immigration advantages of a marriage as a discrete source of corruption that renders the marriage without value. The error is to see the immigration advantages as different in type to the other social advantages that marriage may offer and to ignore the centrality of these in creating 'genuine' marriages. This is in part a professional deformation on the part of the immigration authorities, a tendency to see all actions through the defensive prism of immigration control, but it is also symptomatic of a broader lack of perspective, a failure to appreciate how the world appears to those who enter marriages involving emigration to more developed countries. Looking at marriage migration 'from below' (Beck-Gernsheim 2011: 61) shows how, in an unequal world with few opportunities for movement from poor to rich countries, marriage is an important means of procuring global and thus social mobility, as it always has been. In this light, it is the artificial barrier presented by controls, not the means adopted to surmount it, which represents manipulation and injustice. Marriage to secure the ability to move is no more morally reprehensible and no more sham than aspiring to social advancement through marriage within a state. It is also often the only available avenue for those with relatively little human capital or personal wealth, with gender implications (Palrawala and Uberoi 2008). That it may require a confrontation with state power, the use of intermediaries, displacement over great distances and sometimes sophisticated strategising by individuals and families does not change that.

Although marriage can sometimes be a highly instrumentalised component of a migration strategy (see, for example, Kim 2011), most have substance beyond their immigration purposes and may hold real emotional significance for the parties (Palriwala and Uberoi 2008; Charsley 2012: 7–8). If immigration status represents a considerable material advantage, those who can provide it often appear more glamorous and more desirable. This spouse, in their turn, may be attracted by the chance of a higher status match than they might otherwise aspire to in terms of appearance, education, age and so on or by the embodiment of 'old-fashioned', 'family' or 'simpler' values in an apparently less sophisticated partner. Apparently unlikely intimacies can arise through shared labour market niches or experience of isolation or marginalisation. The 'cultural logic of desire' (Del Rosario 2008) means that emotional attachment is not separate from but enmeshed with the other gains that marriage may bring and these are, in turn, connected to global power relations and their cultural manifestations and, via this route, to immigration status.

The extent to which potential immigration gains means that other disadvantages are overlooked is something which even the parties themselves may not know and certainly cannot easily be uncovered through an administrative process. This is a difficulty which those engaged in the adversarial frontline of immigration control, whether on behalf of the state or of migrants, find it difficult to acknowledge. States often talk about the inherent improbability of certain marriages taking place, concluding that this indicates a sham marriage and no hardship is caused by an immigration refusal. Advocates for migrants will present such marriages as unconnected to immigration; to acknowledge the presence of such motives risks playing into the hands of those advocating tougher controls. Legal scholars will focus on legal definitions and categories. The assumption in all cases is that a marriage is either sham or genuine, and it is a question of drawing the boundaries in the right place.

This discussion however shows that the term 'sham marriage' has little meaning from the perspective of migrant spouses and their partners except in those comparatively few cases where parties enter an arrangement to undergo a marriage ceremony with no consequences for the lives of either beyond an immigration status and, perhaps, a cash exchange. However, states often seek to regulate a much wider range of marriages under the designation of 'sham marriages'. These over-inclusive measures show the weight that is placed on marriage when immigration is involved. As Abrams

(2012) points out, the state expects different things of marriage in different contexts and expects a great deal in the immigration context where the advantages attaching to recognition of a marriage-related claim are regarded as momentous and where the exercise of national sovereign power is considered to trump personal interests.

Of all the possible functions of controls, those connected with culture, morality and national identity have attracted particular attention from scholars, including this author (Wray 2006, 2006a, 2009; Bonjour and de Hart 2013; Strasser et al 2009). Marriage is a social institution, the site of physical, cultural and moral reproduction. Marriage migration permits outsiders into the heart of the nation state and the importation and reproduction of harmful cultural practices, undermining presumed national values of gender equality and individual freedom (Bonjour and de Hart 2013: 64), a 'peaceful penetration' (Abrams 2011) that has the potential to change and corrupt from within. It is unsurprising that controls on marriage migration, including on sham marriage, can be characterised as moral gatekeeping, focusing on accepted models of marriage and excluding those that are culturally or socially deviant. However, moral gatekeeping is not, itself a discrete concept. What is socially or morally unacceptable is closely entwined with questions of social class, race, ethnicity and, in the case of immigration, legal status. As well as marriages that have no meaning or content other than to secure an immigration advantage, sham marriage controls may impact upon marriages in which immigration played a variable role in either the decision to marry or the way that the marriage is conducted. Which of these marriages ends up being included by controls depends not only on the character of the marriage but on the characteristics of the protagonists. As this chapter will show, even marriages in which immigration advantages are entirely absent may be caught by controls that are concerned with the individual, not the marriage.

The relationship between these two factors—individual characteristics and the character of the marriage—is critical. Certain personal characteristics will trigger a closer scrutiny of the marriage (Wray 2006b: 126). This may not always be unjustified; an irregular migrant has more motivation than others to enter a sham marriage. However, this more intense examination itself increases the likelihood of an unfavourable judgement. And what if the additional scrutiny is because the migrant's nationality is associated with non-compliance or because it is believed that there is an economic incentive to emigrate to the host state? While there is extensive attention paid to marriage migration involving some nationalities, others, such as South Africans, Americans and Australians although numerically significant, are rarely mentioned or examined (Charsley 2012: 877–79). Guidance to marriage registrars suggests that some nationalities are over-represented in sham marriages (Charsley 2012a: 17). To what extent is an apparently objective investigation not discovering but constructing a sham marriage because it uncovers an underlying instrumentalism that is present in many or even all marriages but which only becomes visible when placed under such harsh lights?

Focusing on whether or not a marriage is 'sham' is therefore usually not the point. The key issue is to understand the circumstances in which states consider themselves justified in withholding immigration rights from couples engaged in international marriage and, increasingly, in intervening in the wedding ceremony itself. The next part of this chapter attempts to unpack the highly compressed concept of the sham marriage, examining more closely the nature of the marriages that may be affected.

III. A TYPOLOGY OF CROSS-BORDER MARRIAGES

Although their prevalence is uncertain, it is likely that sham marriages do take place. They may be entered for commercial reasons, including as part of an organised scheme, or between two friends or acquaintances in which case money does not always change hands. Such marriages are contracted 'with the sole aim of circumventing the rules on entry and residence' and fall within the narrow EU definition of abuse of rights under which admission may be refused to spouses in marriages contracted by EU citizens exercising free movement rights. Where this occurs, few would argue that governments should be obliged to recognise claims for admission and the issue is more often around burden and standard of proof.[8]

States, however, often wish to restrict a much wider range of marriages. For instance, in the Tribunal case of *Papajorgji*, the parties were refused on the 'sole aim' grounds even though they had been married for 14 years, had two children and were living in a common household, facts which precluded any plausible finding that the marriage had been entered solely for the purpose of obtaining an immigration advantage many years later.[9] National regulation is not so constrained and, as this chapter will show, often controls a much wider range of marriages than those entered solely for immigration purposes. For example, the current guidance to UK immigration officers for determining a sham marriage includes factors associated with forced marriage, itself a concept with blurred boundaries (Siddiqui 2005: 290–94), so that marriages where there is considered to be insufficient equality between the parties may be treated as sham. The sham marriage can easily become

[8] In contrast to the immigration rules where the applicant must show that he meets the criteria, states have the burden of proof of showing a sham marriage under EU law: European Commission *Communication from the Commission to the European Parliament and the Council on guidance for better transposition and application of Directive 2004/38/EC on the right of citizens of the Union and their family members to move and reside freely within the territory of the Member States* (COM 2009 313) 2 July 2009.

[9] *Papajorgji (EEA spouse—marriage of convenience)* Greece [2012] UKUT 38 (IAC).

a free-floating concept capable of being attached to almost any marriage of which there is disapproval, although some marriages are more vulnerable than others to such a designation. Understanding how this is possible requires an understanding of the complex ways in which immigration factors may act upon marriage decisions and how these are regarded, a typology of cross-border marriages (although one in which boundaries are fluid and blurred) on a spectrum between a marriage entered solely for such an advantage and one where it played no part at all.

If the fixed point at the start of the spectrum is a marriage that is solely for immigration purposes, the next broad category is those marriages where the usual characteristics of a married relationship such as cohabitation are present but it is suspected that the marriage would not have happened had the potential advantages of immigration not been present. This is the most complex and controversial category, as marriages that are deemed to fall within it are often treated as sham and, for this reason, it receives most attention here.

One sub-group often placed in this category is arranged marriages. Cross-border arranged marriages are common in some UK minority populations, particularly those from South Asia (see Charsley 2012: 869–72). From the mid-1960s to the late 1990s, they were almost always treated as vehicles for immigration under the primary purpose rule (discussed below). In an arranged marriage, love is expected to follow rather than precede the marriage so that evidence of prolonged courtship and familiarity is not usually available and it was relatively easy to fill the void with a presumption of immigration-related motives. The complex social functions of these marriages were often ignored, as was the parties' personal commitment, even though such marriages often proved themselves resilient and stable during many years' separation when visas were persistently refused (Wray 2011: chapter 5).

Practice did improve during the 2000s although the level of understanding was variable and sometimes unreliable (Wray 2006b; Shah 2010; Wray 2011: chapter 9; Shah 2010). The most recent published guidance to immigration officers, however, contains a renewed focus on a European version of marriage (Carver 2014) or a very narrowly defined version of arranged marriage, and an emphasis on forced marriage, which suggests that arranged marriages are again likely to be treated sceptically although this may be less visible now that other, recently introduced conditions have made marriage migration much harder generally.

Emigration may indeed be one motive for entering an arranged marriage, particularly when other opportunities for migration are not available (Ballard 2008) but that is rarely the only factor. Cross-border arranged marriages are seen as carrying advantages besides immigration, partners are usually carefully selected and they are regarded as a lifelong commitment in which the spouses themselves and their families have invested heavily, emotionally and financially (see, for example, Shaw and Charsley 2006), although the UK parties may now be more willing to contemplate exit if the marriage does not work (Charsley 2013: 11). Although it is a flexible and adaptable practice that evolves in response to other social changes (for a summary of the literature, see Grillo 2011: 85–88), the reasons for such marriages commonly include traditions of caste or cousin marriage, the reinforcement of cultural values, the consolidation or enhancement of family assets and the maintenance of wider affective family ties. However, these non-migration reasons are largely antithetical to the values of individualism and equality represented by the ideal 'pure' marriage, and thus they carry little weight against suspicions of immigration instrumentalism, while the lack of relationship before marriage means that the hardship of refusal may be regarded as insignificant. Even if it is accepted that these marriages are not sham, in the sense that they were not entered solely for immigration purposes, there may be indifference to or even support for their inclusion within that category.

Also within this second group are what might be called 'opportunistic' marriages, including the French concept of *mariage gris* which imagines a unilateral deception; the migrant spouse develops an intimate relationship, enters the marriage and even has children always with the intention of leaving once residency has been attained, a judgement that, by definition, can only be made retrospectively (Kofman et al 2010). In the UK, the term is not used but similar suspicions can be detected in the government's criteria for a sham marriage, which include former sponsorship of an overseas spouse and a previous immigration refusal or irregular status.[10] While prolonged deception may be rare in practice, these suspicions reflect the belief that mixed motives may be involved. Wray (2006a) found that such judgements have a gender dimension, being often made against men marrying older women who were castigated as naive or even foolish for failing to recognise that their only attraction is their passport (see also in respect of the Netherlands, Bonjour and de Hart 2013: 66). Marriages between migrant women from relatively impoverished backgrounds and British men which may involve similar instrumental motives do not receive the same attention, although they are not uncommon. Charsley et al (2012:874), for example, report that women comprise 93 per cent of Thai marriage settlement applicants (compared to 60 per cent overall; Charsley 2012: 866) and their marriages have often been facilitated by British men travelling to Thailand or using introduction agencies for this purpose (see also Sim 2012) but this is rarely problematised or even discussed.

In all the marriages in this category, it is generally established that the parties have a relationship and an assessment of either deceit or opportunism can only be made by drawing on the template of an acceptable marriage or by detecting a lack of commitment in interview, inevitably a subjective

[10] Appendix FM-02, para 3.2.

judgement (Wray 2006a; 2006b). Gender and ethnicity are often implicit factors here; migrant men, particularly from certain countries, have often been regarded as more likely to be calculating and manipulative in their relationships (Wray 2015; Strasser et al 2009; Bonjour and de Hart 2013). Citizen women meanwhile have a particular duty to maintain and reproduce national culture (Yuval-Davis 2008: 43–45, 67) and fail to live up to their responsibilities if they marry 'unsuitably', paying the price through separation or exile.

The danger is that the immigration aspect of these marriages will be over stated because the marriage is scrutinised outside its overall context. It may be that the migrant has chosen a partner who is older, more encumbered or less attractive than they might otherwise expect. However, for an irregular migrant who lacks a settled home and stability, an established family unit may offer much needed emotional security. For an aspiring migrant, including in an arranged marriage, an individual's personal attractiveness may be enhanced by the opportunities they offer for a more interesting and comfortable life. The immigration advantage is entwined with the other social advantages that the relationship offers and these advantages are entwined with, not apart from, the affective ties between the parties.

Such an observation becomes banal once immigration is regarded not as an exceptional circumstance but as one possible social advantage amongst the many that may result from marriage, and once it is appreciated that affective ties between married couples are, in any event, of varying intensity and duration. Where individuals have limited life choices, they will use marriage strategically for the opportunities it offers but they do not regard themselves as any less married or even less loving for that. There is no reason to imagine that marriages in which immigration advantages add lustre to otherwise unlikely partners differ in that respect.

Some such marriages may last and be as emotionally satisfying as marriages in which immigration considerations played no part. Others will end and it is possible that this happens more often than in other relationships but then there are particular strains on cross-border marriages (Charsley 2005) which rigorous immigration controls may exacerbate, creating a self-fulfilling prophecy. The ideal of the 'pure' relationship is anyway predicated on the parties remaining committed only while the relationship offers them non-instrumental benefits so subsequent divorce does not necessarily place the marriage outside that paradigm. Sometimes, the non-migrant partner may consider, in retrospect, that they have been used to some degree or that they were unrealistic in their expectations, but such feelings are not confined to the breakdown of relationships involving immigration. It is anyway not apparent that it is the function of immigration control to prevent people making unwise marital choices.

Further along the spectrum of marriages is another loosely bounded category of relationships which begin with no consideration for immigration factors but whose character or course is partially determined by them. They include marriages that take place sooner than they otherwise might because that is the only way for the couple to stay together or where, since a couple must live somewhere, they decide to go where there are the best economic or other opportunities. In other cases, dowry payments may be inflated in recognition of the benefits that a cross-border marriage represents (Charsley 2012a: 26). Described in this way, few would describe these marriages as 'sham' and it is possible that, if asked, many couples in international relationships would place themselves at this point of the spectrum, reflecting the social ideal of the 'pure' marriage, although Eggebo (2013: 783) found that her interviewees sometimes demonstrated understanding of how motives may be mixed.

Such marriages are not explicitly targeted by restrictions although they may be affected by blanket measures. The difficulty arises in making a reliable judgement that the marriage falls into this category and not the more 'opportunistic' one just discussed, as couples in both categories sometimes have much in common: there is evidence of a relationship between them but they may have married relatively soon after meeting, perhaps in a small ceremony; a larger than average dowry may change hands; the migrant partner lacks status in the UK or comes from a poorer country. The only way to judge the difference is to assess the probability that this couple would have decided to marry irrespective of any immigration considerations, comparing the relationship to the template of the 'genuine' marriage and importing its cultural and social norms.

In this scenario, it is the ability to present the facts of the marriage in a persuasive light that is critical, overcoming the disadvantage of characteristics that cannot be changed such as immigration status, age or ethnicity: 'displaying genuineness' (Carver 2014). An arranged marriage will be accepted into this category only if it complies in all respects with the assumed template for such a marriage, which often includes patrilocal residence although this is a flexible tradition and reversal of gender roles is not uncommon when marriage involves migration (Kofman 2004; Ballard 2005; Charsley 2005). Despite this, men applying for entry are often regarded as having economic or other instrumental motivations, reflected in their higher refusal rates (Wray 2006b; Charsley 2012a: 23), and their marriages are considered to be in the second more opportunistic category. Considerations of who is a 'good' migrant will also affect this judgement; the same facts about a relationship are likely to be differently interpreted depending on the country of origin, immigration status and other factors. Even if it is accepted that a couple falls within this category, that does not necessarily mean that they are excluded from blanket measures directed at sham marriages.

At the end of the spectrum are marriages untouched in any way by immigration factors. These marriages are relatively rare as they require equality of resources and prospects between the parties (or an imbalance in favour of the migrant) that is usually unrealistic given the UK's comparative wealth. As Williams (2010: 83) points out, cross-border marriages are more likely than marriages between citizens to involve inequalities. Arranged marriages and couples where the aspiring migrant spouse party has a relatively impoverished background or does not have an immigration status will usually be unable to demonstrate that they fall into this narrow group, particularly if they cannot present a persuasive relationship narrative that will enable immigration officers to feel comfortable in accepting the marriage (see Wray 2011: 219 for an absurd example of how this can unfold). Those couples also find it hard to show that they belong in the third category for the reasons already discussed and may find that they are regarded as belonging to the second 'opportunistic' category, or that they are caught by blanket measures based on their situation or attributes.

There are thus four broad and porous categories into which a cross-border marriage may be placed: the sham marriage where immigration is the only purpose, marriages where immigration was one purpose, marriages whose course has been partially determined by immigration and marriages in which opportunities for immigration were not a factor at all. In reality, the vast majority will fall into the middle two categories and this creates serious regulatory difficulties. If the right of governments to refuse rights to those in the first category is undisputed, the history of immigration control shows that this is rarely sufficient and governments usually want to go further, bringing into the ambit of the 'sham marriage' the 'opportunistic' marriages of the second category. The problem, however, is that such marriages are not 'sham' and, whatever their initial motivation, the emotional and other costs of refusal may be high particularly but not only if children are involved. A further difficulty is that the boundary between this category and the third one, where the course of events is influenced by the existence of migration controls, is blurred. Deciding which side of the line a particular marriage falls is a subjective judgement which will involve normative assessments of the quality of the relationship and which is likely to be influenced by the inherent value attached to that particular migrant, a product of factors such as nationality, culture and social class. Finally, governments may resort to blanket measures that affect certain categories of migrants irrespective of where they are placed on the spectrum.

IV. REGULATING SHAM MARRIAGE—OR REGULATING MARRIAGE?

This section discusses how the regulation of sham marriages in the UK controls a far wider range of marriages than those entered only for immigration purposes and has expanded its reach beyond the immigration system into the marriage arrangements and ceremony.[11] This enlargement, part of

[11] For a more detailed chronological account up to 2010, see Wray 2011; chapters 2 and 7.

the overall expansion of immigration control beyond the physical border, means that couples where one partner is a non-EEA migrant must overcome protracted and multiple hurdles before they can exercise a right that non-migrant couples take for granted.

A. Pre-Marriage Controls

As already mentioned, section 24 of the Immigration and Asylum Act 1999 required marriage registrars to report suspected sham marriages to the Home Office, although Church of England marriages were excluded, their procedures being regarded as sufficient to deter sham marriages (Stevens 2001: 421). The guidance to marriage registrars is not publicly available but was reported in 2012 to include factors such as the absence of mutual knowledge, use of notes to answer questions about the other person, reluctance to provide personal information, absence of a mutual language, payment to one of the parties, absence of interaction and apparent direction by a third party. Certain national pairings are noted to be common subjects of reports, creating a potentially self-reinforcing cycle (Charsley 2012a: 16–17). While these factors might indicate a sham marriage, they are certainly not conclusive and can only be judged during the brief official interactions that take place before the ceremony.

A report might result in enforcement action at the marriage and this has become more likely since the start of Operation Mellor in January 2013, an 'intelligence-led' enforcement initiative to, amongst other things, disrupt suspicious weddings. Between 14 January and 30 September 2013, there were 500 operations, leading to 334 arrests for immigration offences and 78 removals (Chief Inspector 2014a: 10). Caution is needed in interpreting these statistics. One of the aims of the initiative was to penalise immigration offenders and it may not be the case that the arrests were for sham marriage offences. There has been at least one report of a genuine marriage being raided.[12] A wedding is one of the few occasions when irregular migrants must notify the authorities in advance of their presence at a particular place and time and it is arguable that ceremonies are now an opportunity for pure immigration control, as demonstrated by the arrest at her daughter's wedding of the Colombian cleaner whose illegal employment had caused the resignation of Immigration Minister, Mark Harper.[13]

The approving description of an enforcement operation by the Independent Chief Inspector for Borders and Immigration (2014a) appears excessively complacent about the seriousness of disrupting a wedding ceremony

[12] '"Sham marriage" police storm real wedding', *Camden New Journal*, 7 November 2013.

[13] 'Border police arrest cleaner at heart of Mark Harper immigration row', *The Guardian*, 18 July 2014.

on the basis of unproven suspicions. It describes the entry of uniformed enforcement staff into the waiting room, followed by separate interview to determine if the marriage is sham (depending, for example, on answers to questions about the bedroom flooring), arrest and possible handcuffing. Immigration concerns, and in particular the detection of illegal immigrants, are clearly seen as trumping all other considerations. There appears also to be a performative element here, a display of state power over immigrants at even the most significant moments of life.

Pre-marriage controls developed further with sections 19–25 of the Asylum and Immigration (Treatment of Claimants etc) Act 2004, which provided that all those under immigration control, unless they had indefinite leave to remain or had entered from abroad on a fiancé or marriage visit visa, had to obtain permission to marry through a certificate of approval. The application cost £135, later rising to £295. Irregular migrants, asylum seekers and those who only had short-term leave were routinely refused. Exceptions were made only where there was terminal or long-term illness or inability to travel due to pregnancy. The scheme had an instantaneous effect; by June 2005, four months after implementation, there were 60 per cent fewer notices of marriage in some London Boroughs and around 25 per cent fewer in Birmingham and Leicester. Between 2004 and 2005, the number of marriages celebrated in the UK fell by 10 per cent to their lowest level since 1896 and this was attributed to the scheme (Wray 2011:161–67).

In 2008, the House of Lords held the legislation was discriminatory because of the exemption for Church of England marriages, while the blanket nature of implementation and the financial cost breached article 12 (right to marry and found a family).[14] There were similar findings in the European Court of Human Rights.[15] There were some changes in implementation to meet these objections, but the statute, including the discriminatory provision, was not amended until 2010 when the scheme was finally abolished.

Part 4 of the Immigration Act 2014 has enacted a successor to both the 1999 reporting requirements and the certificates of approval scheme although it has not, at the time of writing, been implemented. It avoids the blanket ban which was one reason the certificates of approval scheme failed by providing that, while all marriages involving non-EEA migrants without indefinite leave, permanent residence or a marriage visa will be referred for possible investigation, decisions on whether to investigate will be made on an individual basis. Closer examination however reveals that the process is not primarily concerned with the nature of the marriage but with administrative compliance. There are increased evidential requirements (and the evidence may be rejected if 'reasonably' believed to be false) before notice of

[14] *R (on the application of Baiai) v Secretary of State for the Home Department* [2008] UKHL 53.

[15] *O'Donoghue v United Kingdom* [2010] ECHR 2022.

the marriage is accepted and the outcome of the investigation (and therefore the ability to marry) depends not on the character of the marriage but on compliance with the investigation.

Pre-marriage controls have become a major element in the regulation of sham marriage. In all cases, however, they seem to be a blunt instrument capable of disrupting or preventing a far wider range of marriages than those that are sham. There is assumed to be a strong correlation between lack of long-term immigration status and a sham marriage. The certificates of approval scheme affected all marriages involving non-nationals, as will the new scheme in the 2014 Act. The reporting requirements, in principle, attempt to identify only sham marriages but rely on external indications coupled with a focus on immigration status as the basis for disruption of a wedding ceremony. In all cases, the process of getting married and even the ceremony itself have become an exercise in immigration control affecting all migrants.

B. Post-Marriage Controls

In 1969, the admission of Commonwealth husbands and fiancés was limited to those 'presenting special features'. The rationale was that, because 1,676 applications had been made during 1968, marriage was being used as a means of entering, working and settling in the UK outside immigration controls. Many (although not all) white Commonwealth men were exempt from controls and the new measures severely affected the non-white Commonwealth husbands of non-white British citizens and residents. The white British wives of non-white husbands were more likely to plead successfully that they could not relocate to places where they would be culturally isolated (Dummett and Nicol 1990: 206–7; Bhabha and Shutter 1994: 57–59 and chapter 4). Nonetheless, white women were adversely affected by the prohibition (only ten Australian and six Canadian husbands were admitted during 1973; Wray 2011: 52, fn 56) and it became the subject of extensive campaigning, based primarily around the hardship endured by these white women. The rule was too crude an instrument to be politically acceptable and was removed in 1974, soon to be replaced by the primary purpose rule.

The primary purpose rule was first introduced into the immigration rules in 1977, was refined over the next period and became a major means of restricting marriage migration, particularly by men, from 1985 when the government was compelled to equalise the immigration rules after the *Abdulaziz* case.[16] It was removed from the rules in 1997. The rule required an applicant to establish that the primary purpose of the marriage was

[16] *Abdulaziz, Cabales and Balkandali v United Kingdom* (1985) 7 EHRR 471.

not admission to the UK. Proving a negative is always difficult and was especially onerous for those in arranged marriages who could not show a prior relationship and the personal familiarity that usually characterises non-arranged marriages. It was widely used against men, particularly from the Indian sub-continent, whose tradition of patrilocal marriage was apparently breached by their desire to move to the UK, raising the inference that the primary reason for the marriage was emigration. The rule was only one way in which non-white spousal migration to the UK was severely curtailed in the three decades before 1997. Other methods included hostile interviews and reliance on minor discrepancies in answers, lengthy delays and protracted application processes, excessive demands for documentation, and dubious medical examinations, including virginity testing (for a more detailed account of the rule and of these practices, see Wray 2011: chapters 3, 4 and 5; Juss 1997: chapters 2 and 3; Sachdeva 1993).

The primary purpose rule, on its face, affected a wider range of marriages than those in the first category outlined in this chapter, drawing in marriages in the second category where there is a relationship but immigration was a factor in the decision to marry. Because of the political and institutional hostility to these marriages and the refusal to acknowledge the complexity of South Asian marriage arrangements, it also drew in couples who were in the third and fourth categories, where immigration was only incidental or had no impact at all. All this is evident from its application to couples who quite clearly had a continuing relationship, including the birth of children and visits over many years. Even where the parties had an alternative explanation for how their marriage came about this was disbelieved, so fixed was the assumption that South Asian families were determined to emigrate even at the cost of unsuitable and unhappy marriages. The consequent distress and loneliness for all concerned was considerable (see, for example, Menski 1999) and caused immense and lasting anger amongst the UK's population of South Asian origin.

One rather unusual example from contemporary reports shows how individuality and attachments were routinely discounted in favour of stereotyped assumptions. A husband seeking to join his wife in the UK was refused on primary purpose grounds. His wife, the sponsor, was a deaf-mute and the immigration officer could not understand why she had been chosen over her non-disabled sister other than because she lived in the UK. In fact, the applicant had been orphaned as a child and taken in by the sponsor's family. Two lonely children had formed an exceptionally close bond, communicating through an invented, private sign language. The sponsor had moved to the UK to access better medical facilities but the separation had left both parties distraught (Powell 1993: 83–98).

The primary purpose rule was finally removed by the new Labour government in 1997. After that the main way of testing for a sham marriage upon first application was the requirement that the parties have a subsisting marriage and intend to live together permanently, requirements that had been present in the immigration rules for many years but only became widely used after the demise of primary purpose. The tests are concerned with the current state of the marriage and the parties' intentions for the future rather than reasons for marriage and do not require a retrospective evaluation of motives. This point was appreciated by the Tribunal but not always by immigration officers who sometimes refused marriages on 'intention' grounds because of their inferences about why the marriage had been entered when the parties lived together and even had children (for a discussion, see Wray 2006a; Clayton 2014: 273–75).

On the other hand, by focusing on one major characteristic of most marriages (cohabitation) and the current state of the relationship, the rule fails to acknowledge the variability and complexity of marriage. Evidence that the relationship has continued in some form during a past period of separation should enable both elements of the rule (subsisting and intention to live together) to be met,[17] but the rule can affect those who are 'living apart together' (Levin 2004) ie maintaining a committed relationship without cohabiting. The Tribunal has found that the rule is satisfied in some such situations (as when couples are separated by work commitments) but not in others (as when separation was due to the husband's imprisonment).[18] There is also potential for cultural normativity: in *AB (Bangladesh)*[19] a husband in a polygamous marriage who intended to divide his time between his UK-based wife and his wife in Bangladesh was found to lack the intention to live permanently with his wife in the UK even though the durability of the relationship was not in question. In *ZB and HB*, intention to live together was found to be absent when the parties had lived together in Pakistan and had a child.[20] However, the sponsor was mentally and physically disabled (capacity was also an issue in this case) and the Tribunal decided that the applicant did not intend to live with him 'as his wife' although the intention to live under the same roof was not questioned. It is not clear if this was a reference to their future sexual relationship (which should have been irrelevant) or the likely nature of the interaction between them in the absence of mutual communication and understanding. This case betrays a preoccupation with marriages that involve an element of caring which has become more prominent in recent years (see below).

[17] *Goudey (subsisting marriage—evidence) Sudan; sub nom Goudey v Entry Clearance Officer, Cairo* [2012] UKUT 00041 (IAC).

[18] *Shabbana Bibi v Entry Clearance Officer, Islamabad* [2002] UKIAT 06623; see discussion at Clayton 2014: 274.

[19] *AB (Settlement—6 months in UK) Bangladesh; sub nom AB v Entry Clearance Officer, Dhaka* [2004] UKIAT 00314.

[20] *ZB and HB (Validity and recognition of marriage) Pakistan; ZB and HB v Entry Clearance Officer, Islamabad* [2009] UKIAT 00040.

The 'subsisting' and 'intention to live together' test is thus capable of being applied to a wider range of marriages than those entered solely for immigration purposes although it comes closer to addressing the issue of sham marriages than some of the other controls discussed in this chapter. It also seems to have been applied in the period after the abolition of the primary purpose rule with some degree of cultural sensitivity (Wray: 2006b; 2011; chapter 9). It relies on a conventional model of marriage based on lifelong cohabitation and has, in practice, been used to refuse marriages where there is an element of disapproval for the reasons of the marriage (see also Wray:2006a). It nudges parties towards the model of the 'pure' relationship but the emphasis on outward characteristics and intention gives it a more pragmatic slant.

In July 2012, the immigration rules were amended as part of a series of changes that made most family migration, including spousal migration, much more difficult. The 'subsisting' and 'intention to live together' tests were separated and are now two separate conditions; applicants must show both that the relationship is 'genuine and subsisting' and that they intend to 'live together permanently in the UK'. More significant is new guidance which sets out factors 'associated' both positively and negatively with genuine and subsisting marriages.[21] While these are said not to be a checklist, it seems that a very wide range of marriages could now be brought within the ambit of the criterion.

Factors which indicate a genuine and subsisting relationship include evidence of a current, long-term relationship, cohabitation, shared responsibility for children, shared financial arrangements, practical arrangements by the parties or their families for living together in the UK and (in the case of an arranged marriage) consent by both parties. There is a much longer list of 22 possible negative indicators which include public statements that the marriage is sham or forced, involvement of other family members in or evidence here of forced marriage, apparent lack of capacity to consent (even if not independently verified), failure to attend or otherwise avoiding an interview, lack of arrangements for living in the UK, the circumstances of the wedding (for example, few guests), lack of mutual knowledge, disagreement as to the 'core facts of the relationship', absence of a common language, exchange of money unless part of a dowry, lack of shared responsibilities or cohabitation, one partner who needs care and the other is a medical professional, and previous entry or sponsorship as a spouse, unlawful residence or refusal of an application to come to the UK.

It is easy to see how some couples, particularly newly-weds without children, any history of cohabitation or joint finances might struggle to show evidence of the positive factors. The negative factors may be present outside a sham marriage. The conflation of forced marriage with sham marriage

[21] Home Office, *Immigration Rules*, Appendix FM 2.0.

reinforces the impression that the decision-maker is being invited to judge the quality of the marriage rather than whether it fits into the narrow category of sham marriages as does the reference to disability and carers. Disability is sometimes a factor in forced marriage but coercion is an independent reason for refusal. Individuals without capacity are already protected by laws on the validity and recognition of marriage.[22] Beyond that, including in this list marriages between those with disabilities and their potential carers implies a strong judgement about what marriage should be for.

There is also scope to make a judgement on the quality of the migrant through reference to factors such as previous sponsorship, refused immigration applications and unlawful residence. This is consonant with the rest of the reforms of July 2012 which also introduced very onerous financial requirements and a long list of suitability requirements which exclude those who have failed to comply even in minor ways with the authorities (for example, recent minor offending, failure to attend for interview or the unknowing submission of false information). There is also the pre-entry English language test, introduced in 2010. Immigration rights, it seems, are to be the preserve of the respectable and capable middle classes.

On the other hand, some of the factors may indeed be present in a sham marriage: the list avoids some crude stereotyping (differences in age, social or cultural background or religion are not mentioned, for example) and the need to make an individualised decision is stressed. The sense that it goes further arises from the number of negative indicators, the emphasis on forced marriage and immigration status, which demonstrate how easily measures against sham marriages blur into other forms of control, and the general anti-immigration context in which they were introduced. At the time of writing, however, there is little evidence as to how this guidance has been operated.

Other post-marriage controls include the probationary period, during which residence is conditional and which has been, at various times, one year, two years and, since 2012, five years. The significance of the probationary period is not only that it tests the durability of the relationship but it tests the level of commitment, as life is more difficult for the couple while it is in place. In particular, the migrant spouse is barred from receiving public funds or benefits such as home tuition fees, a major drawback now that the probationary period is so protracted. It also increases the vulnerability of the migrant spouse to domestic abuse.

Commitment is also tested by requiring migrant spouses in the UK to leave in order to make their application from abroad. This has the added benefit, from a government point of view, of ensuring that those perceived

[22] See, for example, *KC and NNC v City of Westminster Social & Community Services Dept and IC* [2008] EWCA Civ 198.

as having bypassed the immigration system do not 'jump the queue'. The certificates of approval scheme required those refused permission to marry to leave the UK to apply for the necessary visa. The prohibition on those either without leave or with only short-term leave from switching to leave on the basis of marriage, a change made in 2002 and which was explicitly linked to the prevention of sham marriages, had a similar effect (Home Office 2002: 101). The impact of this change was drastic, particularly on failed asylum seekers and irregular migrants who had married and started families in the UK and were now faced with removal at enormous cost to their family lives, often to unstable regions where accessing visa facilities might be dangerous, difficult and costly. Two examples give a flavour of the consequences. In one instance upheld by the Tribunal, the applicant was required to return to a highly unstable Iraq shortly after the Gulf War, obtain travel documents, negotiate Jordanian border controls, endure the cost and danger of travelling from Iraq to Jordan and remain in Jordan to obtain a visa that would previously have been given without his leaving the UK. In another, the father, an overstayer, was deeply involved in the care of his two children, one of whom was disabled. It was unclear that the mother could cope on her own and the family was likely to need welfare support as a result of the father's departure, making a successful application for admission under the rules less likely (Wray 2015). The policy was later found by the House of Lords to breach article 8 although that finding had limited impact in practice (see Wray 2015 for a discussion).

Post-marriage controls have often widened the meaning of the sham marriage to include within controls those outside the first category of marriages discussed in this chapter. The primary purpose rule attempted to include marriages within the second category but often went much wider. The 'genuine' and 'subsisting' and 'intention' tests are related to the task of identifying sham marriages, with a focus on the existing and future relationship rather than the motives for the marriage. However, they involve an assessment of the marriage that permits judgements about the quality of the marriage rather than whether it is sham, while the growing focus on immigration status evident in the recent guidance suggests that immigration motives are being reintroduced as a factor, targeting the 'opportunistic' marriage of the second category. The probationary period and the requirement to leave the UK to obtain leave test the parties' commitment to the marriage with the implicit aim of distinguishing between the second and third categories.

V. CONCLUSION

The controls cited in the previous section demonstrate that sham marriage controls are almost never concerned only with detecting marriages entered with the sole aim of procuring an immigration advantage. Several controls aim to limit the second category: marriages where immigration was a factor in the decision to marry. Sometimes, controls affect all migrants of a particular type, usually those without immigration status or only short-term status.

Controls that aim to determine the quality of the marriage in order to exclude the first and second categories of marriage may compare the marriage to an ideal template (as with 'genuine and subsisting') or require the parties to show their commitment by overcoming additional hurdles and obstacles, as with the ban on switching into marriage from within the UK. These latter techniques shade into blanket controls, such as the certificates of approval scheme (under which an application from outside the UK might eventually be successful) and the ban on Commonwealth husbands between 1969 and 1974. Even if an application has a prospect of succeeding, these tools are blunt instruments and the outcome depends less on the nature of the relationship and more on questions of immigration status, nationality, ethnicity and financial, social and cultural capital. This, it is suggested, is not accidental; controls over sham marriage have always been entwined with the wider purposes of immigration control. Whether parties are able to enjoy married life in the UK (or even to marry at all) depends less upon the genuineness or otherwise of the relationship and more upon the extent to which their presence in the UK undermines those immigration control purposes.

The question that emerges is not the point at which a marriage becomes sham or even the model of marriage that is presented as the template, but the circumstances in which states are justified in interfering with the rights of couples to marry and live together. As discussed earlier in this chapter, the immigration factor in marriages cannot be painlessly identified and neutralised; it is not easy to determine the purposes for which individuals marry and, in any event, these may not correlate to the level of affective commitment. It is unrealistic to imagine that irregular migrants and asylum seekers, often present in the UK for many years, will not form attachments whose disruption will cause hardship not only to them but to their UK partners and children.[23] The right to enjoy family life in one's own home may be regarded as an aspect of citizenship in the broad if not the legal sense. Yet, control over immigration is regarded not only as an aspect of national sovereignty but of government competence. Governments feel unable to abandon their attempts to ensure that immigration is both managed and

[23] The position of children in the UK whose parents do not have leave is a separate issue that has been recently invigorated by the UK's removal of its immigration reservation to the Convention of the Rights of the Child and the enactment of a statutory duty in the Borders, Citizenship and Immigration Act 2009 s 55 to promote and safeguard a child's interests in immigration decisions; see the Supreme Court decision in *ZH (Tanzania) v Secretary of State for the Home Department* [2011] UKSC 4 and subsequent case law.

limited. There is no easy way to resolve these dilemmas and it is not surprising if governments instrumentalise concerns about sham marriage as a way of reconciling these tensions.

The sham marriage is a deeply troubling concept. It does occur, although its prevalence is unclear but it is often also a construct, drawing on an imagined opposition to the imagined ideal of the 'pure' relationship in order to justify wide control measures. By compressing and simplifying a complex and ambiguous term, governments have been able to justify intrusions into the married lives of couples that would otherwise be unacceptable. Such intrusions have usually focused on the granting of immigration rights consequent to marriage. Increasingly, however, the rites aspect, the right even to marry, is also contested.

BIBLIOGRAPHY

ABRAMS, Kerry, 'Peaceful Penetration: Proxy Marriage, Same-Sex Marriage, and Recognition' (2011) (Symposium issue) *Michigan State Law Review* 139.

ABRAMS, Kerry, 'Marriage Fraud' (2012) 100 *California Law Review* 1.

BALLARD, Roger, 'Inside and outside: contrasting perspectives on the dynamics of kinship and marriage in contemporary South Asian transnational networks' in R Grillo (ed), *The Family in Question: Immigrants and Minorities in Multicultural Europe* (Amsterdam, University of Amsterdam Press, 2008).

BECK-GERNSHEIM, Elisabeth, 'The Marriage Route to Migration: of border artistes, transnational matchmaking and imported spouses' (2011) 1 *Nordic Journal of Migration Research* 60.

BHABHA, Jacqueline and SHUTTER, Sue, *Women's Movement: Women under Immigration, Nationality and Refugee Law* (Stoke on Trent, Trentham Books, 1994).

BONJOUR, Saskia and DE HART, Betty, 'A proper wife, a proper marriage: Constructions of "us" and "them" in Dutch family migration policy' (2013) 20 *European Journal of Women's Studies* 61.

CARVER, Natasha, 'Displaying genuineness: cultural translation in the drafting of marriage narratives for immigration applications and appeals' (2013) 3 *Families, Relationships and Societies* 271.

CHARSLEY, Katharine, 'Unhappy husbands: masculinity and migration in transnational Pakistani marriages' (2005) 11 *Journal of the Royal Anthropological Institute* 85.

CHARSLEY, Katharine, 'Transnational Marriage' in K Charsley (ed), *Transnational Marriage: New Perspectives from Europe and Beyond* (London and New York, Routledge, 2012).

CHARSLEY, Katharine, 'Marriages of Convenience and Inconvenient Marriages: Regulating Spousal Migration to Britain' (2012a) 26 *Journal of Immigration Asylum and Nationality Law* 10.

CHARSLEY, Katharine, BENSON, Michaela and VAN HEAR, Nicholas, 'Marriage-Related Migration to the UK' (2012) 46 *International Migration Review* 861.

CHARSLEY, Katharine, *Transnational Pakistani Connections: Marrying 'Back Home'* (London and New York, Routledge, 2013).

CHIEF INSPECTOR OF BORDERS AND IMMIGRATION, *A Short Notice Inspection of a Sham Marriage Enforcement Operation: 14–24 October 2013* (2014).
CLAYTON, Gina, *Textbook on Immigration and Asylum Law*, 6th edn (Oxford, Oxford University Press, 2014).
DEL ROSARIO, Teresita, 'Bridal Disapora: Marriage and Migration among Filipino Women' in R Palriwala and P Uberoi (eds), *Marriage, Migration and Gender* (Delhi, Sage Publications, 2008.
DUMMETT, Ann and NICOL, Andrew, *Subjects, Citizens, Aliens and Others* (London, Weidenfeld and Nicolson, 1990).
EGGEBØ, Helga, 'A real marriage? Applying for marriage migration to Norway' (2013) 39 *Journal of Ethnic and Migration Studies* 773.
GIDDENS, Anthony, *Modernity and Self-Identity: Self and Society in the Late Modern Age* (London, Polity Press, 1991).
GIDDENS, Anthony, *The Transformation of Intimacy* (Cambridge, Polity Press, 1992).
GRILLO, Ralph, 'Marriages, arranged and forced: The UK debate' in A Kraler, E Kofman, M Kohli, C Schmoll (eds), *Gender, Generations and the Family in International Migration* (Amsterdam, Amsterdam University Press, 2011.
HOME OFFICE, *Secure Borders, Safe Haven*, Cm 5387 (London, HMSO, 2002)
JUSS, Satvinder, *Discretion and Deviation in the Administration of Immigration Control* (London, Sweet and Maxwell, 1997).
KIM, Jaeeun, 'Establishing Identity: Documents, Performance, and Biometric Information in Immigration Proceedings' (2011) 36 *Law & Social Inquiry* 760.
KOFMAN, Eleonore, 'Family-related migration: A Critical Review of European Studies' (2004) 30 *Journal of Ethnic and Migration Studies* 243.
KOFMAN, Eleonore, ROGOZ, Madalina and LÉVY, Florence, *Family Migration Policies in France* NODE Policy Report (Vienna, BMWF/ICMPD, 2010).
LEVIN, Irene, 'Living Apart Together: A New Family Form' (2004) 52 *Current Sociology* 223.
MENSKI, Werner, 'South Asian Women in Britain, Family Integrity and the Primary Purpose Rule' in T Barot, H Bradley and S Fenton (eds), *Ethnicity, Gender and Social Change* (Basingstoke, Macmillan Press, 1999.
PALRIWALA, Rajni and UBEROI, Patricia, *Introduction* in R Palriwala and P Uberoi (eds), *Marriage, Migration and Gender*, (Delhi, Sage Publications, 2008).
POWELL, Philip, *Immigration Cases: Volume 1* (1993).
SACHDEVA, Sanjiv, *The Primary Purpose Rule in British Immigration Law* (Stoke on Trent, Trentham Books, 1993).
SATZEWICH, Vic, 'Canadian Visa Officers and the Social Construction of "Real" Spousal Relationships' (2014) 51 *Canadian Review of Sociology/Revue Canadienne de Sociologie* 1.
SHAH, Prakash, 'Inconvenient marriages, or what happens when ethnic minorities marry trans-jurisdictionally according to their self-chosen norms' (2010) 6 *Utrecht Law Review* 17.
SHAW, Alison and CHARSLEY, Katharine, '*Rishtas*: adding emotion to strategy in understanding British Pakistani transnational marriages' (2006) 6 *Global Networks* 405.

SIDDIQUI, Hannana, '"There is no 'honour' in domestic violence, only shame": Women's struggles against "honour" crimes in the UK' in L Welchman and S Hossain (eds), *'Honour': Crimes, Paradigms and Violence Against Women* (London and New York, Zed Books, 2005).

SIM, Jessica Mai, 'Beyond the Stereotype of the 'Thai-Bride': Visibility, Invisibility and Community' in K Charsley (ed), *Transnational Marriage: new perspectives from Europe and beyond* (London and New York, Routledge, 2012.

STEVENS, Dallal, 'The Immigration and Asylum Act 1999: A Missed Opportunity?' (2001) 64 *Modern Law Review* 413.

STRASSER, Elisabeth, KRALER, Albert, BONJOUR, Saskia and BILGER, Veronika, 'Doing Family: Responses to the constructions of "the migrant family" across Europe' (2009) 14 *History of the Family* 165.

WILLIAMS, Lucy, *Global Marriage: Cross-Border Marriage Migration in Global Context* (New York, Palgrave Macmillan, 2010).

WILLIAMS, Lucy 'Transnational Marriage Migration and Marriage Migration: An Overview' in K Charsley (ed), *Transnational Marriage: new perspectives from Europe and beyond* (London and New York, Routledge 2012.

WRAY, Helena, 'An Ideal Husband? Marriages of Convenience, Moral Gatekeeping and Immigration to the UK' (2006) 8 (Autumn) *European Journal of Migration and Law* 303.

WRAY, Helena, 'Hidden Purpose: Ethnic Minority International Marriages and "Intention to Live Together"' in P Shah and W Menski (eds), *Migration, Diasporas and Legal Systems in Europe* (London and New York, Routledge-Cavendish, 2006.

WRAY, Helena, 'Guiding the gatekeepers: Entry clearance for settlement on the Indian sub-Continent' (2006b) 20 *Journal of Immigration, Asylum and Nationality Law* 112.

WRAY, Helena, 'Moulding the Migrant Family' (2009) 29 *Legal Studies* 592.

WRAY, Helena, *Regulating Marriage Migration into the UK: A Stranger in the Home* (Aldershot/Burlington, Ashgate, 2011).

WRAY, Helena, '"A Thing Apart": Controlling Male Family Migration to the UK' in The Invisible (Migrant) Man (Special Issue) *Men and Masculinities* (2015).

YUVAL-DAVIS Nira, *Gender and Nation* (Los Angeles and London, Sage, 1997).

8

Unregistered Muslim Marriages: An Emerging Culture of Celebrating Rites and Conceding Rights

RAJNAARA C AKHTAR

I. INTRODUCTION

APPROXIMATELY HALF OF Britain's 2.6 million Muslims were born in the UK, with almost 60 per cent being below the age of 30 (Office of National Statistics (ONS) Census 2011). Yet this youthful population approaches family ties and marriage in a manner still very much constructed around traditional ideas of matrimony. For example, it remains highly unconventional for a couple to cohabit before a religiously recognised ceremony of marriage. Muslim marriage rites, covering an array of ethnicities, attract lavish attention, sometimes costing the equivalent of a deposit for a house, filled with love, laughter, music, and generosity beyond means. British Asian Muslim weddings, which form the majority,[1] can be a vibrant display of colour and sparkle, easily rivalling Hollywood's most glamorous weddings. Swarovski-studded saris, crystal tiaras, sweeping gowns and five-tier wedding cakes adorned with intricate hand-made flowers can all be seen at numerous stately venues across the British Isles.

In an ever-growing number of cases, this abundance of rites is wholly a public show of devotedness of bride to groom and groom to bride, with no consequential legal rights expected of, or granted by, the state. It is estimated that up to 80 per cent of Muslim marriages in the UK may be 'unregistered' (Duncan Lewis Solicitors Press Release 2014), where religious ceremonial rites are observed while state recognised civil ceremonies are not undertaken. The demand for ceremonial rites to be discharged before

[1] 68 per cent of all British Muslims are of Asian origin. Data from the ONS Census 2011.

a couple is socially accepted as a family unit within Muslim communities perhaps lies at the heart of this practice. This brings to the fore a number of pertinent questions—What rights do British Muslims expect to arise from their marriages, and what occasions their consent solely to an unregistered religiously sanctioned marriage, to which the state and its institutions are not party? How do young Muslim men and women view their 'marriages' and how significant is the performance of religious rites? Finally, to what extent does 'non-marriage'[2] in the eyes of the state impact on this growing cultural phenomenon?

This chapter explores these questions by analysing data drawn from a targeted empirical study in which 20 individuals married according to Islamic traditions were engaged in a survey seeking to ascertain the underlying causes for British Muslims locating their marriages beyond the state's legal jurisdiction.[3] The survey was produced online utilising the 'Survey Monkey' platform where eight questions were posed,[4] and was conducted during the summer of 2014. Answers required qualitative responses, and the survey was publicised using social media (Facebook). The survey was publicised and introduced as follows: 'Survey on Unregistered Muslim Marriages—If you are married according to Islamic traditions (nikkah) but have not registered your marriage in Britain, please can you take a minute to complete this short survey? Please forward to others.'

The survey was disseminated widely using this platform, and responses were received over a four-week period. The survey targeted individuals who had undertaken the '*nikkah*' ceremony and therefore were considered married according to the Islamic traditions. Although this represents a modest sample of a group targeted using a single social media platform, it provides valuable evidence in a much under-researched area for considering the priorities of British Muslims within the matrimonial process. The early indications of this study are fascinating and support the need for further academic study and analysis in the area drawing on a more diverse range of participants engaged at multiple levels and utilising multiple avenues as part of the methodology. The findings from this sample of participants indicate that the elaborate celebration of Muslim marriage rites are commonplace, while acquiring concurrent legal rights as an effect of the marriage is of lesser importance at that juncture.

[2] A ceremony which is far removed from a recognised marriage, making it a non-event, neither valid nor invalid for the purposes of marriage. *Gereis v Yagoub* [1997] 3 FLR 775.

[3] Wider research is being conducted into this phenomenon with a particular focus on marriages which have dissolved and the consequences for each party, however, this goes beyond the scope of this chapter.

[4] The survey questions can be found as an Addendum to this chapter.

II. MUSLIM MARRIAGE RITES

British Muslims face complex and multi-dimensional challenges in navigating the legal and social systems in which they live. The lack of state intervention allows a burgeoning freedom in the application of religious principles, which preserves the dynamism associated with Islamic religious traditions from its very inception (Auda 2008). This dynamism has vanished in many Muslim majority jurisdictions in which the codification of particular legal principles has resulted in inert and stagnant, albeit predictable, sets of rules being applied. British Muslims, conversely, have the potential to map out a new religious culture based on fresh and innovative interactions with the divine source of law—the Quran—and the traditions of the Prophet Muhammad—the *Sunnah*.[5] This is evidenced by contemporary debate on Islamic feminism[6] for example. The Quran is considered an irrefutable source of law, while the *Sunnah* or *Hadith* are also considered a primary source. Hallaq's outline of the pre-eminent position of the Prophetic traditions as a source of law helps place the *Sunnah* in the rubric of a primary source of Islamic laws:

> Outlined in the Qur'an, the Mission was to be propounded and articulated by the Prophet, whose conduct was so consistent with God's will that his sunna was sanctioned, ab initio, as an authoritative source of law. Despite its derivative nature, the Prophet's sunna came to be constituted as a force equal to the Qur'an, but offering a wealth of material barely matched by the concise, revealed text itself. (Hallaq 1995: xvi).

Within the Qur'an, the term *zawj* is used to describe marriage, which can be translated as a 'pairing' and is intended to create a relationship of mutual respect and trust, and allow procreation (Fyzee 1974: 90), thus facilitating the formation of family units.[7] Critiques such as Mir-Hosseini's (2007: 85–113) describe the classical definition of marriage as being purely a contract, which is primarily intended to legalise sexual relations between the couple. However, this minimalises and diminishes the spirit of marriage within the Islamic traditions, which consider it a 'sacred duty' (Esposito 2011: 111) positively encouraged to provide a relationship of tranquillity. Narrations

[5] The *Sunnah* refers to the sayings and actions of the Prophet, and the *Hadith* are the narration/reports of the traditions of the Prophet, which include his sayings and actions. These were compiled into collections by various religious scholars following the death of the Prophet and the compilations were mainly concentrated around the first and second centuries following his death. These form a pivotal source of law for Muslims. However, the nature of the compilation and the time lapse between the death of the prophet and the collection of the *Hadith* have been critiqued by Orientalist writers. A detailed description of methodology relating to the compilation of *Hadith* is provided by Kamali (2005).

[6] See www.islamandfeminism.org for example.

[7] The issue of polygamy from a theological perspective in this doctrine is complex and falls outside the remit of discussion within this chapter.

of the Prophet Muhammad confer an obligation to marry: 'Marriage is my *sunnah*.[8] Whoever keeps away from it is not from me.' (Doi 2008: 196)[9] Further, the sources of Islamic law also carry the following injunctions:

> And among His signs is this. That He created for you mates from among yourselves, that you may dwell in tranquillity with them, and He has put love and mercy between your hearts. Undoubtedly in these are signs for those who reflect. (The Quran: 30:21)

> And Allah has made for you your mates of your own nature, and made for you, out of them, sons and daughters and grandchildren, and provided for you sustenance of the best. (The Quran: 16:72)

These direct injunctions embody the profound depth of the marital union, and are reinforced by the purported existence of an over-arching Islamic culture in which all facets of life are 'effortlessly conceived as religious' (Akhtar 2008: 7), whether social, political or indeed private in the case of marriage. This is strengthened by the idea that Islam is not merely a religion to be followed, but rather a 'complete way of life' to be adopted. Therefore, since there is a religious philosophical dimension to every action of a religiously active Muslim, it can be reasonably expected that marriage when conferred as a sacred duty must be entered within certain parameters to be considered effective. In the Islamic traditions, this is practically manifested in the form of a contract.

Islamic laws confer certain fundamental elements for a marriage to be validly constituted. First, consent is a prerequisite, and so an offer of marriage requires an acceptance (Doi 2008: 228), analogous with most contracts. Marriage is a covenant and each party entering the covenant must freely consent to it (ibid: 208). The Prophet is reported to have said: 'A previously married woman is not to be married until she is consulted, and the virgin is not to be married until her permission is sought.'[10] A lack of consent makes the marriage voidable and examples from the prophetic era reflect evidences which support free consent. For example, the girls married 'off' by their guardians who approached the prophet for redress were allowed to repudiate their marriages (Doi 2008: 208). The example given was of a young virgin whose father had concluded her marriage on her behalf without her consent. When she approached the Prophet, he nullified the marriage for lack of consent, reiterating this pivotal element for validity regardless of gender. Despite such unequivocal parameters, it is clearly evident that cultural norms within some Muslim majority jurisdictions with entrenched patriarchal norms have undoubtedly challenged this autonomy for Muslim girls and women. The infamous *Saima Waheed case* in Pakistan

[8] *Sunnah* means 'way of life' or 'tradition'.
[9] A hadith reported by Ibn Majah from *A'ishah, Bab ma ja'j bi fadl an-nikah*.
[10] Reported by Al-Bukhari in the Book of *Nikkah*.

(Lau 1996) exemplifies the struggle between established religious rulings based on patriarchal and cultural norms, wherein a father challenged the validity of his daughter's marriage on the basis of his own lack of consent as her guardian. The judges considered the competing patriarchal cultural norms and religious jurisprudence, and based on a consideration of Islamic law and the Pakistani constitution the majority did in fact rule that an adult Muslim woman is *Sui Juris* (Ali 1996) and therefore has the right to marry of her own free will (Yefet 2009: 358), creating a national furore. Secondly, *Mahr* must be agreed.[11] A valid marriage requires the payment of a *Mahr* (The Quran: 4:4) which constitutes a nuptial gift to the bride. All references to this payment infer its position as a 'gift' and not a 'bride price' or other customary payment made at the time of marriage in various cultures across the world. Doi opined that the payment of the dowry on the part of the bridegroom is an admission of the independence of the bride, for she becomes the owner of property immediately on her marriage, though before she may not have owned anything. (Doi 2008: 254). The performance of the marriage is called the *nikkah* and the rites associated with how this is conducted are very much dependent on the jurisdiction in which it is taking place. Within Muslim-majority jurisdictions, for example Pakistan and Morocco, state legislation imposes a formal ceremony in the presence of an authorised cleric or registrar, and culminates in registration of the marriage with civil authorities of the state.[12] While this procedure can be circumvented by those seeking a less formal 'marriage' without state recognition, it indicates the advancement towards formality of the *nikkah* in the interests of protecting the rights of the parties. By contrast, in Britain, the *nikkah* remains informal and an indication of normative socio-religious influences which operate within a purely religious framework with no state recognition. This lack of recognition enables unregistered marriages to be conducted beyond the state's jurisdiction, which are considered valid by the Muslim communities.[13]

The *nikkah* is usually conducted in the presence of two witnesses and an *Imam*/religious scholar. However, a valid marriage can in fact be concluded without witnesses[14] and even performed by the couple themselves,

[11] The *Mahr* is a complex issue, and this nuptial gift to the bride is treated as an institution of the Muslim marriage. Many perspectives can be found on *Mahr* including traditional analysis by writers such as Wani (1996) and Fournier (2010), *Mahr* is referred to within the Quran itself in chapter 4, verse 4 which states: 'And give the women (on marriage) their *Mahr* as a free gift; but if they, of their own good pleasure, remit any part of it to you, Take it and enjoy it with right good cheer'.

[12] For example, in Morocco, Article 15 of the *Moudawanam* The Moroccan Family Code 2004, requires registration of the marriage contract with the appropriate authority within three months of being entered.

[13] Such practices are not limited to the UK, and are duplicated in many other jurisdictions including the US despite more stringent criteria. See for example, Welchman (2004: 188–212).

[14] Such a marriage would not be properly constructed but would be considered valid within Islamic law nonetheless.

and can be conducted anywhere—a mosque, a house, a holiday resort, etc. While such informality appears to counter the spirit of marriage within the Islamic legal traditions, which encourages a public celebration of the nuptials, they reflect the contextual reality of modern diverse Muslim communities in which a multitude of potential reasons may influence the manner of conducting the *nikkah*. For example, if the couple's family disapproves of the union, one may conceivably witness a Vegas-style elopement and closed ceremony.

In the case of regularly constituted Muslim marriages, numerous customs that traditionally surround this simple ceremony have now become well-established rituals, which many expect as a rite. These vary according to the culture, and within South Asian cultures, there are often three distinctive days of celebration—the *Mehndi*[15] during which the bride's hands are traditionally decorated with henna; the *nikkah* which comprises the actual wedding ceremony and is often the bride's party; and the *Walima* which follows the *nikkah* by at least a day and is most popularly considered to be a public celebration of the consummation of the marriage.[16]

The default position of all *nikkah* ceremonies is that they constitute unregistered marriages. If the *nikkah* is celebrated in a mosque that has been registered for the solemnisation of marriage,[17] then it may be recognised by the state as a valid marriage where the requisite formalities have been observed. In the absence of this, unless the parties have undertaken an additional civil ceremony, their relationship will not be recognised by the state as constituting a valid legally binding marriage, and thus the couple forego the legal protections that the state upholds for recognised marriages, whether through positive consent or omission through lack of awareness.[18] Thus, for recognition and therefore access to rights, the couple must undertake the additional step of registration of their marriage, which may occur during the *nikkah* if within a solemnised building, or prior to or following the *nikkah* at an appropriate solemnised building.[19] It should be noted that the normative Islamic religious influences around which marriages are conducted do not *exclude* registration of a marriage for the purposes of state recognition. However, arguments may now be advanced which suggest that a conflict has emerged in the UK as legislation no longer defines marriage as between a man and a woman, but rather between one person and another.

[15] The *Mehndi* tradition can be traced in the Asian and Arab worlds. For centuries, this ritual has formed part of the marriage rights for a bride, and is in essence a temporary henna tattoo. In the modern age, the *Mehndi* party has become a well-established tradition.

[16] The *Walima* denotes a feast and the word is of Arabic origin.

[17] Marriage Act 1949, s 41.

[18] This scenario manifests itself in many European jurisdictions, in addition to other countries in which a mono-legal system exists wherein the state does not formally recognise legal pluralism.

[19] This would often be a Register Office.

Strictly orthodox and perhaps even liberal, Islamic scholarly opinion may assert that a valid marriage in the sight of God according to the sources of Islamic law must be between opposite genders.[20] But as this is a relatively recent change in the law, it is unlikely to provide an explanation for the growing numbers choosing not to register their marriages prior to this.

III. TO REGISTER OR NOT TO REGISTER?

The underlying motivations for some British Muslims choosing not to register marriages were investigated by the empirical research undertaken for the purposes of this chapter. Participants were asked: 'If your marriage is unregistered, what are the main reasons for choosing not to register your marriage by participating in a civil ceremony?'. Various explanations were offered in response to this pertinent enquiry, and the most recurring reason submitted by half of the participants was simply not 'getting round to it'. This lack of prominence and urgency placed on the registration of a religious marriage may be due to a number of factors, including a lack of knowledge about the legal consequences of a registered marriage as compared to an unregistered one. Context is clearly an important aspect and at least half of the participants said the time needed to organise a civil ceremony was unattainable, or not a priority in busy modern lives.

Responses to other enquiries about the ceremonial rites, which shall be analysed further below, reflected the level of significance attached to the *nikkah* as the fulfilment of religious traditions. Once completed with an abundance of festivities, any added rites which fall beyond religious and cultural dictates appear to be considered as unnecessary requisites. Many of the participants emphasised the religious ceremony and recognition of the marriage in the sight of God, and explanations offered included the following:

> We don't feel the need to. The most important part was the Islamic ceremony.
>
> We never thought it was important, can't see the need.
>
> The right time has not arisen. We will do once [we] have children. Think I want to maintain maiden name or go 'double barrelled' and adopt both his surname but still keep mine.
>
> No incentive to register. It doesn't change anything at all.
>
> No personal value.
>
> I did not feel the need to have civil ceremony as I felt the nikkah was sufficient to recognise that the marriage is a legal valid marriage in my own life.

[20] While this is undoubtedly the classical Islamic legal position, some commentators now question the premise of this division. See for example: Shannahan (2009).

> Not really required for the purposes of Islam. I am fully aware that a nikkah registered in the UK is not binding in UK law but that is not important. However, I have told my wife we will have to register it later with the registry for tax purposes and also for UK inheritance law purposes.

These comments and the prevalence of simply not prioritising the civil ceremony provide some context to the emergent phenomenon of unregistered marriages. They reflect varying degrees of legal awareness displayed by the participants, which can no doubt be extrapolated wider within Muslim communities. It is apparent that in most cases, far from the decision being precipitated by discussion and reasoning, it is in actual fact a matter of convenience and time. However, to some, there is no value placed on the civil ceremony as it adds nothing to their status as a married couple according to their own perception. Participants' objective knowledge about the legal implications are unclear, and a question on this was deliberately omitted from the survey in order to offset any resultant concerns which may arise between couples which cannot then be addressed. It is clear that the ceremonial rights lavished on weddings occupy a great deal of time and within this busy period, British Muslim couples are not finding the time to register their unions with the state. The consequences of this will usually only become apparent to couples on the breakdown of the marriage, whether by death or divorce.

In order to understand the views expressed by my sample of 20 participants concerning marriage rites, a deeper analysis of the interaction between law and society as a whole for Muslims is necessary; whether this is negotiated between a citizen and their state, or between a citizen and their conscience. The former can be seen in some Muslim majority jurisdictions which assert adherence to religious laws, in which certain rules of law (especially family law) are attributed to a divine source,[21] while the latter emerges in states such as Britain where faith is a personal attribute and coercive forces may be limited to personal convictions and/or community norms. As British Muslims undertake complex navigations between the laws of the state, the norms of their communities and the traditions of their religious convictions, new cultural identities appear to be emerging. This gives rise to the pertinent question of how these new 'cultures' impact on the decision to register and attribute recognition to a couple's marriage.

The empirical survey conducted for the purposes of this chapter provides valuable insight into this emerging practice. Twenty participants in unregistered Muslim marriages were engaged in a survey of a previously under-engaged subject group. Participants self-identified based on the lead into the survey which requested that those married according to the Islamic traditions, but unregistered, partake. Although the research methods originally

[21] The multitude of questions which arise regarding the authenticity of some laws within such states, especially concerning treatment of women, are beyond the scope of this chapter.

envisaged engaging 10 couples within unregistered marriages in a survey by interview, the lack of engagement from the subject group required a reformulation of the research strategy. Enquiring about one's decision not to register a marriage appeared to infringe on the couple's privacy and those who were within higher-ranking professions in particular were unwilling to engage. Thus, the secondary method was employed utilising social media to disseminate the survey with responses being received anonymously from 20 individuals. The online survey guaranteed privacy, and the snowballing technique[22] ensued resulting in the survey being completed by a diverse group of people. While there are limitations of using such a survey, including the lack of personal engagement with the participants, as an initial foray engaging a difficult to identify target group, it has provided some valuable insights. Due to the nature of the questions, the guaranteed anonymity of the responses (King et al 1995; Stanton 1998) positively impacted on the uptake, with the target of 20 participants achieved with relative ease, after a much longer period of time expended unsuccessfully attempting to source couples for interview.

The survey questions were divided into three sections as follows: about you, about your wedding day, and registered and unregistered marriages. The first section requested specific demographic details relating to gender, age, length of marriage, town of residence, profession, ethnicity and religion. The second section posed five questions about the participant's wedding day. The third and final section posed two specific questions: if your marriage is unregistered, what are the main reasons for choosing not to register your marriage by participating in a civil ceremony? And, when interacting with society, do you tell people that you are married or unmarried? The final question specifically identified the following groups in society: employer, doctors/health profession, Muslim friends, non-Muslims, strangers.

The relatively modest number of participants allowed for analysis using the Survey Monkey platform and excel spreadsheets to collate qualitative data from section one, and compare and contrast responses to questions in sections two and three by drawing out common themes, and noting frequency of certain responses.

Of the 20 participants, 13 were female and 7 were male. This discrepancy in gender weighting of participants mirrors a prior study engaging British Muslims on the questions of family law and dispute resolution, in which 250 participants were engaged in a random survey, of which 70 per cent were female and 30 per cent male (Akhtar 2013). The underlying reasons for the limited engagement from male participants are still unclear and enquiries into this field are bound to be defeated by the lack of engagement itself. However, it is highly conceivable that the subject matter provides a

[22] Snowballing (also known as chain referral sampling) is a technique that can be used to access hard to reach populations. See Atkinson (2003).

greater variable of interest to female participants thus resulting in a higher rate of engagement. Studies on response rates in surveys generally have discovered that females are more likely to respond than males which may in itself form the basis of lack of engagement here (Curin et al 2000, Moore and Tarnai 2002, Singer et al 2000).

Participants' ages ranged from 24 to 44, with half being in their 20s and the remainder being in their 30's, with the exception of one participant in their 40s. This reflects a cross-section of age ranges within one generation of British Muslims. The survey results revealed that participants hailed from a cross-section of the country, including Birmingham, Derbyshire, Leicester, London, Manchester, Nottingham, Peterborough, Solihull, and West Midlands. The majority of the participants were professionals, with 11 being doctors, lawyers and teachers. One single participant was a home-maker (educated to degree level), while all others were employed in various roles such as copy-writer, social worker, project manager, etc. This reflects a sample of participants who can legitimately be anticipated to be highly engaged and participating in society.

The duration of the participants' marriages varied, with four being married for one year,[23] three for two years,[24] five being married for between three and five years,[25] a further five between six and nine years,[26] and the three remaining participants for 10, 12 and 15[27] years respectively. This diversity in duration of marriage is a surprising finding as it seems to suggest the practice of non-registration occurs regardless of how long a couple has been married for.

The ethnic backgrounds of the participants were also diverse, and they were represented as follows: three Arabs, one Bangladeshi, six Indians, seven Pakistanis, two Africans and one White English.

One of the participants stated she was a convert to Islam while another stated he was neither born Muslim nor a convert. All other participants were born into Muslim families. This provides an interesting dimension to the responses, allowing for the view of a non-adherent to the faith who is engaged in an unregistered Muslim marriage to be explored.

This diverse group of participants shared one common feature—each undertook the religious ceremonial rites associated with a Muslim marriage while not engaging with the state civil ceremony. Before exploring the reasons underlying their unregistered marriages further, the celebration of the marriage rites as conveyed in the responses to the survey will be analysed in order to better frame the registered/unregistered dichotomy which will be considered subsequently.

[23] Participants were aged 25, 26, 27 and 28.
[24] Participants were aged 24, 28 and 30.
[25] Participants were aged 27, 27, 30, 37 and 39.
[26] Participants were aged 27, 29, 34, 35 and 44.
[27] Participants were aged 36, 34 and 39.

A. Celebrating a Non-registered Marriage

Participants were asked to detail the time spent in planning their weddings, the cost of the celebrations and the number of guests who were invited to participate in/observe the ceremonial rites. The expenses relating to their wedding included the cost of the invitations, reception, food, etc, and they were also asked to detail the cost of gifts presented to their spouse.

The responses revealed that the time spent in planning the wedding was usually between five months and one year. One participant spent two hours planning the nuptials, but provided no details as to the reasons. This can be assumed to be exceptional; weddings are seldom planned and performed on the same day. The responses suggest that the norm is for a great deal of preparation and planning to be undertaken, which is comparable to traditional weddings. A survey by 'Wedding Paper Divas' of traditional weddings in the UK found that on average 27 per cent of participants were engaged for 7–12 months before they married, and a further 40 per cent were engaged for 13–18 months.[28]

The number of guests invited to the wedding varied from a mere five in one case, to an astounding 2,000 in another. Nearly half of all the weddings were attended by between 100–300 guests; a further seven hosted between 301–500 guests; and in two cases there were between 500–1,000 guests. Thus, Muslim marriages are witnessed and celebrated by large numbers of people, with at least 100 people in attendance being the norm. This perhaps reflects the wide social networks common within South Asia, which are maintained in places like Britain. Also, the Muslim birth-rate remains higher in Europe than national averages. For example, in Britain, the national average is 1.8 children per woman (Dorman 2014), while with Muslim women, this is thought to be higher as 9.1 per cent of all under-fives in the population are now Muslim, while the overall recorded Muslim population was 4.8 per cent (ONS Religion, 2013). Thus, Muslim family sizes are generally larger which has a direct impact on the numbers of people one can reasonably expect at a wedding celebration.

The cost of the celebrations ranged from a modest £300 in one case, to a staggering £35,000 in another. Four participants spent over £20,000 on their wedding reception. A further five participants spent between £10,000 and £19,999 on the celebrations. Five more participants spent between £5,000 and £9,100, and the remaining five spent between £2,000 and £4,000. One exception of £300 was spent on the celebrations by the participant whose wedding was planned and completed on the same day.

[28] Huffington Post, (01/04/2013), 'Average engagement length, and other wedding planning statistics', available at www.huffingtonpost.com/2013/01/04/average-engagement-length_n_2411353.html.

Further to this, participants were asked regarding the cost of gifts to their prospective spouses, with no reference made to *Mahr* specifically, but rather focused on gifts given from the bride and groom to each other, and to extended family as is the custom in South Asian and Arab cultures. Responses ranged from no gifts in one case, and £40 in another, to £50,000 being the most spent by any of the participants. Half stated that they spent between £1,500 and £3,000 on gifts. The remainder spent between £4,000 and £7,000. The exchange of gifts between the bride and the groom forms a pivotal part of the celebrations and this is considered as a tradition which now occupies the position of a customary wedding rite. It was clearly treated seriously by the majority of the respondents to the survey.

These vast sums of money both for the wedding celebrations and for gifts are indicative of the significance attached to the ceremonial rites of the religious marriage. While it can be anticipated that the costs of the wedding celebrations are expected to reflect the financial positions of each couple, the evidence provided by these statistics is that an unregistered Muslim marriage attracts the same level of devotion to the big day as most conventional weddings. In 2013, the *Daily Telegraph* reported that the average cost of a wedding was £18,244. Sixteen of the participants appeared to have spent less than the average cost of a wedding, while four spent above it with one being double the average and another being more than triple the average. There are several possible explanations for the difference found in this empirical study, including the Islamic religious traditions, which positively discourage debt, so while a conventional wedding may attract debt, it may be unlikely that this would be the case for a Muslim couple. Further, socio-economic factors may be limiting, as the 2011 census revealed that 45 per cent of British Muslims were not economically active (ONS Religion, 2013). This figure is reflective of a number of factors, including the youthful Muslim population, the higher than average number of Muslim women who are home-makers (31 per cent compared with 17 per cent for people of no religion), and the large number of students (30 per cent of Muslims aged 16 and over) (ONS Religion 2013). Thus, income may reflect the cost of weddings, but this does not weaken the clear emphasis and importance placed on the wedding celebrations by these British Muslims despite them remaining unregistered and therefore without legal status.

B. The Most Important Aspect of the Celebration

Participants were asked to indicate what they considered to be the most important aspect of their wedding day. Half of the participants cited the Islamic ceremonial rite of the *nikkah* contract as the most important part of the day. This contract is the agreement between the couple that they will be joined together in marriage sanctified in the eyes of God; and entering this contract fulfils the requirements for the couple to be considered legitimately married and therefore able to embark on a marital relationship. Without this contract, any form of sexual relationship is prohibited within the Islamic religious traditions.

A further eight participants cited the presence of family and friends as the most significant aspect of the day. Thus, celebrating the marriage with loved ones in a fitting manner, or marking the religious solemnisation of the union were the most important aspects of the wedding day for the majority of the participants.

Of the two remaining participants, for the one who was not a Muslim, the *nikkah* was significant as his wife needed this to verify that the relationship was legitimate to her family; his response thus showed that this was prioritised due to their needs as a couple. For the groom in this case, the issue was of little importance and he was following the rituals required of him to legitimately embark on a relationship with his wife according to her religious beliefs. This demonstrates the possible relevance of unregistered marriages for British citizens who are not Muslim, and for those in relationships with Muslim partners.[29] The last participant failed to respond to this question.

While half of the participants listed the *nikkah* as the most important aspect of their celebration, only marginally fewer participants said the presence of family and friends was the focal point of the festivities, in line with the expectation that most couples wish to share their big day with loved ones. While the celebration of the marriage by family and friends is not strictly necessary within the Islamic traditions, it is wholly feasible that as this forms part of the public announcement of the union and thus validates the marriage in the sight of the Muslim communities to which the couple may belong; perhaps this is indeed an extension of the consideration of religious norms.

Conversely, when asked what participants thought was the most important aspect of the day for parents and close family members, 12 out of 20 stated that the welfare of the guests and the smooth administration of the event were undoubtedly uppermost in their parents' and close families' minds. Six were of the opinion that it was the *nikkah* which was the most important aspect, while the remaining two listed their happiness as the prime concern. One can assume that these may be reflective of the concerns one would expect the families of the bride and groom to have in any traditional wedding scenario, and thus they are very much human concerns. The importance of the ceremonial rite of the *nikkah* was still significant.

[29] This scenario does raise questions about the validity of the *nikkah* where the husband is not a Muslim. However, this cannot be explored as no further details were provided by the participant about his religious beliefs, such as whether he converted to Islam without faith, or as a means to enter the *nikkah* to provide evidence of a valid marriage to his wife's family.

However, this conceivably has the greatest impact on the couple and thus was cited as more of an individual concern.

C. Difference Between a *Nikkah* and a Registered Marriage

Participants were asked to detail their views on the difference between their religious wedding ceremony and registered wedding ceremonies generally. Twelve did not believe there was a difference between their wedding celebrations and that of couples who conducted a registered civil ceremony. Three cited the *nikkah* as the reason for a difference between the two, however, this was simply a ceremonial aspect of the wedding day.

The remainder listed a variety of perceived differences, such as the scale of the wedding, the traditional segregation of the genders, the fact that a civil ceremony is more structured, and that the *nikkah* is considered more of a party than a ceremony. The latter point is accurate to the extent that the ceremonial aspect of the Muslim marriage is very brief and often conducted away from the larger gathering of people. The differences are perhaps more indicative of cultural variances in wedding styles and celebratory norms. However, the effects of the celebration remain the same—the union between the spouses, while the legal consequences are vastly different.

D. Ceremonial Rites of the Muslim Marriage

All participants were asked: 'Can you briefly describe the main events from your wedding day (eg, the arrival of the parties, speeches, food, entertainment, religious ceremony, etc)'. The findings here revealed that many customary norms were visible across each of their weddings, with the ceremony/*nikkah*, food, and photography featuring the most frequently. Each participant briefly detailed the order of events from their wedding day, and the responses to this enquiry revealed what they believed formed part of the actual wedding, as opposed to incidental events of the day. Sixteen of the participants cited the *nikkah* as part of the proceedings and this ceremony featured either as part of a detailed list of proceedings or in one case, the participant simply stated 'The *nikkah* took place at a mosque.' In that example, it is feasible that the *nikkah* was considered to be the sole proceeding of the day which related to the marriage itself.

Further responses to this question included detailed descriptions of the order of events from the arrival of the bride and the groom, to particulars about the order of photography, the types of food served at certain junctures (for example, canapés after arrivals), and dancing and music.

The discharge of the *nikkah* itself varied significantly between each participant. Of those who cited it, four stated that it was conducted at home prior to the arrival at the wedding venue. Four participants stated that the *nikkah* took place at some point before the day of the wedding celebration, and for one couple it took place in February while the wedding party was in July; for the remainder it was conducted up to three weeks before the wedding party.

A further four participants stated that the *nikkah* was conducted in a mosque, away from the wedding venue. In such cases, it is feasible that the ceremony was witnessed by male worshippers as the majority of mosques are gender segregated and the ceremony is performed by a male *imam*. The final five who cited the *nikkah* stated that it occurred at the wedding venue itself, witnessed by the guests. Thus, based on this sample, it appears that it is not necessarily expected that the *nikkah* will be conducted at the time and place of the wedding celebration.

Overall, there was no uniformity in the timing and location of the *nikkah* itself, with this taking place on occasions at mosques, or at the venue of the wedding celebrations. For some couples it occurred weeks or days before the wedding itself, thus did not form part of the days' proceedings. The lack of a large number of witnesses to the *nikkah* did not appear to negate the importance placed on the wedding celebrations themselves. It is apparent that a great deal of significance is placed on the ceremonial rites associated with the *nikkah* from the previous responses from the participants. As such, it forms the pivotal part of the proceedings. However, the timing and location of this seems to be highly variable, suggesting that the wedding celebration is a confirmatory event on the occasion of the *nikkah*, although not necessarily running concurrent to it. The nature and form of the remainder of the festivities was diverse with differences such as the segregation of the genders and the presence of music being factors.

The participants to the survey were from various ethnic groups, and the lack of homogeneity within British Muslim communities was reflected even within this modest sample. The largest representation of Muslims in Britain remains from South Asia, and many studies have considered the legal complexities presented by differing cultural and religious needs. Menski's '*angrezi shariat*' (Menski 1998: 276) and Ballard's '*pardesh riwaj*' (Ballard 2006:51) are two examples of phrases coined by leading academics on the practical manifestation of religious laws within Muslim communities migrating away from South Asia. Both argue that customs which originate in South Asia are transposed from other jurisdictions where Muslims form a minority and these are then amalgamated with some customs and traditions from the home country. The diversity of rites occurring within Muslim weddings can be linked to Werbner's imagery of 'segmented diasporas' (Werbner 2004: 900) wherein 'diasporas may unite together in some contexts and oppose each other in others'. Thus, Muslim communities from diverse ethnic groups may share some commonalities while differing in others, being bound by a shared dominant religion. Within wedding ceremonies, the *nikkah* represents an element of commonality, while the form and nature of the wider celebrations may differ.

This was indeed reflected in the responses received from participants when asked to describe the proceedings on their wedding day. Some distinctive responses to this enquiry included the following, reflecting the diverse range of potential proceedings at Muslim weddings in Britain, reflective of the diversity in customs, cultures and beliefs:

> 'The celebration involved a marching band, and the bride and groom sitting on an elevated position so that photography could ensue. Food was served, followed by more photography'.

> 'The arrival of the groom was followed by the arrival of the bride. There was music and a DJ and a 3 course meal. We lastly cut the cake in front of guests'.

> '*Nikkah* was a small ceremony conducted in a mosque. This was followed by the wedding celebration which occurred in different venues for the men and women (segregated celebration)'.

> 'The *nikkah* occurred 3 weeks before the wedding party, and was held at the bride's parent's home with only a small number of family and friends present'.

> 'The men and the women were segregated during the wedding. However, the bride's father walked her in to the room while the groom's mother walked him into the room. The groom lifted my veil and rings were exchanged. Photography ensued and this was followed by the groom and bride's father leaving the women's room. The absence of men meant there was a lot of dancing and I gave a short speech. After the meal, the men arrived for the cake cutting ceremony. A large motorcade travelled from the wedding party venue to the hotel where we spent the night'.

> 'The Bridal party was the first to arrive, followed later by groom's party. Canapés and drinks were served. This was followed by the *nikkah*. The food was then served followed by the Cake cutting ceremony. Speeches followed before desert was served. Coffee was then served while the bride and groom met their guests for an hour. Everyone left at the same time following the event'.

> 'The *nikkah* was a small ceremony conducted in the mosque. Guests arrived and men and women were segregated. This allowed the women to dance freely. Food was served, and this was followed with more dancing'.

IV. UNREGISTERED MUSLIM MARRIAGE, CAUSES AND CONSEQUENCES

The decision to undertake an unregistered Muslim marriage raises many questions. To what extent are British Muslims consciously navigating between the cultures of the jurisdictions in which they live, the traditions of their own ethnic origins, and/or religious norms? Are these strategies intended to meet the needs of their religious traditions where marriage is concerned, while at a practical level seemingly employing a well-established cohabitation right recognised in wider society affording the same absence of legal rights? Are marriage rites being implemented due to community norms such as undergoing the *nikkah* and celebrating with family (cited by 18 out of 20 participants as the most important aspects of the celebration), while marriage rights are deemed a choice?

Muslim couples in unregistered marriages occupy the same legal space as cohabitants, as their marriages are not recognised by the civil law in the UK (Fournier 2014: 10). The number of couples who live together without marrying has sharply increased in recent years, with 2.9 million opposite sex cohabiting couples being recorded in the UK in 2013 by the Labour Force Survey (ONS Bulletin, Families and Households, 2013). It is unclear how Muslim couples in unregistered marriages would self-identify, whether as married or cohabiting. Thus, it is unclear how many non-registered Muslim couples are included in this figure.

1.9 million cohabiting households have dependent children and cohabiting couples are the fastest growing family type (ONS Families, 2013). The lack of legal protections for cohabiting couples means the law will treat the couple as separate individuals with no special or specific rights and/or obligations to each other reflective of the nature of their relationship, regardless of the duration and presence of children. Conversely, for a married couple, the courts have the jurisdiction to intervene and distribute assets fairly between the spouses. These contributions need not be financial, for example where one partner sacrifices a career to tend to the home and raise the children. For a cohabiting couple, regardless of the partners' contributions, there is no right to maintenance upon the breakdown of the relationship, and any right to a share in the family home will depend on the law of trusts. Where one partner dies intestate, the surviving partner has no guaranteed right to inherit. Within a marriage, intestacy laws mean that the surviving spouse will inherit the estate, ensuring that the spouse and any children are protected from potential consequences such as losing their home, etc.

While unregistered Muslim marriages can be compared with cohabiting relationships in terms of the effects of the arrangements, they differ substantially in terms of the cultural perceptions which give rise to them. Within the Islamic religious traditions, cohabitation is deeply frowned upon and widely perceived as falling outside of religious traditions, wherein sexual relationships between a man and a woman should only take place within the parameters of a marriage. Thus, when a Muslim person is exercising his/her autonomy in opting out of state recognition for their marriage, the normative influences which frame that decision are potentially very much set apart from that of cohabiting couples. They do in fact want a 'marriage' whereas cohabiting couples are deemed to have decided against marriage or deferred one at any rate. The parameters of that marriage are however, distinct from the state's framework and regulatory mechanisms.

Thus, the issue of informed consent to this arrangement becomes a crucial one. A cohabiting couple know that they are not married and although they may have some misunderstanding about their rights, they are aware of the nature of their relationship vis-à-vis a state recognised marriage. Where a non-registered Muslim marriage is concerned on the other hand, it is questionable whether the parties in fact understand that their religious marriage is not recognised by the state and therefore no safeguards are in place.

The parties to an unregistered Muslim marriage have no legal rights unless the couple chooses to enter a cohabitation agreement. Such an agreement would set out the parameters of each party's obligations to the other, and also contain clauses which clarify their respective interests in financial assets considered to be joint, such as their family home. It should be noted that studies of cohabitants (Barlow 2005) reveal that many people engaged in such relationships are unaware of their legal rights (or lack thereof) and it is entirely feasible that the same lack of awareness exists amongst Muslim couples (Fournier 2010).

There has been little empirical research in the area and the number of unregistered Muslim marriages remains speculative, with some citing 80 per cent. However, anecdotal evidence from lawyers involved in Muslim family law issues support the contention that it is rapidly rising. The growth in the number of cases being dealt with by faith-based alternative dispute resolution (ADR) mechanisms further supports this assertion, as many couples approach these fora for expert mediation on religious marriages that fall beyond the state's jurisdiction (Akhtar 2013: 206–34).[30] Referral to faith-based ADR exemplifies the existence of parallel norms within distinct cultural or religious groups within the UK, which are by no means restricted to British Muslims (Douglas et al 2013).[31] These systems operate unofficially and do not occupy any legal space vis-á-vis the state. Unregistered Muslim marriages provide a further example of a parallel 'institution' which exists in a manner which places it beyond the ambit of the state's legal mechanisms.

The marriage rights mediated by such forums are defined within the sources of Islamic law and are distinct from marriage as understood in the state context. For example, Islamic traditions place a positive obligation on

[30] Shariah Councils are plagued with reports of discrimination against women and lack of cultural awareness. 90 per cent of their work-load involves granting Islamic divorces to women whose husbands refuse to grant them in the traditional way, (by uttering the word 'talaq' at three separate intervals). This lack of uniformity in the ability of men and women to obtain divorces has been strongly criticised by women's rights groups. Baroness Cox proposed the Arbitration and Mediation Service (Equality) Bill 2014 in the House of Lords which was intended to address these inequalities. The Bill has it proponents and opponents who argue it is needed to protect Muslim women, and it discriminates against Muslims respectively.

[31] Douglas et al consider ADR from three different faith based forums—A Jewish Beth Din, a Roman Catholic matrimonial Tribunal and a Muslim Shariah Council.

the husband to provide for his family and a right to the wife to expect the basic needs of shelter, clothing and food to be fulfilled (Doi 2008: 315–18). In traditional Islamic law, the duties imposed on women within a marriage are few, and there is no overt equivalent to the obligation placed on the husband to maintain his family, although it can be said that it is socially expected that she will keep the home and raise the children. There is clearly no equivalent to the obligation on the husband within the English law definition of marriage. Within the Islamic legal traditions on the other hand, a failure in this regard can constitute a valid ground for divorce for the wife (Doi 2008: 315–18).

The report of the government-initiated Muslim Marriage Working Group (MMWG) (2012) investigating unregistered marriages, also stated that evidence from community groups suggests that unregistered marriages form a high proportion of their caseload. The Working Group analysed statistics for the number of legally registered Muslim marriages taking place on religious premises, and revealed that the Office of National Statistics figures show only 238 Muslim marriages were recorded for 2009. Putting this into perspective—'Muslims formed 2.78% of the population of Great Britain in 2001 and Sikhs 0.59%, and there were 1,276 Sikh marriages recorded in 2009' (MMWG Report 2012: 3). Gell scrutinises South Asian Jat Sikh wedding rituals, arguing that this community is 'explicitly preoccupied with persuading themselves that they are fully incorporated into the British state' (Gell 1994: 357). Consequently, marriages are described as ceremonialised in two stages beginning with an official ceremony before the state, and followed by a religious ceremony at a temple. The civil registry is described as being of great import, usually video-taped at length. Thus, for the Jat Sikhs, the civil ceremony is very much a valued part of the wedding ceremonies, appearing to set them apart from the marriages of Muslims of South Asian origin.

However, the figures for registered Muslim marriages are more indicative of the number of Muslim religious institutions which are registered to conduct civil marriages rather than the registration of marriages themselves (Haskey, this volume), as it is usual for couples to undergo separate religious and civil ceremonies. However, one aspect of the problem may be a lack of institutions registered to conduct civil ceremonies, as mosques and other centres focus on performing the religious rites of the marriage.

The Working Group detailed a number of possible underlying factors giving rise to unregistered marriages and these provide some interesting factors which potentially explain this phenomenon. First, they considered the impact of countries of ethnic origin wherein religious and civil ceremonies are usually interwoven and thus couples assume they are legally married following a religious ceremony. In such a scenario, the couple will not be aware that they have embarked on an unregistered marriage. Balchin and Warraich (2006) conducted a study in which they discovered that some women who participated in the religious marriage ceremony laboured under the assumption that they were gaining a civil marriage when it was conducted by an *imam*.

Secondly, they suggested that lack of knowledge about the benefits and consequences of registration may undermine the perceived need to take this burdensome step. However, the extent of this awareness gap remains untested. An extension to this, thirdly, is the cost and inconvenience of a civil registration being conducted before or after the more important religious ceremony which has greater cultural and religious significance. The need to take more time out of work and daily life commitments is considered to be a possible underlying factor which deters registration. On this latter point, the respondents to the present survey concurred.

Fourthly, more young people are marrying partners from within the UK now, and thus prior needs for registration to comply with immigration procedures are no longer of concern. Without such a compelling reason, many may simply choose not to register as they perceive no immediate benefit. Fifthly, the Working Group stated that:

> Young Muslims appear to be more likely to not register their marriages. This would seem to be less the result of parental pressure, and owe more to the strengths of Muslim culture, cultural change and peer group norms. In some cases the first religious marriage may be an experimental union of partners not ready for commitment, with the parties to the marriage still living at home. In some cases the women may see religious marriage as testing out the relationship. (MMWG Report 2012: 4)

Thus, an unregistered marriage is a life-style choice which allows a young couple to date and have a sexual relationship, without being tied into a marriage for life with legal consequences in the event of a breakdown. In some cases, this marriage may be privately entered and unbeknown to parents, for example, thus the young couple continue to live in their respective parental homes, while they test out the relationship before it is made more publically visible and recognised by family and community celebrations.

The Working Group reported that:

> [T]he number of unregistered marriages are likely to increase owing to the younger demographic of the Muslim community. Changes in legal aid entitlement may also lead to increasing use of Shariah Councils once a relationship breaks down to facilitate a settlement more cheaply and conveniently than recourse to the family courts. (MMWG Report 2012: 2)

The absence of protection for vulnerable parties, especially in households where one spouse is financially dependent on the other, has led to dismal consequences for some Muslim women where their marriages have broken down. Numerous news reports and documentaries interviewing such women reveal how in a short space of time they can go from a loving relationship and a secure home to being destitute if the marriage breaks down and their home is registered in their husband's name only. The number of

Muslim women who find themselves in this predicament has reportedly risen in recent times, and in response, the Muslim Marriage Project (MMP) led by Baroness Syeda Warsi was set up to investigate this phenomena (Duncan Lewis Solicitors Press Release 2014). The MMP is pursuing two routes as possible solutions to the problem. Firstly, the legal route wherein legislation may be proposed to compel registration of marriages in order to protect vulnerable women and children. Secondly, a drive within Muslim communities to raise awareness of the issue coupled with the drive to encourage Mosques to register as buildings in which the solemnisation of marriages can occur (Duncan Lewis Solicitors Press Release 2014).

Based on the empirical research conducted for this chapter, it is clear that convenience, choice and the freedom to choose play a pivotal role in the manifestation of unregistered Muslim marriages. Consequently, the first of the possible solutions advocated by the MMP becomes problematic. If the analogy of cohabiting couples is used, each couple, whether they undertake an unregistered marriage or choose to cohabit, utilise their basic freedoms to make that choice. It would be discriminatory to force one couple to undergo a state ceremony of marriage while the other is permitted to choose between the two options; and thus this potential solution should be approached with a great deal of caution. Despite the underlying objective of protecting vulnerable women and children, this approach would be deemed an unprecedented infringement on the rights of British Muslims, especially since cohabiting couples face the same potential pitfalls as unregistered Muslim marriages. In order to address concerns about misinformation regarding the rights attached to an unregistered marriage, or the rites to be undertaken for a recognised marriage; the key is education.

Widespread awareness campaigns can provide a solution which allows the spouses to make their own decisions on the rights they will afford themselves in their marriage. In order to prevent the exceptionalising of Muslim communities, such a campaign can also tackle other groups who undergo unregistered religious marriages. A similar campaign was launched addressing cohabiting couples, titled 'The Living Together Campaign' (LTC) launched in mid-2004. A web-site was set up providing detailed advice and guidance for cohabiting couples to make them aware of their legal positions. An evaluation of the project was undertaken by Barlow et al (Barlow et al 2006) in which they concluded that the website set up by the LTC had a generally positive impact on awareness of rights, but needed further promotion for amplified awareness. They also concluded that '[i]nitiatives to encourage cohabitants to make appropriate financial and legal provision are likely to be more successful if they are targeted at the key turning points of relationships (for example, buying or renting a home together, having a child, etc.) when partners are already having to negotiate and take legal steps' (Barlow et al 2006: 10). While the study identified some support for legal reform, there was no obvious consensus on the nature of that reform. Where unregistered Muslim marriages are concerned, it is apparent that British Muslims do need to be engaged on this issue before broad-reaching measures such as legislation is discussed.

VI. CONCLUSION

This chapter does not provide a solution to an issue. Rather, it identifies a norm which is becoming increasingly prevalent—unregistered Muslim marriages. There are many similarities and few differences between marriage under English law and from within the Islamic legal traditions. Both are intended to be the bedrock of society and create a safe environment for raising children. This chapter engaged with the empirical evidence provided by a survey of 20 participants who are engaged in unregistered marriages, and concludes that the decision not to register marriages is often based on practical conveniences, priorities and the demands on time. The majority of participants were clearly fully participating members of society in various professional roles. Their religious marriage ceremonies ranged from modest to lavish, with a great deal of emphasis being placed on their desire to fulfil the traditional rites associated with a religiously recognised marriage. These social occasions allowed their unions to be announced to loved ones and their communities, and the celebrations marked a turning point in their lives from being single individuals to becoming a family unit in which children could be born and raised.

This research supports the contention that there is no fixed social profile for couples choosing to undertake the *nikkah* and forfeit the state recognised civil marriage ceremony. While there is much conjecture surrounding the underlying reasons for the lack of registration of Muslim marriages, this decision appears to be a matter of convenience for many couples and as they have no perceived need to engage with the law as far as their successful marriages are concerned, many are happy to continue with their current arrangement. This optimism may be coupled with a lack of awareness of the legal consequences of non-registration. Busy lives following a lavish religious wedding and honeymoon for which a couple will no doubt have expended substantial holiday entitlements, negates the time and attention required for a civil ceremony of marriage to be planned and accomplished. While some individuals made the choice not to register as they placed little value on state recognition of their unions, for the majority it was merely a lack of opportunity to complete the process. If there are any normative influences that give rise to the decision to marry only within the Islamic traditions, this cannot be traced to religious doctrine.

Those within successful marriages where there are no requirements to engage with laws of immigration or other potential legal considerations, appear to feel no urgency in registering their marriages, with one participant stating that it would be a concern once they had children, and another, who cited inheritance and tax implications. Thus, key turning points in a relationship may give rise to registration and there certainly appears to be a clear lack of any ideological aversion to undertaking a civil marriage ceremony for British Muslims. The models of intervention provided by the LTC may be a framework for consideration, however, successful deployment would be dependent upon the extent of its dissemination. Whether there is the political will for such a project, and the availability of requisite funding from the Ministry of Justice remains to be seen. It is improbable that awareness in itself will be an adequate solution. It is nevertheless the most vital and imperative first step.

BIBLIOGRAPHY

AKHTAR, Rajnaara, *British Muslims and the Transformative Processes of the Islamic Legal Traditions; Negotiating Law, Culture and Religion with Specific Reference to Islamic Law and Faith Based Alternative Dispute Resolution* (University of Warwick, PhD Thesis, 2013).

AKHTAR, Shabbir, *The Quran and the Secular Mind: A Philosophy of Islam* (London and New York, Routledge, 2008).

ALI, Shaheen Sardar, 'Is an Adult Muslim Women Sui Juris? Some Reflections on the Concept of "Consent in Marriage" without a Wali (with Particular Reference to the Saima Waheed Case)' (1996) 3(1) *Yearbook of Islamic and Middle Eastern Law Online* 156.

ATKINSON, Rowland and FLINT, John, 'Sampling, snowball: accessing hidden and hard-to-reach populations' in RL Miller and JD Brewer (eds), *The A-Z of Social Sciences* (Sage, 2003, available at: srmo.sagepub.com/view/the-a-z-of-social-research/n94.xml.

AUDA, Jasser *Maqasid Al-Shariah as Philosophy of Islamic Law* (Washington DC, IIIT, 2008).

BALCHIN, Cassandra and WARRAICH, Sohail Akbar, Recognising *the Unrecognised: InterCountry Cases, Muslim Marriages and Divorces in* Britain, available at: www.wluml.org/node/566.

BARLOW, Anne, DUNCAN, Simon, JAMES, Grace and PARK, Alison, *Cohabitation, Marriage and the Law, Social Change and Legal Reform in the 21st Century* (Oxford, Hart Publishing, 2005).

BARLOW, Anne, BURGOYNE, Carole and SMITHSON, Janet, 'The Living Together Campaign—An investigation of its impact on legally aware cohabitants' *Ministry of Justice Research Series 5/07*, available at: http://lawcommission.justice.gov.uk/docs/living-together-research-report.pdf.

BALLARD, Roger Ethnic Diversity and the Delivery of Justice, the Challenge of Plurality in P Shah and W Menski (eds), *Migration, Diasporas and Legal Systems in Europe* (London, Routledge-Cavendish, 2006.

CURIN, R Richard, PRESSER, Stanley and SINGER, Eleanor, 'The effects of response rate changes on the index of consumer sentiment' (2000) 64 *Public Opinion Quarterly* 413.

DOI, Abdur-Rahman and CLARKE, Abdassamad, *Shariah; Islamic Law*, 2nd edn (London, TaHa Publishers, 2008).
DOUGLAS, Gillian, 'Britain's Religious Tribunals: Joint Governance in Practice' (2013) 33 *Oxford Journal of Legal Studies* 263.
DUNCAN LEWIS SOLICITORS, 'Press Release, Aina Khan and Baroness Warsi kickstart Muslim Marriage Project' (2014) available at: www.duncanlewis.co.uk/IslamicLaw_news/Aina_Khan_and_Baroness_Warsi_kickstart_Muslim_Marriage_*Project* _(14_January_2014).html.
ESPOSITO, John, *What Everyone needs to know about Islam,* 2nd edn (New York, Oxford University Press, 2011).
FOURNIER, Pascale, *Muslim Marriage in Western Courts, Lost in Transplantation* (Farnham, Ashgate, 2010).
——, '*Family law, state recognition and intersecting spheres/spaces: Jewish and Muslim women divorcing in the* UK'. A submission to the Centaur Conference, McGill University, available at www.pascalef.com/wp-content/uploads/2014/05/Centaur-April-2014-FINAL.pdf.
FYZEE, Asaf *Outlines of Mohammadan Law*, 4th edn (Delhi, OUP, 1974).
GELL, Simeran Man Singh, 'Legality and Ethnicity, Marriage among the South of Bedford' (1994) 14(4) *Critique of Anthropology* 355.
HALLAQ, Wael (ed), *The Formation of Islamic Law* (Farnham, Ashgate, 1995).
KAMALI, Mohammad, *A Textbook of Hadith Studies: Authenticity, Compilation, Classification and Criticism of Hadith* (Markfield, Islamic Foundation Publishing, 2005).
KING, Wesley and MILES, Edward, 'A quasi-experimental assessment of the effect of computerizing noncognitive paper-and-pencil measurements: a test measurement equivalence' (1995) 80(6) *Journal of Applied Psychology* 643.
LAU, Martin 'Opening Pandora's Box: The Impact of the Saima Waheed Case on the Legal Status of Women in Pakistan' (1996) 3 *Yearbook of Islamic and Middle Eastern Law* 518.
MIR-HOSSEINI, Ziba, 'Islam and Gender Justice' in V Cornell and O Safi (eds), *Voices of Islam: Vol 5: Voices of Diversity and Change* (Westport, Greenwood, 2007).
MUSLIM MARRIAGE WORKING GROUP, *Report of Working Group* (2012) available at: www.whatdotheyknow.com/request/179578/response/444442/attach/7/MMWG%20SUBMISSION%20AND%20FINAL%20REPORT%20 11.10.12.pdf.
OFFICE OF NATIONAL STATISTICS, *Childbearing of UK and non-UK born women living in the UK—2011 Census Data*, ONS, 2014), available at: www.ons.gov.uk/ons/rel/fertility-analysis/childbearing-of-uk-and-non-uk-born-women-living-in-the-uk/2011-census-data/index.html.
——, *Full Story: What does the Census tell us about religion in 2011?* (ONS, 2013a), available at: www.ons.gov.uk/ons/rel/census/2011-census/detailed-characteristics-for-local-authorities-in-england-and-wales/sty-religion.html.
——, *Families and Households* (ONS, 2013b), available at: www.ons.gov.uk/ons/rel/family-demography/families-and-households/2013/stb-families.html.
SANDBERG, Russell, DOUGLAS, Gillian, DOE, Norman, GILLIAT-RAY, Sophie and KHAN, Asma, 'Britain's Religious Tribunals: Joint Governance in Practice' (2013) 33 *Oxford Journal of Legal Studies* 263.

PEARL, David and MENSKI, Werner *Muslim Family Law* (London, Sweet and Maxwell, 1998).

SHANNAHAN, Dervla 'Sexual Ethics, marriage, and sexual autonomy: the landscapes for Muslimat and lesbian, gay, bisexual, and transgendered Muslims' (2009) 3 *Contemporary Islam* 59.

SINGER, Eleanor, VAN HOEWYK John and MAHER Mary P, 'Experiments with incentives in telephone surveys' (2000) 64 *Public Opinion Quarterly* 171.

WANI, Afzal *The Islamic Institution of Mahr* (New Delhi, Qazi Publishers, 1996).

WELCHMAN, Lyn *Women's Rights in Islamic Family Law* (London and New York, Zed Books Ltd, 2004).

WERBNER, Pnina, 'Theorising Complex Diasporas: Purity and Hybridity in the South Asia Public Sphere in Britain' (2004) 30(5) *Journal of Ethnic and Migration Studies* 895.

YEFET, Karin Carmit, 'What's the Constitution got to do with it? Regulating Marriage in Pakistan' (2009) 16 *Duke Journal of Gender Law & Policy* 347.

ADDENDUM

Survey Questions

Thank you for giving me a few minutes of your time to complete this survey. I am researching registered and unregistered Muslim marriages in the UK, and my interest is in marriage rites and how Muslim couples celebrate their marriages.
Dr Rajnaara Akhtar

1. About you
   About you: Are you Male or Female?
   How old are you?
   How long have you been married?
   Is your nikkah registered as a civil marriage?
   Where do you live (name of town or city)?
   What is your profession/job?
   What is your ethnic background?
   Were you born in a Muslim family or did you convert to Islam?

ABOUT YOUR WEDDING DAY

2. What was the most important aspect of your wedding day to you?

3. What do you think was the most important aspect of the wedding day to your parents or close family members?

4. Can you briefly describe the main events from your wedding day (eg the arrival of the parties, speeches, food, entertainment, religious ceremony, etc).

5. Do you think your wedding was different to other weddings that are then registered through a civil ceremony? If so, how.

6. Cost of your wedding and planning:
   - How much did your wedding celebration cost in total (Wedding reception, invitations, etc. NOT gifts) (An approximate figure is acceptable)
   - How much did gifts given from the bride and groom to each other and extended families, cost (an approximate figure is acceptable)
   - How long did you spend planning your wedding?
   - How many people were present at your wedding?

REGISTERED AND UNREGISTERED MARRIAGES

7. If your marriage is unregistered, what are the main reasons for choosing not to register your marriage by participating in a civil ceremony?

8. When interacting with society, do you tell people that you are married or unmarried?
   Employer
   Doctors/Health Profession
   Muslim Friends
   Non-Muslim
   Strangers

9

Forced Marriage: Rites and Rights

PERVEEZ MODY

I. INTRODUCTION

I MET MISHKA,[1] a self-described 'survivor' of a forced marriage who had grown up in Manchester. She told me how when she was a young girl, gossip at home suggested she was being lined up to marry a cousin in Pakistan. A trip to Mirpur in Pakistani Kashmir involved the hustle and bustle of food and relatives arriving and wedding preparations. Naively, Mishka asked whose wedding it was only to be told it was her own. She was shocked, resistant; but when her protests were brushed aside she recognised that she had little option but to go through with the marriage. She was threatened that if she didn't, she would be kept in Mirpur until she agreed to toe the family line. Mishka went through with the marriage and made a pact with her cousin-husband that she would bring him over to Britain so long as he didn't expect this to be a 'real' marriage in any sense and agreed 'to leave her alone'. She kept to her side of the bargain and brought him over, getting a job to support him to prove to the immigration authorities that they would be economically self-sufficient. However, when he came to Britain and demanded that she play the social and sexual role of his wife she phoned the local police who arrived at her home, escorted her out of the door and took her to a women's refuge.

Mishka suffered enormous loneliness and missed her family desperately, despite fearing their anger and knowing their disappointment at her actions. Nothing had prepared her for the shift from a South Asian household full of its intimacies to the harsh, controlling and lonely world of refuges. Like many other young women I have spoken to in the course of my fieldwork, she spoke of silent and unanswered phone-calls made to her home and of her longing memories of siblings and family; wondering when her isolation would ever end.

[1] Throughout this chapter I maintain the anthropological convention of anonymity for all my informants, who are given pseudonyms.

This chapter examines the ethnographic complexity of 'consent' in the context of forced and arranged marriage and its relevance for our understandings of marital rights and rites for South Asians in England and Wales today.[2] The argument pursued is twofold. The first section will look at some of the presumptions underlying the current law and the complexities arising from it. I will propose that the emphasis on ascertaining legal 'consent' to a marriage (to repudiate or establish claims of coercion) has exhibited the way in which consent itself is un-theorised in terms of its anthropological significance for British South Asian marriage. In this chapter, I present an anthropological argument based on ethnographic cases of forced marriage in the UK to argue that we may find that obligation is a forceful element in the construction of marital consent and, furthermore, that it is difficult to determine whether consent is borne of a 'genuine change of mind' where opposition has previously been expressed. My argument here is that consent and resistance to marriage are part of the intimate coercions that parents and children exercise upon each other. This discussion draws on the interplay between consent and the categories of love, arranged and forced marriages. The second part of the chapter presents some anthropological conceptions of consent, coercion, force and obligation through the lens of specific ethnographic cases to ask whether coercion is useful in thinking about the right not to marry.

Using popular classification, 'love-marriages' are self-arranged marriages and frequently take place across more carefully guarded social boundaries of class, caste, community, linguistic or ethno-religious group than those marriages that are parentally arranged. 'Arranged marriages' are arranged by the couple's parents and usually conform firmly to notions of community and caste endogamy (including amongst Muslims, for whom the *biradari* or clan serves as an endogamous group). In some instances of "love-cum-arranged marriage", parents may agree to endorse publicly the love choice of their child through domesticating acts of arrangement (for instance, throwing a reception to signal their support of the marriage choice) thus drawing love-marriages into a culturally acceptable repertoire of arrangement.

To the legal mind, forced marriages are those in which either (or both) parties to the marriage do not give their full and free consent and so the marriage can be annulled.[3] The difficulty of applying this legal clarity to

[2] I am restricting this discussion to England and Wales because there is a different law for Scotland. The Forced Marriage (Protection and Jurisdiction) (Scotland) Act 2011 provides legal protections for those facing forced marriages and makes the breach of a protection order a criminal offence, punishable by two years in jail.

[3] Lack of valid consent to marry arising from duress is a ground upon which a marriage is voidable in English law: Matrimonial Causes Act 1973, s 12(1)(c); this finding and result is conceptually distinct from divorce, in which a valid marriage is terminated—a finding of nullity, by contrast, typically rests on some flaw present from the inception of the marriage, which invalidates it.

South Asian marital forms arises in the first instance in the identification of 'the parties' and the agency the law attributes to the party as an individual. Underlying the consent of the individual in a typical arranged marriage is the social/cultural conceptualisation of the 'two parties' to a marriage as the two *families* who consent to it (not merely the marrying individuals). It is the active desire of these collectivities that is widely understood to 'cause' marriages to happen (Dumont 1988; Ballard 2011). Rituals of South Asian marriages across diverse caste or ethno-religious groups often express the active agency of the parents and families involved in the marital rituals by presenting the agency of the bride, groom (and couple) as merely dutifully acquiescing to their parents' wishes (Gell 1994). This interaction of kinship at the forefront of arranged marriage creates a spectrum of agency which has problematised the development and practice of the legislation intended to circumscribe consent and distinguish acquiescence from coercion. In short, how can the law treat the presence or absence of consent as determinative when the concept of consent is so socially complex?

II. THE LAW AGAINST FORCED MARRIAGE

Whilst it is difficult to pinpoint exactly how or when forced marriage began to figure in public discourse in the UK, it is clear that a series of high-profile cases extensively publicised in the media sparked widespread interest (Briggs 1997; Sanghera 2007, 2009) and led to state intervention centred on the issue of 'forced marriages'. Forced marriage had long been invalid under English law—as noted above, such a marriage can be brought to an end with a decree of nullity. However, the more recent publicity led to the Forced Marriage (Civil Protection) Act 2007, which was designed to enforce the state's intolerance of families coercing their children to marry, and to prevent such marriages in the first place, by creating civil remedies directed against those using force for this purpose. The law is described as making provision for 'protecting individuals against being forced to enter into marriage without their free and full consent and for protecting individuals who have been forced to enter into marriage without such consent'.[4] Under this law, to 'force' is defined in section 63A(6) as to 'coerce by threats or other psychological means'. By this definition, physical and emotional threats designed to coerce can attract civil redress in the shape of 'protection orders'. Furthermore, the violation of a forced marriage protection order or, indeed, using any form of coercion for the purpose of causing someone to

[4] For the full text of the law, see: www.legislation.gov.uk/ukpga/2007/20/introduction.

enter into a marriage is now a criminal offence under Part 10 of the Anti-Social Behaviour, Crime and Policing Act 2014.[5]

The Home Office-commissioned report into forced marriages, *A Choice by Right* (Uddin and Ahmed 2000) emphasises the definitional boundaries between arranged marriages and forced marriages. Arranged marriages are described as 'traditional' and legitimate forms of marriage in numerous parts of the world and within certain minority communities in the UK (ibid: 10). Such marriages are arranged by the parents but nonetheless require the consent of both partners to the marriage. In the language of the report: 'In the tradition of arranged marriages, the families of both spouses take a leading role in arranging the marriage, but the choice whether to solemnise the arrangement remains with the spouses and can be exercised at any time' (ibid: 10). 'Forced marriage' is sharply distinguished from arranged marriage as a mutation from the (approved) arranged set-up, in which one or both parties to the marriage do not consent or have been coerced or forced into giving consent (ibid). As the report succinctly puts it, 'In forced marriage, there is no choice' (ibid: 10). One of the problems with that statement is that while it is objectively true that in a situation of force there is no choice, it does not account for the complex range of circumstances that prevent individuals from being able to identify the forcefulness of obligation that they feel bearing down upon them.

When complex and contested cases involving forced marriage allegations reach the courts, whether under this civil/criminal legislation or in the context of a petition for a decree of nullity of the marriage, the interpretive burden placed upon judges to decide precisely what counts as legitimate kinship obligation and pressure (consistent with the giving of consent) and what counts as psychological coercion (invalidating consent) is very great indeed. This tension was fore-grounded in the Home Office report, *A Choice by Right*:

> There is a spectrum of behaviours behind the term forced marriage, ranging from emotional pressure, exerted by close family members and the extended family, to the more extreme cases, which can involve threatening behaviour, abduction, imprisonment, physical violence, rape and in some cases murder. People spoke to the Working Group about 'loving manipulation' in the majority of cases, where parents genuinely felt that they were acting in their children and family's best interests (Uddin and Ahmed, 2000: 11).

[5] Forced marriage was already a criminal offence in Scotland. Critics of criminalisation argue that it has further impeded the possibility of people seeking help from legal sources as they fear that their own kin will be arrested. It has also had the inadvertent outcome that people minimise the experiences they have had, again because they fear bringing more trouble upon their families if they confess all. The 2014 Act criminalises conduct related to forced marriage wherever in the world the marriage takes place (or is intended to take place). See also Wilson 2014: www.opendemocracy.net/5050/amrit-wilson/criminalising-forced-marriage-in-uk-why-it-will-not-help-women.

In this vein, Anitha and Gill (2009) draw attention to a Scottish case that pre-dates the passing of the Forced Marriage (Scotland) Act 2011 in which the validity of a marriage had to be determined. In *Mahmud v Mahmud*,[6] a 30-year-old British Pakistani man (Mr Mahmud) argued that he had succumbed to parental pressure (crucially, *without* a genuine change of mind) and married his cousin from Pakistan at a Register Office in Glasgow only after 12 years of resisting this arranged marriage. He did not reveal his marriage to his non-Muslim girlfriend whom he had plans to marry, and with whom he had had one child and was expecting a second. On the day of the marriage, he went to the register office on his way to work on his own and in his work clothes; following the ceremony, he left the register office alone and went to work. The fact that he had gone through the ceremony but had not consummated the union or agreed to long-term cohabitation was important in drawing the inference that the apparent consent to marry that was given was piecemeal, and forced. Soon after the marriage, Mr. Mahmud informed the immigration authorities that this was a 'pretended marriage', entered into under duress and so his cousin-'wife' was deported. She having been deported, the wife made no appearance at the hearing of Mr Mahmud's case for the marriage to be annulled for want of valid consent.

Lord Prosser, in granting his order of nullity of marriage, asked why Mr. Mahmud married in this way. He drew attention to the 'general cultural and social background of the parties involved', and the fact that 'the family maintained the tradition of parental authority and the obedience of children to their parents' wishes, including their wishes in relation to marriage'. As soon as Mr Mahmud left school, he began to experience pressure to marry his cousin, but unlike his brother (whose view on his own arranged marriage and its attendant family pressures was 'fair enough') he resisted, and hoped his parents would have a change of heart. Unfortunately, they did not and his father died of a stroke, expressing—as his dying wish—that his son should marry his cousin. Consequently, Mr Mahmud was blamed by the family for his father's death and suffered from the knowledge of the shame his mother would experience if he continued to resist the marriage. For Lord Prosser, the crucial question was one raised by Ormrod LJ in the case of *Hirani v Hirani*,[7] 'whether the threats, pressure or whatever it is is such as to destroy the reality of consent and overbears the will of the individual'.

But Lord Prosser also stressed that parents are entitled to apply pressure upon a person refusing to marry, with a view to producing a change of mind. Lord Prosser argued:

> [I]n my opinion parents, and indeed others, are well entitled to exert their influence, and indeed to apply pressure, upon a person who is refusing to marry, with

[6] *Mahmud v Mahmud* 1994 SLT 599.
[7] *Hirani v Hirani* [1982] 4 *Fam Law* 232.

> a view to producing a change of mind ... I would also emphasise that if under pressure—and perhaps very considerable pressure—a party does indeed change his or her mind and consents to a marriage with however ill a grace and however resentfully, then the marriage is in my opinion valid. It will only be invalid if the consent which has thus been induced cannot sensibly be described as a genuine change of mind or a genuine expression of will, but is rather to be categorised as an act contrary to the party's own true intent, and an unwilling surrender to a pressure which the individual is no longer able to resist.[8]

In reading this judgment, two things become very clear. The first is that the law had to draw a line between what counted as persuasion and what counted as coercion. The judge annulled the marriage, but nevertheless recognised the possibility that parental pressure (and their children's deference to it) is a relevant fact of kinship and that it need not amount to coercion if the person capitulates to that pressure, even if it is with 'ill grace'.[9] Thus, the court recognises that sometimes this pressure will invalidate consent, and sometimes it will not, depending on the particular circumstances and individual involved.[10] Despite the finding that the marriage is invalidated, this judgment draws attention to the cultural primacy of deference and the centrality of the exercise of parental will upon the marriages of their offspring in discerning whether the individual parties to such marriages can properly be said to have 'consented' to them.[11]

III. COMMUNITY RITES AND RIGHTS

The debates over forced marriages and honour crimes have sought to make vitally important inroads into ethno-religious and kinship practices, as they seek to underline that forced marriage is intolerable and that there is no place for it to hide. In the unequivocal terms expressed by Mike O'Brien (then Home Office Minister for Community Relations) in a parliamentary debate on women's human rights: 'Multicultural sensitivity is not an excuse for moral blindness' (Uddin and Ahmed 2000: 10). It is easy to see how South Asian communities in this country are facing a crisis: internally, from the attractiveness of forms of resurgent religion that are demonstratively

[8] *Mahmud v Mahmud* 1994 SLT 599, 601.

[9] 'If one ignores traditions of authority and deference between parent and child, or the normal custom of arranged marriages, no judgment will be possible as to the point where pressure should be called force, or deference becomes *unwilling* capitulation. Anyone ignorant of these traditions would perhaps be inclined to make an assumption that arranged marriages involve an inherently 'forceful' imposition of the parents' will, overbearing the will of the child. I see no general basis for that view' (emphasis added) (ibid, 601).

[10] See Mody (2013) for an anthropological discussion of capitulation in South Asian marriages, and Harris-Short, Miles & George (2015), pp 86-91 for a survey of the case law on duress as a factor rendering marriage voidable in English law.

[11] See *Singh v Kaur* (1981) 11 *Fam Law* 152 for example, for a case in which pressure was not found to have invalidated consent.

'modern', politically-charged and consequently attractive to some of their young; and externally, through a widespread perception of a policy and media-led critique that their kinship values are somehow 'backward' and need to change. Increasingly then, communities and individuals are becoming aware of the message against forced marriages, and are taking it upon themselves to ensure that such unhealthy practices are rooted out of their communities. So, for instance, I have heard of one Asian police officer of the South Yorkshire police force who, in his capacity as secretary of his local mosque, has taken it upon himself to attend every marriage solemnised there to ensure that there is full and free consent of all the individuals marrying.

However, whilst the tide appears to be slowly turning in favour of internal 'community' vigilance in ensuring no-one is *forced* into a marriage, there is no consensus on whether young South Asians in Britain should be *free to choose whom* they want to marry, or *how* they should marry, a key concern of this chapter. As someone who has worked on love-marriages in South Asia, I find this silence unsurprising because it indicates that there is still an enormous unease about publicly condoning self-arranged or 'love-marriages', even though, in private, young people are increasingly able to convince their families to support their own choice of spouse, especially if that person was carefully chosen and of the same background. Samad (2004) points out that by resorting to textual Islam some women are able to argue with their parents that they should have the right to marry whom they want and that they cannot be forced into an arranged marriage. Whilst this linguistic conjunction of force with arrangement is bewildering to lawyers who see clear definitional demarcations between 'forced marriages' and perfectly acceptable (ie consensual) 'arranged marriages', the anthropological evidence on the ground is that South Asians who may be angling to be permitted to marry out of love frequently express their frustration by using these conjoined terms ('forced into arrangement'), as if to mark the absence of choice entailed. Indeed, this appears to be the empowering message of one of the women's groups at the forefront of tackling forced marriage in Derby, which identify Islamic organisations through which they hope to bring about 'Islamic understanding' and through this, help women get *khulla* or Islamic divorce. They openly support love-marriages, saying that you could not marry someone who you do not even know.[12]

In general, however, such self-selected marriages are often deplored. For example, one speaker, a female Muslim chaplain, at a 'Forced Marriage Road Show' in Manchester argued that she was 'fed up' with young people in Bradford who, she claimed, were now making allegations of forced marriages against their parents in order to 'lead their Clark Gable lifestyles'.[13]

[12] *Apna Haq* (Your Rights) event, Derby, 24 May 2008.

[13] This was the opening shot of Z Khan, a reflexive and rather exuberant female Muslim chaplain in Bradford.

She said that an association of Imams in Bradford has decided not to solemnise any *Nikkahs* (Islamic marriage contracts, creating marriage under Islamic law, though not under English law) if the parents do not accompany the couple who wish to marry: these marriages would be assumed to be love-marriages that had no parental blessing. Here we see the full extent of the crisis precipitated by this debate over forced marriages in the realm of kinship values and marital rites. Simeran Gell in her seminal work on British South Asian religious and register office marriages in the early 1990s argued that immigration practices had so affected the marital rites of British-born South Asians that many communities such as Jat Sikhs in Bedford had come to adopt what may appear to be a superfluous two-marriage sequence in the UK (civil register office marriage followed by religious marriage in a Gurudwara approximately six months later). She observes that despite the 'technical marriage' in the register office that legally effected the union, such marrying couples would not subsequently behave as though they were married in any socially meaningful way, maintaining appropriate distance as though they were still merely betrothed or engaged. The second 'religious' marriage took place in temples that were registered places of worship and here the cultural form and demeanour of bride and groom were in keeping with the convention that arranged-marrying couples are indifferent but consenting partners to the union. Gell argues that the first part of the two-marriage sequence—the civil marriage registration—is culturally as significant for her Jat Sikh informants as the religious ceremony that marries them, since the incorporation of these rites allows them to legally 'smile at the state' to demonstrate British values and show that their parentally-arranged religious marriages were not false, forced or sham marriages just because they were not based on the metropolitan motivations of pre-marital romantic love. On the other hand, marriage itself is meaningfully embarked upon only after it receives religious sanction in culturally appropriate ways through blessings in the Gurudwara. Gell's work in the early 1990s demonstrates the ways in which South Asians in the UK can be seen to have been navigating their relationship with Britain through innovations in their marital rites.

Both the example of the Yorkshire police officer who attends all marriages to ensure they are not coerced and that of the Bradford Imams who seek to protect parents from unwanted love-marriages indicate the emergence of new 'rites' of marriage that are being shaped by the exigencies of the forced marriage law. Ethno-religious communities are feeling the need to regulate themselves to ensure that there is no 'force' in play, whilst also having to balance carefully the relations of power between generations so that young people are made to talk to their parents and make them agreeable if they wish to have a love-marriage. Clearly, the effects of the discourse of forced marriage have begun to be experienced in the realm of marital rites even if they have not led to overt calls to support love-marriages instead of parentally arranged ones.

As a result of the intense politicisation of the forced marriage debate, a whole range of issues are not being raised yet within the British South Asian community—most notably, the right not to marry at all, and secondly, the right to marry out of love or choice rather than arrangement. The literature on 'forced marriage', as it has developed in the past few years, is heavily focused upon arranged marriage and is almost completely silent about the large number of South Asians whose loving relations with *non-South Asian* partners abruptly end when the South Asian partner comes under intense pressure to find a more appropriate or 'suitable' spouse. The extent of this problem can be seen by the fact that boyfriends and girlfriends are increasingly contacting agencies, with or without the support of their partner, to complain about 'forced marriages' of their partners to a third party.[14] The excessive emphasis on young South Asian *women* in need of rescue by the state has also meant that there is a dearth of mixed-sex refuges in the UK that can provide refuge to *a couple* escaping violence or threats of violence, even though many of those supporting such couples have increasingly noted this need.[15] Since such couples are invariably in loving relationships that are threatened by the impending forced marriage, it is striking that among the many silences surrounding self-choosing in marriage is that regarding the extent to which both parties to the intimate relationship (even non-South Asian partners) may experience threats and violence.[16]

IV. CONSENT OR COMPROMISE?

The forms and forming of individual consent reveal how extensively the ties of kinship obligation are experienced and felt, not just by the marrying parties but by all the immediate kin who shape marriage proceedings.

The many instances of 'loving coercion' that litter the anthropological record but remain unseen by the legal gaze alert us to the inherent confusion between kinship coercion and the practice described in short-hand as 'arrangement'. The paradox is encapsulated by the frequently heard complaint amongst informants who seek relief from a forced marriage and who describe their situation as one in which they have been 'forced into an arranged marriage'—thus highlighting the fact that with such coercive arrangement, not marrying ceases to be a viable alternative to arrangement or love.[17] One of the issues that is being seriously discussed in the emerging

[14] Interviews with members of the Forced Marriage Unit, Foreign and Commonwealth Office, London, November 2012.

[15] Interview with former Male Support Worker, December 2009.

[16] For a chilling account of the lack of protection available to couples on the run in England, see Briggs and Briggs (1997).

[17] I am grateful to Kaveri Sharma for bringing this to my attention (personal communication).

literature is the fact that, as in studies of domestic violence, many people condemn 'forced marriages' and yet find it difficult to 'see themselves in the picture' (Khanum 2008: 10). Whilst government and legal luminaries are keen to emphasise that the new law is about 'force', not 'arrangement', in practice the forcefulness of obligation, the internally coercive nature of kinship and the sexual and romantic attachments of lovers often co-mingle. Forceful arrangement may often be the outcome of the parents' sudden discovery of their child's romantic love, or other signs of a loss of parental control (for instance, sexuality and independence amongst young women, as well as children getting involved in drugs and petty crime).[18] Equally, young people may find themselves morally and psychologically bound to follow a course of arrangement they say they want no part in. The elasticity, or reflexivity, of coercion may well express itself in the form of freer second marriages that may often follow more socially constrained (even forced) first marriages.

In practice, however, young British South Asians tend to experience the boundaries between force and arrangement, between coercion and choice, as much more blurred, precisely because a common understanding of marriage is that it is an expression of wider kinship values that are shared by the whole social group, and at least to some extent, by the couple involved. As one of my Sikh informants (herself a victim of a 'forced marriage') said in response to my question about her own mother's arranged marriage: 'You know, she is a bit confused about it. She says, you have to marry when your parents tell you to. In my opinion, it sounds like a forced marriage, if you ask me!' Note how this definition is technically true ('In a forced marriage, there is no choice'), but that for many South Asians, such obedient consent is part of a kinship matrix that many grow up with, with no expectation that it will be otherwise (note, for example, that in *Mahmud v Mahmud*, Mahmud's own brother's reaction to an arranged marriage was that it was 'fair enough').

Conversely, a British Bangladeshi mother of one of my informants in Tottenham, London, reflecting on her own daughter's forced marriage said this about her husband's motivations:

> His mother was Hitler Number 1! My husband kept his word to his mother [about arranging his daughter's marriage to his eldest brother's son]. She could have stopped him at any point if she wanted to. My husband felt, my parents have told me to do something, I respect them, so I must do it. Our religion is that we must help others [our kin]. He did not think that he was about to unleash a storm into his own daughter's life.

Here the mother spells out in hindsight the force of obligation upon her husband that made him seek an arrangement despite the trouble he unleashed

[18] See Samad and Eade (2002: 53–67); Forced Marriage Unit in Khanum (2008: 6–10).

upon their daughter. She saw the agent of coercion as her mother-in-law, a 'Hitler Number 1' who held the key to stopping the cursed marriage.

Another informant, a 27-year-old British Kashmiri woman who had lived through a forced marriage at the age of 17 said to me:

> If I didn't marry, I would be cast aside; I would bring shame on the family, my parents would lose their sisters and brothers—no-one would speak to them. So, it was almost as if it was a duty for me to get married.

It is important to note the emphasis in these cases on the strength of kinship obligation owed by the parents to other relatives to arrange a suitable marriage (even if the matter must be forced). Shaw, in her work on transnational cousin marriage amongst British Pakistanis (2001) reveals that she found the parents of British offspring blaming the marriage itself upon pressure from their own siblings in Pakistan. She draws analytic attention to the peril of parents ignoring the obligation to consider the children of their siblings in Pakistan as potential marriage partners, showing us the important ways in which sibling bonds may play a part in causing parents themselves to experience pressure that they then transmit onto their children.

Forcefulness clearly need not be violent; as I have argued elsewhere, ethnographically force is sometimes revealed as a sort of profound fatalism that forecloses dissent—refusing to consider that obligations can be questioned (Mody 2013). Take the example of Ayesha, one of my informants, a university-educated British Bangladeshi woman who had a forced marriage from which she escaped. One summer, her parents took her to Bangladesh to marry her 21-year-old cousin, but instead she fell in love with a younger cousin who was just 18. They would meet by the riverbank in the village where she stayed, and he would give her gifts of Hindi music cassettes to express his feelings to her. She asked her father to let her marry the boy she loved but he refused, saying that he had promised his elder brother that their children would be married. Consent was not assumed but discussed and debated over a prolonged period of time in numerous domestic, kinship and social contexts, including the censorious stage whispers of aunts and uncles who would say that her parents had 'put Ayesha on a pedestal' by not putting their foot down and insisting that she should marry immediately as she was told. Ayesha explained that after the discovery of her romance with her younger cousin in Bangladesh, her father flew to Bangladesh to speak to her and try and arrange the marriage of his choosing with the older cousin. This is how she described the conversation with her father to me:

> We were at my *mama*'s house [mother's brother] by the railway tracks. My father said to me: '*Abbu* [father] has never asked you for anything, so I am going to ask you for one thing…' He didn't even have to say it. I automatically said 'yes' [to marry her older cousin]. So I did say 'yes'. I felt … like an obligation—he has given me everything I want. OK, he hasn't given me my freedom, but I know in the Asian community freedom is not what one is given, it is what is earned when you get married.

Nazia Khanum, in her case study of 'forced marriage' in Luton argues that preventing a love-marriage or forcing someone not to marry is as great a violation as forcing the person into an arrangement not of their making. Forced marriage then, sits close to a widely felt but frequently inchoate sense that resisting a marriage (exercising the right not to marry) is really resisting the obligations one has to one's most immediate kin. Conversely, acceding to such a marriage reinforces the moral worth of a person who is socially recognised as having retained their family's love and earned their 'freedom' (in the terms of Ayesha above).

This dilemma, framed differently, is posited by Marilyn Strathern (2005) in her article about a legal dispute—the 'Compo girl case'—fought between two Papua New Guinean Minj sub-clans, one of whom demanded a girl, 'Miriam', in compensation from the other. The notion that the issue of rights that people have in relations (ie in relatedness itself, claims on each other in the sense of kinship) is one that is profoundly productive in anthropology. Strathern anticipates some of the issues that I am grappling with in this chapter on forced marriage. She says by way of comment on the judge who ruled against Miriam being part of a 'head payment' to her mother's clan that '[t]o acknowledge claims as obligations in the context of kinship looks to modern eyes as perpetuating dependency, control and coercion' (2005: 129). Simplifying her argument enormously for the purposes of this chapter, Strathern's contention is that the Euro-American mode of thinking sets up groups opposed to each other and communities as opposed to the individual. Her contribution is to encourage us to consider the ways in which we can see obligation not as external but as *inhering* in all social interactions so that we can bring ourselves to entertain the prospect that Miriam 'might like to be able to fulfil her obligations' (2005: 132). In this construction, what is at stake is not so much Miriam's agency in abstraction, but her sense of self as mediated through her relationships (ie her rights in relations and relatedness).

In the case of Ayesha whose father pleads with her to marry his brother's son, her acquiescence to her father's wishes, pre-empting even his question, reveals how she too regards her sense of self as mediated through her relationship with her parents. She isn't free to marry the man she loves, because she understands freedom as a bequest from her parents in recognition for having dutifully fulfilled her kinship obligations—in her words, 'freedom is not what one is given, it is what is earned when you get married'. Ayesha is confronted by a beloved and much admired father asking her for something, 'for the first time in her life'. However, in reality his request that she marry as arranged is not a single question, just as the marriage itself is not a single event (even if the law deems it so). The marriage is the summation of multivalent kinship relations and the question posed by the father is whether Ayesha will submit (continue to submit) to the lifelong role that he has prepared for her. Ayesha says yes and in so doing she intends to surrender her love for her other cousin, reinforce her love for her father and—she feels—fulfil the self for which she has been prepared.

However, her consent was short-lived, and during the marriage ceremony (being conducted in her absence in another village), she escaped with her younger cousin and married him in a hasty ceremony conducted by a local Imam. After the wedding she remembered thinking of her father who would have had a search party out for her, and of her mother, wondering what she was feeling.

As it turned out, Ayesha's marriage to her younger cousin also failed and when she called her father for his help she was flown back to the UK and lived at home with her family albeit never in the stereotypical role imagined by her parents. Strathern's comment about Miriam's case is poignant here: 'Human rights discourse—grounded in equality between individuals sweeps all this [dependency, control, coercion] away. [The] question was whether it were also to sweep away kinship as such' (2005: 129). What I have tried to show in this chapter is that the emphasis on individual consent presupposes people who see themselves as singularly masters of their own agency, who must know their minds one way or another and be able to demonstrate this in a court of law. Whilst most British South Asians certainly could see themselves in this picture (and politically, it is important that they do), they would also recognise in the context of the discourse around forced marriage, that at the level of *values*, the abstraction of a rights-bearing individual (who must exercise their rights in favour of freedom at the expense of what looks like a surrender of one's closest kin) is a somewhat pyrrhic victory. The self that emerges in this discussion of consent in cases of forced marriage—whether the self is consenting to or repudiating collective values—is not a unified being, but a self built upon a series of painful compromises, each weighed and stacked against the other in a contingent and shifting universe of events and choices.

I began this chapter with the story about Mishka and her forced marriage in Pakistan. This forced marriage came to light when the freedom she sought (from the deal she had made with her cousin to disregard this as a 'true' marriage) was no longer available to her. Having fulfilled her obligation to her family, she felt she could not compromise herself any further and she left home and rebuilt her life in a different city. After almost a decade of forging a life of her own after her escape from her forced marriage, a few weeks prior to my interview with her, her work colleague had taken a phone-call from Mishka's little sister. Mishka described this to me by smiling brightly and prefacing her words with the following caveat—'So, now my story has a happy ending!' Her 'happy ending' began when she picked up the phone and spoke to her sister. In one moment, the long years of her kinship exile and isolation ended. Her family had finally tracked her down and was reeling her in. Her mother was in hospital and the whole family desperately wanted her back to be with them. She was incredibly scared and nervous and spoke to me of her delight in seeing her baby brother whose eczema she had tended for years when he was little, wrapping him in wet gauze to protect his bleeding body from the onslaught of inflammation. He was now a grown man and one of the first things he told her was that he was proud of her for standing up to their parents. Her little sister had struck out and declared to her parents that she wanted to have a love-marriage and this was now accepted. Mishka described with happiness *and* bitterness how much things had changed within her family and how sad she felt that she hadn't been able to benefit from any of it; she had to make the break and suffer much of the pain for things to change for her little siblings. She laughed and cried as she recounted to me the first thing her mother said to her when she arrived at the hospital to see her: 'You shouldn't have done what you did to us'.

This sentence in my mind captures the complexity of what is at stake in an anthropological study of forced marriage, consent and the right not to marry. Mishka's reaction to her mother's words was a mixture of surprise, disbelief and knowing. After everything Mishka had been through, her mother described her own heart being broken by her daughter's actions. Even in her shock and pain at hearing this, Mishka laughed as she recognised the enormous love that her mother's words also expressed towards her. Mishka's is a simple tale, where the 'happy ending' she declared to me in a life scarred by a forced marriage wasn't a Bollywood romance in which she married her boyfriend but rather a much dreamt of family reunion with her siblings and father around her mother's hospital bed. As with many of my informants (including Ayesha above), the contestations and compromises that bind individuals to their families and loved ones despite marriages, are equally strong, if not stronger than the ones that bind them to the state with its loving law against forced marriage.

BIBLIOGRAPHY

ANITHA, Sundari and GILL, Aisha, 'Coercion, Consent and the Forced Marriage Debate in the UK' (2009) 17 *Feminist Legal Studies* 165.

BALLARD, Roger, 'Honour Killing? Or just plain homicide?' in L Holden (ed), *Cultural Expertise and Litigation: Patterns, Conflicts, Narratives* (London, Routledge, 2011).

BRIGGS, Jack and BRIGGS, Zena, *Runaways: A True Story of Love and Danger* (London, Vista, 1997).

DUMONT, Louis, *Homo Hierarchicus* (New Delhi, Oxford University Press, 1988).

GELL, Simeran Mansingh, 'Legality and Ethnicity: Marriage among the South Asians of Bedford' (1994) 14 *Critique of Anthropology* 355.

HARRIS-SHORT, Sonia, MILES, Joanna and GEORGE, Rob, *Family Law: Text, Cases, and Materials*, 3rd edn (Oxford, Oxford University Press, 2015).

KHANUM, Nazia, *Forced marriage, family cohesion and community engagement: National learning through a case study of Luton* (Watford, Equality in Diversity, 2008).

MODY, Perveez, 'Marriages of Convenience and Capitulation: South Asian Marriage, Family and Intimacy in the Diaspora' in J Chatterji and D Washbrook (eds), *Routledge Handbook of the South Asian Diaspora* (London, Routledge, 2013).

SAMAD, Yunus, 'Muslim Youth in Britain: Ethnic to Religious Identity' presented at the Centre for Comparative Religious Studies, Turin, 11 June 2004, available at: www.cestim.it/argomenti/02islam/02islam_uk_sanad.pdf.

SAMAD, Yunas and EADE, John, *Community Perceptions of Forced Marriage* (London, Foreign and Commonwealth Office, Community Liaison Unit, 2002).

STRATHERN, Marilyn, *Kinship, Law and the Unexpected: Relatives are Always a Surprise* (Cambridge, Cambridge University Press, 2005).

SHAW, Alison, 'Kinship, Cultural Preference and Immigration: Consanguineous Marriage among British Pakistanis' (2001) 7 *Journal of the Royal Anthropological Institute* 315.

SHAW, Alison and CHARSLEY, Katherine, 'Rishtas: Adding Emotion to Strategy in Understanding British Pakistani Transnational Marriages' (2006) 6 *Global Networks* 405.

UDDIN, Paola and NASIR, Ahmed, *A Choice by Right: The Report of the Working Group on Forced Marriage* (London, Home Office Communications Directorate, 2006).

Part III

10

Church of England Weddings and Ritual Symbolism

SARAH FARRIMOND

I. INTRODUCTION

CHURCH OF ENGLAND weddings have been much on my mind this week. Last Friday was 14 February, St Valentine's Day, and in my capacity as an Anglican ordinand,[1] I assisted at a wedding in a parish church in a village in West Yorkshire. The church was full, guests were dressed up: men in suits, women in smart dresses and often hats. There was a warm friendly atmosphere in marked contrast to the cold, grey weather outside. The wedding couple themselves were 'traditionally' dressed: bride in a long white gown and groom in morning dress (Tobin et al 2003). There were bridesmaids and ushers and a best man. The bride was escorted down the aisle and given away by her father. After the ceremony there were photographs and then the couple and their guests continued the rites and celebrations of this special day with a reception at a hotel, speeches and a dance. The priest, the church wardens[2] and I tidied up the church and left to continue our ordinary working days.

On Saturday 15 February the House of Bishops of the Church of England issued a statement on same sex marriage (House of Bishops 2014), including the statement that the Church would not be prepared to ordain anyone who was married to someone of the same sex, which was to become possible in England from 29 March 2014, following the Marriage (Same Sex Couples) Act 2013. This was despite the fact that from July 2005 clergy have been allowed to be in civil partnerships (House of Bishops 2005) and caused considerable distress to many, including clergy in civil partnerships, who would like to be able to marry, but, as gay Anglican clergy, may not

[1] An ordinand is someone training to be an ordained minister in the Church of England.

[2] A church warden is a senior elected officer in an Anglican parish church with responsibility for practical aspects of the running of the church.

now do so. This concern extended well beyond my own circle of acquaintance to conversation threads on social media sites, which in addition to reflections on exclusion, and on the legitimate interpretation of tradition included debates around whether the English civil law of marriage and the understanding of marriage within the Church of England had hitherto been at variance.

On Sunday 16 February I attended a church service celebrating marriage, a theme suggested to the vicar by St Valentine's Day. Couples who had been married in the churches over the previous year were invited to attend. The services took the basic shape of the usual Sunday worship of those churches: a communion service, but with a particular focus on marriage (though mindful in spoken sections of the liturgy of the fact that for various reasons marriage was a difficult or sad topic for many present). The sermon was the place where this was most clearly evident, the priest addressing the subject with a particular focus on the marriage service and especially the vows. In the course of this he mentioned, with approval, the fact that '80 per cent of couples' in weddings he conducted opted to use the version of the wedding vows where the bride promises to obey and the groom to worship.[3] I was very surprised by this and some days later took up the issue with him, arguing against the practice. He was convinced that retaining the promise to 'obey' neither had unfortunate pastoral consequences—that it was neither playing into the hands of those who either abuse women or connive at it, as I argued—nor was it to be understood as suggesting men and women were not intellectual and spiritual equals.

So it is business as usual for the Church of England wedding. It is the ritual symbolism of these weddings that is the subject of this chapter: both the ritual and symbolism contained within such weddings and what the phenomenon of the Church of England wedding as a whole might signify. The chapter will begin by drawing out of the events described above a sketch of the character of the Church of England as it pertains to weddings, historically and at the present time, including, but not limited to, its legal status. This will be followed by a critical account of Anglican wedding ritual: texts and their performance; paying attention to the values embodied and performed; noting points of similarity and difference with other wedding ritual, religious or secular; and the contribution of the Church of England to wedding ritual in general. The chapter will conclude with a brief consideration of what draws people to Church of England weddings and how the Church of England understands its involvement in weddings.

[3] The Alternative Service Book (Church of England 1980), no longer authorised for public worship, though still occasionally used, required the grooms of brides promising to obey to promise to worship. Current authorised wedding services retain the option of the bride promising to obey but no longer balance this with the groom promising to worship.

II. WEDDINGS IN THE CHURCH OF ENGLAND

The events outlined above suggest three areas of significance for the ritual symbolism of the Church of England wedding. First, weddings in Anglican churches in England are a familiar phenomenon, unremarkable either to the regular congregation of the church or to those wedding guests who live secular lives. They are a familiar phenomenon in two distinct ways. As will be explored below, they share a material culture and many ritual acts with other kinds of weddings and partnership ceremonies, religious and secular, with and without legal force. As well as being a familiar aspect of contemporary ritualisation, Church of England weddings use texts that have changed remarkably little since the sixteenth century, having undergone only three revisions in that time. Indeed the sixteenth century 'Service of Holy Matrimony' in the *Book of Common Prayer* drew heavily on Medieval English Catholic rites. But there have been changes, prompted by shifts in theological thinking and by a changing social context.

Secondly, the nature and the manner of a religious body's response to social change depend on its own internal discourse about its identity and values. They also depend on the sorts of issues the surrounding context (of which members of the religious body in question are also members, of course) presents at any given time. But the political status of the religious body in question is also important. In the case of the Church of England the status is that of the established church of England. Anglican churches exist in other parts of the United Kingdom (and indeed the world), part of the same Christian denomination, but without established status. This established status gives the Church certain privileges and responsibilities at a local level: Church of England clergy often have an 'in' to institutions, on the strength of their status rather than their individual wisdom or character. Conversely they have a pastoral responsibility for all, not just worshipping Anglicans, and so are expected to baptise, to conduct funerals and to marry anyone resident within a given area who asks. Nationally the Church and state are connected: the monarch is the 'Supreme Governor' of the Church, the Archbishop of Canterbury crowns any new monarch, Bishops sit in the House of Lords. And beyond parliament the House of Bishops[4] understands part of its role as responding to 'national issues affecting the Church of England' (House of Bishops 2014). Because of its status this response does not just consist of broad theological principles or ethical recommendations, but specific policies around, amongst other things, the implications of participation in certain life-cycle rituals. This has two aspects: the offering and

[4] The House of Bishops is one of 3 'houses' of the General Synod, the national governing body of the Church of England. The House of Bishops consists of the 44 diocesan bishops, various assistant bishops (all men) and from April 2013, 8 regionally elected senior women clergy (Church of England 2013).

withholding of Church of England rituals for particular individuals and the disciplinary implications for participating in rituals performed by bodies other than the Church of England. In the past, being divorced, with a former spouse still alive, debarred a person from getting married in church. So such august Anglicans as CS Lewis and Dorothy Sayers had civil weddings when they married partners who had been divorced. Even today individual priests are at liberty to refuse to conduct such weddings, and some do. More generally all divorced persons wishing to marry in church are supposed to submit to a process of directed reflection on the end of their previous marriage before being permitted a church wedding. In particular, where the present relationship contributed to the breakdown of the previous one (beginning as an extra-marital affair) then a church wedding is supposed to be withheld (Church of England 2002). It is for this reason that Prince Charles and Camilla Parker-Bowles were married in a civil ceremony. While some clergy prefer not to question couples closely, others are more rigorous than formal policy dictates, extending a refusal to conduct the weddings of divorced people to those co-habiting prior to marriage (without suitable public expressions of penitence). While this is not a policy recommended by any official Church document, as a practice it provides a further illustration of the way in which the Church of England uses ritual as a sanction to discourage behaviours it disapproves of.

Thirdly, the opening account included references to aspects of weddings that occasion particular controversy. Marriage has been much contested in the Church of England. Debate has turned from the sacramental status of marriage, through parental consent and what rendered a marriage rite efficacious, the degree of consanguinity within which marriage should be forbidden, the possibility or impossibility of divorce, the equality or inequality of men and women, the acceptability or unacceptability of artificial contraception, to the status of same sex sexual relationships. While some of these debates have been resolved and others lost their critical edge, many remain live issues, despite occasional statements from the House of Bishops and elsewhere concerning what has 'always' been understood about marriage. All have left their mark on Church of England wedding ritual, from who is to be permitted a church wedding, what values are to be expressed in the texts of services, to the relative importance of the Church of England wedding when compared with other kinds of English wedding. The simple availability of non-Anglican weddings reduced the proportion of people marrying in Church of England weddings at various points. This occurred with the introduction of civil weddings in the 1830s (and weddings in non-Anglican places of worship). In addition the long reluctance of the Church of England to permit divorcees to marry in church meant that, as with more readily accessible divorce the divorce rate and by extension the number of second marriages increased, so the overall proportion of marriages in the Church of England decreased. More recently, the expansion of possible civil venues for weddings from simple, generally quite small register offices to hotels, stately homes and other venues suitable for large-scale celebrations has seen a particularly sharp decline in the proportion of weddings taking place in Church of England ceremonies. Whether such declining enthusiasm for Church of England weddings constitutes evidence of 'secularisation' is beyond the scope of this chapter. But it must be noted that people do not choose a civil ceremony simply because they have a secular world view; nor do they choose a Church of England wedding because their understanding of the world or of marriage coincides with that of the Church of England, even assuming a consensus Anglican view can in fact be identified, which is doubtful.

III. TEXTS AND THEIR PERFORMANCE

While Anglican theologies of marriage vary considerably, Church of England wedding services have changed very little, at least as far as the texts are concerned. Such weddings are built around authorised Anglican liturgical texts; and in this context, and for the Anglican liturgy more generally, 'authorisation' is a concept with some weight. Canon law requires ministers only to use authorised forms of service, with a few, specified, exceptions (Church of England 2014). At present, for marriage these are the 'Form of Solemnization of Matrimony' in the 1662 *Book of Common Prayer* (hereafter *BCP*), the 'Series 1: Form of Solemnization for Matrimony' (Church of England 1999), which is a limited revision of the *BCP* and the 'Marriage Service' of *Common Worship* (hereafter *CW*) (Church of England 2005, 101–72).[5]

The *BCP* of 1662 was the product of 100 or so years of wrangling about the identity of the English Church following the Reformation. The finished text combined reformed, protestant theology with liturgical forms that owed much to earlier catholic patterns. This was especially the case with the 'Form for the Solemnisation of Holy Matrimony'. Much of this, notably the two sets of vows and most of the pastoral introduction, follows very closely the form and words of the Sarum rite, the most widely used of the pre-Reformation English rites. The wedding vows were brought into the church from their medieval location at the church door and the idea of a 'nuptial mass' was lost, although the couple were encouraged to attend Holy Communion together as soon as possible after their wedding (Stevenson 1982: 134–52). The service consists of a pastoral introduction outlining the nature of marriage in Christian thinking, which excludes sacramental language, but instead speaks of marriage as 'instituted of God', a 'holy estate', 'signifying unto us the mystical union that is betwixt Christ and his church'

[5] Full texts of all authorised Church of England wedding services are available at: www.churchofengland.org/prayer-worship/worship/texts/pastoral/marriage.

(*BCP* 1662: 183–87). It goes on to outline a Christian vision for the marital relationship. Marriage exists so that children can be born and brought up within the Christian faith. Marriage is a 'remedy against sin', being the legitimate context for sex, and offers 'mutual society, help and comfort'. This is followed by two sets of vows that the couple take. The first, 'espousals', derives from betrothal rites and consists of promises made in the future tense: promises to get married at some point. The second set of promises, the 'nuptials', are vows made in the present tense, something introduced into Christian wedding ritual in the twelfth century following the conviction on the part of such thinkers as Peter Lombard that consent to marriage on the part of the couple should be articulated and not just assumed (Stevenson 1982: 68). These vows put the duties of husbands and wives, outlined in the pastoral introduction, into the mouths of the couple. Then the groom puts a ring on the fourth finger of the bride's left hand with a set form of words, which extends the relational themes of the vows into the economic unity of the household: 'With this ring I thee wed, with my body I thee worship, and with all my worldly goods I thee endow'. The celebrant then says a prayer of blessing for the couple, followed by the statement 'what God hath joined together let no man put asunder' and a declaration of the marriage. Other prayers and set psalms follow, and possibly a sermon or briefer set scriptural exhortation. The symbolic implications of this service are clearest when it is contrasted with the medieval rites it replaced and the puritan wedding practices it overturned at the Restoration. In contrast with medieval rites it is a service that is entirely conducted in the vernacular; confidence in the efficacy of the right words made up for a grave scepticism about the propriety or usefulness of ritual acts and symbolic objects. A very high value is accorded to scripture in particular. The wedding as a whole, rather than just the nuptial blessing, is brought into the body of the church from the church porch. This move is difficult to interpret. The Reformers rejected the idea that marriage was a sacrament, while still symbolically connecting marriage and the Church. A similar symbolic ambivalence is evident in the retention of the wedding ring, but in replacing its blessing by the priest with simply placing it on the prayer book. This retention of intentional symbolic action contrasts with English puritan practices that removed any such gesture and movement and simply added scriptural exhortation to a bare exchange of vows (Stevenson 1982: 155).

The *BCP* rite was used to conduct weddings from its publication until 1965[6] and remains an option. From the early twentieth century there was a considerable movement for liturgical reform. This was motivated, variously, by a desire to incorporate scholarly findings into liturgical practice, to develop forms of worship that were more culturally relevant to

[6] Although a revised version from 1928 was rejected, it was used quite often, the Bishops having let it be known that despite its unofficial status they would not protest its use.

the contemporary context, and to establish a more flexible 'common worship' so that clergy might be less likely to use unauthorised, illegal forms. 'Series One' is the designation for various alternative forms of worship that received legal recognition in March 1965 under the 'Prayer Book (Alternative and Other Services) Measure' (Jasper 1989: 244). This service replicates very closely the marriage service from the ultimately unsuccessful 1927–28 attempts to revise the *BCP*. The *Series One* service differs slightly from the *BCP*. The structure is unchanged. Sexuality is presented rather more positively (or less crudely), the references to 'brute beasts' and 'carnal lusts' being removed from the pastoral introduction and the second 'cause for which matrimony was ordained' being completely re-written. So '[i]t was ordained for a remedy against sin, and to avoid fornication; that such persons as have not the gift of continency might marry, and keep themselves undefiled members of Christ's body' was replaced with 'it was ordained in order that the natural instincts and affections, implanted by God, should be hallowed and directed aright; that those who are called of God to this holy estate, should continue therein in pureness of living'. The bride is no longer required to promise to obey. The 1928 text removed the promise to obey completely, though this was re-instated as an option in later services. The groom was to 'honour' rather than 'worship' his wife in the promise associated with the ring giving. Other changes from the 1662 text involved various additional prayers and set readings in the event of a nuptial Eucharist. Underlying this process of liturgical revision, which went on to produce the *Alternative Service Book* (hereafter *ASB*) and *CW*, is a history of often acrimonious disagreement and debate.

In 1954 the Convocations of Canterbury and York agreed to appoint a Liturgical Commission, which would be responsible for overseeing liturgical revision, including an on-going process of experimentation. This process led to the publication and 'experimental' use of what came to be known as 'Series One', 'Series Two' and 'Series Three', each of which included an incomplete range of services. The last of these saw the first services in modern English. In 1980 the *ASB* was published, with services for all occasions in contemporary English, and its use, as an official alternative to the *BCP* was authorised until the end of 1990, a period subsequently extended to the end of 2000. During these years the more permanent rites of *CW* were developed (Jasper 1989).

CW, unlike like the *BCP* or the *ASB*, is not entirely contained in one book, from which individual services can be extracted where necessary (particularly important for weddings). It is a series of texts of services that are bound into different configurations for reference and available on the internet, so clergy and others leading worship can produce orders of service from this material for actual liturgical use. A fair degree of variety is possible, although it remains the case that Anglican worship is supposed to conform to the patterns, albeit more flexible, which are formally authorised.

The *CW* marriage service draws heavily on that in the *ASB* and its overall structure differs little from that of the *BCP*. This service is the primary liturgical text around which the contemporary Anglican wedding is constructed. It begins with a prayer, emphasising the wedding as an act of worship. A pastoral introduction follows. There are many similarities with that in the *BCP*: a declaration of the purpose of the service, an outline of the nature of Christian marriage, into which the three purposes of marriage are inserted. The *BCP* order of children, sex and comfort is altered, with sex taking first place, then children and then 'strength, companionship and comfort' (*CW Pastoral Services* 2005: 105). The *ASB* order was 'comfort and help', sex and then children (*ASB* 1980: 288). The *ASB* pastoral introduction has been retained as an alternative to the new *CW* one. Commentators attribute this change of order to a more positive theological appreciation of sex (or of companionship) (eg Everett 2006: 186) but whether this was the intention of the revisers is not recorded.[7]

The final reading of the banns is followed with the 'spousal' vows, or 'declarations', where the priest asks first the bridegroom and then the bride the following:

> *N* will you take *N* to be your wife [husband]?
> Will you love her [him], comfort her [him], honour and protect her [him],
> And forsaking all others,
> Be faithful to her [him] as long as you both shall live?

Each responds 'I will' and then a question is put to the congregation, requesting their support for the couple in their future marriage, in the same basic form as the declaration. The collect is followed at this point with one or more Bible readings and a sermon. Then there are the marriage vows. This differs from previous rites, which concluded the marriage before moving on to the readings and the sermon. The couple stand before the celebrant and the groom and then the bride make their vows. Three alternative sets of vows are given. The preferred option, in the main body of the text, rather than the 'alternative vows' appendix, is as follows:

> I, *N*, take you *N*,
> to be my wife [or husband],
> to have and to hold,
> from this day forward;
> for better for worse,
> for richer for poorer,
> in sickness and in health,
> to love and to cherish,
> till death us do part;
> according to God's holy law.
> In the presence of God I make this vow. (*CW Pastoral Services* 2005: 108)

[7] See also Herring, chapter 13 in this volume.

The vows for husband and wife are the same and differ from the *ASB* vow only in the concluding line, the *ASB* having 'and this is my solemn vow' (*ASB* 1980: 290), instead of 'in the presence of God I make this vow'. The alternatives (listed in an appendix and not in the text as in the *ASB*) consist of a form as above, but adding 'and obey' after 'cherish' in the bride's vows. Again, this largely replicates the *ASB* vow, except that there, in the event of the bride promising to obey, the husband was to promise to 'worship' his wife. The ongoing controversy on the appropriateness of such a promise long precedes the *ASB*. The other set of vows are those from the *BCP*, with the option of omitting the 'obey' clause.

The exchange of vows is followed by the blessing and giving (or where both partners have rings, exchange) of rings, these acts being accompanied with set forms of words:

> *N*, I give you this ring
> as a sign of our marriage.
> With my body I honour you,
> all that I am I give to you,
> all that I have I share with you,
> within the love of God,
> Father, Son and Holy Spirit.

Where only the bride has a ring, her words differ only by replacing 'I give' with 'I receive'. The celebrant then 'proclaims' the marriage and blesses it, using one of a number of prayers of blessing. The marriage is then registered, either at this point or at the end of the service. Then there are prayers. If there is going to be a Eucharist this follows. In such circumstances, the marriage can be blessed immediately before the breaking of the bread and distribution of the bread and wine. The service ends with a 'dismissal' and a blessing of the whole congregation.

A liturgical text expresses ideas. The text of a marriage service is the product of what Adrian Thatcher would describe as both the 'internal and the external discourses on marriage' (Thatcher 1999: 31); respectively, the conversation within the churches about the nature and purpose of marriage in Christian faith and practice, and the conversation between the Church and the wider world. So, the Church of England wedding expresses the view that marriage is a good thing for society as a whole and also for the marriage partners. Marriage is a permanent, lifelong thing. It is a serious commitment: not only is it to be undertaken seriously, but it is also an arena for the acquisition and the practice of certain qualities of character. Marriage is in some sense symbolic of the relationship between God and the world, though not explicitly as a sacrament.

Contemporary marriage rites attempt, with other recent exercises in liturgical revision, to reflect contemporary sensibilities about the human person and marriage in society. As we have noted, these are far from uncontested areas, not least within the Church. Nevertheless, recent liturgical innovation reflects an increasing appreciation of a fundamental equality between the sexes that extends to roles within marriage and in society. There is, however, a decided ambivalence about this, which is evident in the contemporary Anglican texts: the 'obey' clause' remains an option; attempts to remove it altogether, as has happened in the wedding rites of other Churches, have not been successful. It is hard to determine exactly what this might mean. Liturgical texts offer an insight into such attitudes, but it is often not possible to read them as straightforward, normative statements, especially when more than one such statement is being made, in this case that wives should not (or should) promise to obey their husbands. This issue will be revisited below.

An additional question is the vexed one of the 'giving away' of the bride, to which many Anglican liturgists are hostile (Spinks 1998: 209). Traditionally the bride enters the church with her father, and is 'given away' following the final reading of the banns and the couple's declarations of willingness to marry. This is a part of the *BCP* service: 'Who giveth this Woman to be married to this Man?' (*BCP* 1662: 292). The *ASB* notes that the 'Giving Away' ceremony is optional, and provides no form of words to accompany it. The notes to the *CW* service say 'the bride may enter the church escorted by her father or a representative of the family. Or the bride and groom may enter church together' (*CW Pastoral Services* 2005: 133). It goes on to observe that the 'traditional ceremony' of 'Giving Away' is optional, and offers a form of words: 'Who brings this woman to be married to this man?' The terms 'escort' and 'bring' are intended to remove the implication that the bride is the property of her father and then her husband. *CW* offers an additional optional section at this point, as an alternative to 'giving away'. The celebrant asks the parents of both bride and groom:

> *N* and *N* have declared their intention towards each other.
> As their parents, will you now entrust your son and daughter to one another as they come to be married?

Both sets of parents respond: 'we will'.

All of this reflects a desire, in the words of Stevenson, to incorporate 'many of the insights of the marriage relationship of the present age, in particular, the complementarity[8] of the sexes' (Stevenson 1982: 191). It also indicates a considerable degree of ritual conservatism and reluctance to dispense with familiar liturgical and ritual forms. Many couples marrying in church are

[8] Complementarity is a term much in use in contemporary debates in the Church of England about sexuality and gender, focused on the issues of same sex marriage and women bishops. In these debates the term indicates an understanding of humanity in which men and women are equal, but different, with distinct roles to play in Church and society. The term is also sometimes used, less precisely, to indicate the view that women and not just men have value before God; any differentiation according to gender being left vague. It is likely that Stevenson was using the term in the second way.

deliberately choosing a 'traditional' ceremony. For such people a sense of continuity with the past is very important and the repetition of familiar words and actions contributes to this sense of continuity. The source of the reluctance to dispense with the 'obey' clause is hard to locate, but seems to derive from conservative individuals in the Church, whether involved in the synodical processes of liturgical revision or in parish ministry. The rite of 'giving away' is very different. While some individual clergy might personally like the practice, its retention is largely motivated by the desires of marrying couples, who consistently requested its inclusion even where there was no textual provision for it. While only a small minority of brides now promise to obey, the vast majority are still 'given away' (Farrimond 2009: 248). It is doubtful that brides understand this practice as indicative of their being the property of either father or future husband. The performative aspect of the 'giving away' is very important to brides, being a part of the very important bridal procession down the aisle and also involving the bride's father in a distinct role. What attracts almost no attention is the fact that the words associated with this action no longer refer to it as a 'giving away', but rather as 'bringing'. Retention of cherished performative practices should not necessarily be understood as agreement with the ideas such practices originated to express.

Church of England weddings cannot be reduced to the texts from which they are performed: their performance is crucial to any understanding of their significance. Some clues as to their performance are to be found in the rubrics and notes in the texts, others in wider legislation. In the *BCP* the respective sides on which bride and groom stand, for example, are specified—'The man on the right hand and the woman on the left'—as is their location in the body of the Church. Considerable attention is paid to the exchange or the giving of a ring:

> The bridegroom places the ring on the fourth finger of the bride's left hand and, holding it there, says ... If rings are exchanged, they loose hands and the bride places a ring on the fourth finger of the bridegroom's left hand and holding it there, says ... If only one ring is used, before they loose hands the bride says ... (*CW Pastoral Services* 2005: 109).

It is possible to speculate on the origins of exact location, choreography and symbolic objects, but unfortunately it is not possible to identify definitive solutions to such puzzles. Specific commentators or reformers give reasons for their proposed continuation or revision of practice, but other interpretations are always possible. Indeed speculation on various aspects of wedding ritual forms a part of the popular culture of marriage, as of other ritual behaviour (Grimes 1990). The examples given, and others like them, represent a broader Anglican pattern which includes continuity with pre-Reformation practice on the one hand and protestant innovation on the other in pursuit of an ecclesiastical identity both catholic and reformed. The fact that these aspects of ritual behaviour are prescribed within the marriage service of the Church of England suggests not some particular understanding of bridegrooms that they stand on the right, or of wedding rings being worn on the fourth finger of the left hand; rather, the persistence of these particular practices, century after century, has associated them, whatever their origin, with weddings, and specifically with weddings in the Church of England.

This applies more broadly to aspects of the performance of Church of England weddings for which the texts themselves offer no guidance. So, Church of England weddings take place in an Anglican church, which will be, with rare exceptions, a parish church. Such a church has a particular relationship with its locality because locality is the principle on which the Church of England organises its pastoral care, including its conducting of weddings. The whole country is geographically divided into dioceses, which are sub-divided into parishes. Primary pastoral responsibility in the Church of England, as an episcopal church,[9] lies with diocesan bishops, who delegate to the 'incumbents' (rectors, vicars or priests-in-charge) of parishes. Incumbents may have more than one parish, but in each of their parishes they have responsibility for the 'cure of souls' of all residents, irrespective of their involvement with the Church of England. A wedding can be performed by a priest other than the incumbent, but only at the incumbent's invitation. Individuals have a right to marry in a church if either of them lives within the parish boundary, attends the church on a regular enough basis to be admitted onto the 'electoral roll' (the nearest thing to a list of members that the Church of England keeps), or can demonstrate an association with the particular church or parish. Such associations include having lived there in the past, and having wider family connections there, including relatives having had their own weddings, baptisms or funerals there (Farrimond 2009: 258–59). So in its wedding practice the Church of England continues to promote the idea that a sense of geographical belonging is an important aspect of human identity and one that is to be properly honoured at key moments in life.

Having a wedding in a church with which one has, in principle, a demonstrable—and generally a geographically demonstrable—connection connects weddings with a locally-based understanding of pastoral care. Having weddings in church buildings at all and celebrated by ordained ministers indicates the view that weddings are properly the business of the Church. Though the Church was quite slow to develop wedding-related ritual, the location of weddings in church buildings is a highly symbolic practice. The contemporary wedding is a complex ritual whole, but it includes within it two originally distinct ritual practices. Couples were encouraged to have a nuptial blessing for their marriages pronounced at the Mass from the fourth

[9] One with bishops.

century CE (Stevenson 1982: 26). Much later the parish church door, as a highly visible location, became the place where marriage vows were properly to be made (Stevenson 1982: 76–83). The church as a focal point of a locality and the church as a place of divine encounter in which God's blessing might be sought are both reasons why weddings might properly take place in church.

The opening paragraph of this chapter sketched a Church of England wedding ceremony that, while neither universal nor mandatory, is common enough to constitute normal practice. Symbolic objects such as special clothing, rings, and flowers are employed to designate role, to suggest key themes in weddings (especially displays of wealth, and fertility), and even more so because such objects, along with music, serve to identify the occasion as a wedding and transform the church from its ordinary aspect into a church in which a wedding is taking place. In this space and using these artefacts the wedding takes place and the words of the wedding service are spoken. But the wedding consists of movement as well as speech: there is choreography, not just lines. The groom and best man wait at the front, the bridal party (bride, her father and attendants) enter in a procession to music, the two 'sides' of the bride and groom sitting separately. When the bride stops at the front of the church, bride and groom stand next to each other. The bride passes her bouquet to a bridesmaid. The service proceeds with or without a verbal 'giving away' formula, after which congregation, bride and groom sit, stand, and kneel as directed by the priest. After the vows, when the marriage is registered, the couple, their witnesses and parents all go to the table where the registers are laid out, either in a vestry or, more commonly in some place in full view of the congregation. During the signing of the register music is played and the couple then return to the front of the church for the prayers and a final blessing by the priest. The bride and groom then lead the wedding procession out of church, bride's and groom's 'sides' of the church now recombined: bridesmaids now paired up with ushers and best man, the mother of the bride walking with the father of the groom and vice versa. There follow photographs outside the church (or inside in inclement weather), often complemented by a video of the service. Then bride and groom leave the church for a wedding reception elsewhere.

None of this movement is mandated by any official church, or other, document, but it forms as much a part of the Church of England wedding as do the authorised texts. This kind of intentional physical movement is by no means peculiar to this kind of wedding: social movement is embodied and displayed in physical movement. Anglican churches do, however, often lend themselves particularly well to the choreography described, with grand doors and long central aisles affording the necessary space for processions. Not only are these buildings the contexts in which such ritual developed, but also they have such features in abundance as tend to be regarded as especially attractive for weddings. It is not only a kind of generalised social movement that is embodied in a wedding, but a focused re-calibration of social relationships. This extends across the total performance (Schechner 1993) of the wedding and also applies in a narrower sense to the church service. Bride's and groom's friends and family are distinguished from each other and clearly separated prior to the wedding by such events as hen and stag parties and by very gendered patterns of wedding consumption (Farrimond 2009: 199ff). This intensifies on the day of the wedding, with not only bride and groom sleeping apart the previous night (even where, as is mostly the case now, they live together) but each of them accompanied by members of their own 'side'. This continues into the start of the church service, as noted above. A transformation happens after the signing of the register and the final prayers, with the ordering of personnel in the wedding procession embodying a re-alignment of relationships in the face of the new marriage. This re-alignment continues into the reception, with some attempt usually made to get 'both sides to mix' (Farrimond 2009: 236). Photography and video provides a visual record of this whole process. This kind of performance, featuring marked periods of separation and then re-integration, separated by transformative, liminal spaces, marks out a wedding as a proto-typical rite of passage (Van Gennep 1909). Rites of passage theory identifies weddings as serving a social function (allowing for social change while leaving fundamental social structure unchallenged) and highlights the connections between weddings and other life-cycle ritual, especially, in an Anglican context, infant baptisms and funerals. However it does not offer an exhaustive interpretation of wedding ritual: more is going on here.

Weddings are certainly rites of passage. They are also rites of intensification,[10] providing opportunities to intensify bonds of affection and to display and enact values (Davies 2008: 9). Values enacted in Church of England weddings vary considerably, as will be explored below in a consideration of why couples choose such weddings. Certain things can be said generally, however. Weddings are occasions for display. This includes the conspicuous use of objects and performance of actions 'proper' to a wedding: clothing, rings, flowers for example; the capacity to 'do things properly' (Farrimond 2009: 265–66). One aspect of this display of propriety is the performance of gendered identities. Even where the wedding vows and other aspects of the service are egalitarian, bride and groom are distinguished throughout, in the language used, by their gender. What being male or female signifies may not be spelt out, but being male or female seems very important. This is extended significantly by material culture: brides and grooms are visibly very distinct, both from each other and, in the case of the bride, from all others present. Wedding guests likewise are dressed, whether members of the wedding party or ordinary guests, according

[10] See Probert, chapter 3 in this volume for more on this.

to a dress code which distinguishes men from women very sharply, much more so than is commonly now the case for either work or recreation. Some of this display is also a matter of conspicuous consumption (Veblen 1899) in a monetary sense too: *expensive* clothing, cars and flowers. Weddings in Anglican parish churches furthermore display a connectedness to a particular locality and community, again something often regarded as a quality worth showing off. But display and sociability are not distinct categories. Weddings display social relationships, and significantly also the admirable quality of sociability in a couple, with their desirable social success evident in the number of relatives and friends present at the wedding. Lastly, in the strategic display of children in the wedding service as bridesmaids and pages, as well as the extensive use of flowers, weddings accord a high value to fertility, whether evident in the couple's existing children or hoped for in the future.

Of course much of this does not only apply to weddings in the Church of England, or even to British weddings. Indeed some continuity of ritual, and especially material culture, from religious weddings to civil weddings, and indeed from heterosexual weddings to same sex weddings or civil partnerships, can blur the distinctions between types of weddings.[11] As has been shown, the ritual and material culture of the Church of England wedding operates both as a symbolic system pointing to particular values and as a set of defining characteristics of such a wedding. The Church of England wedding, having been the most common kind of wedding in England for several centuries, was the context in which modern English wedding ritual developed, around, for most of those years, an unchanging textual core. The *BCP* 'Form for Solemnization for Matrimony' became over that time not only a Christian theological and liturgical text, but an English cultural artefact. Actual Church of England weddings similarly embodied the values of which the text speaks, but also became extremely familiar cultural events, paradigmatic scenes (Needham 1971), possessed of distinctive performative and especially visual characteristics associated with a 'proper wedding'. Widening options for wedding venues have allowed some of these performative and visual characteristics to be transferred to a secular context, which has proved very attractive to many couples.

IV. WHY CHOOSE A CHURCH OF ENGLAND WEDDING?

Despite attractive alternatives a significant minority of marrying couples still choose to marry in the Church of England. What follows is a brief consideration of what motivates this choice, deriving from empirical research by the present writer among officiating clergy and marrying couples in a Yorkshire town (Farrimond 2009). Couples choose Church of England weddings

[11] See Peel, chapter 5 in this volume for a contrasting perspective on this issue.

for a wide variety of reasons. Religiosity is a factor, but by no means the only one, and one that operates in a number of ways. Some couples marry in Anglican wedding services because they have an articulate Christian commitment. These are by no means necessarily Anglican. Some of them express dissatisfaction at the ritual limitations of the Church of England wedding, or at the way its use by non-religious people rather undermines its 'spiritual' significance. Others define their beliefs less unambiguously but speak of 'special places' either in the general sense of being atmospheric in some way, or in the locally specific sense of being associated with important personal and family events, not least other weddings, christenings and funerals. For these people, belonging to a particular place and to particular people had enormous significance, one which the Anglican parish church was able to symbolise in a way that a 'commercial' venue could not. Family were a deciding influence in other ways too. Sometimes this took the form of older relatives actively promoting a Church of England wedding (or sometimes a wedding in another Christian church—a Church of England wedding operating as a compromise choice). Sometimes couples just wanted to please parents or grandparents. More generally couples liked to replicate details of previous family weddings, especially if those weddings were believed to have led on to happy marriages. Of course this last only encourages religious weddings if older generations had such weddings. The same is true of the more general stated motivation for church weddings: a desire to do things 'properly'. Propriety lies very much in the eyes of the beholder and in the immediate circumstances in which they make their decisions.

While couples may *choose* to participate as key actors in Church of England weddings, ordained clergy *must* do. Clergy nevertheless often speak positively about the experience of conducting weddings. Weddings can be pleasurable occasions for officiating clergy, making a change from involvement in the sadder times of people's lives. They also, moreover, provide clergy with an opportunity to exercise their ritual expertise, both in the conducting of the wedding ceremony and in educating the couple in the protocol of the occasion. Weddings are understood as ways in which the Church can reach out to those outside its regular worshipping community, whether to encourage people to think more seriously about the Christian faith, or to offer hospitality and service. Clergy expressed little desire to promote a particular understanding of marriage to marrying couples, but expressed some frustration on occasion with various policies that they were obliged to implement, mainly around the remarriage of divorcees. Weddings were widely understood as one of several categories of life-cycle ritual. As such they were key points of contact with the community in which the clergy person worked and in which the church was located, the local sensibility of the priest often resonating with that of some couples.

Actual weddings are occasions which embody and perform values, both of the Church of England and of the couples marrying in its churches. They are heavy with symbolism, and packed with objects and actions understood as important or meaningful, in hugely divergent ways, by couples, by officiating clergy, by guests and by friendly and hostile observers alike. But the Church of England's involvement with weddings in general is also something that is heavy with symbolism, and again what this involvement might symbolise is profoundly contested (Earey 2012). Is it a vehicle for gentle, pastoral companionship with people on their life course? Is it a means of maintaining a didactic and controlling influence on society? Is it a way of keeping holy stories and sacred places, both those of the Church and those of individual women and men, alive? And can it change again, as it has before, to face new realities in a new world?

BIBLIOGRAPHY

CHURCH OF ENGLAND, *The Alternative Service Book* (London, SPCK, 1980).
——, *The Book of Common Prayer* (Oxford, Oxford University Press, 1662).
——, *Marriage in Church after Divorce* (London, CHP, 2002).
——, *Common Worship Pastoral Services* (London, CHP, 2005).
——, *House of Bishops* 2014, available at www.churchofengland.org.
DAVIES, Douglas, 'Cultural Intensification: A Theory for Religion' in A Day (ed), *Religion and the Individual: Belief, Practice, Identity* (Aldershot, Ashgate, 2008).
EAREY, Mark, *Worship that Cares. An Introduction to Pastoral Liturgy* (London SCM, 2012).
EVERETT, Henry, 'Marriage' in P Bradshaw (ed), *A Companion to Common Worship Volume 2* (London, SPCK, 2006).
FARRIMOND, Sarah, *Ritual and Narrative in the Contemporary Anglican Wedding* (University of Durham, PhD Thesis, 2009).
GRIMES, Ronald L, *Ritual Criticism: Case Studies in Its Practice, Essays on Theory* (Columbia SC, University of South Carolina Press, 1990).
HERRING, Jonathan, 'Why Marriage Needs to be less Sexy' chapter thirteen in this volume.
HOUSE OF BISHOPS, *Pastoral Statement on Civil Partnerships* 2005, available at www.churchofengland.org.
——, *Pastoral Guidance on Same Sex Marriage* 2014, available at www.churchofengland.org.
JASPER, RCD, *The Development of the Anglican Liturgy* (London, SPCK, 1989).
NEEDHAM, Rodney, *Circumstantial Deliveries* (Berkeley CA, University of California Press, 1981).
PEEL, Elizabeth, 'Civil Partnership Ceremonies: (Hetero)normativity, Ritual and Gender' chapter five in this volume.
PROBERT, Rebecca, 'From This Day Forward: Pre-Marital Cohabitation and the Rite of Marriage' chapter three in this volume.
SCHECHNER, Richard, *The Future of Ritual: Writings on Culture and Performance* (New York, Routledge, 1993).

SPINKS, Bryan D, 'Revising the Marriage Liturgy in the Church of England' (1998) I *Anglican Theological Review* 13.
STEVENSON, Kenneth, *Nuptial Blessing* (London, SPCK, 1982).
THATCHER, Adrian, *Marriage After Modernity: Christian Marriage in Postmodern Times* (Sheffield, Sheffield Academic Press, 1999).
TOBIN, Shelley et al, *Marriage a la Mode. Three Centuries of Wedding Dress* (London, National Trust, 2003).
VAN GENNEP, Arnold, *The Rites of Passage* (Chicago IL, University of Chicago Press, 1960 [first published 1909]).
VEBLEM, Thorstein, *The Theory of the Leisured Class* (Oxford, Oxford University Press, 2007 [first published 1899]).

11

Playing 'House of Lords Bingo': A Critical Discourse Analysis of Hansard *Debates on Civil Partnership and Same Sex Marriage*

ROSIE HARDING

I. INTRODUCTION

AT THE TIME of the 'marriage rights and rites' workshop in April 2014, we had just witnessed the very first English same sex marriages, which took place on 29 March 2014. As with when the first civil partnerships took place in 2005, the national news media had a brief flirtation with images of same sex couples celebrating their relationships (Jowett and Peel 2010). There were brides and brides, grooms and grooms, some rainbows, a few cakes, and a lot of confetti. There was even a live-filmed same sex wedding, set to an original musical, shown on national broadcast television (Till and Taylor 2014). The tenor of the debate surrounding the Marriage (Same Sex Couples) Act 2013 as it journeyed through Parliament, on the other hand, was quite different from that which accompanied the Civil Partnership Act 2004. Whereas in 2004, civil partnership was constructed primarily around access to formal equality rights (Harding and Peel 2006; Harding 2006), much of the House of Commons' discourse on the Marriage (Same Sex Couples) Act was focused on ideas of 'love' and on procreation/raising children (Harding 2015). In this chapter, I explore the differences and continuities between the discourse in the House of Lords during the passage of the 2004 Act and the 2013 Act. I begin in Section II with a reading of Stonewall's 'House of Lords Bingo' card, exploring its memetic character, and the cultural ideas that it draws upon, before moving on in Section III to explore the House of Lords' debates themselves through a content and thematic analysis of the House of Lords' Second Reading debates on each bill. Through this analysis, I argue that though explicitly homophobic speech has all but disappeared from parliamentary discourse, heterosexist tropes about appropriate familial relationships regularly appear in these debates.

II. PLAYING HOUSE OF LORDS BINGO

Figure 1 is a reproduction of the online 'bingo card' that the Lesbian, Gay, Bisexual and Trans (LGBT) campaigning organisation Stonewall[1] first circulated

Figure 1: Stonewall's House of Lords #equalmarriage bingo card

[1] www.stonewall.org.uk.

via the social networking tools Facebook[2] and Twitter on the day of the House of Lords' Second Reading of the Marriage (Same Sex Couples) Bill.[3] The image has circulated online on a number of occasions since, including during debates on the implementation regulations for the Marriage (Same Sex Couples) Act in February 2014. Whilst a straightforward reading of this image might point towards expressions of homophobia and anti-gay sentiment, there are some complexities to the terms in the image that I will discuss in this chapter. I will argue that there are, in fact, a range of cultural ideas that flow from this image, including: exposing the limitations of stereotypes of homosexuality alongside constructions of the House of Lords as a 'homophobic' space; and creating a 'spectacle' of politics through gaming.

In many respects, this 'bingo card' is best conceptualised as a *meme*—which we can understand as 'a prism for shedding light on aspects of contemporary digital culture' (Shifman 2012: 189), drawing on memetic methods of imitation or copying. Perhaps the most interesting aspect of contemporary memetic cultural practice is its relationship to parody. Parody has long been a part of LGBT sub-culture, and is particularly associated with performativity including drag and 'camp' (Kleinhans 1994). Often, internet memes seek to ridicule, and frequently in ways that are fundamentally incompatible with any understanding of equality.[4] Another recent connected example would be the circulation of images of floodwater, or weather forecasts with terms like 'gay floods' or 'UKIP weather', following the publication of a letter from UKIP councillor David Sylvester that gay marriage was to blame for the storms and floods experienced in Britain in early 2014 (Marszal 2014).[5] On its most straightforward reading then, the parodic nature of this image seeks to remove the 'sting' from some of the perceived hostility that would be expected to emerge when the House of Lords debates gay rights issues. For the purposes of understanding the meme, it is helpful to divide the terms on the bingo card into four broad categories: homophobic language, discourse on the function of marriage; the consequences of gay marriage; and 'fairness' arguments, which primarily cohere around taxation (see table 1).

Some of the more unusual or novel terms in the 'bingo card' are drawn from discourse in contemporary media accounts of same sex marriage: the reference to 'lesbian queen' is from an interview Lord Tebbit gave to the *Big Issue*, published just days before the Lords' Second Reading debate

[2] The image and comments on Facebook are available at: www.facebook.com/stonewalluk/photos/a.209844060398.169557.18933990398/10151649269770399/?type=1andref=nf.

[3] HL Deb 3 June 2013, vol 745, col 937.

[4] For those of you who are unfamiliar with internet memes of recent times, a short browse of www.knowyourmeme.com may be enlightening.

[5] Perhaps even more entertaining is Nigel Farage's own parody related to this meme, where he presented the UKIP Weather: www.youtube.com/watch?v=V1LpHODOgjM.

Table 1: 'Bingo Card' themes

Homophobic Language	Function of Marriage	Consequences of gay marriage	'Fairness' arguments
perversion, bestialists, marry your pet, unnatural, sodomy, deviants/deviance, 'aggressive homosexuals'	family, children, procreation, 'traditional' marriage, 2,000 years old! 'enduring values'	slippery slope, lesbian queen, handcart to hell, constitutional outrage, polygamy, incest, devalued, 'new intolerance'	inheritance tax, spinster sisters, marry your son

(Delaney 2013); the term 'constitutional outrage' can be attributed to backbench Conservative MPs following announcement of the Bill, in reference to the lack of electoral mandate for the legislation, as it had not been a manifesto commitment (McCormick 2012); and 'hell in a handcart' has made appearances in the coverage of same sex marriage in the *Daily Mail* (Lefever 2012). Another key source for the words and phrases on Stonewall's bingo card were the House of Lords' debates on previous legislation, where the tenor of the debate has, in the past, been rather heated, sometimes verging on offensive. Perhaps the most challenging anti-gay House of Lords' discourse appeared during the debates surrounding the equalisation of the age of consent (Baker 2004). Terms including 'perversion', 'unnatural', and 'sodomy' were used with alarming regularity by contributors speaking against the proposed equalisation of the age of consent for gay sex at the age of 16 in 1998, 1999 and 2000 (Baker 2004). The House of Lords repeatedly refused to pass the legislation, and the Sexual Offences (Amendment) Act 2000, which lowered the age of consent for gay male sexual activity to 16 years, eventually became the sixth of just seven Acts ever to come into law following use of the Parliament Acts.[6]

The term 'aggressive homosexuals' was used during the Report stage debate on the Marriage (Same Sex Couples) Bill in the House of Commons by Sir Gerald Howarth MP,[7] and is reminiscent of the tenor of language from debates on the introduction of Section 28 of the Local Government Act in 1988. The 'fairness' arguments are, of course, familiar to anyone who remembers the debates on civil partnership, and the House of Lords' short-lived 'wrecking amendment', which sought to extend the possibility of

[6] The other six being: Government of Ireland Act 1914; Welsh Church Act 1914; Parliament Act 1949; War Crimes Act 1991; European Parliament Elections Act 1999; and the Hunting Act 2004.

[7] HC Deb 20 May 2013, vol 563, col 943.

civil partnership to carers, siblings and other family members as a means to avoid inheritance tax. The exclusion of these types of relationship from civil partnership legislation was also tested in the European Court of Human Rights.[8]

Some of the other terms in Stonewall's bingo card are, however, less familiar from previous debates. Take, for example, the relatively new trope of 'traditional marriage', which has appeared recently within the English debates. This term appears to be rooted in discourse that has travelled across from the US Christian Right. Whilst its use is designed to be a reference to (contemporary, monogamous) heterosexual marriage, the internet has been quick to point out the flaws with using such an ambiguous term, through various critical memes. For example, one graphic designer blogger created an infographic depicting the different ways that marriage was depicted in the Old Testament, including polygyny and forced marriage (Long 2008). Others highlight the historical use of marriage as a way of ensuring appropriate transfers of wealth. Another more recent addition is talk of the 'new intolerance', which speaks to a sentiment that intolerance, rather than being experienced by LGB people, is now being directed at those who oppose homosexuality because of their religious beliefs. I will return to a much fuller discussion of these two tropes in Section III, below.

As well as the substantive content of the 'bingo card', the terms that spectators were to look out for in the House of Lords' debate, there are two other memetic cultural ideas drawn on in this image. First, there is the idea of the House of Lords (and Parliament in general) as a homophobic space. By placing these terms (particularly those that would fall into the 'homophobic language' category above) visually 'inside' an image of the silhouette of the Houses of Parliament, the image cleverly conveys Parliament as the place where these terms reside. The construction of the House of Lords as a homophobic space has been touched on above, when discussing the discourse used in previous debates. But it is important to point out that the tenor of House of Lords' debates since the Parliament Acts were used to force the enactment of the Sexual Offences (Amendment) Act 2000 has been quite different. Searches of *Hansard* suggest that explicit use of 'homophobic' speech has all but disappeared from more recent debates. Whereas in the late twentieth century it was quite usual for explicitly anti-gay sentiment or terms to be expressed in both Houses where such matters were discussed,[9] language in debates on more recent legislation, including

[8] *Burden and Burden v United Kingdom* (Application no 13378/05) [2007] ECHR 723.

[9] For some examples, readers could refer to the contributions by Sir Nicholas Fairbairn (HC Deb 21 February 1994, vol 238, col 98), or Mr Nicholas Winterton (HC Deb 22 June 1998c vol 314c col 769).

the Marriage (Same Sex Couples) Act 2013 has been much more temperate. This is not to say, of course, that the sentiment has completely disappeared, rather that the language and arguments have changed. I return to this issue below.

The final cultural idea that this image draws on is the relatively recent phenomenon of mass viewing of live televised broadcasts of parliamentary business. Prior to the launch of parliamentlive.tv, the only live content was that which was broadcast over the cable (subscription TV) parliament channel, then the Freeview BBC Parliament TV channel, initially as a small, quarter-screen image. Interestingly, the Marriage (Same Sex Couples) Bill debates were not broadcast on the BBC's Freeview service, but rather were streamed live online. Whilst the UK television news media have regularly broadcast important votes (for example the memorable Government defeat on the issue of tuition fees), the prospect of large numbers of viewers watching parliamentary debates streamed live across the Internet seems rather astonishing. In addition to the live streaming, Stonewall staff undertook 'live tweeting', highlighting key moments from the debate as it unfolded. It is hard to imagine how such mass engagement with the business of Parliament could ever have been facilitated prior to the digital age. Yet the creation of a 'bingo card' to accompany watching the debates seems to take things a step further. The very existence of this meme designed to draw attention to the live broadcast of Parliament to the masses, alongside live commentary by interested parties through the medium of Twitter, may itself limit the possibilities of the use of explicitly homophobic speech within Parliament.

III. DEBATING SAME SEX RELATIONSHIP RECOGNITION IN THE HOUSE OF LORDS

A. Methods

John Eekelaar (2014) has provided a fascinating account of the road to same sex marriage in England and Wales, and the content of the debates throughout the Bill's parliamentary journey. As such, rather than explore the whole of the parliamentary discourse on the Marriage (Same Sex Couples) Act 2013 and the Civil Partnership Act 2004, I have chosen to limit my focus for this chapter to the Second Reading debates in the House of Lords for each Bill. The primary reason for this is that the Second Reading debates are the first point at which each chamber of the House has the opportunity to debate the merits of a particular bill, and this is where the key arguments on either side of the debate are generally aired. A second reason is that Second Reading debates where there has been a free vote are considered to be the closest approximation to the norms and requirements of deliberative democracy (Weale, Bicquelet and Bara 2012). I have also restricted the debates analysed here to the House of Lords, for three reasons: first, because the Lords have been (historically) less supportive of lesbian and gay rights than the Commons; secondly, because the constitutional position of the Lords as an unelected chamber makes for an interesting juxtaposition of lobbying and representation which can be seen in the text of the debates; and thirdly, because the Stonewall bingo card directs attention towards the House of Lords, rather than the other stages of parliamentary proceedings.[10] The House of Lords Marriage (Same Sex Couples) Bill 2013 Second Reading debates were extensive, took place over two days, and occupied nearly 10 hours of parliamentary time.[11] The debates include some 85,853 words, over 146 pages of single spaced text. In contrast, the Civil Partnership Bill [HL] 2004 Lords' Second Reading debate[12] took just three hours, and amounts to 25,980 words, over 45 A4 pages of single-spaced text. The entire dataset for this chapter is therefore 111,833 words of parliamentary speech.

The debates were analysed using a combination of content analysis and thematic analysis. The content analysis consisted of counting the number of times each word or phrase from the Stonewall 'bingo card' appears in the respective debates. Derivatives and similar words were used in the count to ensure that all relevant expressions were counted.[13] Table 2 provides the output from the content analysis. In the content analysis, speakers were coded as to whether their speech was 'positive' (in support of the legislation) or 'negative' (against the legislation). There were 17 speeches in the Civil Partnership Bill Second Reading debate, with the vast majority (n=15) taking a broadly 'positive' view. Just two of the 17 speeches were 'negative': the contributions from Baroness O'Cathain and Lady Saltoun of Abernethy. In contrast, the House of Lords' Second Reading of the Marriage (Same Sex Couples) Bill included 91 speakers, 42 of whom spoke against the Bill, and 49 in favour.

Thematic analysis was undertaken on the deductive themes identified from the Stonewall bingo card of 'Homophobic Language', 'Function of Marriage', 'Consequences of Gay Marriage' and '"Fairness" arguments'. The debates were read and coded for these themes, which are discussed in turn below.

[10] For analysis of the House of Commons debate, see Harding (2015).

[11] HL Deb 3 June 2013, vol 745, cols 937–969 and cols 980–1048; HL Deb 4 June 2014, vol 745, cols 1059–1109.

[12] HL Deb 22 Apr 2004, vol 660, cols 387–433.

[13] For example, searches for 'sodomy' included 'sodom, sodomite'; for 'bestialists', searches were undertaken to cover 'bestiality' and other derivatives and on 'cat', 'dog' 'animal'; '2000 years old' includes 'millenia'; 'inheritance tax' includes reference to 'death duties'.

Table 2: Content Analysis

		Civil Partnership Bill 2004	Marriage (Same Sex Couples) Bill 2013
Theme	**Word/Phrase**	**Count**	**Count**
Homophobic language	Perversion	0	0
	Bestialists	0	1
	Marry your pet	0	0
	Unnatural	1	0
	Sodomy	7	0
	Deviants/Deviance	0	0
	'Aggressive homosexuals'	0	1
Function of marriage	Family	23	50
	Children	35	152
	Procreation	0	29
	'Traditional marriage'	0	15
	2,000 years old!	0	3
	'Enduring values'	0	18
Consequences of gay marriage	Slippery slope	0	0
	Lesbian queen	0	1
	Handcart to hell	0	0
	Constitutional outrage	0	19
	Polygamy	1	14
	Incest	2	7
	Devalued	0	3
	New intolerance	0	2
'Fairness' arguments	Inheritance tax (death duties)	18	2
	Spinster sisters	8	3
	Marry your son	1	1

As will be apparent from the content analysis set out in Table 2, few of the words and phrases on Stonewall's 'bingo card' appear in the *Hansard* record for either the Civil Partnership Act 2004 or the Marriage (Same Sex Couples) Act 2013. Just nine of the 24 Stonewall's words and phrases appeared in the Civil Partnership Act debate; and no spectator would have been able to call 'full house', as eight of these tropes do not appear in the Marriage (Same Sex Couples) debate either. Indeed, if my thematic arrangement of the terms were to be constructed as a bingo card, the only theme where a winner would be found would be that of the 'fairness' arguments around inheritance tax, spinster sisters and other caring relationships.

A notable feature of the content analysis from these debates is the clearly very different emphasis within each debate. For example, the Civil Partnership Act debates were replete with discussions of inheritance tax (n=18), yet in the equivalent debate on the Marriage (Same Sex Couples) Act, inheritance tax was only mentioned twice. The first mention was from Lord Campbell-Savours,[14] who intimated that though he has 'no problem with pension-splitting, inheritance tax management or anything that seeks equality with heterosexual couples', he is clear that: 'my problem is over the use of the word "marriage". I see it as distinct from civil partnership'. The second mention was from Lord Edmiston,[15] whose concern in mentioning inheritance tax was with the 'interesting possibilities for inheritance tax planning' that he argued arose from the lack of a consummation requirement in same sex marriage. A second clear difference between these debates can be seen in the number of mentions of family, children and procreation, all of which feature much more strongly in the debates on the Marriage (Same Sex Couples) Bill. We can infer from this that, whereas civil partnership was viewed as a legal framework solely concerned with regulating relationships between adults, marriage is constructed as the foundation of and for *family* life.

B. Homophobic Language

Of most note from the content analysis is the lack, in either debate, of explicit discourse that can be considered 'homophobic language'. Whilst the term 'unnatural' appeared in the Civil Partnership Bill debate, and 'bestiality' in the Marriage (Same Sex Couples) Bill debate, the context of these is somewhat surprising. The relevant passages are quoted in Extracts 1.

[14] HL Deb 3 June 2013, vol 745, col 990.
[15] HL Deb 3 June 2013, vol 745, col 1003.

Extracts 1

My Lords, I want to say how much I welcome the Bill. After I joined this House, the first major debate in which I participated was on 13 April 1999. I stood up at 10.29 p.m. to make my first major speech in the House. The subject was the equalisation of the age of consent ... I sat through many speeches about gay men and women—noble Lords may recall some of them—referring to us as sick, abnormal, unnatural and ruined. I remember starting my speech. Bravely—some would say naively—I stood up and said that I was 34 and proud to be gay, and that I was gay when I was 24, 20, 19, 18, 17 and 16. I looked around me, and I felt very vulnerable—but there was also a huge warmth in the House that night from colleagues all around it. I ended my speech by saying:

> 'In tonight's vote I should like your Lordships to speak out for me and millions like me, not because you agree or disagree with who I am or, "because you approve or disapprove", of what I do, "but because if you do not protect me in this House you protect no one"'.—[Official Report, 13/4/99; col 738.]

We lost that vote, and I walked away from this Chamber feeling pretty wretched. (Lord Alli)[16]

There are 20,000 homophobic crimes annually and 800,000 people in five years have witnessed homophobic bullying at work. An even more dreadful statistic is that 96 per cent of young LGBT people in secondary schools routinely hear homophobic language. Three in five who experience homophobic bullying say that teachers who witnessed it never intervened.

We have heard lots of references to letters and e-mails, some of which I was proud to receive. Unfortunately, some of those letters and e-mails to me also provided evidence, which I am sure your Lordships have seen, of continued prejudice towards me and my community. Being defined as immoral and evil is just for starters. Statements made by many public figures recently have compared same-sex relationships with child abuse, slavery and bestiality. I have heard those comments. There is no point in noble Lords shaking their heads; those opinions still resonate in our society. Comments like that fuel aggression and homophobic bullying and cause damage to the self-esteem not only of people such as me but of young people in particular. (Lord Collins of Highbury)[17]

[16] HL Deb 22 April 2004, vol 660, col 408.
[17] HL Deb 4 June 2013, vol 745, col 1089.

There are two points to make about these contributions to the respective debates. First, as will be evident from the text of each extract, both of these speeches were from openly gay peers. These two are not the only 'out' gay members of the House of Lords. Lord Smith of Finsbury, Lord Black of Brentwood and Baroness Barker all made reference to their own sexuality in their contributions. Indeed Baroness Barker, a Liberal Democrat peer, used her speech to 'come out' publicly.[18] I hope that it is not too much of a stretch to assume that the presence of openly gay and lesbian members of the House of Lords may have impacted on the tenor of the debate. The second point is that the ways that the terms in question are portrayed in these speeches makes it quite clear, discursively, that to use explicitly homophobic language in these debates would be felt as personally offensive by these members of the House.

Similarly, the seven mentions of 'sodomy' in the Civil Partnership Bill debates were all from two supporters of the Bill, both of whom sought to point out the limitations of the modern usage of the term (see Extracts 2).

Extracts 2

> Part of the problem is that the Christian Church has been in the most appalling muddle over homosexuality ever since it was founded. The Old Testament says 'do not eat lobster', 'do not eat crab', and 'stone adulterers to death'. If we were to do so, I suspect it would have the same effect on the countryside as the Black Death. God spoke to Abraham, or so we assume, six hundred years after it is assumed to have happened. Abraham changed the spelling of his name, his wife could have children at the age of 99, and they could then go and inhabit the best piece of real estate on the Eastern Mediterranean littoral. Not unsurprisingly, Abraham said 'Yippee. What's the catch?' God replied: 'Chop off the end of your penis with a stone axe and those of all your 10,000 slaves as well'. This is called the authority of the Old Testament
>
> The noble and much-loved late Lord Hailsham had a story of a French friend of his who said to him: 'On sait tres bien ce qui est arrive a Sodome, mais qu'est-ce qu'on a fait a Gomorrhe alors?', assuming that people knew what actually happened at Sodom. Well, they did not, as the Church could not make up its mind. Luther, of course, got

[18] 'My Lords, I declare an interest. Many years ago, I had the great good fortune to meet someone. She and I have loved each other ever since—that is, apart from the occasional spectacular argument, usually about driving or DIY'. (Baroness Barker, HL Deb 3 June 2013, vol 745, col 951).

in a terrible rage about sodomy, because he said it was all to do with celibate priests in Rome. Funnily enough, the Spanish Inquisition also burnt 150 sodomites without the benefit of strangulation as well as heretics, because it was classed as heresy. There was a wonderful Venetian journalist-editor who wrote a thundering Sun-like leader in a local newspaper in 1508, blaming the catastrophic defeat of the Venetians in some battle upon randy nuns and Venetian sodomites. So one can show that the attitude on homosexuality up until very recently was based on a series of slightly hysterical myths. (The Earl of Onslow)[19]

My Lords, in supporting the Bill, I draw to the attention of the noble Earl, Lord Onslow, the fact that Ezekiel says that the sin of Sodom and her daughters is that they, 'had pride of wealth and food in plenty, comfort and ease, and yet she never helped the poor and the wretched'. It is not the sin that was often ascribed to them. (Lord Beaumont of Whitley)[20]

Explicitly homophobic language in the House of Lords is not present in these debates. Indeed, many contributors went to significant lengths to disclaim that their opposition to the Bill, or their opposition to same sex marriage in general was rooted in homophobia. It would be folly, however, to dismiss the elements of Stonewall's bingo card that construct the House of Lords as a homophobic space purely on the absence of such express discourse. As with explicit or overtly racist speech (Every and Augoustinos 2007), explicitly homophobic speech is now less common in public discourse (though not entirely eradicated). Instead, we must look more carefully at everyday language in order to excavate the different layers of privilege and oppression that imbue discourse. In so doing, we can understand the 'mundane heterosexism' that passes unchallenged in everyday language (Peel 2001). Whereas 'homophobia' carries the definitional meaning of an 'irrational fear of homosexuals' (Weinberg 1972), 'heterosexism' shifts the focus to 'consideration of more covert forms of homonegativity' (Peel 2001: 544). Heterosexism, as distinct from homophobia, and in common with concepts such as sexism and racism, seeks to highlight the everyday forms of privilege and discrimination that are embedded in the social world, as well as individual feelings of distaste, condemnation or hostility towards lesbians and gay men (Herek 1996).

[19] HL Deb 22 April 2004, vol 660, col 416.
[20] HL Deb 22 April 2004, vol 660, col 417.

The final phrase in the homophobic language theme, 'aggressive homosexuals' speaks to some of this form of prejudice. This idea appeared as follows:

> It is all too possible that, even if the law is totally robust, a teacher or a priest who has tried to opt out, or somebody else who is, or should be, protected under the Bill, may be attacked at law by a possibly aggressive gay rights organisation. (Lord Davies of Stamford)[21]

The issue to which Lord Davies refers is the question, which was the subject of much discussion during the Lords' debates, of whether persons who are employed in roles which include discussion of marriage (particularly teachers and religious officials) could be sued or prosecuted for expressing a view of marriage which excludes same sex couples. The two sides of this particular argument can be highlighted by the contributions on the issue by Baroness Stowell on the one hand, and Lord Tebbit on the other (see Extracts 3).

Extracts 3

> Some people are concerned that the Bill will impact on freedom of speech, that people such as teachers—or, indeed, anyone while at work—will not be able to criticise same-sex marriage. I can reassure the House that this Bill does not in any way affect the perfectly legitimate expression of the perfectly legitimate belief that marriage should only be between a man and a woman. Teachers will be expected to teach the factual and legal position when teaching about marriage, as with any area of the curriculum, but they will not be expected to promote or endorse views that go against their own beliefs. It will be unlawful to dismiss a teacher purely for doing so. (Baroness Stowell of Beeston)[22]
>
> Finally, I must express my concern for those employed in schools and churches. Would their jobs be at risk should they question the new orthodoxy? Section 28 of the Education Act prohibited teachers from promoting homosexuality and was denounced by the liberal establishment. This Bill seems to require teachers to promote marriage between homosexuals. What will the liberal establishment say then? There must be some explanation for that. (Lord Tebbit)[23]

[21] HL Deb 3 June 2013, vol 745, cols 1020–1021.
[22] HL Deb 3 June 2013, vol 745, col 940.
[23] HL Deb 3 June 2013, vol 745, col 1018.

This discourse, drawing on the spectre of public sector workers of faith who are persecuted or prosecuted for expressing views that are not in keeping with the legal and social reality of same sex marriage, highlights a key remaining fault-line in public talk about lesbians and gay men: the appropriate limits that should be placed on freedom of expression in the conflict of rights between religious belief and sexuality.[24]

Leaving aside the issue of conflict of rights, or the legitimate and proportionate constraints that may be placed on freedom of expression, the construction of the talk on both sides is interesting here. Looking more closely at Baroness Stowell's attempt to pre-empt the argument, we see her speak of 'the perfectly legitimate expression of the perfectly legitimate belief that marriage should only be between a man and a woman', but then go on to say that all teachers will be expected to teach the 'factual and legal position' but 'will not be expected to promote or endorse views that go against their own beliefs'. The issue of 'promotion' of homosexuality of course has echoes of that much reviled legislative provision, Section 28, which purported to outlaw the teaching of homosexuality as a pretended family relationship. Lord Tebbit refers explicitly to the now repealed provision, but suggests that the legalisation of same sex marriage will require teachers to 'promote marriage between homosexuals'. The interesting thing about this particular flashpoint in the debates, however, is that neither contributor is entirely wrong. The factual reality is that the enactment of same sex marriage will require teachers (and anyone else who expresses a view) to admit that same sex marriage is recognised in law. Conversely, rights to freedom of expression permit that anyone can express their view that same sex marriage is contrary to their values, beliefs or ideals (whether these are founded in religious belief or otherwise). That is not to say, of course, that they will not face public or private censure for expressing heterosexist views. In contrast to the lack of expressly homophobic language in these debates, there was no shortage of heterosexism in these debates.

C. Function of Marriage

One area where heterosexism is evident is in the contributions that focused on family, children and procreation. The term 'procreation' did not appear at all in the Second Reading debate on the Civil Partnership Bill in 2004. Indeed, the question of children was not considered at length during the passage of the Civil Partnership Act. The issue of same sex couples adopting children had been considered at length during the debates on the Adoption

[24] There is not the space to deal adequately with the interesting and complex literature on this point here. See Stychin (2009a) for more detailed discussion of how this issue could play out in the future.

and Children Act 2002. Legislation allowing for the same sex civil partner of a woman who gives birth to be named on that child's birth certificate as a parent came later (in the form of the Human Fertilisation and Embryology Act 2008). There were just 35 mentions of child or children in the Second Reading debate on the Civil Partnership Bill. These mentions can be split into two main themes: first, references to same sex couples raising children together (n=21); secondly, discourse that equates children with (different sex) marriage (n=9). An example of the latter type would be the assertion, from Baroness Scotland of Asthal when introducing the Bill, that 'it is important for us to be clear that we continue to support marriage and recognise that it is the surest foundation for opposite sex couples raising children'.[25] In general, however, children did not feature heavily in the Civil Partnership Bill debates. There are two plausible explanations for this absence. The first is the pervasive assumption that same sex couples do not have or raise children. Clearly this is an erroneous assumption, but it does appear to permeate the debate. The second is that the stereotypical image of the 'homosexual' that is constructed in Parliament is that of a gay man; lesbians are largely absent from parliamentary discourse, and arguably in public discourse more generally. The limited statistics that are available on lesbian and gay parenting suggest that it is lesbian couples who are more likely to have children (Harding 2011), which may account for some of the invisibility of parenting by same sex couples in this discourse.

In contrast, the mentions of children (n=152) and procreation (n=29) together in the Second Reading debate on the Marriage (Same Sex Couples) Bill constituted a significant discursive theme. The vast majority of these mentions constructed having and raising children as the preserve of different sex couples only. Within this discourse, the main thrust of the arguments cohered around one of the few continuing, substantive differences between same sex and different sex marriage: consummation. A flavour of these mentions is reproduced at Extracts 4.

Extracts 4

> One is that marriage is given for the conception, nurture and upbringing of children—that is what it is naturally there for, as other speakers have said. I accept that other family arrangements can successfully bring up children, but there is something naturally given about marriage in relation to children. (The Lord Bishop of Chester)[26]

[25] HL Deb 22 April 2004, vol 660, col 387.
[26] HL Deb 3 June 2013, vol 745, cols 995–996.

> The reason marriage is limited to one man and one woman is that it takes no more and no less to produce children. If we were to accept that love is the precondition for marriage, why should we restrict it? If there is no possibility of genetic offspring or indeed no requirement for consummation, why should not close relatives get married? If that were to happen, I can see all sorts of interesting possibilities for inheritance tax planning. We would open a Pandora's Box. I do not believe we have looked closely enough at the unintended consequences. (Lord Edmiston)[27]
>
> The one fact of life is that we are all different. We all differ in our physical and mental attributes, and in our dislikes and preferences. Most people form opposite-sex partnerships, giving birth to children and nurturing them in the family unit. This type of relationship, defined by the parameters of declared commitment, consummation of the relationship and social commitment for the nurture and care of the family, has long been defined as marriage. Difference should be respected. While same-sex partnerships are primarily for adult companionship, they do not share the same social responsibilities and parameters that define 'marriage' in so many different religions and cultures. What I fail to understand is the pretence that marriage, with its clearly defined parameters and attached responsibilities, is the same as same-sex adult companionship when everyone outside Westminster knows there is a world of difference. (Lord Singh of Wimbledon)[28]
>
> The defining process of marriage is consummation, which is for the entirely practical purpose of bringing children into the world—the creation of families which have been the building block of society for centuries. The marriage of two men or two women cannot naturally bring about the purpose of marriage; legally perhaps, but naturally not. (Lord Dannatt)[29]

Consummation has been well discussed in the academic literature on both civil partnership and same sex marriage (see eg, Barker 2006, 2012; Stychin 2006). Herring (this volume) provides a detailed overview of the law relating to consummation, and an interesting argument about the need to de-sex family law. In short, however, consummation is currently a requirement of different sex marriage, but not of same sex marriage. Whether this difference has arisen for reasons of principle or prudishness, there has been no attempt to define any particular same sex sexual acts as the legal equivalent

[27] HL Deb 3 June 2013, vol 745, col 1003.
[28] HL Deb 3 June 2013, vol 745, col 1009.
[29] HL Deb 3 June 2013, vol 745, cols 1013–1014.

of heterosex for the purposes of consummation of marriage. The attempts by supporters of the Bill to rebut these discussions of divinely sanctioned procreative activity were generally somewhat rhetorically perfunctory. The most common approach was to highlight the recognition of marriage between those who are infertile, or who are past childbearing age, or who are voluntarily childless. The following contribution from Baroness Mallalieu is indicative of this form of argument:

> I have had people say in letters, e-mails and, indeed, in this House that homosexuals cannot consummate a marriage; marriage is meant for the creation of children; homosexuals cannot commit adultery. Those are the strains of objections voiced by a number of your Lordships, including the noble Lord, Lord Tebbit. We do not stop women over childbearing age or some disabled people from marrying, or those who cannot have or do not want children—of course not. As the right reverend Prelate the Bishop of Leicester conceded, such people are no less married—so why not homosexuals? (Baroness Mallalieu)[30]

Aside from the question of consummation, and given the obvious limitations of arguments that only heterosexual couples have children, these claims that the function of marriage is to support 'the family' are clearly speaking to a different set of concerns. The underlying concerns about marriage as the most appropriate location for expressions of adult (hetero)sexuality, and the related moral values that are inherent in such a concern lie barely below the surface of this discourse.

Extracts 5

> When we hear two people exchange their marriage vows, whether in a place of worship or at a registry office, we know that we are witnessing a couple commit to the kind of values that we associate with the special enterprise of shared endeavour—loyalty, trust, honesty and forgiveness. (Baroness Stowell of Beeston)[31]
>
> This is a hugely important milestone for equality, respect and dignity in our society, which rightly values stable relationships within the framework of marriage. (Baroness Royall of Blaisdon)[32]
>
> My Lords, I am a passionate supporter of the Bill. I support it because I believe in the institution of marriage, which is the bedrock of society and should be open to all. I support it because I believe in the values of the family, and the Bill will, in my view, strengthen them.

30 HL Deb 3 June 2013, vol 745, col 1035.
31 HL Deb 3 June 2013, vol 745, col 938.
32 HL Deb 3 June 2013, vol 745, col 948.

I support it because I am a Conservative. Respect for individual liberty is at the core of my being and this is a Bill that will add to the sum of human freedom. I support it because I am a Christian and I believe we are all equal in the eyes of God, and should be so under man's laws. I support it because I am one of those people who I fear were rather glibly derided by the noble Lord, Lord Dear, as being part of a tiny minority and, I think, were praised by my noble friend Lady Knight as being delightful, in that I am gay. (Lord Black of Brentwood)[33]

For 40 years my life has been driven by Christian and Conservative convictions, and now I am led to believe that because I continue to hold those values and principles I am a swivel-eyed loon. I want to raise a flag for swivel-eyed loons, because at the very heart of our country and our party is a commitment to time-tested values and principles. (Lord Mahwinney)[34]

My main reason for opposing this Bill and for being disquieted about its content is its likely impact on children. The values which will influence their own attitudes in life could be influenced by the Bill. Small children have a need for the warmth and love of their natural mother. Boys, as they struggle to find their way in an increasingly competitive and challenging world, need the guidance and sense of values given by their father. All children, of whatever age, benefit from the security, stability and discipline of a loving family home. Children experience many pressures in school and these could be made much worse if the sort of material I have seen being prepared by Stonewall for use in primary schools ever gains wider usage. It would cause confusion and distress. (Lord Eden of Winton)[35]

As can be seen from Extracts 5, 'values' were drawn on by both sides in the same sex marriage debate. The values of stability, monogamy and longevity were drawn on as both an argument for and an argument against same sex marriage. There are interesting parallels here to the academic literature that argues for the recognition of same sex marriage as a way to domesticate gay male sexuality (Sullivan 1996; 1997). Missing from this debate is any question that conservative values such as these are in any way problematic. In contrast, this has been the topic of significant discussion within feminist and queer circles as to the limitations of arguing for access to same sex marriage (eg, Auchmuty 2004; Barker 2012; Spade 2013). Perhaps the discourse in

[33] HL Deb 3 June 2013 vol 745, cols 987–988.
[34] HL Deb 3 June 2013 vol 745, col 1016.
[35] HL Deb 4 June 2013 vol 745, col 1073.

this debate that most brings to mind those feminist critiques is that from Lord Eden excerpted above. The issue is, in essence, that the conservative arguments in favour of marriage (whether of same or different sex couples) are rooted in an understanding of marriage that is understood by many feminist and queer commentators to be oppressive of women, economically conservative (in the sense of supporting private, rather than public, responsibility for care and welfare), and therefore fundamentally unequal. Indeed, this conservative argument in favour of the family was made explicitly in the course of the debates:

> When Beveridge introduced the welfare state, he foresaw that the national form of social security might well undermine the family. He was right. We increasingly see the state taking over family care, looking after grandfathers and grandmothers in their dotage, rather than it being the duty of the offspring. As our nation's ability to fund the welfare state comes increasingly into question and above all shows itself up as a hideously expensive substitute for our fractured western families, it is surely inappropriate at this time to weaken the nature of marriage and the family, which have always been the bedrock of society. (Lord Vinson)[36]

In contrast, the economic consequences of marriage were not mentioned in the contributions to the debate that were *in favour* of the marriage bill. For those arguing for the same sex marriage bill, marriage was about love and recognition of that love; not money.

D. Consequences of Gay Marriage

The question of which values do or should underpin marriage, irrespective of the gender of the parties involved, leads us to the themes in the debate which focus on the consequences, socially and legally, of recognising same sex marriage. Again, and as may be expected, critical and feminist voices were largely absent from this debate. No contribution to the debate outlined the radical potential of same sex marriage. No contribution explored the merits of Nan Hunter's (1991) argument that same sex marriage provides a positive opportunity to redefine the place of gender in marriage and consequently to improve the equality credentials of marriage more generally. There were, however, contributions that hinted towards the de-gendering of marriage. Consider this contribution from Lord Vinson:

> Not only will the word 'marriage' be expected in future to cover numerous different sexual relations, but at the same time the terms 'husband' and 'wife' will lose their current meaning. They will become sexless words. (Lord Vinson)[37]

[36] HL Deb 4 June 2013 vol 745, col 1078.
[37] HL Deb 4 June 2013 vol 745, col 1077.

I am sure that there are many feminist commentators who would join me in cheering this outcome of same sex marriage, should it materialise. Importantly, of course, Lord Vinson does not see the de-sexing of marriage as a positive consequence of same sex marriage. Rather, his view is that this will 'have a destabilising and confusing effect on children and the existing concept of family'.[38] Importantly none of the contributors who spoke in favour of same sex marriage appeared to recognise that there was any possibility that same sex marriage would or could affect the place or performance of gender within marriage. This is not surprising. It has been noted that feminist voices have been absent from law reform debates on same sex marriage in other jurisdictions (Young and Boyd 2006).

Perhaps more surprising is that arguments such as the one put forward by Lord Vinson were not directly challenged by the pro same sex marriage contributions to the debate. It appears from reading the contributions in favour of the Bill that same sex marriage would have no impact on heterosexual marriage at all. This may be because it would be very difficult rhetorically to make an argument in favour of same sex marriage, whilst concurrently being critical of marriage. To do so would either be considered internally contradictory, or would otherwise run the risk of providing critical fodder for those on the other side of the debate. As Young and Boyd (2006) have argued, critiques of marriage are unthinkable, or at the very least 'unhearable' in formal equality debates about access to marriage for same sex couples.

A second consequence of gay marriage that was raised by those critical of the Bill was the potential that the recognition of same sex marriage would inevitably lead to calls for the recognition of polygamy. This was not a significant discourse within the debates, but it was drawn upon by a few contributors. There were 14 mentions of polygamy or polyamoury in the 2013 debate, a marked increase on the single mention of it in the Civil Partnership Second Reading debate. During the 2004 debate, the sole mention of polygamy was to demonstrate that it was historically permitted and/or mentioned positively in the Old Testament. In the debates on the Marriage (Same Sex Couples) Bill, this historical context was also raised (n=4), usually in contributions by supporters of the Bill. The existence of recognition of polyamorous relationships in other jurisdictions was mentioned twice. The largest number of mentions (n=5) of polygamy/polyamoury were, however as potential consequences of legislating at the top of the 'slippery slope' of same sex marriage. In spite of the large increase in discourse around polygamy since the 2004 debates, it is difficult to see the potential for recognition claims from those in polyamorous relationships as a major discursive theme in these debates.

[38] Ibid.

E. Fairness Arguments

The final theme in Stonewall's 'bingo card' were the 'fairness' arguments about inheritance tax exemptions, and the recognition of caring relationships between family members (spinster sisters, or sons and daughters caring for their parents). This issue exercised the Lords to such an extent in 2004 that at Report stage they passed an amendment to the Civil Partnership Bill which would have enabled family members in interdependent relationships of care to register a civil partnership. Indeed, civil partnership was constructed by those who opposed the recognition of same sex relationships in 2004, as primarily concerned with exemptions from inheritance tax:

> The obvious solution to all the problems caused by inheritance tax is to abolish it altogether. An inheritance tax abolition Bill would be much more popular and benefit many more people than the Civil Partnership Bill, and would prevent hardship for many more people. (Baroness O'Cathain)[39]

In contrast, the majority of the mentions of this issue in the Marriage (Same Sex Couples) Bill came during the speech made, early in the debate, by Baroness Barker:

> Some noble Lords say that allowing gay people to get married is unfair because it leaves other sorts of relationships, such as those of siblings, without the same legal rights as those who choose a marital status. If enabling gay marriage will be unfair to another relationship, such as that of two sisters, then existing marriage laws are unfair. I think we all understand that relationships which adults enter into voluntarily are wholly distinct from relationships which are determined by consanguinity. If family members could become civil partners, it would be really easy for a bullying parent or sibling to force a member of their family into a relationship simply in order to protect property. I do not think that any of us want to legislate for that. (Baroness Barker)[40]

This difference between the debates on the Civil Partnership Bill and those on the Marriage (Same Sex Couples) Bill can be explained in two ways. First there has been a change in the liability to inheritance tax for family members following the death of a surviving spouse or civil partner since 2007 which effectively doubled the threshold for persons in that situation. This would not have an impact on 'spinster sisters', but may well have provided additional tax planning opportunities for those who were concerned about the inheritance tax liability faced by their children. The second explanation is that marriage is not socially constructed in relation to the legal rights and responsibilities that are embedded in it. By this, I mean that whereas the Civil Partnership Bill itself laid bare the multiple social and economic benefits that same sex couples had been excluded from, these were not so

[39] HL Deb 22 April 2004, vol 660, col 407.
[40] HL Deb 3 June 2013, vol 745, col 952.

obvious on the face of the Marriage (Same Sex Couples) Bill. As a result, Baroness Barker's bold statement that 'if enabling gay marriage will be unfair to another relationship … then existing marriage laws are unfair' highlights the ineffectiveness of the sorts of arguments that were used against civil partnership. In order to make the argument that those in caring (but not sexual) relationships should benefit from the economic advantages of marriage would be to admit that marriage confers economic advantages, and to open up to scrutiny the ideological basis of such different treatment.

IV. CONCLUDING REMARKS

Same sex marriage is now a social and legal fact in England. The Marriage (Same Sex Couples) Act 2013 was passed with overwhelming support in both Houses of Parliament, and is now part of our law. The parliamentary debates on the same sex marriage legislation highlighted a good deal of support for, as well as opposition to, marriage for same sex couples. It is perhaps fair to say that Stonewall's 'bingo card' ultimately missed the mark in terms of its representation of the content of the debates. Yet the themes, of homophobia, the function of marriage, the consequences of marriage and the 'fairness' arguments from the civil partnership debates still hold cultural value. In many respects it does not matter that no spectator would have been able to call 'full house' on the bingo card; indeed it is a relief that one could not. But the questions that the 'bingo card' raises about the function of marriage, and the implicit questions about the future of marriage remain salient. What is marriage for? Will same sex marriage change marriage in the future? How? Importantly, as a meme and as a campaigning tool, Stonewall's bingo card was highly successful. It engaged an audience on social media with the parliamentary debates on same sex marriage, and facilitated discussion about the substantive content of those debates. It is just perhaps a shame that the discourse the meme uncovered, particularly the opportunities for same sex marriage to influence different sex marriage positively were not fully explored.

It is refreshing to look at these debates and not see the sort of language about LGBT people that was prevalent during the debates on the age of consent in the last years of the twentieth century. Overtly homophobic speech appears to have no place in our contemporary legislature, which can only be a positive development. Yet heterosexism (alongside sexism) is still a mundane part of everyday speech, both inside and outside Parliament. Now that same sex marriage is a reality in our jurisdiction, it is time to begin the feminist work of interrogating the extent to which marriage has changed not just through the inclusion of same sex couples, but also to reflect other aspects of contemporary life. The big questions now are not about whether same sex marriage should be recognised, but are focused on what marriage means, and whether the legal recognition of intimate relationships is the best or most appropriate way to distribute societal benefits. The next pressing question, for family lawyers and for feminist academics, is to ascertain exactly what marriage *is* for. We need to be clear about the social, economic and cultural values that marriage should contain, and make sure that the next evolution of marriage supports equality in the widest possible sense.

BIBLIOGRAPHY

AUCHMUTY, Rosemary, 'Same-sex marriage revived: Feminist critique and legal strategy' (2004) 14(1) *Feminism and Psychology* 101.

BAKER, Paul, '"Unnatural Acts": Discourses of homosexuality within the House of Lords debates on gay male law reform' (2004) 8 *Journal of Sociolinguistics* 88.

BARKER, Nicola J, 'Sex and the civil partnership act: the future of (non) conjugality?' (2006) 14 *Feminist Legal Studies* 241.

——, *Not The Marrying Kind: A Feminist Critique of Same-Sex Marriage* (Baskingstoke, Palgrave Macmillan, 2012).

DELANEY, Sam, 'Lord Tebbit: Gay marriage, a lesbian queen—full interview' (2013) *Big Issue*, available at: www.bigissue.com/features/interviews/2438/lord-tebbit-gay-marriage-lesbian-queen-full-interview.

EEKELAAR, John, 'Perceptions of Equality: The Road to Same-Sex Marriage in England and Wales' (2014) 28 *International Journal of Law Policy and the Family* 1.

EVERY, Danielle and AUGOUSTINOS, Martha, 'Constructions of racism in the Australian parliamentary debates on asylum seekers' (2007) 18 *Discourse and Society* 411.

HARDING, Rosie, '"Dogs are 'registered', people shouldn't be": Legal consciousness and lesbian and gay rights' (2006) 15 *Social and Legal Studies* 511.

——, *Regulating Sexuality: Legal consciousness in lesbian and gay lives* (Abingdon, Routledge, 2011).

——, '(Re)Inscribing the Heteronormative Family: Same-sex relationships and parenting "after equality"' in R Leckey (ed), *After Equality* (Abingdon, Routledge, 2015).

HARDING, Rosie and PEEL, Elizabeth, '"We Do"? International perspectives on equality, legality and same sex relationships' (2006) 7 *Lesbian and Gay Psychology Review* 123.

HEREK, Gregory M, 'Heterosexism and homophobia' in RP Cabaj and TS Stein (eds), *Textbook of homosexuality and mental health* (Washington DC, American Psychiatric Press, 1996).

HERRING, Jonathan, 'Why Marriage Needs to be Less Sexy' chapter thirteen in this volume.

HUNTER, Nan D, 'Marriage, Law and Gender: A Feminist Inquiry' (1991) 1 *Law and Sexuality* 9.

JOWETT, Adam and PEEL, Elizabeth, '"Seismic cultural change?": Media representation of same-sex "marriage"' (2010) 33 *Women's Studies International Forum* 206.

KLEINHANS, Chuck, 'Taking out the Trash: Camp and the politics of parody' in M Meyer (ed), *The Politics and Poetics of Camp* (London, Routledge, 1994).

LEFEVER, Robert, 'Some complain we're going to hell in a handcart, but gay couples deserve the same rights as anybody else' (2012) *Mail Online* available at: www.dailymail.co.uk/debate/article-2152048/Some-complain-going-hell-handcart-gay-couples-deserve-rights-anybody-else.html.

LONG, Ryan G, 'Marriage in the Bible' (2008) available at: ryangrantlong.blogspot.co.uk/2011/01/marriage-in-bible.html.

MARSZAL, Andrew, 'UKIP Councillor who blamed floods on gay marriage expelled from party' (2014) *The Telegraph*, available at: www.telegraph.co.uk/news/politics/ukip/10619383/Ukip-councillor-who-blamed-floods-on-gay-marriage-expelled-from-party.html.

MCCORMICK, Joseph P, 'Backbench Tory MPs Speak Out against 'outrageous' marriage equality plans' (2012) *Pink News* available at: www.pinknews.co.uk/2012/12/11/backbench-tory-mps-speak-out-against-outrageous-marriage-equality-plans/.

PEEL, Elizabeth, 'Mundane Heterosexism: Understanding incidents of the everyday' (2001) 24 *Women's Studies International Forum* 541.

SHIFMAN, Limor, 'An anatomy of a YouTube meme' (2012) 14 *New Media and Society* 187.

SPADE, Dean, 'Under the Cover of Gay Rights' (2013) 37 *NYU Review of Law and Social Change* 79.

STYCHIN, Carl F, 'Not (quite) a horse and carriage' (2006) 14 *Feminist Legal Studies* 79.

——, 'Faith in the future: Sexuality, religion and the public sphere' (2009a) 29 *Oxford Journal of Legal Studies* 729.

——, 'Closet Cases: "Conscientious Objection" to Lesbian and Gay Legal Equality' (2009b) 18 *Griffith Law Review* 17.

SULLIVAN, Andrew, *Same-Sex Marriage: Pro and Con: A Reader* (New York, Vintage, 1997).

——, *Virtually Normal: An argument about homosexuality* (London, Picador, 1996).

WEALE, Albert, BICQUELET, Aude and BARA, Judith, 'Debating Abortion, Deliberative Reciprocity and Parliamentary Advocacy' (2012) 60 *Political Studies* 643.

YOUNG, Claire FL and BOYD, Susan B, 'Losing the Feminist Voice? Debates on the legal recognition of same sex partnership in Canada' (2006) 14 *Feminist Legal Studies* 213.

Part IV

12

Let's Talk About a Divorce: Religious and Legal Wedding

PETER W EDGE[1]

I. INTRODUCTION

THE EXTENSION OF marriage to same sex couples is an important policy concern in a number of jurisdictions across the world. This is not necessarily framed as a religious rights issue, at least in the constitutional discourse. In *US v Windsor*,[2] for instance, the US Supreme Court managed to discuss the constitutional position of same sex marriage without any consideration of religion; the High Court of Australia has managed much the same in *Commonwealth of Australia v The Australian Capital Terrority*.[3] In this chapter, however, rather than seeking to engage with marriage as part of the canon of family law (Hasday 2004), I will be putting same sex marriage very much in a religious frame, that is, as an issue which raises religious interests.

Following Wintemute (Wintemute 2002), I consider love rights as going beyond recognising the right to share sexual activity, to enabling and recognising the development of a partnership. I argue that the contested areas in England have become the symbolic and ceremonial side of the creation of marriages—love rites rather than love rights. This emphasis on the symbolic and the ceremonial should not be misinterpreted as an emphasis on the trivial or the easily resolvable. Rather, it has generated a considerable public debate. I argue that the current debate may usefully be understood as a debate over co-production of legal marriage by the state and religious organisations, which has become more problematic as the conceptions of marriage increasingly diverge. I argue that the time has come for a divorce between legal and religious production of marriage, with religious weddings

[1] Thanks to participants at the Cambridge Workshop, and to Brigitte Clark of Oxford Brookes, for their comments on an earlier draft of this chapter.

[2] *United States v Windsor* 570 US 12 (2013).

[3] *Commonwealth of Australia v The Australian Capital Territory* [2013] HCA 55 (No C13 of 2013). On the Australian context more broadly see Grossi (2012).

having purely religious consequences for all religious communities. A consequent question is where the term marriage should then reside. One possibility is for marriage to remain a technical term in English law, albeit one which co-exists with other usages of the same word in social and religious discourse. Another, more radical, way forward is for the state to cease to have any role in the production of marriage whatsoever, and instead to reinvent both legal marriage and legal civil partnerships as a single category of legal civil partnerships, with marriage ceasing to be a legal construction in England. Adopting the latter, I ultimately argue for civil partnerships for all as the best way to address both equality and religious liberty.

II. THE DEVELOPMENT OF CIVIL PARTNERSHIPS IN ENGLISH LAW

English law in relation to marriage developed from local Anglo-Saxon custom but came to be increasingly regulated by Christian religious law, which was relatively stable by 1300 (Helmholtz 2004: 522–56). For a considerable period, 'the regulation of marriage was largely a matter for the Church' (Masson, Bailey-Harris and Probert 2008: para 1-002). After marriage law ceased to be a matter for ecclesiastical courts from 1836–60,[4] religious organisations and communities contributed to marriage particularly through the process by which marriage came to exist, which I will refer to throughout as wedding (Edge and Corrywright 2011). Focusing on the end of the twentieth century, there were two primary types of wedding—civil and religious.

Civil weddings could occur in the office of a Superintendent Registrar.[5] As the statute states baldly, 'No religious service shall be used at any marriage solemnized in the office of a superintendent registrar'.[6] This key passage has not been interpreted by the courts, with the only appellate decision on the section exploring a different issue.[7] There is, perhaps, tangential guidance elsewhere in the Act. In a section dealing with weddings of the housebound and detained, provision is made for use of the 'relevant form, rite or ceremony' where the wedding is being conducted as if in a registered place of worship.[8] This is defined in the statute as

> a form, rite, or ceremony of a body of persons who meet for religious worship in any registered building being a form, rite or ceremony in accordance with which members of that body are married in any such registered building.[9]

[4] Marriage Act 1836, Ecclesiastical Courts Act 1855, Matrimonial Causes Act 1857, Ecclesiastical Courts Jurisdiction Act 1860.
[5] Marriage Act 1949 s 45(2).
[6] Marriage Act 1949 s 45(2).
[7] *Miles v Wakefield* [1987] AC 539 (HL).
[8] Marriage Act 1949 s 45A(2), cf s 45A(4).
[9] Marriage Act 1949 s 45A(5).

Even this section, however, has not been the subject of judicial consideration. Civil weddings could also occur in 'approved premises', where the wedding took place in a venue registered for weddings 'according to such form and ceremony as the persons to be married see fit to adopt'.[10] This is not as broad as it sounds, however, as '[no] religious service shall be used at a marriage on approved premises'.[11]

Four routes provided for explicitly religious solemnisations of marriages. Three of them were specific to particular religious communities, allowing marriages to be created by the usages of the Society of Friends,[12] Jews,[13] and the Church of England.[14] An important point to note here is that these were not marriages within the context of these three religious groups—for instance by occurring in a place of worship dedicated to the religion—but by the usages of each. The canon law of the Church of England is part of English law, and so its usages may be determined legally.[15] For the other two communities, explicit statutory mechanisms existed to determine the question of whether the marriage was according to their usages.[16] The last, and most general, route emphasised not the way in which the wedding was carried out, but the premises on which it occurred. Marriages may occur at certified places of worship[17] whose governing body may authorise a person to be present at the solemnisation of marriages without the presence of a registrar.[18] Such ceremonies must include a brief, statutory form of words,[19] and must be with the consent of the governing body,[20] but otherwise may be 'according to such form and ceremony as [the couple] see fit'.[21] Interestingly, this does not necessarily require that the ceremony takes place in accordance with the particular religion practised at the place of worship.

Entering the twenty-first century, then, marriage was seen as a legal institution which could be created either purely by state activity, or, less commonly, by a partnership between the state and certain religious communities (Haskey 2015). The structure of the relationship was determined by the state, as were the rules concerning the ending of the relationship, that is, the rules for divorce. It was an institution that was limited to opposite sex couples only.[22]

[10] Marriage Act 1949 s 26(1)(a).
[11] Marriage Act 1949 s 46B(4).
[12] Marriage Act 1949 ss 26(1)(c), 47.
[13] Marriage Act 1949 s 26(1)(d).
[14] Marriage Act 1949 Part II.
[15] Marriage Act 1949 Part II.
[16] Marriage Act 1949 s 55(1).
[17] Marriage Act 1949 s 41. See further *R (Hodkin and another) v Registrar General of Births, Deaths and Marriages* [2013] UKSC 77.
[18] Marriage Act 1949 s 43.
[19] Marriage Act 1949 s 44(3), (3a).
[20] Marriage Act 1949 s 44(1).
[21] Marriage Act 1949 s 44(1).
[22] *Hyde v Hyde and Woodmansee* (1866) LR 1 P & D 130; Matrimonial Causes Act 1973 s 11(c).

The Civil Partnership Act 2004 created new 'civil partnerships' which had many similarities to marriage. The legislation has been criticised for seeking to replicate marriage (Stychin 2006; Bendall 2013), but also for failing to do so closely enough to eliminate sexual-orientation discrimination in this area (Wright 2006). To portray civil partnerships as 'gay marriage' was often seen as over-simplistic (see Barker 2006; Kitzinger and Wilkinson 2004), although a concept with tremendous cultural traction (see also Farrimond 2015; Peel 2015). That it is a close analogy was less contested. Like marriage, civil partnership creates far-reaching legal incidents (Wright 2006), acts as a relationship ritual (Harding and Peel 2004), is legally incompatible with a subsisting marriage,[23] and is not open to individuals within prohibited degrees of relationship.[24] In a recent Supreme Court decision, Lady Hale found that 'Civil partnership is not called marriage but in almost every other respect it is indistinguishable from the status of marriage in United Kingdom law'.[25]

Unlike marriage weddings, however, civil partnership weddings were initially constructed as purely civil. The standard procedure for creation of a civil partnership required the signing of a civil partnership document in the presence, inter alia, of a civil partnership registrar.[26] As with the routes to civil marriage outlined above, '[n]o religious service is to be used while the civil partnership registrar is officiating at the signing of a civil partnership document'.[27] The wedding could, with an important exception discussed below, happen in a place approved by the registration authority, which could also provide a place in its area for the registration of civil partnerships.[28]

It is significant to note that there was no religious route for the creation of a civil partnership, a position which survived the prohibition of sexual orientation discrimination in relation to the provision of goods and services.[29] The provisions allowing marriage by the usages of the Church of England, Society of Friends, and Jews, were not extended to civil partnerships. Strikingly, the more general provisions concerning the certified place of worship were expressly excluded from the legislation. Registration of a civil partnership is formally separate from any ceremony,[30] but the separation between civil partnership registration and religious ceremony was reinforced by a separate rule that registration may not take place in religious premises.[31]

23 Civil Partnership Act 2004 s 3(1)(b).
24 Civil Partnership Act 2004 s 3(1)(d).
25 *Bull and Another v Hall and Another* [2013] UKSC 73, [26]. This is not a view shared by the applicants in *Wilkinson*, discussed below (n 56).
26 Civil Partnership Act 2004 s 2(1)–(4).
27 Civil Partnership Act 2004 s 2(6).
28 Civil Partnership Act 2004 s 6(5).
29 See Department for Communities and Local Government 2007.
30 Civil Partnership Act 2004 s 2(1).
31 Civil Partnership Act 2004 s 6(1)(b).

Civil partnerships, then, were constructed as a form of especially secularised civil ceremony. Specifically religious ceremonies were excluded from the process, as with civil marriage, but without the possibility of religious routes. This exclusion of religion was deliberate:

> [O]pposite-sex couples can opt for a religious or civil marriage ceremony as they choose, whereas civil partnership is an exclusively civil procedure. The government has been very clear throughout the process that it has no plans to bring in same sex marriage. Marriage is an institution for opposite couples with its own historical traditions. Civil partnership provides a separate and distinct relationship, which is secular in nature and only open to same sex couples. (Lord Falconer of Thoroton 2007: 5–6).

The exclusion of religion from the creation of civil partnerships began to be queried by couples who wished to form a civil partnership through a religious ceremony, and by religious communities who wished to create such partnerships as a religious act.[32] As a result, a 2011 change in the law allowed religious premises to be used for those communities which wished to do so, but the ceremony remained a civil one, which could not 'be religious in nature'. The first religious community to take advantage of this was the Cross Street Unitarian Chapel in Manchester, but the first civil partnership ceremony in a place of worship appears to have been carried out by the Quakers at Friends House in London. Some religious communities may be willing to extend their services to civil partnerships, but may have been deterred by the additional process and fee,[33] but obviously many communities who did not accept same sex unions within their religious thinking deliberately choose not to register.

III. SAME SEX MARRIAGE IN ENGLISH LAW

It will be recalled that the fundamental distinctions between civil partnerships and marriage were the gender polarity of the couple, and the exclusion of religious possibilities from civil partnerships. Both may have been less stable than anticipated. Opposite sex couples sought access to civil partnerships,[34] and same sex couples sought access to marriage.[35] The 2011

[32] Notably by the Quakers in 2009, whose Yearly Meeting, resolved 'to enable same sex marriages in a meeting for worship under the care of a meeting as we currently do for opposite sex marriages' (see Yearly Meeting, 'Epistle from Britain Yearly Meeting Gathering 25 July to 1 August 2009': www.ymg.org.uk/; see also FLGBTQC (Friends for Lesbian, Gay, Bisexual, Transgender and Queer Concerns), 'Collection of Marriage Minutes': flgbtqc.quaker.org/marriageminutes.html.

[33] As discussed in General Register Office, *Civil partnerships on religious premises: Some Frequently Asked Questions*, GRO, November 2013.

[34] For instance Stephanie Munro and Andrew O'Neill, who have petitioned the European Court of Human Rights as part of the Equal Love case—see further equallove.org.uk/the-legal-case.

[35] For instance Sharon Ferguson and Franka Strietzel, who also form part of the Equal Love case, referred to above.

amendment to the law had itself begun to recognise that the complete exclusion of religion from civil partnerships should not be maintained.

In 2012 the Home Office consulted on extending marriage to same sex couples. It received over 228,000 responses. The concept was rejected by bodies such as the Coalition for Marriage, the Catholic Bishops' Conference, the Church of England, the Muslim Council of Britain, and the Evangelical Alliance, as misunderstanding the nature of marriage, which was exclusively heterosexual. The Government proposed to enable same sex couples to have a civil marriage, and to permit religious organisations that wished to conduct same sex marriages to do so, but with explicit protection for religious organisations and clergy that did not wish to do so;[36] and to retain civil partnerships for same sex couples only, but allow existing civil partnerships to be converted to marriage. In response, more than one thousand Roman Catholic clerics signed an open letter arguing that same sex marriage would return them to persecution, rendering them unable to teach 'the truth about marriage in their schools, charitable institutions or places of worship'.[37]

The Government proceeded with the Marriage (Same Sex Couples) Bill 2012–2013. The Bill included specific protection for religious organisations and individuals who did not wish to solemnise same sex marriage. The Church of England, by virtue of its constitutional position, was not entitled under the Bill to decide for itself on same sex marriage, but instead was prohibited from carrying out such marriages without further legislation. Controllers of places of worship, as well as Quakers and Jews, could 'opt in' to religious marriage of same sex couples, but no organisation could be compelled to opt in, and no one could be compelled to carry out a same sex marriage. The Bill passed its key second reading in the House of Commons in February 2013, with a very significant majority of MPs voting for the Bill.

The Marriage (Same Sex Couples) Act 2013 extends marriage to same sex couples,[38] and provides routes for conversion of existing civil partnerships to marriages.[39] The Church of England does not thereby become required to, or entitled to marry same sex couples,[40] nor do any clergy otherwise required to solemnise marriages become required to solemnise the marriage of a same sex couple.[41] Other religious organisations are protected by the detailed provisions of section 2. This protects organisations from any compulsion, including enforcement of a legal requirement, concerning an opt-in

[36] This responded to a long-standing concern, significant in the passage of the Human Rights Act 1998, that allowing same sex partnerships would lead to religious organisations being compelled to religiously sanctify them—see Cumper 2000.

[37] See Scottish Catholic Observer, 'A vow to protect freedom' (2013) January 18.

[38] Marriage (Same Sex Couples) Act 2013 s 1.

[39] Ibid, s 9.

[40] The Church in Wales, with a different constitutional position, has an opt-in power under the Marriage (Same Sex Couples) Act 2013 s 8.

[41] Ibid, s 1(3)–(5).

activity.[42] Further, a similar protection from compulsion exists where a person refuses to conduct, participate in, or consent to a marriage because a same sex couple is getting married.[43] The same section amends the Equality Act 2010, the principal equality statute in UK law, to exclude the provision of religious marriage of same sex couples.[44] The principal purpose of Section 2 is to protect religious organisations from being compelled to exercise the opt-in powers later in the Act. Sections 4 and 5 amend the Marriage Act 1949 to allow a same sex couple to be married in a registered place of worship 'according to such form and ceremony as the persons to be married see fit to adopt', but only where the governing authority has given written consent to marriages of same sex couples.[45] The governing authority is an internal one—'the persons or persons recognised by the members of the relevant religious organisation as competent for the purpose of giving consent for the purposes of this section'.[46] Similar provisions continue the practice of treating religious marriages by the Society of Friends and by Jews specifically, but mirror the requirement of a positive decision in writing by the 'relevant governing authority'.[47] Belief organisations, that is organisations 'whose principal or sole purpose is the advancement of a system of non-religious beliefs which relate to morality or ethics' remain unable to carry out religious weddings of any type, because of their inability to register a place of worship.[48] The statute requires that their position must be reviewed by the Secretary of State before January 2015.[49]

IV. RELIGIOUS AND LEGAL MARRIAGE: TIME FOR A DIVORCE[50]

The flashpoint for the recent debate in the UK was not open disagreement between the substantive incidents which should follow from a legal partnership between a same sex couple as opposed to an opposite sex couple, or disagreement about the morality of same sex relationships (Jowett 2014). Although no doubt some of the opposition to same sex marriage was from those who considered the Civil Partnership Act a poor piece of legislation, this was not the battleground upon which the debate took place. Nor were specific concerns about the position of religious communities which did

42 Ibid, s 2(1).
43 Ibid, s 2(2).
44 Ibid, s 2(5), (6).
45 Marriage Act 1949 s 26A, as amended.
46 Marriage Act 1949 s 26A(4) as amended.
47 Marriage Act 1949 s 26B, as amended.
48 This restriction has recently been reaffirmed by the Supreme Court—see *R (Hodkin and another) v Registrar General of Births, Deaths and Marriages* [2013] UKSC 77, Lord Toulson at [57]–[59].
49 Marriage (Same Sex Couples) Act 2013 s 14.
50 See also Presser (2012).

not wish to carry out same sex religious marriages central to the debate. Religious communities were discussed primarily in relation to protecting the autonomy of religious communities to 'opt in', or not, as they choose. The Catholic Church, for instance, is no more compelled to create a same sex pathway to religious marriage than it has been compelled to create an opposite sex pathway for divorcees. Instead, the recent debate has focused on symbol, ceremony, and language. As discussed below, the decision of the state to define 'marriage' in a new way was resisted in Parliament. Strikingly, we can see parallels in similar debates outside the UK. In the case before the High Court of Australia for instance, the Commonwealth of Australia phrased its opposition to the ACT legislation singularly narrowly:

> Of course, the ACT Marriage Act could have validly extended rights under ACT law to same sex couples *as if* they were in a marriage—thereby accepting and acting upon the demarcation of status effected by the Commonwealth Acts. But what it purports to do instead is to authorise and clothe in legality as a *marriage or equal form of marriage* that which under Australian law cannot be such.[51]

It should not be thought that this reduces the importance of the debate. Symbol, ceremony, and language matter (see further Barker 2011; Bamforth 2007; Auchmuty 2008). Indeed, this moving of the debate to a relatively high level of abstraction and principle may reduce the scope for pragmatic compromise between different groups. The emphasis on principle increases the difficulty of developing a 'family law [which] would decide this important question without unduly denigrating or devaluing any particular social front' (Huntington 2013: 646). The 2013 Act, for instance, was welcomed by Ben Summerskill of Stonewall as 'the last piece of the legislative jigsaw providing equality for gay people',[52] but criticised by Sir Roger Gale MP as 'Orwellian almost, for any government ... to seek to come along and rewrite the political lexicon'.[53] Let me state an abstract version of the two positions—it should be stressed that I am not seeking to précis either Ben Summerskill or Sir Roger Gale.

From the perspective of a supporter of same sex marriage, a distinction between civil partnership and marriage was a violation of equality norms because it treated similarly placed persons differently. Love rights are love rights regardless of the gender of the loving, and former distinctions between opposite sex and same sex unions needed to be recognised as arbitrary discrimination and removed. Even if civil partnership and marriage were identical in every way except nomenclature and sexual polarity, this would still constitute discrimination. By excluding same sex couples from marriage

[51] Federal argument, para 37 (submitted 13 November 2013).

[52] Stonewall, 'Same Sex Marriage Bill Storms through House of Commons' (Press Release, 5 February 2013) at: www.stonewall.org.uk/media/current_releases/8461.asp.

[53] Roger Gale MP, Hansard HC vol 557 col 152 (5 February 2013).

the law carried the message that the relationship was less authentic—in the words of pivotal former law, a 'pretended family relationship'.[54] It sought to police a separation between the modern era and the past, severing same sex couples from their family traditions of marriage, which would typically emerge from an opposite sex couple.[55] While it was acceptable to allow religious organisations and people some space to set their values against equality norms here, by not requiring them to provide religious marriage services to same sex couples, religious organisations could not exercise a monopoly over the definition of marriage. As one commentator has put it, '[t]he law cannot, and probably should not attempt to, change the doctrinal understandings of such religious bodies—but nor may it reflect such understandings in its own rules' (Norrie 2011: 98–99).

From the perspective of an opponent of same sex marriage, a distinction between civil partnership and marriage respected equality norms because it treated differently placed persons differently. While it was important to ensure that people of all sexual orientations were treated decently, for instance by according the incidents of civil partnerships to those who enter into them, same sex and opposite sex relationships were not the same.[56] In particular, marriage was intrinsically limited to opposite sex couples. The distinction may arise from the relative ease of reproduction for the stereotypical opposite sex couple; essentialist constructions of the different sexes in partnership; tradition and culture; or religion, particularly a long theological tradition which sees the family as prior to the state. Whatever its source, this distinction was a given that the state needed to recognise—it could not simply change the definition of marriage.

The key to draw from these abstractions is that both poles neglect the history of marriage in English law, as a history of co-production of marriage between the state and religious organisations and communities.[57] In England, marriage is both a religious and a national legal concept in a sense that, say, *nissuin*[58] and *nikah*[59] are not. The controversy over the definition of 'marriage', particularly by those seeking change, has not given sufficient weight to this co-production. Both the state, and religious organisations who use the term, have a stake in 'marriage' which is not easily replicated elsewhere across the law/religion scene.

[54] Local Government Act 1988 s 28; repealed by Local Government Act 2003 s 122.

[55] This is an area the importance of which I consistently underplay in my writing. I am grateful to Michael Holdsworth, formerly of Oxford Brookes University, for his insights on this point.

[56] This is the view of government policy taken in *Wilkinson v Kitzinger and Others* [2006] EWHC 2022 (Fam), [2006] HRLR 36.

[57] For a broader reflection on similar ideas, see Nichols (2012).

[58] The Jewish religious term normally translated as marriage.

[59] The Muslim religious term normally translated as marriage.

This co-production should not be caricatured as a unified front between the state and significant religions. As the Church in Wales has recently noted:

> It is true that church and state have already disagreed profoundly. The first dispute was in 1835 (until 1907) on the Table of Kindred and Affinity (can a man marry his deceased wife's sister?), and again in 1937 on the liberalization of divorce by the state. Archbishop Lang felt that this was a watershed. It was only in 2002 that the Church of England allowed divorced people to marry in church under certain circumstances, and so came into line with civil law (the Church in Wales always had some discretion from the 1990s). Now the introduction of same sex marriage causes further tensions. That leaves a major challenge for how the church will relate to the state on their doctrine of marriage.[60]

Neither is the new understanding of marriage contained in the legislation incompatible with all religious stances. As noted in relation to the development of religious routes to civil partnership, some religious organisations and individuals take exactly the positive view of same sex marriage I have sketched above. It is fair to say, however, that the understandings of the state and demographically significant religious communities about marriage have now diverged to an unusual degree—and the extent of this divergence is what has given the debate about symbol, ceremony, and language such heat.

One way of understanding the 2004 Act is as an attempt to address the discrimination faced by same sex couples without requiring the cooperation of religious groups in the co-production of marriage. In the passage quoted earlier, Lord Falconer said that civil partnership differed from marriage in being for same sex couples, and exclusively civil. Let me recast the last ground in terms of co-production—civil partnerships were *not* co-produced with religious communities and organisations. Not only did they not depend upon religious communities for their implementation, but in the first iterations of the law, religious communities were positively, and strongly, excluded from the production of civil partnerships. The justifiable scepticism about 'separate but equal' or even 'separate but same' strategies when dealing with a historically persecuted minority (see further Barker 2011; Baker and Elizabeth 2012), as well as the call for change by religious communities who found their powers over religiously wedding couples divided by the state in a way they found arbitrary, rendered this resolution to the problem of co-production of marriage unstable. At the time of writing the state has chosen to redefine marriage in line with state values of non-discrimination on the grounds of sexual orientation, rather than in line with the values of the demographically significant religious communities who opposed this definition in the consultation process.

[60] Standing Doctrinal Commission of the Church in Wales, 'The Church in Wales and Same Sex Partnerships' (March 2014), para 29.

There was a pressing need to reform the law to recognise that 'lesbian, gay, bisexual and transgendered individuals are generally entitled to equal treatment with heterosexual individuals' (Wintemute and Andenaes 2001: 4). From my perspective, the new legal position is much better than the previous distinction between civil partnership and marriage. But there is another way of resolving the problem which gives better weight to both equality and religious freedom: that is the removal of religious marriage from the legal sphere entirely, and the universalising of a creature purely of state law, which for the moment I will refer to as civil partnership.[61] Co-production would be ended by recognising that civil partnerships are an exclusively legal concept which the state is exclusively entitled to shape according to its own values, which will of course involve how it constructs religious liberty; and that religious marriage (as *nissuin*, *zawadj* and other religious partnerships) is an exclusively religious concept which different religious communities are exclusively entitled to shape according to their own values.[62] This would lead, as the religious think tank Ecclesia has put it, to 'a mutually beneficial disentangling of the roles, interests, and practices of church and state' (Barrow 2006).

As to the argument from equality, the current regime means that some religious weddings create legal incidents, and some do not—as Chatterjee observed of the post-1837 marriage landscape, '"choice" has indeed been extended in the realm of marriage laws, but different kinds of *religious* choices still result in different status in law' (Chatterjee 2010: 535). With the recent, overdue, liberalisation of the law concerning registration of places of worship in *Hodkin*, religious communities sufficiently well-resourced to be able to operate a place of worship are largely able, if they choose, to access a route to marry. Religious communities which are not so placed cannot. Additionally, there is some evidence that the distinction between purely religious marriage, and legal marriage, is not recognised with equal clarity across different communities (see Douglas 2011). The removal of legal effect from all religious weddings, regardless of the access of a community to a registered place of worship which carries out legal marriages, would simplify and equalise the legal consequences of religious wedding.

In relation to the argument from religious freedom, the state has a strong interest in determining the content of its partnership law, and inevitably this will be in accord with its fundamental values. Within a religiously plural state, the issue then arises of how it is to deal with communities whose values conflict. Within a co-production model, there is a distinction between religious communities whose values are sufficiently aligned to allow co-production, and those who are not. The potential for entanglement between religion

[61] My conclusion, although not my argument, can also be found in Norrie (2011).

[62] For a detailed argument against this separation of law and religion in the specific context of the family, see further Shachar (2010).

and state is high. Removing legal effect from religious weddings removes this potential, and allows religious communities to shape marriage without the influence of legal recognition for particular shapings. It may be argued, however, that removing legal effect actually reduces religious liberty in two ways—the liberty of religious organisations who want their religious ceremonies to have legal effect in state law, and the liberty of a marrying couple who want their religious ceremony to have this effect. I have already suggested that a state demand to confer a religious ceremony is unlikely to succeed on religious liberty grounds; the same approach suggests that a religious demand for conferment of particular state benefits through a religious ceremony is also unlikely to succeed.

One issue arising from this 'civil partnerships for all' approach is how to articulate religious wedding, which will create in the religious law or understandings of the community a marriage, *nissuin*, *zawadj* and the like; with the civil partnership ceremony which will create a legal civil partnership. This concern with articulation is not particularly novel. In Australia, the Commonwealth's current Marriage Act includes provision for allowing a legal marriage to be followed by a second 'religious ceremony of marriage', which is predicated upon the proving of the legal marriage.[63] There are a number of possible forms of articulation, the simplest being none whatsoever—couples are free to carry out whatever religious ceremonies they wish, which are completely immaterial to the legal creation of a civil partnership. Another is to allow some degree of articulation, as we saw in the 2011 reforms to civil partnerships and religious places of worship. This opens up the possibility of distinguishing between different religions by different degrees of articulation.

One concern for those who did not see same sex partnerships as religiously identical to opposite sex partnerships was that allowing religious routes to such partnerships would pressure them to change their stance. At its most blunt, there are arguments that once marriage is defined in a way which does not depend upon sexual polarity, equality law can be used to compel religious sanctification of same sex marriage. Although an abiding concern for religious communities which would fear such an outcome, this already weak argument has been dealt with explicitly in the new legislation. More subtly, and more accurately, it may also be that once religious communities *can* carry out same sex marriages, a debate will take place within the communities as to whether they *should* carry out such marriages. So by opening up the possibility of same sex religious weddings, the state nudges communities which do not currently endorse these views on a journey towards compliance with state values. Articulation could be used to take this nudge further, to allow religious communities whose vision of marriage is compatible with that of the state to move more smoothly into the

[63] Marriage Act 1961 s 113(5) (Commonwealth of Australia).

creation of legal civil partnerships. Allowing this to operate at the level of the individual couple may be too complex, and in any case would not be a particularly effective nudge. The organisation would need to be assessed for its congruence with the legal definition of civil partnership generally to secure this preferential status.

I have argued elsewhere that using state power deliberately to encourage theological change within a community in order to bring it into line with state values and aims should always be a cause for concern (Edge 2010; cf for instance Jackson 2009). As may be expected, therefore, I do not advocate the adoption of this mechanism to distinguish between state-compliant religions and others, and seek to reward transition into state-compliance with legal incentives. If, however, this approach is not seen as objectionable it should at least be applied consistently—which of course is not the case in the current regime, with its explicit protections for religious autonomy in relation to sexual polarity, but not other conflicts between religious and state values. So not only would this articulation need to be withheld from communities who distinguish on sexual polarity when the state does not, but also from communities which refuse to marry people of different religions or races, people with particular disabilities except where the state also refuses marital status, and of course divorcees. Religious communities with different views of marriage in terms of ending of the commitment, or the compatibility of the commitment with multiple partners, would also be excluded. A strikingly small number of communities may, ultimately, qualify for this preferential treatment.

VI. BUT WHO GETS THE HOUSE? ABANDONING MARRIAGE AS A LEGAL TERM

The Act includes provision for turning civil partnerships into marriages, which came into force in December 2014. In this final section I argue for the opposite. It is perhaps worth my being frank that the remaining differences between civil partnerships and opposite sex marriage seem to me to favour civil partnerships as a structure. Marriage, but not civil partnership, keeps an emphasis on consummation. A similar emphasis can be found in adultery, one of the routes to leave it (although technically this opposite sex activity will also justify divorce in a same sex marriage). Along with Herring, I find this emphasis on a very particular kind of sexual activity unnecessary (Herring 2015). My preference for civil partnership over marriage seems, it is also worth noting, to be a minority view for heterosexuals in Britain.[64]

[64] See the 2013 Yougov poll at yougov.co.uk/news/2013/05/19/public-supports-civil-partnerships-all/.

If there is to be a distinction between religious marriage, etc, and intimate partnerships recognised by law, one possibility is to leave the terms as they are. There will be legal ideas of what a marriage is, religious ideas, and social ideas, and they may bear very little relationship to one another. This leaves open the possibility of confusion. It also suggests a degree of continuity with former ideas of intimate partnerships which may hamper the development of this area of law. It would also mean that the legal system was using a term shared with a particular subset of religions in the jurisdiction, but not others. It may be better for a purely legal institution to have a distinct linguistic identity, and to leave 'marriage' to the religious communities with which it has been shared.

It may be argued that by moving the state out of marriage, I am giving insufficient weight to the social goods that marriage provides. If I were to argue not only for the abolition of legal marriage, but also civil partnerships, this would be a strong criticism. By retaining state involvement in civil partnerships, however, the state role in supporting 'the social bases of caring relationships' (Brake 2010: 173) is maintained. Additionally, crafting civil partnerships as a purely legal institution opens up the possibility for more radical changes in this institution—for instance to move away from Brake's amato-normativity to support other forms of caring relationship (see further Herring 2015); or to move towards Ristroph and Murray's 'disestablished family' (Ristroph and Murray 2010). The remaining force of this criticism, however, concerns the cultural significance of marriage, and the 'intangible benefit' of 'access to a deeply meaningful institution—it is about equal participation in the activity, expression, security and integrity of marriage'.[65] While the abolition of legal marriage for opposite sex couples would address the issue of equal participation, it would not meet the needs of couples—both same sex and opposite sex—who see legal marriage as more significant, or more binding, than a civil partnership (see Merin 2002: 274–77).

It may also be argued that the term 'marriage' should remain a state possession, and that the state giving up this property is not a neutral way of resolving the (religious) disputes as to the definition of marriage which have characterised the current debate. There is some strength in this. Advocating a removal of a legal position is not the same as advocating that such a legal position should not be adopted. Marriage at the moment clearly is a legal institution, and changing that will not satisfy those who wish to use state power to resolve the definitional arguments.

More concretely, it may also be argued that there is a legal right to marriage,[66] as opposed to civil partnership. In practice, arguments which engage with this frequently move between a right to marriage per se, and

[65] *Halpern v Canada (AG)* (2002) CanLII 427949.
[66] Article 12 of the ECHR.

the discrimination inherent in some couples being able to marry and others not, with the emphasis on the latter. A good example is the witness statement of Susan Wilkinson, who sought to have her Canadian marriage to another woman recognised as a marriage, rather than a civil partnership.[67] She argued that she did not wish her relationship to be recognised as a civil partnership:

> [I]t is simply not acceptable to be asked to pretend that this marriage is a civil partnership. While marriage remains open to heterosexual couples only, offering the 'consolation prize' of a civil partnership to lesbians and gay men is offensive and demeaning. Marriage is our society's fundamental social institution for recognising the couple relationship and access to this institution is an equal rights issue … to have our relationship denied that symbolic status devalues it relative to the relationships of heterosexual couples.[68]

Discrimination aside, is there a right to marry? The European Convention on Human Rights provides, under Article 12, that 'Men and women of marriageable age have the right to marry and found a family, according to the national laws governing the exercise of this right'. Is this a fatal obstacle? The ECHR has been reluctant to intervene too closely in national marriage law, as we see in *B&L v UK* for instance, where the Court states that:

> Article 12 expressly provides for regulation of marriage by national law and given the sensitive moral choices concerned and the importance attached to the protection of children and the fostering of secure family environments, this court must not rush to substitute its own judgment in place of the authorities that are best place to assess and respond to the needs of society.[69]

Nonetheless, Article 12 has some effect, and would prevent a state imposing some bans on marriage. In *Goodwin*,[70] for instance, the court found 'no justification for barring the transsexual from enjoying the right to marry under any circumstances'.[71] It is probably not open, therefore, for the state to remove the legal framework allowing for recognition of a legal couple.[72] The specific question here is whether it requires that the legal relationship between a couple who are covered by Article 12 be called 'marriage'.

The official languages of the ECtHR are English and French, although other languages are used by the Court. As may be anticipated, the word 'marry' is not used in both the, equally definitive, versions of the Convention. The English language version of Article 12 uses 'marry', the French 'marier'—English and French for the same concept in the respective

[67] See *Wilkinson v Kitzinger and Others* [2006] EWHC 2022 (Fam).
[68] Ibid, at [5].
[69] *B & L v United Kingdom* (Application no 36536/02), 13 September 2005, [2006] 1 FLR 35, at [36].
[70] *Goodwin v United Kingdom* (1996) 22 EHRR 123 (ECtHR).
[71] *Goodwin*, at [103].
[72] See also *Van Oosterwijck v Belgium* (1981) 3 EHRR 557.

languages, but obviously not the same word. Beyond the official text itself, there is much diversity in Member States' practice. In Germany, for instance, the Basic Law of 1949, under article 6(1) states: 'Ehe und Familie stehen unter dem besonderen Schutze der staatlichen Ordnung', normally translated as 'Marriage and the family shall enjoy the special protection of the state' (Sanders 2012). So a right to have a relationship entitled 'marriage' would not seem to be contained in the ECHR.

This may fairly be rejected as an excessively lawyerly form of pedantry. Might Article 12 guarantee the right to form a 'marriage' recognised as such in the official language of the State party in question? Even this is not, to me, a rejection of abolitionism. If marriage ceases to be a legal term in England, and is replaced throughout with the term 'civil partnership', it may then be argued that that term becomes the term which parties have a right to have their relationship recognised as.

The case law is, similarly, not supportive of an insistence on a right to a particular term. In *Schalk and Kopf v Austria*,[73] it is true, the Court rejected an argument by Austria that the case be struck out because of the availability of registered partnerships for a same sex couple who sought the right to marry. The differential treatment inherent in the existence of opposite sex marriage was, however, clearly relevant to this decision: 'the said Act allows same sex couples to obtain only a status similar or comparable to marriage, but does not grant them access to marriage, which remains reserved for different-sex couples'.[74]

The abolition of marriage would not, of course, be without its practical problems. Most significant of these is the issue of recognition of legal relationships internationally (see further Curry-Sumner 2005; Frimston 2006; Curry-Sumner 2007; Curry-Sumner 2008). These were not seen as insurmountable when civil partnerships were the only forms of love rights available to same sex couples, however; and it is not clear to me that they are more insurmountable when they are the only form of love rights available to *anyone*.

VII. CONCLUSIONS

As a final word, during the passage of the Civil Partnership Act through Parliament, the responsible minister, Jacqui Smith, was pressed on whether the government supported same sex marriage. She replied:

> I recognise that many hon. Members on both sides of the House understand and feel very strongly about specific religious connotations of marriage. The Government are taking a secular approach to resolve the specific problems of same sex couples. As others have said, that is the appropriate and modern way for the 21st century.[75]

[73] *Schalk and Kopf v Austria* (2011) 53 EHRR 20 (ECtHR).
[74] Ibid, at [37].
[75] Hansard HC vol 425(35), col 177 (12 October 2004).

If I can remove 'same sex' from her words, and look to treat both same sex and opposite sex couples the same in law, then we are in agreement.

BIBLIOGRAPHY

AUCHMUTY, Rosemary, 'What's so special about marriage? The impact of *Wilkinson v Kitzinger*' (2008) 20 *Child and Family Law Quarterly* 475.

BAKER, B and ELIZABETH, V, 'Second-class marriage? Civil union in New Zealand' (2012) 43 *Journal of Comparative Family Studies* 633.

BAMFORTH, Nicholas, 'The benefits of marriage in all but name?' (2007) 19 *Child and Family Law Quarterly* 133.

BARKER, Nicola, 'Ambiguous symbols Recognising customary marriage and same sex marriage in South Africa' (2011) *International Journal of Law in Context* 447.

——, 'Sex and the Civil Partnership Act: The future of non-conjugality' (2006) 14 *Feminist Legal Studies* 241.

BARROW, Simon, 'What future for marriage?' (Ekklesia, 2006), available at: www.ekklesia.co.uk/files/sgmarriageconsult.pdf.

BENDALL, Charlotte, 'A break away from the (hetero)norm?: *Lawrence v Gallagher* [2012] 1 FCR 57; [2012] EWCA Civ 394' (2013) 21 *Feminist Legal Studies* 303.

BRAKE, E, *Minimising marriage: Marriage, morality and the law* (Oxford, Oxford University Press, 2010).

CHATTERJEE, Nandini, 'English law, Brahmo marriage and the problem of religious difference: Civil marriage laws in Britain and India' (2010) 52 *Comparative Studies in Society and History* 524.

CUMPER, Peter, 'The protection of religious rights under section 13 of the Human Rights Act 1998' [2000] *Public Law* 254.

CURRY-SUMNER, Ian, 'European recognition of same sex relationships: We need action now!' (2008) *International Family Law* 102.

——, 'Private international law aspects of homosexual couples: The Netherlands Report' (2007) 11.1 *Electronic Journal of Comparative Law*.

——, *All's well that ends registered? The substantive and private international law aspects of non-marital registered relationships in Europe* (Antwerp, Intersentia, 2005).

DOUGLAS, Gillian, DOE, Norman, GILLIAT-RAY, Sophie, SANDBERG, Russell and KHAN, Asma, 'Social cohesion and civil law: Marriage, divorce and religious courts' (Cardiff, Cardiff Law School, 2011).

EDGE, Peter W, 'Hard law and soft power: Counter-terrorism, the power of sacred places, and the establishment of an Anglican Islam' (2010) 12 *Rutgers Journal of Law and Religion* 382.

EDGE, Peter W and CORRYWRIGHT, Dominic, 'Including Religion: Reflections on Legal, Religious and Social Implications of the Developing Ceremonial Law of Marriage and Civil Partnership' (2011) 26 *Journal of Contemporary Religion* 19.

FALCONER OF THOROTON, Lord, 'Church, state and civil partners' (2007) 9 *Ecclesiastical Law Journal* 5.

FARRIMOND, Sarah, 'Rights and rites: Church of England Weddings and Ritual Symbolism' chapter ten in this volume.

FRIMSTON, Richard, 'Marriage and non-marital registered partnerships: Gold, silver and bronze in private international law' (2006) *Private Client Business* 352.

GROSSI, Renata, 'The meaning of love in the debate for legal recognition of same sex marriage in Australia' (2012) *International Journal of Law in Context* 487.

HARDING, Rosie and PEEL, Elizabeth, 'Civil partnerships: A new couple's conversation' (2004) 14 *Feminism and Psychology* 41.

HASDAY, Jill Elaine, 'The canon of family law' (2004) 57 *Stanford Law Review* 825.

HASKEY, John, 'Marriage Rights—Trends in Marriages by Manner of Solemnisation and Denomination in England and Wales, 1845–2012' chapter two in this volume.

HELMHOLZ, Richard H, *The Oxford History of the Laws of England, volume 1: The Canon Law and Ecclesiastical Jurisdiction from 567 to the 1640s* (Oxford, Oxford University Press, 2004).

HERRING, Jonathon, 'Why Marriage Needs to be Less Sexy' chapter thirteen in this volume.

HUNTINGTON, Clare, 'Staging the family' (2013) 88 *New York University Law Review* 589.

JACKSON, Bernard, '"Transformative accommodation" and religious law' (2009) 11 *Ecclesiastical Law Journal* 131.

JOWETT, Adam, '"But if you legalise same sex marriage…": Arguments against marriage equality in the British press' (2014) 24 *Feminism and Psychology* 37.

KITZINGER, Celia and WILKINSON, Sue, 'The re-branding of marriage: Why we got married instead of registering a civil partnership' (2004) 14 *Feminism and Psychology* 127.

MASSON, Judith, BAILEY-HARRIS, Rebecca and PROBERT, Rebecca, *Cretney Principles of Family Law* (London, Sweet & Maxwell, 2008).

MERIN, Yuval, *Equality for same sex couples* (Chicago IL, University of Chicago Press, 2002).

NICHOLS, Joel A (ed), *Marriage and divorce in a multicultural context: Tiered marriages and the boundaries of civil law and religion* (New York, Cambridge University Press, 2012).

NORRIE, Kenneth McK, 'Religion and same sex unions: The Scottish Government's consultation on registration of civil partnerships and same sex marriage' (2011) 16 *Edinburgh Law Review* 95.

PEEL, Elizabeth, 'Civil Partnership Ceremonies: (*Hetero)normativity, Ritual and Gender' chapter five in this volume.

PRESSER, Stephen B, 'Marriage and the law: Time for a divorce?' in JA Nichols (ed), *Marriage and divorce in a multicultural context: Multi-tiered marriage and the boundaries of civil law and religion* (New York, Cambridge University Press, 2012).

RISTROPH, Alice and MURRAY, Melissa, 'Disestablishing the Family' (2010) 119 *Yale Law Journal* 1236.

SANDERS, Anne, 'Marriage, same sex partnership and the German Constitution' (2012) 13 *German Law Journal* 911.

SHACHAR, Ayelet, 'Faith in law? Diffusing tensions between diversity and equality' (2010) 36 *Philosophy and Social Criticism* 395.

STYCHIN, Carl F, 'Not (quite) a horse and carriage: The Civil Partnership Act 2004' (2006) 14 *Feminist Legal Studies* 79.

WINTEMUTE, Robert, 'From "sex rights" to "love rights": Partnership rights as human rights' in N Bamforth, *Sex Rights: The Oxford Amnesty Lectures*, 2002.

WINTEMUTE, Robert and ANDENAES, Mads (eds), *Legal recognition of same sex partnerships* (Oxford, Hart Publishing, 2001).

WRIGHT, Wade K, 'The tide in favour of equality: Same sex marriage in Canada and England and Wales' (2006) 20 *International Journal of Law, Policy and the Family* 249.

13

Why Marriage Needs to be Less Sexy

JONATHAN HERRING

I. INTRODUCTION

IN A RECENT letter to *The Times* (Hamilton 2014) there is a report of a conversation between two male legal academics, one married and one unmarried. The unmarried one is reported as saying the other was lucky to be married. The reason? His wife could read him law reports in bed!

The law on marriage itself takes no account of such marital joys. Indeed one of the striking things about the law on marriage is that although there is extensive regulation on how to marry and the role of courts on divorce, what happens during the marriage in-between is very largely unregulated (although see Probert 2007). This chapter will focus on one odd exception to that: the requirement of consummation. For opposite sex marriages, once all the marriage rites are over and the couple drive off into the sunset, in legal terms the marriage is still in an inchoate state. Not until consummation does the marriage become a secure legal entity.

Consummation has become a live issue following the Marriage (Same Sex Couples) Act 2013, where, as we shall see, Parliament has struggled with consummation within the context of same sex marriage. Indeed conservative commentators have emphasised the consummation issue in their arguments opposing same sex marriage and claiming that even after the new legislation, same sex and opposite sex marriages should be regarded as different.

This chapter will explore the role of consummation in marriage. It will examine the traditionalist argument that the nature of the sexual act justifies a difference between same sex and opposite sex couples. It will argue in favour of removal of the consummation requirement and a rethinking of what it is that makes marriage different from other relationships.

The chapter will start by setting out the law on consummation prior to the 2013 legislation. It will then explain what the new legislation says about consummation in the context of same sex marriages. It will explore why consummation has come to play the role it has and whether it can now safely be abolished as a requirement.

II. THE LAW ON CONSUMMATION

A detailed summary of the law on consummation can be found elsewhere (Herring 2013). The key points are these. Under section 12 of the Matrimonial Causes Act 1973 a marriage is voidable on eight grounds, including that the marriage has not been consummated due to the incapacity of either party or the wilful refusal of the respondent.[1] A single act of 'ordinary and complete intercourse'[2] is sufficient to consummate a marriage. It should be emphasised that an unconsummated marriage, although capable of being nullified, is as valid as any other marriage. It is simply that it is vulnerable to being nullified by an application to the court by one of the parties. Where the marriage is annulled it is treated as (largely) having not existed.[3] That is because there was a flaw in its inception which means that it is legally suspect. Nullity is therefore different from a divorce, where the law brings a valid marriage to an end.

The fact that failure to consummate renders a marriage voidable, rather than void, indicates that there is no public policy objection to unconsummated marriages, as there is to bigamous marriages, for example. Such void marriages are invalid without any application to the court having been made. Anyone with a legitimate interest can complain about a void marriage, but only the parties themselves can complain about the unconsummated marriage. This suggests that the flaw in the unconsummated marriage is significant to the law only if it is so regarded by the couple themselves.

Consummation is then the final element of the rite for an opposite or same sex marriage. As Heather Brook explains:

> Consummation is a corporeal performative, a sex act whose performance brings that which it names into being. It is a kind of practical sexual test which newlyweds must pass if they want to protect their marriage from challenges to its validity. (Brook 2014: 52).

Yet it is surprising that consummation is included within the requirements for a full marriage. The fact that the act takes place in private and is therefore not readily susceptible to proof (as a legion of cases demonstrate (see Moran 1990)) makes it not a natural contender for the law on the formalities on marriage, which are otherwise designed to make it crystal clear to an outside observer whether a valid marriage has taken place.

III. SAME SEX MARRIAGE

The Marriage (Same Sex Couples) Act 2013 at last permits same sex couples to marry. Section 1(1) is refreshingly straight forward:

> Marriage of same sex couples is lawful.

[1] The Matrimonial Causes Act 1973 provides for bars to relief in certain cases.
[2] *D-E v A-G* (1845) 1 Rob Ecc 279, 163 ER 1039.
[3] Although a voidable marriage is treated as valid until such time as it is annulled.

Anyone hoping that this simplicity will be matched in the rest of the statute is in for a disappointment. In particular the promise of equal marriage is marred, at least for the more pedantically minded. There are some notable differences between same sex and opposite sex marriage. These primarily involve sexual matters. Paragraph 4 of Schedule 4 states that same sex couples will not be able to rely on the consummation grounds for having a marriage annulled. Paragraph 3(2) of Schedule 4 states that in respect of the law of divorce

> [o]nly conduct between the respondent and a person of the opposite sex may constitute adultery for the purposes of this section.

Hence same sex marriage is de-sexed. The court need not gaze on same sex marital sexual behaviour to ensure that there is consummation; or on non-marital same sex activity to see if it constitutes adultery. The courts can coyly look away. But why did it ever want to look in the first place? And why was there a problem with defining consummation in same sex relationships?

IV. WHY DOES THE LEGISLATION NOT INCLUDE CONSUMMATION?

At first it seemed that the Government intended to have the consummation requirements apply to same sex marriage. In the Equal Marriage Consultation Paper (HM Government 2012a) it was suggested that the legislation would not define consummation in the context of a same sex marriage but would allow the courts to develop a definition through case law. However, following consultation it was decided not to include the consummation requirement for same sex couples. The explanation offered hardly deserves that name:

> Same sex couples cannot currently annul their civil partnership on the basis of non-consummation. Opposite sex couples will continue to be able to annul their marriage on the grounds of non-consummation. By maintaining this position, we are not altering the legal position unnecessarily (HM Government 2012b: para 9.10).

It may have been that the Government felt uncomfortable in defining what amounted to consummation within the context of a same sex couple. There would, of course, have been no technical difficulty in doing so. The Sexual Offences Act 2003 contains descriptions of a wide range of sexual acts which could have been drawn on. It may be, as intimated above, that the refusal indicates a latent homophobia, or at least an unwillingness to acknowledge gay and lesbian sexuality openly. More charitably, it may be an acknowledgement that gay sexuality expresses itself in range of sexual acts and one particular act cannot be selected as indicative of a gay or lesbian sexual relationship. A similar point could, of course, be made about heterosexuality.

The more obvious solution might have been to remove the consummation requirement from marriage altogether. However, the paper in its discussion on consummation refers to the evidence of the Catholic Bishops' Conference of England and Wales, indicating there was pressure from religious groups not to remove the requirement (Compton 2013).

V. SEX, MARRIAGE AND THE LAW

Opponents of same sex marriage have argued that in legalising it the Government has changed the nature of marriage. The lack of a consummation requirement for same sex marriages has been pointed to by opponents as revealing that there is a fundamental distinction between same sex and opposite sex marriages. It has been claimed that the de-sexing of marriage, through the downplaying of the significance of heterosexual intercourse to marriage, has left marriage without any real meaning or role. For example, Patrick Parkinson, a leading Australian family law academic, claims:

> A consequence of extending marriage to same sex relationships is that there will be almost nothing left of the legal definition of marriage as a union of a man and a woman for life to the exclusion of all others. Robbed of its distinctiveness, and detached from its cultural and religious roots, marriage as an institution is unlikely to retain its cultural importance and vitality. We simply won't know what marriage is any more. (Parkinson 2011: 1).

A major stream in the traditionalist opposition to same sex marriage has been that there is something special about heterosexual intercourse that marks marriage as separate from all other relationships and provides a justification for its special status. Before exploring these arguments at a general level I want to look at what the courts have said about the role of sex in marriage.

VI. CONSUMMATION

What is the purpose of the consummation requirement? In truth the courts have struggled to answer that question. In *Dickinson v Dickinson (otherwise Phillips)*[4] Sir Samuel Evans found the answer in considering the reasons why we have marriage in the first place. Unsurprisingly, given the vintage of the case, he turned to the Book of Common Prayer of the Church of England to find three reasons: 'firstly for the procreation of children, secondly for a remedy against sin, and to avoid fornication, and thirdly for the mutual society, help, and comfort, that the one ought to have of the other'. This was

[4] *Dickinson v Dickinson (otherwise Phillips)* [1913] P 198, (1913) 109 LT 408.

in line with earlier case law which saw the following reasons for marriage: 'a lawful indulgence of the passions to prevent licentiousness, and the procreation of children, according to the evident design of Divine Providence'.[5]

The cases seem to assume that these reasons explain the consummation requirement. But they hardly do. A single act of consummation is unlikely to result in children, particularly given the House of Lords' decision in *Baxter v Baxter*[6] that intercourse using contraception could amount to consummation. That is reinforced by the finding in one case that (because penetration had not occurred) there was no consummation in the marriage even though the wife had become pregnant.[7] Lady Hale recently acknowledged that it can no longer be claimed that the law on marriage is based on the production of children. In *Ghaidan v Godin-Mendoza*[8] she stated that 'the capacity to bear or beget children has never been a prerequisite of a valid marriage in English law. Henry VIII would not otherwise have had the problems he did'.

As to the prevention of licentiousness, it might be doubted whether a single act of consummation would satisfy a lifetime of sexual desire. This leaves only the argument that consummation plays an essential role in the 'mutual society, help and comfort' of marriage. However, these can all be provided without the need for vaginal penetration. Further, we know enough now about marital rape to be aware that marital intercourse is not necessarily linked to help or comfort (Herring 2011).

The truth is that the law in its consummation requirement was following the Ecclesiastical Courts. The explanation for the consummation requirement, if any, lies in theology. One explanation is that the physical union reflects and completes the spiritual union of the couple, reflected in the Biblical statement: 'That is why a man leaves his father and mother and is united to his wife, and they become one flesh'.[9] The Catechism of the Catholic Church places the importance of consummation in the requirement of conjugal love:

> Conjugal love involves a totality, in which all the elements of the person enter—appeal of the body and instinct, power of feeling and affectivity, aspiration of the spirit and of will. It aims at a deeply personal unity, a unity that, beyond union in one flesh, leads to forming one heart and soul; it demands indissolubility and faithfulness in definitive mutual giving; and it is open to fertility. In a word it is a question of the normal characteristics of all natural conjugal love, but with a new significance which not only purifies and strengthens them, but raises them to the extent of making them the expression of specifically Christian values.[10]

[5] *D-E v A-G (falsely calling herself D-E)* (1845) 1 Rob Ecc 279, 298, 163 ER 1039, 1045.
[6] *Baxter v Baxter* [1948] AC 274.
[7] *Snowman v Snowman* [1934] P 186.
[8] *Ghaidan v Godin-Mendoza* [2004] UKHL 30.
[9] Genesis 2: 24.
[10] *Catechism of the Catholic Church*, Part II, Section 2, Ch III, Art 7, V: The Goods and Requirements of Conjugal Love, para 1643.

Whatever the merits or otherwise of the theological doctrine of the spiritual union, they can hardly be said to justify a legal requirement in a modern secular state.[11]

It may therefore be asked why consummation has managed to continue to exert its influence on the law. It may be that the best explanation is that the consummation requirement reflects and reinforces a series of patriarchal assumptions. First, only penile sexual penetration of a vagina is taken to amount to consummation. This privileges heterosexual relations and a particular form of heterosexual activity. Only the 'approved' forms of sexual behaviour have the magic of conjugality. The mystical quality of the heterosexual vaginal penetration enables it to be shrouded in a special light and thus clearly distinguished from the 'disgusting acts' (Eskridge 1999: 17) of same sex or extra-marital activity.

Secondly, a detailed analysis of what amounts to consummation in the case law provides an horrifically male-centred notion of the act (Moran 1990). Consummation is understood as the male penetrating the female. It is the man who must do the penetrating and 'take possession' of the wife. The act is described in entirely physical terms with no response required from the wife. For consummation there must be 'male penetration of the female body: intercourse must be ordinary and complete, not partial and imperfect'.[12] This involves penetration for a reasonable length of time. Notably, the detailed definition of consummation reflects the image of the passive female. All that seems required of her is that she has a vaginal tract of a sufficient length for the penis to enter. This most clearly came out in the open in the *SY v SY*[13] case where it was unsuccessfully argued on behalf of the husband that the wife's 'stunted' vagina was no more than a 'pouch', that sexual intercourse would be 'nothing but masturbation inside the wife's body' and consequently the marriage could not be consummated. These points all reinforce Moran's argument that consummation 'is of considerable significance as a site relating to the emergence of male heterosexual sexuality within the institution of marriage' (Moran 1990: 171). The male is the active one (it is he who penetrates) and woman's role is entirely passive, limited to being able to accommodate the male penis.

Thirdly, consummation has been central to the legal definition of sex (Chau and Herring 2004). Sex for the purposes of marriage has been defined in terms of a person's capacity to engage in heterosexual intercourse. So a person with a penis which is capable of consummating a marriage will be regarded as a man and a person with a vaginal passage that can 'accommodate' a penis is a woman.[14] It is extraordinary that something as

[11] It may, of course, be used to say that there are fundamental differences between the legal and theological understanding of marriage.

[12] *D-E v A-E* (1845) see n 2 above.

[13] *SY v SY* [1963] P 37, 48.

[14] *Corbett v Corbett* [1971] 2 All ER 33.

fundamental as a person's sex is defined in terms of their capacity to engage in one particular form of sexual behaviour. There is much more that could be said about this approach to the definition of sex, but again it reflects the elevation and centralisation of heterosexual intercourse.

Fourthly, consummation has played a role in the prevalence of marital rape. Until the marital rape exception was removed in *R v R*[15] the husband could not be convicted of raping his wife. As marital sex was seen as part of the essence of marriage, consent to marriage was interpreted as consent to sex. This raised the interesting point that one of the founding events necessary to create a full marriage in effect lay exclusively in the control of just one of the parties.[16] There is little disguise in the link between consummation and rape in the comments of Lord Dunedin in *G v G*[17] in a 1924 case where non-consummation was said to be due to the wife's reluctance:

> It is indeed permissible to wish that some gentle violence had been employed; if there had been it would either have resulted in success or would have precipitated a crisis so decided as to have made our task a comparatively easy one. But the husband's answer to the complaint that he did not so act, when put to him in cross-examination, is that he was very anxious to awaken the sexual instinct; that he had found her on many occasions hysterical and tearful, and that he felt that any attempt with even mild and gentle force would only hinder and not help the end which he desired.

It might be thought that we have moved well beyond that, but consider these comments by the influential Evangelical blogger Andrew Lilico:

> If we say that the law should not recognise permanent and ongoing consent to sexual intercourse, we are creating a wedge between the legal obligations of marriage and the undoubted moral obligations of Christian marriage. Christian spouses are not entitled to withhold their bodies from one another and are specifically instructed by Paul not to do so unless for some agreed temporary spiritual purpose (e.g. see I Corinthians, 7:1–5) … That means that a Christian marriage—a moral and indissoluble contract of permanent and ongoing consent to sexual intercourse—is profoundly different in nature from a legal marriage—a dissoluble contract that does not imply permanent or ongoing consent to sexual intercourse. (Lilico 2014).

No doubt this is a minority view, even within conservative Christian circles, but it reveals the on-going influence of the view that consummation is a central aspect of marriage, upon assumptions about consent to sex.

In conclusion, the case law on consummation provides little justification for the requirement. Indeed the judgments reveal an understanding of consummation which reinforces stereotypes about male and female sexuality and the privileging of heterosexuality and a phallocentric understanding of sex.

15 *R v R* [1992] 1 AC 599.
16 I am grateful to the editors for this observation.
17 *G v G* [1924] AC 349, 357.

VII. CAPACITY

The centrality of sex to marriage is also emphasised in a more recent line of cases concerning mental capacity to marry.[18] In *YLA v PM*[19] Parker J considered the position of a woman with an IQ of 49 who had been assessed as having moderate to severe learning difficulty. The judge was clear that the capacity to consent to sex relations was a 'component part' of the capacity to consent to marriage. Concluding her judgment she stated:

> She does not have the capacity to consent to marriage (i) because she cannot consent to sexual relations and (ii) she does not understand the obligations and responsibilities of marriage, and she is unable to weigh up the options.

Mostyn J in *D Borough Council v AB*[20] held:

> the test of capacity to marry must be very closely related to the test of capacity to consent to sexual relations. And it would be a very strange thing if the latter were set higher than the former, for it would be an absurd state of affairs if a person had just sufficient intelligence to consent to marriage but insufficient capacity to consent to its (generally speaking) intrinsic component of consummation.[21]

The different expectations of what marriage entails were well demonstrated in *IC v Westminster*,[22] where the family of a severely disabled man arranged a marriage with a woman from Bangladesh. It was clearly expected that the wife's role would primarily be one of carer. However, the English courts, in finding the marriage void, focussed primarily on any sexual relationship and the ability of the husband to consent to that.

These cases are in line with precedent, but are questionable. First, it should be remembered that sexual relations are not required for a valid marriage and so it is hard to see why it should be regarded as intrinsic to marriage.[23] The law will not invalidate a marriage in which there is no sex, without the application of either party. In an earlier case Munby J, at least on one reading, did not place sex at the heart of marriage:

> there must be understanding of the nature of the marriage contract, and the duties and responsibilities attached to marriage; they are that marriage is a contract, formally entered into, which confers on the parties the status of husband and wife, an

[18] *X City Council v MB, NB and MAB (by his Litigation Friend the Official Solicitor)* [2006] EWHC 168 (Fam) (which linked the two); *PC (by her Litigation Friend the Official Solicitor) and NC v City of York Council* [2013] EWCA Civ 478; *Sandwell Metropolitan Borough Council v RG, GG, SK, SKG* [2013] EWHC 2373 (COP).

[19] *YLA v PM and MZ* [2013] EWHC 4020 (COP).

[20] *D Borough Council v AB* [2011] EWHC 101 (COP).

[21] Ibid, para 15.

[22] *KC and NNC v City of Westminster Social & Community Services Dept and IC* [2008] EWCA Civ 198.

[23] It is true that there is a social expectation that sex will ordinarily be part of marriage, but it is not clear whether most people would see a sexless marriage as an invalid marriage or a sad one.

> agreement to live together, to love one another as husband and wife, to the exclusion of all others, creating a relationship of mutual and reciprocal obligations, typically involving the sharing of a common home and domestic life and the right to enjoy each other's society, comfort and assistance.[24]

Given that the law has acknowledged that a couple are entitled to marry without having sexual relations it is hard to see why it should be a requirement for the capacity to understand what marriage is. Nonetheless, the current, mainstream view of the courts is that sex is integral to marriage and so a party who lacks capacity to consent to sex ipso facto lacks capacity to marry. This indicates how the courts have elevated the sexual element as central to its nature. It will be interesting to see if the same approach is taken in relation to capacity to enter a same sex marriage, given that consummation is not required. What is really going on in these cases is that the courts are wishing to protect people they fear will simply be sexually abused during their marriage. It is interesting that the courts are shying away from being open that marriage can be a site for abuse and prefer to deal with the cases in terms of capacity.

VIII. SEX AND THE TRADITIONALIST ARGUMENT AGAINST SAME SEX MARRIAGE

As already mentioned the consummation issue played a major role in the traditionalist arguments against same sex marriage. I will focus on three.

A. The Indistinguishability of Marriage

First, it is argued that consummation is what marks a marital relationship as different from other relationships. In short, the sexual element is central to what makes marital relationships different from others. If the sexual element is removed as a defining feature of marriage, it becomes impossible to distinguish marital relationships from every other. Ormrod J in *Corbett*[25] commented:

> sex is clearly an essential determinant of the relationship called marriage because it is and always has been recognised as the union of man and woman. It is the institution on which the family is built, and in which the capacity for natural heterosexual intercourse is an essential element. It has, of course, many other characteristics, of which companionship and mutual support is an important one, but the characteristics which distinguish it from all other relationships can only be met by two persons of opposite sex.

[24] *Re E* [2005] 1 FLR 965.
[25] *Corbett v Corbett* [1971] P 83, 105–6.

Charles Cooper, a traditionalist advocate, argues: 'No societal purpose of marriage other than procreation and child-rearing can plausibly begin to explain the institution's existence, let alone its ubiquity' (Cooper 2012: 2).

There is a grain of truth in these arguments. In the past marriage was regarded as being the approved location for sexual relations and the raising of children. Neither of these has much resonance in our current society. Few attach opprobrium to sexual relations outside marriage and the notion that sex is solely for the production of children is a very much minority view. But what then is the central role of marriage?

One of the benefits of same sex marriage is that is requires us to face that question directly. The pat answers in the past—producing children and authorising sexual relations—should never have been convincing, but now there is no hiding behind them. I will offer later in this chapter an argument as to what can replace sex as being at the heart of marriage.

B. The Goodness of Conjugality

One of the most common arguments raised by opponents of same sex marriage was that marital sexual relationships produce a unique good, which was not found in same sex relationships. This good explained why it was appropriate to privilege marriage and exclude same sex couples from it. In its most sophisticated form this is found in the writing of Sheif Girgis, Robert George and Ryan Anderson, who set out what they see as the conjugal view of marriage:

> Marriage is the union of a man and a woman who make a permanent and exclusive commitment to each other of the type that is naturally (inherently) fulfilled by bearing and rearing children together. The spouses seal (consummate) and renew their union by conjugal acts—acts that constitute the behavioural part of the process of reproduction, thus uniting them as a reproductive unit. Marriage is valuable in itself, but its inherent orientation to the bearing and rearing of children contributes to its distinctive structure, including norms of monogamy and fidelity. This link to the welfare of children also helps explain why marriage is important to the common good and why the state should recognize and regulate it. (Girgis, George and Anderson 2011: 245–46).

They contrast the 'revisionist view':

> Marriage is the union of two people (whether of the same sex or of opposite sexes) who commit to romantically loving and caring for each other and to sharing the burdens and benefits of domestic life. It is essentially a union of hearts and minds, enhanced by whatever forms of sexual intimacy both partners find agreeable. The state should recognize and regulate marriage because it has an interest in stable romantic partnerships and in the concrete needs of spouses and any children they may choose to rear. (ibid: 246).

Much has been written to indicate the flaws in these arguments (eg Bamforth and Richards 2011) and it is not my aim to add to that. The argument seems to take one particular view of the nature of sexual intercourse, one which not everyone will share, let alone entrench in law. However, I would make the following two points.

First, they elevate sexual intercourse as being a central, indeed defining, act of marriage. This is strange given that according to one recent survey the average married couple has sex three times every four months (Woods 2013).[26] A 2004 study suggested the average was two or three times a month (Blanchflower and Oswald 2004). An earlier study in the United States found only 26 per cent of couples having sex once a week or more often (Call, Sprecher and Schwartz 1995). Whether such surveys are accurate is impossible to ascertain, but they clearly indicate that other features of marital life are more clearly markers of its essence than sexual intercourse for many couples. One leading psychologist notes that 'affection (hugging, kissing, holding hands) was a more important predictor of intense love for both men and women in long-term relationships than sexual intercourse' (Muise 2012). It seems surprising to seek to justify the goodness of marriage in what is, if the surveys are correct, not exactly an everyday activity for most couples; and not locate it in more common and concrete forms of fulfilment.

Secondly, the vision presented by the traditionalists of sexual penetration represents only one particular view. By contrast Michelle Madden Dempsey and I (2007) have argued that a penile penetration is a prima facie wrong. I will not repeat the arguments we make about the harmfulness associated with the act, but would emphasise we accept that there are circumstances which justify it. The point to make is that the 'conjugal' view of sexual penetration seems blind to the disadvantages associated with sex. Further, it seems to ignore the many benefits that can be associated with sexual activities that fall outside their paradigm.

C. The Goodness of Male-Female Relationships

In England, perhaps the most vocal opposition to same sex couples came from conservative evangelicals. For them same sex marriage poses problems beyond an understanding of sexual intercourse. The Coalition for Marriage (2014) claims 'Marriage reflects the complementary natures of men and women'. The biological differences in sex reflect the differences in the roles of husband and wife. Same sex marriage challenges this image of sex-defined roles being central to marriage. Hence Mark Highton complains:

> Marriage has from the beginning of history been the way in which societies have worked out and handled issues of sexual difference. To remove from the definition of marriage this essential complementarity is to lose any social institution in which sexual difference is explicitly acknowledged. (Highton 2014).

[26] Woods (2013) describes those who have sex three times a month as 'sex crazed'.

On such a view sexual difference is expressed in marriage. Andrew Goddard, a prominent evangelical theologian, writes of 'a new social unit based on the union of two individuals who together embody the fundamental created distinction or "otherness" within humanity—being male and female' (Goddard 2013: 3). The two sexes in their differences complement each other. Goddard might be correct in suggesting that one of the things that makes relationships interesting is that it introduces new ways of looking at and relating to the world. One might, therefore, see some benefit for people entering relationships with people who are somewhat different from themselves. What is surprising is Goddard's assumption that it is sex that has to be that difference. Two people may be similar or different in many ways: why should one factor (sex) be elevated as a distinguishing feature of significance? (Cornwall 2011).

The answer, of course, lies in a host of assumptions that are made about a person's sex. The complementarian argument only makes sense if one holds on to a host of stereotypes about men and women. To give one example, Dr Trayce Hansen argues:

> Men and women bring diversity to parenting; each makes unique contributions to the rearing of children that can't be replicated by the other. Mothers and fathers simply are not interchangeable. Two women can both be good mothers, but neither can be a good father ... A father teaches a boy how to properly channel his aggressive and sexual drives. A mother can't show a son how to control his impulses because she's not a man and doesn't have the same urges as one. A father also commands a form of respect from a boy that a mother doesn't—a respect more likely to keep the boy in line. And those are the two primary reasons why boys without fathers are more likely to become delinquent and end up incarcerated. (Hansen 2013).

In this quotation we see that the difference argument is often based on a host of assumptions and stereotypes about what men and women, or mothers and fathers, are like (Feinberg 2012).

For other evangelicals the argument is not based on a stereotype about gendered behaviour. Lurking behind much evangelical opposition is the view that husbands and wives have different roles. Based on St Paul's infamous instruction that wives are to submit to their husbands and that the husband is the head of the wife, this view is that there are very particular roles in marriage for the husband and wife. For some the significance of male headship is more spiritual. It is seen as part of Godly order in the world, reflecting the relationship between Christ and the Church and God the father and God the son (Grudem 2012). Not all Christians would agree with that interpretation by any means, but it is important for a strand of thought for conservative evangelicals. Of course this clear demarcation between the roles for husband and wife, if seen as central to marriage, is challenged if same sex marriage is permitted.

What we see, therefore, from this examination of some of the traditionalist objections to same sex marriage and claims about the unique goodness of heterosexual marriage, is that these rest on assumptions about the nature of sex or particular views about the roles that gender should play.

Indeed this is precisely why some commentators have warned of the dangers of same sex couples seeking marriage (Polikoff 1993). Claire Young and Susan Boyd have commented that:

> Underpinning their opposition to same sex marriage was a neoconservative view of marriage and the family as inherently patriarchal and hierarchical institutions. For them, the imperviousness of marriage and the family to the critique of feminists and others was crucial to the health of society and the nation. These interventions represented a 'performance of heterosexuality', revealing the anxiety of many men (and women) in society about the fact that 'being straight' is an increasingly contested status, as is masculinity ... Allowing lesbians and gay men to marry would strike at the most abiding and important aspects of marriage in their eyes, that is, the hierarchical nature of the relationship in which women and men have clearly defined gender-based roles based on the male breadwinner and the stay at home wife and mother. (Young and Boyd 2006: 233).

What, however, this discussion also shows is that the traditionalist opposition to marriage, while dressed up in the language of natural law and tradition, is based on particular views about sex and gender roles. Consummation is typically identified as the marker of those, and that in itself is revealing. Even if the traditionalist arguments are persuasive to an individual, they are based on a particular theological perspective; they do not reflect the views of a majority of the population, nor even of a majority of the population that would describe themselves as religious.

IX. MOVE TO ALLOW CONSUMMATION

What, in the light of these debates, should be done with the consummation requirement? The most obvious response is to remove it as an outdated and unjustifiable requirement. But we should hesitate before taking that route. Susan Boyd and Claire Young have noted the irony that 'as soon as lesbians and gay men begin to acquire spousal status, the move is to erase sex from that status' (Boyd and Young 2003: 769). They see this as reflecting an unwillingness to acknowledge or speak of same sex sexual behaviour. It is especially contrasted with the willingness of the courts to talk in agonising detail of opposite sex behaviour in relation to consummation. As Lucy Compton notes of side-lining consummation of same sex relationships:

> This attitude is grist to the mill of the homophobes who tolerate gay lifestyles as long as they are not visible and who claim no objection to gay sex as long as it remains behind closed doors. (Compton 2013: 565).

She argues we could readily use the term 'sexual intimacy' for consummation in all marriages. This would, Compton claims, avoid the difficulties with the definition of consummation and some of the negative assumptions behind it listed above.

Nonetheless, I would argue that the consummation requirement should be abandoned, as it has in many jurisdictions. The assumption behind the consummation requirement is that sex is central to marriage. But if sex is what marriage is all about it is far from clear why we need marriage, in a legal sense. Sex itself is not an activity the state benefits from; nor is it an activity which in itself creates disadvantages which require legal remedies to intervene. In short people are quite able to get on with having sex without the need for any legal framework.

X. CARE-BASED MARRIAGE

If sexual relationships are no longer regarded as at the heart of marriage and as a unique marker of it, what is to be? I would answer caring relationships.[27] Care is enormously valuable in our society. The meeting of the needs of others in a caring relationship should be a central goal of any society. A sexual relationship between two parties may be fun for the parties involved, but is not itself producing any great social benefit.[28] Care does. If the Government announced a no sex week and the citizens complied no great loss would arise. If the Government announced 'no care week' and the citizens complied, significant harm would result. There is much more that can be said about the benefits of care, which I will not expand on here (see Herring 2013).

There is a particularly strong reason for regarding care as the hallmark of marriage for lawyers. If we look at the role of the law in marriage, it is primarily involved in ensuring that if a relationship breaks down there is a fair sharing of the family property, to ensure that one party does not unduly benefit or lose out from the relationship. This protects the rights of those in the relationship and encourages others to enter into such relationships. I have argued that it is care work which is the primary source of economic disadvantage caused in a caring relationship. The primary justification for financial orders on divorce lies not so much in the marriage itself but in the care work performed in the context of an intimate relationship. Again, much can be said on this issue and I have written on it elsewhere.

Most relevant for this book is a particular criticism of moving to a care-based marriage. That is proof of 'marriage'. If marriage is to protect caring

[27] It may be that some people would prefer not to use the word marriage if this is done. I don't have a particular view on that. My interest is in the use of the functions achieved through marriage law being used for caring relationships.

[28] It is true that if a child is produced then there may be a social benefit, but most sex does not produce a child and there are other ways of child production.

relationships, what are to be the rites that define the entry into status? John Eekelaar writes of a proposal that relationships of dependency should define marriage:

> It is hard to see how marriage law could be replaced by definitions of dependency. These are essentially retrospective decisions, requiring evidence that responsibilities have been assumed, or dependency has arisen, over time. They could not realistically be the basis for a system of prospective identification of a relationship (not necessarily involving dependency), which marriage is. (Eekelaar 2012: 326).

One response, which he foresees, is simply to agree that a care-based model of marriage will only be identifiable retrospectively. So when a person seeks a legal remedy (eg a financial order at the end of the relationship), the court will determine whether there has been sufficient care to render such a remedy appropriate. The alternative, requiring parties who intend to enter caring relationships to register their relationships, is problematic because the nature of care is that its extent and impact are impossible to assess. As I have written elsewhere,

> intimate lives are messy and unpredictable. The sacrifices called for can be unforeseen and obligations without limit. The marriage might bring children, it might not; care of a demented parent may become a major task, it may not; a disabled child may take up all the energies of one spouse, they may not. The best laid plans for the marriage may need to be discarded at a moment's notice. (Herring 2014: 33).

However, as Eekelaar notes, this model of retrospective assessment of whether the relationship was sufficiently caring to deserve the label marriage is problematic. How will it deal with questions where currently marital status may be relevant, such as tax, social security, immigration, medicine, pensions or employment? One response is simply to say that marriage should cease to be relevant in these issues. However, if we are seeking to use marriage to promote caring relationships we might not readily jettison these tools. I doubt it is overly onerous for social security officials, for example, to ask about a person's caring role. Provision could be made for a person in a caring relationship to be assessed and have a formal evaluation of whether they are in a caring role. Indeed many carers are current assessed for benefits based on their caring role and the assessment could be a way into giving them an acknowledged status. I accept that the current family law legal system with its focus on marriage and civil partners has an ease of use which would be lost by a focus on care and commitment. Nevertheless I believe that there are many relationships of care in which there is a need for family law's remedial, protective and supportive functions, but which fall outside its scope. The plight of those whose care goes unrecognised and unrewarded justifies the increased bureaucratic difficulties.

But my argument is that those in non-caring relationships do not need the kind of support family law offers. I am not opposed to the idea of marriage being retained as a religious and social idea; but the focus of the law should be on care. So we can either redefine marriage as being about care, which would be my preference, or refocus family on a new category of relationships.

There is a second and important issue, which may flow from what I have just said. As stated, at the start of the marriage one of the notable features of marriage is the lack of regulation or assessment of what happens during the relationship. The model I have just promoted from a care-based marriage would involve some kind of state or court investigation into whether the relationship is one marked by care. There is a danger that if caring relationships are the focus of legal attention then only those relationships which are analogous to a traditional form (parent/child; spouse) will be recognised (Brake 2012). Relationships which do not fit the standard model—and Barker (2012) argues this may particularly be true of gay and lesbian relationships—will lose out. There clearly is a danger, but there is no reason why that must take place. If we focus on the doing of the work of care, this should ensure outdated assumptions about the proper nature of family life fade away.

XI. CONCLUSION

This chapter has explored the place of consummation in the rite of marriage. It started with an examination of the role consummation has in opposite sex marriages. It found no adequate justification for its role in the current law. Indeed as developed by the courts it played a role in glorifying certain forms of heterosexual behaviour and a particular image of the male heterosexuality. The chapter highlighted the difficulties the Government had in integrating consummation within same sex marriage. These were to be expected given the assumptions underpinning consummation in the law.

The chapter then turned to the role played by consummation in the arguments of traditionalist opponents of same sex marriage. It was argued that underpinning their arguments that consummation was key to marriage, and that the benefits of penile vaginal penetration explain the status of marriage and why it should not be open to same sex couples, is a particular understanding of gender and sex that is based on stereotypes about what is expected of men and women and gender-specific roles in marriage.

The chapter concluded that we need to refocus the law on marriage on care rather than sex. It is caring relationships which generate vulnerability to abuse and disadvantage and so need the protection of marriage law. Caring relationships are the ones that deserve being promoted through the law on marriage and which are key to societal well-being. It is care that that is the good of marriage. We should displace sex from being at the heart of marriage and replace it with care.

BIBLIOGRAPHY

BAMFORTH, Nicholas and RICHARDS, David, *Patriarchal religion, sexuality and gender. A critique of new natural law* (Cambridge, Cambridge University Press, 2011).
BARKER, Nicola, *Not the Marrying Kind: A Feminist Critique of Same-Sex Marriage* (Basingstoke, Palgrave, 2012).
BLANCFLOWER, David and OSWALD, Andrew, 'Money, sex and happiness: An empirical study' (2004) 106 *Scandinavian Journal of Economics* 393.
BOYD, Susan and YOUNG, Claire, '"From same-sex to no-sex"? Trends towards recognition of (same-sex) relationships in Canada' (2003) 1 *Seattle Journal for Social Justice* 757.
BRAKE, Elizabeth, *Minimizing marriage: Marriage, morality, and the law* (New York, Oxford University Press, 2012).
BROOK, Heather, 'Zombie Law: Conjugality, Annulment, and the (Married) Living Dead' (2014) 22 *Feminist Legal Studies* 49.
CALL, Vaughn, SPRECHER, Susan, and SCHWARTZ, Pepper, 'The incidence and frequency of marital sex in a national sample' (1995) 57 *Journal of Marriage and Family* 639.
COALITION FOR MARRIAGE, 'Marriage is unique' available at: c4m.org.uk/.
COOPER, Charles, 'The constitutional argument for traditional marriage' in C Cooper and W Eskridge (eds), *Marital Strife: Same-sex marriage and the constitution* (Washington DC, National Constitution Centre, 2012).
COMPTON, Lucy, 'Where's the sex in same-sex marriage?' (2013) *Family Law* 564.
CORNWALL, Suzanne, *Controversies in Queer Theology* (London, SCM Press, 2011).
EEKELAAR, John, 'Book Review: Marriage proposals: Questioning a legal status' (2012) 8 *International Journal of Law in Context* 320.
ESKRIDGE, William, *Gaylaw: Challenging the apartheid of the closet* (Cambridge MA, Harvard University Press, 1999).
FEINBERG, Jessica, 'Exposing the traditional marriage agenda' (2012) 7 *Northwestern Journal of Law & Social Policy* 301.
GIRGIS, Sherif, GEORGE, Robert and ANDERSON, RYAN, 'What is marriage?' (2011) 34 *Harvard Journal of Law and Public Policy* 245.
GRUDEM, Wayne, 'Biblical Evidence for the Eternal Submission of the Son to the Father' in D Jowers and H Wayne (eds), *New Evangelical Subordinationism?* (Eugene, PR, Pickwick, 2012).
GODDARD, Andrew, 'Reframing The Same-Sex Marriage Debate' (2013), available at klice.co.uk/uploads/Ethics%20in%20Brief/Goddard%20v.18.4.pdf.
HAMILTON, Adrian, 'Letter' *The Times*, 27 January 2014.
HANSEN, Trayce, 'Love Isn't Enough: 5 Reasons Why Same-Sex Marriage Will Harm Children' available at www.nomblog.com/19953/.
HERRING, Jonathan, 'No more having and holding: The abolition of the marital rape exemption' in S Gilmore, J Herring and R Probert (eds), *Landmark cases in family law* (Oxford, Hart Publishing, 2011).
——, *Caring and the law* (Oxford, Hart Publishing, 2013a).
——, *Family Law* (Harlow, Pearson, 2013b).

——, *Relational autonomy and family law* (Heidelberg, Springer, 2014).
HERRING, Jonathan and CHAU, P-L, 'Men Women and People' in B Brooks-Gordon et al (eds), *Sexuality Repositioned* (Oxford, Hart Publishing, 2004).
HIGHTON, Mike, 'Disagreeing about marriage—and gender' available at: mikehigton.org.uk/disagreeing-about-marriage/.
HM GOVERNMENT, *Equal civil marriage: a consultation* (London, The Stationary Office, 2012a).
——, *Equal marriage: The Government's response* (London, The Stationary Office, 2012b).
LILICO, Andrew, 'Should legal marriage imply consenting to sex?' available at: www.peter-ould.net/2014/02/27/guest-post-should-legal-marriage-imply-consenting-to-sex/.
MADDEN DEMPSEY, Michelle, and HERRING, Jonathan, 'Why sexual penetration requires justification' (2007) 27 *Oxford Journal of Legal Studies* 467.
MORAN, Les, 'A study in the history of male sexuality in law: non consummation' (1990) 1 *Law and Critique* 155.
MUISE, Amy, 'The ins and outs of sexual frequency' (8 June 2012) *Psychology Today*.
PARKINSON, Patrick, 'Marriage at the heart of a crucial commitment to children' available at: www.smh.com.au/federal-politics/society-and-culture/marriage-at-the-heart-of-a-crucial-commitment-to-children-20110907-1jxr5.html.
POLIKOFF, Nancy, 'We will get what we ask for: why legalizing gay and lesbian marriage will not "dismantle the legal structure of gender in every marriage"' (1993) 79 *Virginia Law Review* 1535.
PROBERT, Rebecca (ed), *Family life and the law: Under one roof* (Aldershot, Ashgate, 2007).
WARDLE, Lynn, 'The boundaries of belonging: allegiance, purpose and the definition of *marriage*' (2011) 25 *Brigham Young University Journal of Public Law* 287.
WOODS, Judith, 'National sex survey: "Three times a month? Who are these crazed sexpots? Are they Scandinavian?"' available at www.telegraph.co.uk/women/sex/10475999/National-sex-survey-Three-times-a-month-Who-are-these-crazed-sexpots-Are-they-Scandinavian.html.
YOUNG, Claire and BOYD, Susan, 'Losing the feminist voice? Debates on the legal recognition of same sex partnerships in Canada' (2006) 14 *Feminist Legal Studies* 213.

Index

www.ingramcontent.com/pod-product-compliance
Ingram Content Group UK Ltd.
Pitfield, Milton Keynes, MK11 3LW, UK
UKHW020134290926
15471UKWH00003B/489